S0-DQW-975

POCKET *A*DVENTURES
GUATEMALA

POCKET *A*DVENTURES
GUATEMALA

Shelagh McNally

HUNTER

HUNTER PUBLISHING, INC,
130 Campus Drive, Edison, NJ 08818
732-225-1900; 800-255-0343; fax 732-417-1744
www.hunterpublishing.com

Ulysses Travel Publications
4176 Saint-Denis, Montréal, Québec
Canada H2W 2M5
514-843-9882, ext. 2232; fax 514-843-9448

Windsor Books
The Boundary, Wheatley Road, Garsington
Oxford, OX44 9EJ England
01865-361122; fax 01865-361133

Printed in the United States

ISBN 1-58843-528-8

© 2006 Hunter Publishing, Inc.

This and other Hunter travel guides are also available as e-books
in a variety of digital formats through our online partners,
including Netlibrary.com and Amazon.com.

All rights reserved. No part of this publication may be reproduced, stored in
a retrieval system, or transmitted in any form, or by any means, electronic,
mechanical, photocopying, recording, or otherwise, without the written
permission of the publisher.

This guide focuses on recreational activities. As all such activities contain
elements of risk, the publisher, author, affiliated individuals and companies
disclaim responsibility for any injury, harm, or illness that may occur to
anyone through, or by use of, the information in this book. Every effort was
made to insure the accuracy of information in this book, but the publisher
and author do not assume, and hereby disclaim, liability for any loss or
damage caused by errors, omissions, misleading information or potential
travel problems caused by this guide, even if such errors or omissions
result from negligence, accident or any other cause.

Cover photo © David M Barron/Oxygen Group Photography
Index by Mary Ellen McGrath

Maps by Kim André © 2006 Hunter Publishing, Inc.

1 2 3 4

www.hunterpublishing.com

Hunter's full range of guides to all corners of the globe is featured on our exciting website. You'll find guidebooks to suit every type of traveler, no matter what their budget, lifestyle, or idea of fun.

Adventure Guides – There are now over 40 titles in this series, covering destinations from Costa Rica and the Yucatán to Tampa Bay & Florida's West Coast, Ecuador, Switzerland, Paris and the Alaska Highway. Complete with information on what to do, as well as where to stay and eat, *Adventure Guides* are made for the active traveler, with comprehensive coverage of the area's history, culture and wildlife, plus all the practical travel information you need. Details on the best places for hiking, biking, canoeing, horseback riding, trekking, skiing, watersports, and all other kinds of fun, are included.

Alive Guides – This ever-popular line of books takes a unique look at the best each destination offers: fine dining, jazz clubs, first-class hotels and resorts. In-margin icons direct the reader at a glance. Top-sellers include *St. Martin & St. Barts*, *The US Virgin Islands* and *Aruba, Bonaire & Curaçao*.

And Hunter has long been known for its **one-of-a-kind** travel books that focus on destinations and vacations rarely found in travel books. These include *The Best Dives of the Caribbean; Golf Resorts; Cruising Alaska; A Traveler's Guide to the Galapagos* and many more.

Full descriptions are given for each book at www.hunterpublishing.com, along with reviewers' comments and a cover image. You can also view pages and the table of contents. Books may be purchased on-line via our secure transaction facility.

Acknowledgments

Many thanks to Eugenio Gobbato in Rio Dulce for your great information and help, Lucille van Straaten for your kind suggestions and comments, Shannon McNally, for the Spanish translations (and lessons), and my exceedingly patient and efficient editor, Kim André.

Contents

◆ Maps

DEDICATION

This book is dedicated my mother, Lynne Colvey.
Thanks, Mom for all your support.

THE EFFECTS OF HURRICANE STAN

When Hurricane Stan struck Guatemala in October 2005, it caused massive flooding and mudslides along the Pacific coast and in the Central and Western Highlands. Fifteen of the 22 provinces in both areas were hit and over 700 communities were affected. Several villages were completely destroyed, including the small village of Panabaj, near Santiago Atitlan on Lake Atitlan. Roads were washed out and bridges swept away, along with thousands of acres of crops. It's estimated that 24,000 homes were lost and over 3.5 million people suffered loss of property.

Since these areas already have a higher poverty rate, many communities were left quite vulnerable. But once again the Maya proved their resilience and resourcefulness by immediately re-building roads and bridges as well as their own homes. The main tourist areas of Chichicastenango, Tikal, Yaxha, Copan, Quirigua, Rio Dulce, Antigua, Quetzaltenango and most of Lake Atitlan were not affected. If you are traveling to these areas you may not notice any differences, except for the usual changes with some businesses closing and others opening.

If you are venturing off to the smaller and more remote communities, be patient. The roads may not be in the best conditions and traveling will be slower than normal. While every effort is being made to restore most roads, the work might take a long while in rural regions.

Introduction

Guatemala is the heart of the Maya world and it is mysterious, compelling, magical and tragic all at once. Layers of history envelop this country like a patchwork quilt. There are enigmatic Maya ruins alongside grandiose cathedrals built by the Conquistadors. The diversity of the landscapes is as-

tonishing. In a matter of hours you can go from a windswept mountain peak to steamy mangroves by tropical waters. But the real reason we come to Guatemala is for the Maya people. In this age of anonymous, mass-produced culture, they are unique. The Maya have held onto their language, culture and traditions against an onslaught from the Western world that began with Conquistadors and continues with the United States. Guatemala offers incredible adventures, not only with the nature, but also with the Maya themselves. Coming here will change you, and that is exactly what travel is all about.

History

◆ Historical Timeline

BC

3114	On August 12th, the world is created, according to the Maya Long Count.
3000	The Olmec arrive on the Pacific Coast in Guatemala.
2600	Maya civilization begins to form Cuello, in Belize, is occupied by the Maya.
2000	Peak of the Olmec civilization.
1500	Start of the Pre-Classic period.
300	Maya create a hierarchical society ruled by nobles and kings Maya cities Tikal, Uaxactún, Abaj Takalik are built. The Maya calendar is completed into its final form.

AD

200	The Classic period starts.
292	Maya date recorded on Stela 29 at Tikal.

300	Cities along the Usumacinta River, Kaminaljuyu and Piedras Negras are built.
400	The Maya highlands fall to Teotihuacan and the disintegration of Maya culture and language begins in some parts of the highlands.
500	The Maya city of Tikal becomes the first great Maya city.
600	An unknown event destroys the civilization at Teotihuacan Tikal becomes the largest Maya city with as many as 500,000 inhabitants.
738	Copán is conquered by Quiriguá.
869	Construction ceases in Tikal, marking the beginning of the city's decline.
899	Tikal is abandoned.
900	Classic Period ends, with the collapse of the southern lowland cities Maya cities; Terminal Classic begins and lasts until 1000 AD. This era represents the collapse of the Classic Maya, especially in the Petén and along the Usumacinta River.
1200	Northern Maya cities begin to be abandoned. The Dresden Codex is written at Chichén Itzá. The Itzá flee to what is now Flores and form the Kingdom of Petexbatún.
1283	Mayapán becomes the civil capital of the Yucatán.
1470	Iximché, Capital of the Chaquiels is created.
1523	Pedro de Alvaro arrives on the Pacific Coast.
1524	Alvaro sets up first Spanish capital near Imixche.
1543	Antigua becomes Spanish capital.
1605	The Annals of Cakchiquel were written in the Cakchiquel language. Similar in content to the Popol Vuh.
1650	Smallpox and flu epidemics kill off 85% of the Maya population.
1695	The ruins of Tikal are discovered by Spanish priest Father Avedaño and his companions, who becomes lost in the jungle.
1773	Antigua is destroyed by a series of violent earthquakes.
1776	Capital is moved to Guatemala City.
1821	Guatemala declares its independence from Spain.
1823	Guatemala joins El Salvador, Honduras, Nicaragua and Costa Rica to form the United Provinces of Central America that abolishes slavery.
1829	Francisco Morazán comes into power and starts taking land away from the church to give to European settlers.

1838	The United Provinces break up into the five individual countries.
1839	First civil war. Government is brought down and Rafael Carrera is elected.
1847	Guatemala is declared a sovereign republic.
1871	The "Liberal Revolution" brings Justo Rufino Barrios. He restructures the economy to benefit coffee, cotton and sugar plantations but passes restrictive laws that discriminate against the Maya.
1901	United Fruit Company invited to invest in Guatemala.
1931	USA backs election of General Jorge Ubico.
1940	Infant mortality in at an all time high. United Fruit profits flourish.
1944	Jorge Ubico is forced from power. Juan Jose Arevalo is elected president and initiates many reforms.
1950	Jacobo Arbenz wins the presidential election and institutes the Agrarian Reform Law.
1954	The United Fruit Company gets the US government to stage a coup and replace Arbenz with Colonel Carlos Castillo Armas who arrests 9,000 people peasants and labor leaders, many of whom are killed and tortured. Castillo Armas repeals the Agrarian Reform Law.
1958	Civil war begins.
1962	Disgruntled army officers create FAR and launch a guerrilla war against the military government. The United States sends Green Berets to train Guatemalan army.
1966	Julio Cesar Mendez Montenegro is elected and starts the first paramilitary death squads. Napalm is first used.
1969	FAR is defeated but the death squads continue to round up people and execute them.
1970	Colonel Carlos Arana Osorio elected.
1971-74	Osorio initiates a second wave of "pacification" and 15,000 civilians disappear. Guerrilla Army of the Poor (EGP) is formed.
1976	A 7.5 Richter earthquake destroys much of a Guatemala City and the surrounding area, including Antigua. 25,000 are killed and over one million are left homeless.
1978	Colonel Romeo Lucas Garcia is elected and the Organization of the People in Arms (ORPA) is formed. Over one million have fled the country pursued by death squads. President Carter cuts off US military aid.
1980	The Committee for Peasant Unity (CUC) peacefully occupy the Spanish Embassy to call attention to their

unmet demands. The government burns the embassy down, killing both the peasants and Embassy staff.

1982 General Efraín Ríos Montt is elected and, despite promises of reform, begins his scorched earth policy. The four rebel armies, FAR, OPRA, EGP and PCT, form the Guatemalan National Revolutionary Unity (URNG).

1984 General Oscar Mejia Victores ousts Rios Montt in a coup. The scorched earth policy continues and over 400 villages are destroyed, 1,000 people per month are executed and 200,000 civilians flee to Mexico. The human rights organization, Mutual Support Group (GAM), is formed by the wives and mothers of the "disappeared."

1985 Elections are held. Civilian rules returns with the election of Christian Democrat Vinicio Cerezo.

1991 Jorge Serrano Elias is elected president. The URNG and the government begin peace talks.

1992 Maya leader Rigoberta Menchu wins the Nobel Peace Prize, bringing worldwide attention to Guatemala.

1993 President Serrano attempts to suspend the Constitution and close down Congress. He is forced out the country and Ramiro de Leon Carpio, head of the governmental human rights office, is chosen interim president.

1994 Peace negotiations continue.

1996 Alvaro Arzú Irigoyen is elected president and purges upper ranks of the Military. The Final Peace Accord is signed.

1998 Monsignor Juan Gerardi the driving force behind the Human Rights Movement and the Recovery of Historical Memory (REMHI) is assassinated.

2000 A crack is discovered in the crest of Temple IV at Tikal National Park. Trials begin for the Gerardi murder. Coffee prices are the lowest since 1973.

2001 The Ministry of Energy announces oil exploration will begin and issues licenses to foreign companies.

2002 The International Monetary Fund and the government sign one-year US$105 million stand-by loan agreement to support new economic program.

2003 General Efraín Ríos Montt runs again for president. Oscar Berger wins the presidential elections.

2004 Berger acknowledges the state's role in the political killings.

2005 Bush resumes military aid to Guatemala.

Geography & Land

Guatemala is a relatively small country covering 42,355 square miles (108,430 square km), but it has a very diverse landscape. Limestone plateaus sit next to majestic mountain ranges dotted with pristine lakes and rivers; active and inactive volcanoes are located alongside rainforests and tropical beaches. What's great for travelers is that they can easily move from one environment to another in a short period of time.

Because of it location and geography, Guatemala possesses great biological diversity. In order to protect this natural heritage the Guatemalan government began establishing protected national parks, reserves and biospheres. The first park was created in 1955 and the most recent one was designated in 2002. Today, there are over 30 protected areas and another 40 are being proposed.

◆ Borders

Guatemala is the northernmost country in Central America. It shares its northwestern border with **Mexico** and its northeastern border with **Belize**. To the south it touches **El Salvador** and **Honduras**. The eastern coastline has only a small section that opens up in the **Bay of Honduras**, providing access to the **Caribbean Sea**. The western coastline is much larger and stretches along the **South Pacific Ocean** with beaches of black volcanic sand.

◆ Regions

Guatemala is divided up into 22 **departments**, the equivalent of states or provinces. Often, the capital city has the same name as its department. For the purpose of this book, we have divided the country into seven regional chapters, plus a separate chapter for Guatemala City.

Central Highlands

Made up of the departments of Chimaltenango, Sololá and Sacatepéquez, the Central Highlands is very popular with tourists. The **Sierra Madre Mountain Range**, which runs through the area, has created volcanoes, deep valleys, ravines, mountain plains and plateaus. Despite two major fault lines and a propensity for earthquakes and eruptions, this area is the most densely populated in Guatemala. There are two active volcanoes – **Pacaya** and **Fuego** – and three extinct volcanoes that surround **Lake Atitlán**. Many villages around this famous lake have become popular tourist destinations. The beautiful colonial city of **Antigua** is found in the Panchoy Valley. The capital, **Guatemala City**, is nestled in the Ermita Valley, surrounded by mountains and volcanoes.

Los Altos

Los Altos is the most mountainous and remote area in the country and includes the departments of Quetzaltenango, San Marcos, Totonicapán and Huehuetenango. Between the volcanic mountain chain of the **Sierra Madre** in the south and the **Cuchumatánes Mountains** in the north are pine forests, lakes, streams and deep valleys. There is one active volcano, **Santiaguito**. Traditional Maya villages are located in the valleys and plateaus. Temperatures are much colder here due to the high altitudes. Guatemala's second largest city, **Quetzaltenango**, also known as Xela, is located here in the Quetzaltenango Valley. The area grows coffee, maize, apples, rice and cardamom. Cattle and sheep ranches, as well as factories, also play an important role in the economy. The area is famous for its weavers.

Northern Highlands

Mountains make up 60% of Guatemala's land mass. The highlands are the most populated area in Guatemala and also receive the most tourists.

The Northern Highlands encompass the departments of Quiché, Alta Verapaz and Baja Verapaz. To the east, the **Sierra de Chuacús mountain range** joins the **Cuchumatánes Mountains** and gives way to the virgin rainforests of the north. To the west are the **Sierra de las Minas Mountains**. Because of its location at the foot of two mountain ranges, the Northern Highlands are filled with rivers and the area is one of the wettest and greenest in Guatemala. The mighty **Río Cahabon** and **Río Polochíc** flow through this department, fed by the Chioxy-Usumacinta river system that originates in the Gulf of Mexico. And the rivers flowing in and out of the mountains have created a series of underground grottoes and caves considered to be some of the natural wonders of Guatemala. The Northern Highlands is primarily a rural area, producing coffee, cardamom, rice, broccoli, corn and black pepper.

El Petén

El Petén is the most northern and largest of the departments sharing a western border with Chiapas, Mexico; a northern border with Campeche, Mexico; and an eastern border with Belize. It is a vast area filled with savannas, swamps, tropical jungles and ancient Maya ruins. In fact, the largest temples and cities are found here. El Petén remains the least populated region and, with a high unemployment rate, is one of the poorest. The influx of people into the rainforests has begun to threaten the wildlife, while oil and timber companies are waiting to move in and start development of the region. The **Maya Biosphere Reserve** was created in 1990 to prevent further destruction of the rainforest here. El Petén's capital city is **Flores**, located on an island in the middle of **Lake Petén**. It serves as the jumping-off point for visiting various ruins, including the famous **Tikal National Park**, **Uaxactún**, **Dos Pilas** and **Ceibal**.

Departments

N

MEXICO

Lago Petén Itza

Petén

BELIZE

Huehuetenango

Quiché

Alta Verapaz

Izabal

Lago de Izabal

San Marco

Totoni-capán

Baja Verapaz

Zacapa

Quetzaltenango

Solola
Atitlán

Chimaltenango

El Progreso

Guatemala
• City

Guatemala

Jalapa

Chiquimula

Suchite-pequez

Retalhuleu

Antigua
Guatemala

Santa Rosa

Jutiapa

HONDURAS

Escuintla

EL SALVADOR

Pacific Ocean

© 2006 HUNTER PUBLISHING, INC

NOT TO SCALE

Izabal

East along the Caribbean coast is the department of Izabal. The city and its surroundings are also called the Guatemalan Caribbean. The area is a combination of plains and hills, with Guatemala's largest lake in the middle feeding many small rivers and lagoons. **Río Dulce** meets the lake near the coast and eventually flows out into the **Amatiqué Bay** and the **Caribbean Sea** near the Garífuna town of Lívingston. There are acres of wetlands, mangroves and aquatic ecosystems in this department. The capital city is **Puerto Barrios**, a commercial port and the launching point for exploring reserves in the area. The ruins of Quiriguá, an UNESCO World Heritage Site, are also found in this department.

Eastern Plains

The only desert in Central America is found in the Eastern Plains of Guatemala (departments of Jutiapa, Jalapa, Chiquimula, Zacapa, and El Progresso), where several rare cacti have been found. The desert landscape soon gives way to rolling hills with subtropical forests, volcanic peaks and sulfur lakes. The lush valleys here produce sugar cane, tobacco, cocoa, bananas, melon okra, sesame seeds, grapes, corn, fruits and black beans. The **Sierra de las Minas Mountains** yield minerals such as barium, zinc, fluorite, gold, silver, lead, iron, titanium and nickel.

Pacific Coast

Escuintla, Retalhuleu, Santa Rosa and Suchitepequez make up the tropical Pacific Coast region. The upper part of this area is formed by a range of volcanoes that descends down into fertile lowlands. This is another agricultural area, producing sugar cane, cotton, bananas, coffee, cattle, cardamom, corn, black beans, soybeans, sesame seeds, fruits, shrimp and rubber. The coastline has black volcanic ash and mangrove wetlands that are the breeding grounds for many water birds as well as sea turtles. The **Monterrico Natural Reserve** is found in this area along with ancient Olmec ruins dating back to 1500 BC.

Flora & Fauna

Guatemala's unique position between two continents and two oceans makes it one of the most bio-diverse countries in Latin America. This "land of eternal spring" has the perfect climate for over 19 ecosystems ranging from the mangrove forests on both coasts to the pine forests and cloud forests of the mountains to the desert thorn forests found in between.

◆ Plants

For the most part, it is an incredibly lush country, with over 8,000 species of plants, including 600 species of **orchids**. Orchids are plentiful and beautiful in Guatemala. They belong to the family of **epiphytes**, a class of plants that do not root in soil but live off sunlight and the moisture in the air. These "air plants" attach themselves to other plants, not as a parasite, but simply to position themselves closer to the rain and sun. Many mosses, lichens, algae, and liverworts are also epiphytes, including the **Spanish moss** (*Tillandsia usneoides*) seen in the cloud forests. Of course, the most famous epiphyte is the national flower, the **monja blanca** (white nun) orchid. Another striking species found in the cloud and humid mountain forests are the delicate **maidenhair ferns** of the family *Polypodiaceae*, easily identified by their dainty fronds on thin stalks.

Warm humid forests also have the ideal growing conditions for dozens of **palm** species. These plants are easily recognized by their distinct single trunk that fans out into leaves. Many types of palms are important economic crops used for their food, fiber and oil. The largest export is the xate (sha-tay) palm, used as a fill in for commercial flower arrangements. The commercial farming of xate is now causing serious degradation of the ecosystems in the Alta Verapaz and El Petén regions.

Guava plants are found everywhere in Guatemala, except in the cloud forests, which are too high up for this plant to flourish. It belongs to the myrtle family, characterized by lovely green leaves and beautiful fragrant flowers and fruit. Over 450 varieties grow in Guatemala. Another genus found throughout is the **jacaranda**. There are over 50 different types of jacaranda, but the most common is a plant with periwinkle blue clustered flowers. **Cassava**, also known as **yucca**, is a large bush with greenish-yellow flowers. It's the primary source of tapioca, but its roots are also used to make bread or eaten as a vegetable.

PARKS & RESERVES	
Volcano Parks	**Location**
Acatenango-Fuego Complex	Sacatepéquez, Chimaltenango
Agua Volcano	Sacatepéquez
Tajumulco Volcano	San Marcos
Pacaya Natural Park	Escuintla
Wetlands, Woodlands, Rainforest & Cloudforest Parks	
Bocas del Polochíc (freshwater wetlands)	Izabal
Cerro San Gil Wildlife Refuge (tropical rainforest)	Izabal
Lachua National Park	Alta Verapaz
Laguna El Tigre-Río Escondido Protected Biotope (wetlands)	El Petén
Maya Biosphere Reserve (rainforest)	El Petén
Sierra de Las Minas Biosphere (cloud forest)	El Progreso, Las Verapaces Zacapa, Izabal

Archeological Parks	
Ceibal and Aguateca-Dos Pilas Cultural Monuments	El Petén
Iximché Cultural Monument	Chimaltenango
Quiriguá Cultural Monument	Izabal
Tikal National Park, Archeological	El Petén
Nature & Wildlife Parks	
Cerro Cahui Protected Biotope (wildlife refuge)	El Petén
Chocón Machacas Biotope (manatee reserve)	Izabal
El Zotz Protected Biotope (bat reserve)	El Petén
Lake Atitlán (natural reserve)	Sololá
Mario Dary Biotope (quetzal refuge)	Baja Verapaz
Monterrico Natural Reserve-Hawaii National Park (mangrove reserve/turtle sanctuary)	Santa Rosa
Tikal National Park (archeological/wildlife refuge)	El Petén
Punta de Manabique Biotope (marine/coastal wetlands)	Izabal
Semuc Champey Natural Monument (river)	Alta Verapaz
Sierra de Los Cuchumatánes (mountain range)	Huehuetenango, Quiché

◆ Forests

Despite numerous plants and flowers, it is the trees that really define Guatemala. The actual word "Guatemala" comes from the Nahuatl language and means "Land of Trees." Fifty-one percent of the country is forest, either coniferous, broad-leaved, tropical or mixed. The mountain forests are filled with **pine** and **cypress** and the cloud forests have some of the largest specimens found in Central America. Many of these trees are prized for their wood and Guatemala has had a long struggle with logging companies over their depletion of the forests. **Logwood** (*Haematoxylum campechianum*) is a native tree that was prized for its dark red sap. It was used to produce a purple dye highly sought-after in the 19th century. Another popular tree is the **caoba mahogany**, a favorite tree for furniture and other wooden objects because of its strength and attractive grain, resistant to both rot and termites. **Teak** is another tree prized for its hard wood. The magnificent **ceiba** is the sacred tree of the Maya, who use it to explain the universe (the limbs and leaves represent heaven, the trunk is earth and the roots are the underworld). The ceiba can reach a height of 130 feet (40 m).

In the tropical zones of Izabal, the Petén and Pacific, the trees are more likely to be fruit-bearing, such as the **breadfruit** (*Artocarpus altilis*). This incredibly useful plant has a fruit that resembles an oversize mango, valued for its pulp and juice. The **calabash** (*Crescentia cujete*) tree grows to 30 feet (nine meters) and is used for its tough and flexible wood, as well as for the fruit that resembles a gourd. Everyone enjoys the fruit of the **cashew**, a tropical evergreen found throughout Guatemala. The **coconut** is another tropical tree found in the coastal regions. **Tamarind** is a tropical evergreen tree that reaches heights of 80 feet (24 m). Its acidic fruit is used as a spice as well as a candy and tamarind juice sweetened with sugar is a popular drink in Guatemala.

Also in the tropical areas are the swamps filled with red, white and black **mangroves**. These trees have a special root system that allows them to filter salt water and thrive in the shallow, brackish waters of the tropical swamps. They are easily recognized by their tangle of roots that arch above the water. The red mangrove belongs to the family *Rhizophoraceae* and is classified as *Rhizophora mangle*. The white mangrove belongs to the family *Combretaceae,* while the black mangrove belongs to the family *Verbenaceae* and is classified as *Avicennia germinans*.

◆ Crops

Guatemala's commercial crops include banana, coffee, melon, tobacco, sugar, potato, tomato, watermelon, papaya, Chile pepper, pineapple, corn, yucca, cucumber, beans, pineapple and guava.

◆ Wildlife

Guatemala's wildlife is equally diverse, with over 600 species of birds living alongside 250 species of mammals, 200 species of reptiles and amphibians and hundreds of species of butterflies and insects.

The forests are filled with deer, foxes, monkeys, peccaries, jaguars, tapirs, coatis, tepezcuintles and pumas.

Baird's tapir is a native of Guatemala. This nocturnal, herbivorous mammal resembles a large pig, but with a flexible snout and short legs. It can reach up to 600 pounds, but is an extremely agile runner and swims quite fast. They are shy animals and are hunted by locals for their meat.

The **jaguar** is one of the most revered animals in the Maya world and consequently there is much religious iconography associated with the animal. The most common type is yellow with black spots. The black jaguar is extremely rare. The jaguar is currently on the endangered species list and its numbers are dwindling due to hunting and loss of habitat. The **ocelot** is another jungle cat, much smaller than the jaguar. It resembles an overgrown house cat, with black stripes on a gray background. Its most notable features are large black eyes.

The loud, ferocious howling heard in the jungle at sunrise and sunset is the cry of the **howler monkey** (*Mono Congo*). Despite their seemingly murderous yells, howler monkeys are actually gentle vegetarians living in family groups. The male can grow to 15 pounds and he protects his family by the ferocious howls used to both warn his family and intimidate his enemies. They are very curious creatures and will sometime follow groups of humans. The **spider monkey** is another breed of smaller primate, with slender limbs and a prehensile tail that it uses to swing from branch to branch. Locals also call this monkey "capuchino" because its brown face with white eyes resembles the outfits worn by the Capuchin religious order.

The **coatimundi** is a member of the raccoon family and, like most raccoons, will eat anything. It lives in the trees and on the ground and is easily recognized by its long white nose and bushy tail. The **kinkajou** (*Potus Flavus*) is a funny looking creature with the face of a koala bear and the body of a raccoon. It's a nocturnal creature that comes out after sunset to feed on fruit and insects, using its prehensile trail to leap from treetop to treetop. It's the easiest animal to spot in the jungle. The **tepezcuintles**, also known as the **paca**, is a nocturnal rodent that lives in the forest. It is found throughout the country wherever there is water. It's easily hunted and the meat is considered a delicacy. Guatemala is also becoming famous for the various types of **bats** that live here, particularly in the El Zotz region of the Petén.

Crocodiles, manatees, fish and crustaceans fill the fresh water lakes and rivers of Guatemala. The shy **manatee** is a sea cow that inhabits the waters of the Izabal and is difficult to spot. So are the **caimans** or crocodiles, often mistaken for logs since they can lie for hours with just their nostrils and eyes above water. They are found in many of the mangroves and fresh water rivers and can grow up to 17 feet in length (5 m). Check with locals before swimming. The most common fish found in the fresh waters throughout Guatemala is **bass** and **perch**. On the coast it is mojarra (**perch**), robalo (**snook**), tarpon machaca (**shad**), **white mullet**, **catfish** and **lizardfish**. Also on the Pacific coast you will find big game fish such as **swordfish**, **tuna**, **wahoo**, **dorado** and **blue marlin**.

One of the defining animals of the jungle is the iguana. The friendliest and most abundant is the common **green iguana**. Although they can grow up to six feet (1.6 m), they are harmless creatures and can be found resting in branches of trees or sunning on large rocks. Locals hunt them for their meat and eggs. One of the more amusing lizards is the **Jesus Christo (Jesus Christ) lizard**, named for its ability to stand on two legs and skim across the water to escape predators.

As with any tropical area, there are plenty of snakes here. Fortunately the vast majority are not venomous and nocturnal. However, the **coral snake** should be avoided. It is easily recognized by its bright rings of red, yellow and black. Probably the most feared snake is the "barba amarilla" (yellow beard or **fer-de-lance**). This aggressive snake is known for attacking without provocation.

◆ Insects

There is no shortage of insects in Guatemala. There are hundreds of butterflies in a variety of sizes and colors. One of the most flamboyant is the **blue morpho**, which grows to five inches and is a bright electric blue. Like most butterflies, it has an underside that is quite drab. You have to wait for it to open its wings before you can see the color. Other common butterflies are the **monarch**, with orange and black wings, and the **red butterfly**, with wings of silver and red. While walking in the forest, keep an eye out for the industrious **leaf cutter ants**, who snip pieces of leaves and carry them back to their nest. Their trails can be a quarter-mile long. **Red ants**, with their vicious bites, are the only ones you will need to avoid.

Likewise, stay away from the **tarantula**, **black widow** (*latrodectus*) and **brown recluse** (*loxosceles*). All three of these spiders are poisonous. The large, hairy black and orange tarantula is known locally as the "araña de caballo" (horse spider). Although painful, its bite is not fatal. However, both the black widow and brown recluse can cause serious tissue damage from their bite. Both are found in dark, hidden places. The brown recluse spider (*Loxoceles reclusa*), sometimes referred to as the violin spider, is identified by the black violin-shaped mark on its head.

◆ Birds

Probably the most spectacular fauna in Guatemala are the birds. With so many different ecosystems, there is a wide range of songbirds, predators and waterfowl. Around the flanks of volcanoes, you will spot such colorful species as the azure-rumped, black-capped **siskin**, **tanager**, **rufous saberwing**, **maroon-chested ground-dove** and **Pacific parakeet**. As you climb higher, you will spot the magnificent predatory birds, such as the **great black hawk** and **grey-headed kite**. In the cloud forests there are a number of brilliant birds, such as the **pink-headed warbler**, **blue-throated motmot** and **horned guan**, as well as the resplendent **quetzal**, the national bird of Guatemala. The mangroves are the nesting grounds for such birds as the **blue** and **white heron**, **white ibis**, **blue kingfisher**, **chachalaca**, **roseate spoonbill**, **pygmy kingfisher** and **collared plover**.

> **AUTHOR NOTE:** *The scarlet macaw is one of the most brilliantly colored birds in these woods.*

For a list of conservation organizations operating in Guatemala, see the *Appendix*, page 269.

Government & Economy

◆ Politics

Politics is a complicated business in Guatemala; there are now over 40 political parties in action. Guatemala had its first democratic election in over 50 years in November, 1999. The election came down to a race between Oscar Berger of the Frente Republicano Guatemalteco (FRG), the opposition party with 33% support, and Alfonso Antonio Portillo Cabrera of the Partido de Avanzada Nacional (PAN), the conservative party in power, which had 30% of the vote. Alvaro Colom of the Alianza Nueva Nación (ANN), a party of ex-guerillas, was the third candidate. Portillo was a controversial candidate because of his connection to Ríos Montt, also running on the FRG ticket. Montt was executor of the scorched-earth policy that destroyed entire villages and left thousands of Guatemalans either homeless or dead. Portillo himself has been quite open about killing several people, claiming it taught him how to protect Guatemala and bring about an end to violence and crime in the country. Amazingly, the voters responded to Portillo and elected him with an overwhelming majority. Oscar Berger and the PAN obtained enough votes to remain the official opposition.

The last few years since the elections has seen a continuation of human rights abuse. However, the government has acknowledged the abuses of the previous FRG regime, particularly after the 1998 investigation by the Catholic bishop Juan Gerardi (who was then assassinated). In 2001, several trials began against those accused of human rights abuses. Montt himself faced a jury in the fall of 2002. A verdict has not been reached. In the meantime Portillo remains President of Guatemala and Montt has been named President of the Parliament.

◆ Economy

Guatemala GDP for 2001 was an estimated $20 billion. Since the signing of the peace accord in 1996, Guatemala's economy has been growing rapidly. Eighty-five percent of the economy is generated by the private sector. Most of the manufacturing is light assembly and food processing, geared to the Central American marketplace as well as the US. The majority of Guatemala's exports are agricultural goods – **sugar**, **bananas** and **coffee** are the main exports. Recently, the country has started exporting textiles, apparel, winter vegetables (such as broccoli and potatoes), fruit and cut flowers. **Tourism** is also becoming important.

The **United States** remains Guatemala's biggest trade partner, with **Canada** a close second. The government sector is small and underfunded, and many of the public utilities, such as the telephone, ports and airports, have been privatized, which has driven up costs further.

The international community is helping Guatemala with its recovery from the civil war. France, Italy, Spain, Germany, Japan, Canada and the United States are all donating resources and financing projects. The major challenges to Guatemala's economy are the high levels of illiteracy (30% of men and 50% of women), lack of capital and a weak infrastructure. The transportation, telecommunications and electricity sectors are all poor.

Despite the growing economy there is still a great deal of poverty. According to the United Nations, 87% of all Guatemalans currently live in poverty, 60% lack basic health care and 30% have no access to potable water. Infant mortality remains high. The gulf between the rich and poor is wide and unequal land distribution has resulted in two percent of the population owning 68% of all cultivable land. The wealthy, who make up only 10% of the population, receive two-thirds of all the income. The remaining 90% must live on what is left. International aid is contingent upon the government's continued dedication to economic reforms and improvements in human rights.

Money

◆ Currency

The currency is the **quetzal**, named after the famous bird. In June of 2001 the American dollar was also recognized as an official currency. Consequently, it is difficult to exchange any other foreign currency (you have to take it to the National Bank of Guatemala in Guatemala City, which is extremely annoying). You can change money at the airport, but rates are very poor. The solution is to travel with American dollars. If you're traveling overland, you can change Mexican pesos or Belizean dollars at the border with moneychangers who offer decent rates.

> **AUTHOR NOTE:** *At the time of writing, the rate of exchange was Q7.5 to US $1.*

◆ Credit Cards & ATMs

Your ATM card can be used in Guatemala as long as it's linked to a banking system such as Plus or Interact. Many of the ATM machines have instructions in both Spanish and English. The machines often run out of money in the afternoons and on weekends.

Visa credit cards are accepted throughout the country at most upscale hotels and restaurants. However, **MasterCard** is rarely accepted and

AMEX is taken only in the larger tourist areas. The easiest **traveler's checks** to cash are Thomas Barclay. You will have a hard time finding a place to cash AMEX traveler's checks, even if they are issued from a reputable bank.

◆ Tipping & Taxes

You should tip waiters 10-15% and leave the hotel cleaning staff a dollar a day tip. Restaurants charge a 10% IVA (value-added tax), while hotels charge a 10% tourist tax on top of the IVA tax for a whopping 20% addition to your hotel bill.

> **AUTHOR NOTE:** *The only place you can barter is in the markets. Shops, restaurants and hotels usually have fixed prices.*

The People

◆ Cultural Groups & Religion

Over 55% of the population is **Maya Indian**, 35% is *Ladino* (Maya and European descent), and the remainder is of mixed heritage. There are 24 recognized Maya dialects and tribes throughout the country. The Maya have held onto their traditions and proudly celebrate their heritage through everyday dress, religious rituals, music and dance. Each village has its own *traje*, or handmade clothes, woven and embroidered with brilliant colors. The origins of *traje* are not clear. Some believe it was an invention of the Spanish used to keep track of the Maya, but others think the costumes are too elaborate to be created solely for that reason. Either way, *traje* is part of the Maya heritage and people wear theirs with pride. Each village has its own *traje* and language, creating a rich cultural mosaic. The common thread connecting all village is **Market Day**, the most important event of the week. Guatemala has become famous for its markets, and visitors come in search of the beautiful textiles, pottery, masks and wooden carvings that have become icons of the country. The Central Market in Guatemala City and the Market in Chichicastenango are the two largest, with the widest selection of crafts. Panajachel also has a large outdoor market.

Sadly, most Maya survive through subsistence farming and supplement their income by selling their weavings or working on large coffee and fruit plantations for meager wages.

For the most part the *Ladino* culture is urban and eagerly embraces everything modern. Most of the economic and political power lies in their hands.

Guatemala has been hard on its indigenous people, ignoring their human rights, but not hesitating to shamelessly exploit their exotic hold on tourists. The good news is that the Maya are now participating in the growing eco-tourism industry, which allows them to preserve their way of life and have a decent income.

The country is predominantly **Catholic**, with a growing population of **Evangelists**. The Maya in particular are quite conservative and you should dress with respect for this. Women should dress modestly when traveling to the more rural areas. Tight clothes that reveal a lot of flesh will be frowned upon. Often, Maya women will not talk to strangers, particularly gringo men. If you need to ask for directions, approach someone of the same sex.

On the whole, Guatemalans are much more polite than the average American. Too many tourists forget to use "please" and "thank you." Learn a few polite phrases in Spanish (see page 281) and you will be amazed at the warm reception you receive. Rude behavior, such as loud demands or impatience with someone giving you service, will get you ignored.

Festivals and religious holidays and fiestas are an integral part of Guatemalan social life. There are over 371 festivals celebrated throughout the country, so on any given day there is some kind of celebration going on. The holidays are a blend of religion and history, celebrating past events as well as the culture itself. For a more detailed description of the holidays please refer to the Holidays & Festivals section (page 22).

◆ Language

Spanish is Guatemala's official language, although the majority of the Maya learn their own language first; in more remote villages, Spanish is a second language spoken by few. There is little English in Guatemala, except in the more tourist-oriented areas.

If you don't speak the lingo, use the Spanish glossary in the *Appendix*, page 280, to help with some basic requests. If you want to learn Spanish while visiting Guatemala, several towns have excellent schools that offer language education, room and board. These include La Antigua, Panajachel, San Pedro La Laguna, Xela, Cobán, Huehuetenango and the nearby village of Fundación Cuchumatán; recommended schools are listed in the appropriate section.

> ### ❖ OFFICIALLY RECOGNIZED LANGUAGES
>
> Guatemala recognizes as official a number of Mayan languages, including Achi', Akateko, Awakateko, Chalchiteko, Ch'orti', Chuj, Itzá, Ixil, Popti', Kaqchikel, K'iche', Mam, Mopán, Poqoman, Poqomchi, Q'anjob'al, Quiché, Sakapulteko, Sipakapense, Spanish, Tekiteko, Tz'utujil, Uspanteko, Garífuna and Xinka.

◆ Food

Every region in Guatemala has its own specialty dishes, but the staple of any Maya diet are **beans** and **tortillas**, which are served at every meal.

Frijoles, kidney-shaped beans, can be cooked in a variety of ways. The most popular method is *refritos*, in which the beans have been boiled, mashed and then refried, or *enteros*, where the beans are served whole in their cooked juices with sliced onions. Breakfast beans are served with a dollop of cream on top.

Tortillas are made from maize, a sturdy variety of corn that is too tough to eat on the cob but, when ground, makes a delicious flour. The flour is shaped into a small round pancake (the best are handmade) and cooked over a flame. A variety of stuffings – such as beans, rice, guacamole, cheese, chicken, beef and pork – are served alongside. Tortillas are best eaten warm. If you get a chance, try the blue corn tortillas, the most delicious of all.

The most popular snacks are **tamales**, flavored cornmeal stuffed with either chicken or pork, wrapped in a banana leaf and then steamed. A good tamale can be a meal in itself and being able to create the perfect tamale is a source of pride among Maya women.

Chile rellenos are stuffed chile peppers; these are usually filled with cheese, rice and chicken. **Chiles** also show up in a variety of salsas, or can be pickled. Approach anything made with chiles with a certain amount of caution as the average gringo palate is not used to such heat.

Stews and **soups** made with turkey are especially popular in the chilly north. The most popular breakfast in the highlands is *mosh*, oatmeal cooked with milk and cinnamon.

Traditional breakfasts include eggs, beans, tortillas and coffee. Lunch is the main meal of the day and many restaurants will offer a daily special that consists of soup, roast chicken, rice, beans, tortillas and a drink. This *comida del dia* is the most economical way to eat. Dinner tends to be a smaller meal featuring soups, stews, beans and tortillas. The *Ladino* population seems to prefer hamburgers, pizza, pasta and Chinese food and there are plenty of restaurants to meet their needs.

Vegetarians will have a hard time finding food in the more remote areas. The places that see a lot of tourists will have vegetarian restaurants. In fact, you can gauge how much tourism a place gets by the number of vegetarian restaurants.

◆ Drinks

You'll be able to take your choice from a variety of soft drinks almost everywhere in Guatemala. Pepsi is battling it out with Coca-Cola and it appears to be winning in popularity. You can also find Sprite and Fanta. Natural fruit drinks, called **licuados**, are made in almost all the restaurants. *Con agua* means the fruit is blended with water; *con leche* means milk is added. In the colder regions, **atol** is offered. This warm, sweet drink is made from rice, oat or corn water sweetened with honey or sugar and a pinch of cinnamon.

No one drinks the local **water** and neither should you. Bottled water is sold under half a dozen brand names; these vary according to the region.

AUTHOR NOTE: *Make sure the bottle's seal is not broken –*
there is a sideline business of bottling tap water as purified.

Ice cubes made from purified water usually have a hollow center, but this is not always the case. You don't really need to worry too much about getting pure water; since the locals don't drink tap water, there is always purified water available. If you're in a very remote area with no clean water, boil your water for 20 to 30 minutes to kill bacteria. If your plan includes travel in remote areas, consider bringing water purification tablets, sold at most hiking or outdoor stores.

There are only two brands of **beer** sold in Guatemala: **Gallo** is the light beer and **Mazo** is the dark beer. The Mexican beer **Tecate** is becoming very popular in the larger cities as well.

Rum is the favored hard liquor, along with *aguadiente* or *guaro*, home-made moonshine. Be careful of this. It has a very high alcohol content and leaves you with a wicked hangover and plenty of dead brain cells. Locally made **wine** is an acquired taste. It tastes more like a sweet sherry. Imported wines are probably a better option.

> ❖ **INSIDER TIP: ASKING FOR DIRECTIONS**
>
> When asking for directions, don't rely on a single person for a correct answer. Many Guatemalans won't admit they don't know where the place is because they don't want to seem unhelpful. Instead, they will make directions for you. The rule of thumb is to ask three people and take the best two out of three. If you get three different answers, keep asking until you get a consistent answer.

INTRODUCTION

Travel Information

When to Go

◆ Climate

Although Guatemala is advertised as the land of eternal spring, it actually has a varied climate. The Highlands have warm days and cool nights, and in the higher altitudes the temperature can fall as low as 32° F (0° C) between December and February. The average annual temperature in this area is between 68° and 76° F (20-25° C). The Petén lowlands, as well as the Pacific and Atlantic coastal regions, have a tropical, hot and humid

climate with an average temperature of 83° F (28° C), and heavy rainfall year-round. The Eastern plains are hot and dry, with an average temperature of 86° F (32° C).

◆ Seasonal Concerns

Guatemala doesn't really have any terrible seasons. There is *invierno* (winter) from April to November, followed by *verano* (summer) from November through April.

The true **rainy season** starts in June and lasts until the end of September. During this period, the sunny mornings are followed by rain and cloud in the late afternoons. If you don't mind getting up early in the morning to do your sightseeing before the rain, then travel during this season can be great. The biggest problem is roads getting washed out. The more remote areas of Guatemala, particularly Los Altos and El Petén, are often inaccessible during the rainy months, as are many of the more remote ruins in El Petén. If you plan to visit any of these ruins, you should check to see if they can be reached during the rainy season. Contact INGUAT, 4 Calle 4-37, Zone 9, Ciudad Guatemala, ☎ 502/331-1333 or check with the tour companies handling individual ruins.

Invierno (winter) is a good time to visit since there are fewer tourists, hotel prices are low and there are plenty of bargains around.

Verano (summer) is the best time to visit, when the days are sunny and warm. August gets busy for a few weeks when Italians, Germans and French come over to visit. Of course, the highlands are always chilly, particularly Los Altos and Las Verapaces.

The busiest time in Guatemala is during **Semana Santa** (Holy Week). Travelers from Central America, Mexico and South America come to Guatemala to celebrate Easter and enjoy the many festivals. The Passion Plays and pageantry in Antigua are world famous and shouldn't be missed. The area gets very crowded during this time and hotel prices are raised, so plan ahead.

◆ Holidays & Festivals

Guatemala is a country of fiestas and religious holidays. Integral parts of any fiesta are the music, food and drink. Public and religious holidays are celebrated throughout the country. Government agencies, banks, schools and universities are usually closed on public holidays.

Each village also has a patron saint and when that saint's day arrives (once a year), the entire village takes a weeklong holiday to celebrate with religious processions, parades, dances, music, performances, fireworks and a carnival. Large quantities of liquor are consumed, including *guaro* (white lightening) or *aguadiente* (firewater), a drink made from fermented sugar cane. No fiesta in Guatemala is complete without lots of fireworks – the noisier the better. Marimbas are the favorite instrument, along with harps and drums. Dances play an important part in any fiesta, but especially in the religious feasts. Many of these dances date back to before the Conquest in the 16th century. Some are rooted in Mayan traditions, while others have African roots, with Moorish and Iberian influences. Each village has its own special dance and certain villages are famous for their folkloric dances.

Religious holidays are also celebrated with processions of the *cofradias*. Each town has a *cofradia*, a group of men or women elected by the town to uphold the religious traditions that are a blending of the ancient Mayan religious practices and Catholicism. Cofradias are responsible for carrying the town's religious icons during the processions that mark these holidays. Many of the traditional Mayan holidays and ceremonies are closed to foreigners and you should respect this condition. If you are fortunate enough to see a Mayan ritual, then refrain from taking photos and keep a respectful distance.

These fairs are great fun, but you should keep in mind that everything slows down during a fiesta, particularly a saint's day celebration. In smaller, more remote villages, this includes the bus service, since the driver will be out celebrating with his bottle of white lightening. Don't look for peace and quiet during the fiestas either. They are all-night affairs.

There are so many festivals that it's best to check each department individually to see what is upcoming. The most extensive list divided by departments can be found at The Maya Paradise, Rio Dulce Information site (www.mayaparadise.com/fiestas/fiestas.com), which also lists future events.

Official Holidays

These holidays are celebrated throughout the country.

January 1:	New Year's Day
January 6:	Dias de los Tre Reyes Mago (Feast of the Three Kings)
February 1-5:	Canadeleria (Candlemas)
March:	Carnaval, just before Lent
March/April:	Semana Santa (Holy Week)
May1:	Labor Day
June 30:	Anniversary of the Revolution
September 15:	Independence Day
October 12:	Day of the Races
October 20:	Revolution Day
November 1:	Dios de los Muertos (Day of the Dead)
December 24-25:	Christmas
December 31:	New Year's Eve.

Customs & Immigration

◆ Documents

Visitors from Western Europe, Canada, the USA, Mexico, Central America, Brazil, Chile, Paraguay, Uruguay, Venezuela, Australia, Israel, Japan and New Zealand do not need a visa to enter Guatemala. You must, however, be in possession of a valid passport. The majority of visitors will automatically be given a 90-day tourist visa on arrival (grouchy officials tend to give only 30 days). If you want to stay longer than the length of your visa, you must apply for an extension in Guatemala City. To renew your visa you must submit a solicitud de prórroga de visa de turista o visitante *(request for renewal of tourist or visitor visa)*, the form for which you can download at www.migracion.gob.gt/ingles/serv/form/proturvi.pdf. You must present the completed form, an international credit card or sufficient travelers's checks (in your name), evidence of a round-trip airplane or bus ticket and a signed statement, accompanied by an authenticated photocopy of the personal identification stating your name, nationality, personal identification document number, address, phone, and economic capacity to the Subureau of Foreign Proceedings, 7 avenida 1-17, zona 4, 2nd floors, INGUAT Building, ☎ 502/5-361-8476, fax, 502/5-361-8479, 8 am-

4:30 pm, Mon-Fri (they do close for lunch). They will give you another form that you must take to the bank and pay a fee of Q75 to stamp the form. Then you bring all your forms back to the office so you can be registered in the database system of Immigration Services. If you are not on Guatemala's most wanted list then the officer will stamp all your papers and issue you another visa. Except to spend at least a day doing this – if all goes well. It's such a hassle and colossal waste of time that most people get around the paperwork by simply leaving the country for a day and re-entering to get a new visa. Make sure you ask for an entry stamp on your passport because without one you will be forced to pay a large fine (or bribe) to leave the country.

◆ Departure Tax

If you leave by plane, you are required to pay whopping Q237 exit fee (about US $30 per person). If you leave by land the exit fee is Q10 (about $1.50 per person). Most locals leave the country by bus, which is the reason for the huge difference. There is no fee to enter the country.

Getting Here

◆ Overland

The majority of travelers arrive in Guatemala overland via Mexico or Belize. There are three main border stations from Mexico: Ciudad Cuauhtemoc/La Mesilla in Huehuetenango; Tapachula/El Carmen in San Marcos; and Ciudad Hidalgo/Ciudad Tecún Umán in San Marcos. The most convenient route is through Tecún Umán. The road from Huehuetenango (the Pan American Highway) is really mountainous and travel is slow going. There are direct buses from the border to Guatemala City and certain tourist shuttles offer rides to and from San Cristóbal de las Casas, Chiapas, Mexico.

Shuttles from Antigua to Mexico

Monarca Travel, Calzada Santa Lucia Norte #7, ☎ 502/7-832-1939, monarcas@conexion.com.gt. This company also offers shuttle service from San Cristobal de las Casas, Chiapas, Mexico to Antigua Guatemala. Tickets start at $40 per person and include help with border crossings.

Sin Fronteras, 5a Avenida Norte#15A, ☎ 502/832-1017, fax 502/832-8453, offers a special bus pass to and from Mexico for up to 14 days starting at $94.

You will need to make reservations for the shuttle buses.

Public Buses from Guatemala City to the Mexican Border

Public Buses leave regularly from Guatemala City for the Mexican border in Tecun Umán, San Marcos:

Galgos leaves from 7 ave. 19-44 Zona 1 at 7 am to 1:30 pm.

Fortalezas leaves from 19 ave. 0-70 Zona 1, 2:30 am to 6:30 pm every hour.

Rapidos del Sur leaves from 20 ave. 6-55 Zona 1, 2:30 am to 6:30 pm every half-hour.

Rutas Lima leaves from 6a. calle 8-63 Zona 1, 5:30 am to 4:30 pm every hour.

Velasquez leaves from 20 calle 2a. ave. Zona 1, 5:30 am to 4:30 pm every hour.

Tacana 2a. leaves from ave. 20-42 Zona 1, 5:30 am to 4:30 pm every hour.

Only one main line handles the trip from the capital to La Mesilla, Huehuetenango:

Transportes Velázquez leaves from 20 Calle y 2a. Avenida, Zona 1, 1, 2:30 am to 6:30 pm every hour.

Tickets will be about US $15 per person. No reservations are allowed.

Buses from Chiapas, Mexico to La Mesilla, Huehuetenango

UNO, ☎ 52-51-55-533-2424 or toll free throughout Mexico, 800/702-8000, www.uno.com.mx.

Colon Cristobal, toll free in Mexico, ☎ 800/849-6136.

ADO, ☎ 51-55-533-2424 or toll free in Mexico, 800/702-8000.

Prices will vary according to the bus line, but tickets usually start at around $30 to get to the border. Your seat is guaranteed when you buy a ticket and reservations can be made online.

If you are entering Guatemala from Belize, take a bus from the border town of Melchor de Mercos to Flores. At Flores you will have to transfer to another bus that will carry you east to Río Dulce and on to Guatemala City. You will need to transfer a second time if you are heading to Antigua.

Public Buses from Guatemala to Flores

Buses leave at 4:30am, 8:30 am, 8:30 pm.

La Petenera leaves from 16 calle 10-03 Zona 1.

Lineas Maxima leaves from 5a. ave. 17-26 Zona 1.

Maya Express leaves from 17 calle 9-36 Zona 1.

Fuentes de Norte leaves from 17 calle 17-01 Zona 1.

Prices start at US $8 per person.

Shuttle Services to Flores

You have the option of leaving from Antigua or Guatemala to get to Flores. You must make reservations for the shuttles and they will pick you up at your hotel.

Adventure Travel Center . . . . ☎ 502/7-832-0162
Horizantes . . . . ☎ 502/7-832-1530
Monarca Travel . . . . ☎ 502/7-832-1939
Guatemala Res/Rainbow Travel . . . . . . ☎ 502/7-832-4202

First Class Express Service from Guatemala City to Flores

This private bus services offer some very good deals on travel to the border with first class service aboard well equipped buses as far as Flores. From Belize and onwards the service is strictly second class though.

Fuentes del Norte, 17 calle 17-01 Zoan1 1. 3:20 am until 2 pm every hour. US $18 per person.

Linea Dorada, Main Bus Terminal, Zona 4, ☎ 502/2-232-9658 for reservations, 9 am and 10 pm. You can make arrangements to travel as far as Chetumal, Mexico on this line.

From Chetumal Mexico to Flores, Petén

Mundo Maya has a bus leaving the Main Terminal, Chetumal City to Flores leaving every day at 6 am and 3 pm for US $22 per person. You can also catch this bus in Belize City. ☎ 51-55-533-2424 or toll free in Mexico, 800/702-8000.

From Belize City to Flores

You can pick up any of the Mexican buses going into Flores in Mexico City. You can also contact:

Batty Brothers Bus Line, ☎ 501-2-73354 for more details on schedules and reservations. They change frequently.

> **❖   INSIDER TIP: CUSTOMS RIP-OFFS**
>
> Gangs of sleazy guys hang out around the borders offering to be your "friend" and help you get through Customs or change money. They may pretend to be border officials and ask for a Q70 ($9) fee. Don't pay them and don't let them help you. They often end up stealing your documents or money. If you need assistance, go into the Customs office where the genuine officials will help for free. No Customs official will ever ask for money.

If you want exchange money, look for men with money pouches or with money wedged in between their fingers (each finger holds a different currency). These moneychangers offer good rates and are fairly honest.

◆ By Air

All international flights land at **La Aurora International Airport**, ☎ 502/2-331-3283, in Zona 13 in the southeastern part of Guatemala City. Taxis wait outside the terminal on the Arrivals level. Taxi rates are set and are quite reasonable: US $7 to Zona 9 or 10, US $10 for Zona 1 to the bus terminal. (See the *Walking* section on page 52 for details on the city's various *zonas*).

Guatemala is well serviced by a number of airlines:

Aerolineas Argentinas, 10a. Calle 3-17, Zona 10, Nivel 1, Edificio Aseguradora General, ☎ 502/2-331-1567 fax 502/2-334-6662.

AeroMexico, 10a. Calle 6-21 "A," Zona 9, Nivel 3, ☎ 502/2-331-9507 fax 502/2-334-3313, discover-guate@guate.net.

Air Canada, 18 Calle 5-56, Zona 10, Edificio Unicentro, Nivel 3 y 7, ☎ 502/2-366-9985, fax 502/2-366-6415.

Air France, Avenida Reforma 9-00, Zona 9, Plaza Panamericana, Planta Baja, ☎ 502/2-334-0043/5, fax 502/2-331-1918.

Air New Zealand, Avenida Reforma 9-00, Zona 9, Plaza Panamericana, No. 8, ☎ 502/2-331-2070, fax 502/2-331-2079.

American Airlines, Avenida Reforma 15-54, Zona 9, Edificio Reforma Obelisco, No. 401-A, ☎ 502/2-334-7379, fax 502/2-360-6084.

British Airways, 1a. Avenida 10-81, Zona 10, Edificio Inexa, Nivel 6, ☎ 502/2-332-7402 al 4, fax 502/2-332-7401.

Cathay Pacific, 10a. Calle 60-21 "A," Zona 9, Nivel 3, ☎ 502/2-331-9507, fax 502/2-334-3313.

Continental Airways, 18 Calle 5-56, Zona 10, Edificio Unicentro, Niveles 3 y 7, ☎ 502/2-366-9985, fax 502/2-336-6415.

Delta Airlines, 15 Calle 3-20, Zona 10, Edificio Centro Ejecutivo, Nivel 2, Oficina 201, ☎ 502/2-337-0642/70/80/88, fax 502/2-337-0670.

Iberia (Lineas Aereas de España), Edificio Galería Reforma, Avenida Reforma 8-60, Zona 9, ☎ 502/2-332-0911, fax 502/2-334-3715.

KLM, Edificio Plaza Marítima, 6a. Avenida 20-25, Zona 10, ☎ 502/2-367-6179, fax 502/2-337-0227.

Lan Chile, Avenida Reforma 9-00, Zona 9, Edificio Plaza Panamericana, No. 8, ☎ 502/2-331-2070, fax 502/2-331-2079.

Lufthansa, Diagonal 6 10-01, Zona 10, Nivel 8, Centro Comercial, Las Margaritas, Torre II, ☎ 502/2-336-5526, fax 502/2-339-2994.

United Airlines, Avenida Reforma 1-50, Zona 9, Edificio El Reformador, Nivel 2, Oficina 201-202, Nivel 3, Oficina 301-302, ☎ 502/2-332-2995, fax 502/2-332-3903.

US Airways, 10a. Calle 6-21 "A," Zona 9, Nivel 3, ☎ 502/2-331-9507, fax 502/2-334-3313.

Getting Around

◆ By Air

There are a number of airline companies that service Guatemala internally. The most popular route is the one from Guatemala City to Tikal. Although there are other routes offered, they are quite unreliable since they are not frequent, are often overbooked or cancelled at the last minute. Aside from the Aurora Airport, the only other modern airport is in Flores. Most of the domestic airlines offer at least one trip per week to Tikal, with the exception of Tikal Airlines, which has daily flights. The domestic airlines all have offices at the Aurora Airport.

Aeroquetzal	☎ 502/2-334-7689
Aviateca	☎ 502/2-470-8222
Lineas Aereas Maya	☎ 502/2-331-1841
Racsa, SA	☎ 502/2-361-7056
Taca	☎ 502/2-470-8222
Tikal Airlines	☎ 502/2-332-5070
Taca Inter Regional	☎ 502/2-279-5821
Mexicana	☎ 502/3-333-6001
Copa	☎ 502/2-361-1567

◆ By Bus

There are two kinds of buses in Guatemala: public and private.

Public buses are known as "chicken buses" since they accept livestock as well as people. Fares are dirt cheap and the buses go anywhere, no matter how remote or how bad the roads. They are also incredibly uncomfortable, since most are refurbished school buses. A second-class chicken bus is one with no missing parts, seats still bolted to the floor and windows that sometimes open. Third-class buses are those that should have been condemned but haven't stopped running. All buses are kept very clean, no matter how old.

Something you will never hear from a chicken bus driver is "sorry, we are full." Drivers will cram as many people into a bus as humanely possible – and then some. Expect to rub elbows, hips, thighs and other unexpected body parts with the locals while traveling on a chicken bus. There are usually three or four people to a seat and sometimes you will end up holding the odd parcel (or chicken) for your neighbor. It's always an adventure riding a chicken bus and it's a great way to meet the locals. To explore the more remote areas of Guatemala, you will need to travel by chicken bus. A short chicken bus ride is fun, but the long hauls can be nightmarish, particularly on roads with the hairpin turns. Chicken bus drivers don't slow down for anything.

For a fun read, pick up a copy of Vivien Lougheed's **Central America by Chicken Bus**. It's out of print, but worth finding a used copy for sheer entertainment value. At last check, used copies were available at www.amazon.com.

❖ BUS SAFETY

Unfortunately, chicken buses attract **thieves**. Keep your valuables next to your body in some kind of money pouch. Never put anything valuable or breakable in your luggage. Use a generic, inexpensive bag to avoid having your good one stolen. If you are going on a day-trip, leave your passport and money in the hotel safe and bring photocopies of your important papers. Avoid traveling at night on chicken buses, since that is the most dangerous time. Generally, you are safe in more rural areas, but avoid using the bus in bigger cities and tourist areas. Fortunately, these areas have plenty of tourist shuttles as an alternative.

You pay for a **ticket** when you are *on* the chicken bus. A recent rip-off has involved ticket sellers who stand outside the buses and sell you fake tickets as you board. Of course, the bus driver won't take the fake ticket – you won't know the difference – and you will have to pay a second time. All buses have an official seller who collects fares and provides tickets once the bus is on its way. Bus travel is cheap. Short runs will cost $1-$5; longer routes, $8-$12.

Another type of chicken bus are the *colectivos* or micro-buses. These are passenger vans that do short, frequent runs between villages. They are very inexpensive and are used primarily by workers heading to the local *fincas* or to town. You will still be crammed in, but with fewer people. You can flag down *colectivos* on any road. In the more remote areas, pick-up trucks act as the *colectivos* and you will be crammed in the back of the truck standing up.

Chicken bus schedules are subject to change without notice for a variety of reasons. Breakdowns are frequent and during the rainy season the roads may get washed out. Fiestas are another reason for delays, as bus drivers will often join in on the party and not be able to drive the next day. There is nothing you can do except enjoy your surroundings and be patient. Delays are part of travel in Guatemala.

Guatemala's **private, first-class buses** run less frequently than chicken buses. If you have a long journey, I recommend booking a seat on a first-class bus. They are regular-size buses with one seat per person, bathrooms and windows that work. The run from Guatemala City to Flores even has a "luxury" bus, with stewards who offer fresh complimentary coffee and snacks, comfy seats with pillows, blankets and Hollywood movies. The drivers appear to be sane as well.

TRAVEL INFORMATION

Private companies also offer shuttle services, which are **mini-vans**. They keep regular schedules and you get a seat all to yourself. They aren't as much fun, but they are certainly quicker and more comfortable than the other options. They are expensive when compared to chicken buses and, if you are traveling on a budget, they can eat up your cash quickly. But for those long hauls the shuttle is sometimes the only way to go. Reservations are recommended. Contact the companies below to book your place.

❖ SHUTTLE SERVICES

A number of companies offer shuttle services in and around Guatemala City, Copán Honduras, Panajachel, Chichicastenango and the surrounding areas. The companies listed below are all based in Antigua.

Adventure Travel Center Viareal, SA, 5a Avenida Norte #25B, ☎/fax 502/7-832-0162, viareal@guate.net.

Atitrans, 6a Avenida Sur #8, ☎ 502/7-832-1381, fax 502/7-832-0644, paraisomaya@yahoo.com.

Monarca Travel, Calzada Santa Lucia Norte #6a, ☎/fax 502/7-832-1939, monarcas@conexion.com.gt. This company also offers shuttle service from San Cristóbal de las Casas, Chiapas, Mexico to Antigua Guatemala. Tickets start at US $40 per person and include help with border crossings.

Rain Forest, 4a Avenida Norte #4A, ☎ 502/7-832-5670, fax 502/832-6299, www.rainforest.guate.com.

Sin Fronteras, 5a Avenida Norte #15A, ☎ 502/7-832-1017, fax 502/832-8453, www.sinfront.com.

Turansa, 9a Calle (inside Hotel Villa Antigua), ☎ 502/7-832-2928, fax 502/832-4692, www.turansa.com.

Guatemala Reservations/Rainbow Travel, 3 Avenida Norte #3, ☎ 502/7-832-4202, www.guatemalainfo.com.

◆ Hitchhiking

Everyone hitchhikes in Guatemala at some time. In remote areas, such as Los Altos, Quiché or Las Verapaces, hitching is sometimes the only way to get around. Rides are not free, though, and you will be expected to pay the same price as for a bus ticket – ranging from about 50¢ to a few dollars. Sometimes, truck drivers will overcharge tourists by a few dollars. If you argue the point they will usually back down.

The only place it isn't safe to hitchhike is through El Petén. Take the bus in that department. Women should never hitchhike alone.

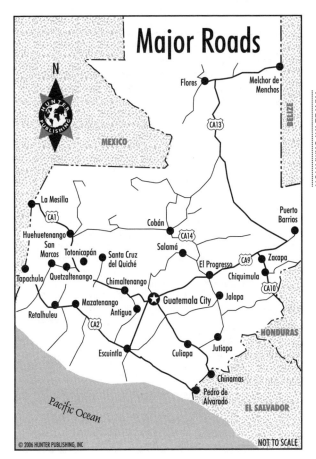

Major Roads

NOT TO SCALE

© 2006 HUNTER PUBLISHING, INC

◆ By Car

Renting a car gives you freedom and more time to explore. If you proceed with caution and don't drive long distances, you will be fine.

Guatemala measures distances and speeds in kilometers. The average speed on the highway ranges between 50 and 65 mph (80-100 kmph), but you may want to go slower through the mountain roads. The small white crosses you see on the roads mark where someone has died in a car accident.

There are lots of car rental companies. The best prices and selection are found at La Aurora airport in Guatemala City and at the Flores Airport in El Petén. You'll have a choice of cars, 4WD trucks and mini-vans. Prices start at US $50 per day, usually with some kind of distance allowance known as *kilometraje*. Read the fine print in your contract carefully and be sure to check the car thoroughly for dents and other damage before signing. Be aware that many insurance policies don't cover damage to the vehicle. The largest rental companies are **Hertz**, ☎ 502/2-334-7421, 800-654-3131, www.hertz.com; **Avis**, ☎ 502/2-331-2750; and **Tabarini** ☎ 502/2-332-2161, 2-334-5906.

Most cars have standard gear shift. If you must have an automatic, request it ahead of time. If you want to explore off the beaten path, you should invest in a four-wheel-drive vehicle. Before you head off into the wilds, be sure to check road conditions, particularly during the rainy season. There are no local tow trucks and no AAA in Guatemala. If you get stuck in a remote area, you are on your own.

❖ DRIVING SAFETY

Parking and **security** can be problematic in urban areas. Never park on the street, even in broad daylight. Robbers have perfected the art of smashing a window and grabbing anything within reach. Always use a car park with security and don't leave any valuables inside. **Carjacking** and **highway robberies** are becoming more of a problem, to the point where the US State Department is recommending that you caravan, that is, travel together in a group of cars. Depending on your travel plans, this may not be a practical option. The best precaution is to stay on the main highways and travel during the day.

Driving Tips

Driving is a challenge. **Defensive driving** is a must and you need to stay alert. There is no driver's education here, so there are plenty of bad drivers who don't use signals, tailgate and weave in and out of traffic. Stop signs, speed limits and traffic lights are frequently ignored. If you are not going fast, some drivers will start to tailgate while leaning on their horn and shining the high beams in your mirror. Maintain your cool. Unfortunately, tailgaters are often found on winding one-lane highways passing through the steep mountains. If someone is being really aggressive, pull over and let them pass. Don't try to challenge the road machos here. It's not worth ruining your vacation.

Another annoyance are the **diesel buses** and **trucks**. After about 10 minutes of following one of these stinky trucks you will probably start to feel sick from the fumes. Fortunately, truck and bus drivers are really cooperative. If they see you want to pass, they will blink their lights to let you know it is safe to pass. But proceed with caution because this signal also can mean they are about to stop, change lanes or turn.

The main highways are fairly well maintained, which means potholes the size of small meteors have been fixed, leaving holes just small enough to rip out your transmission. The Inter-American Highway (CA-1) and the road from Guatemala City to the Caribbean coast (CA-9) are dangerous due to heavy traffic, including large trucks and trailers. The Pacific Highway is also dangerous due to the many drunk drivers coming back from partying at the beach.

❖   INSIDER TIP: EMERGENCY HELP

There are no emergency roadside services, but you can contact the police by dialing 120 or the fire department at 122 or 123.

RULES OF THE ROAD

- ❖ Don't drive at **night**.
- ❖ **Drinking** and driving is against the law. If you are involved in an accident and have been drinking, you go directly to jail and stay there until a judge has determined who pays for the damages. A re-enactment of the accident will have to be performed in order for the judge to make his decision. This process can take up to two years to complete. Plenty of time to perfect your Spanish with your cellmates.
- ❖ Always get **insurance**. It's not required by law, but if you are involved in an accident and injure or kill a Guatemalan, you will be responsible for damages to the whole family.
- ❖ A valid US driver's **license** is acceptable ID to rent a car. You may also want to get an international driver's license since traffic officers seem to prefer them.
- ❖ Always carry your **license**, a photocopy of your **passport** and **car rental agreement** with you. All personal documents, including vehicle registration, are private property and may not be kept by the police for any reason. If a police officer insists on keeping the documents, ask that he escort you to the nearest police station to clear up the problem.
- ❖ Guatemala's road safety authorities are the Department of Transit and the Joint Operations Center of the National Police. You can contact them by dialing 120.
- ❖ Turning **right on red** is not permitted unless otherwise posted.
- ❖ Drivers must **yield** when entering a traffic circle. Those in the inner circle have right of way.
- ❖ Adults must wear **seat belts**, but they are optional for children.
- ❖ It's against the law to drive and use a **cellular phone** at the same time.

❖ If you are involved in an **accident**, don't move the car
and wait until your insurance representative arrives
before signing anything or giving out information.

◆ By Taxi

Taxis are plentiful. Every small village will have some kind of vehicle operating as a taxi, even if it is someone's personal truck or van. Taxis are a
good option if you want to visit a ruin or other site where there is no regular
bus service. Always settle on the price before you get into the cab.

In larger urban areas the driver must carry an ID card and must use the
meter for trips less than seven miles (12 km). For longer trips, you'll need
to negotiate the fare beforehand.

Don't flag down a cab in Guatemala City. Instead, phone for one from
your hotel or restaurant. That way, it can be traced if there's a problem.
Gypsy cabs often roam the streets looking for tourists to rob.

Staying in Touch

◆ Telephones

The entire country uses **area code 502**. The telephone company, called
TELGUA, has a monopoly on the market – there are no alternatives. All
phones work with a calling card, which can be bought in local grocery
stores and pharmacies in blocks of 20, 30, 50 and 100 quetzals. The
phone system is quite good and the lines are very clear. The cheapest
way to call home is to buy one of the calling cards and dial direct. You may
be able to use your private calling card purchased in the States, but you
need to check with that company to determine if the card is accepted in
Guatemala. If it is, you'll need a special access code in order to charge the
call to your card. You may have to purchase a local phone card to make
the initial call. Most calling cards follow the same procedure where you
dial the International Access number for the country and then give the international operator your card number or follow the prompts you are
given.

❖ INTERNATIONAL ACCESS NUMBERS FOR CALLING CARDS

MCI Call USA: ☎ 99-99-189. Check codes or for more information ☎ 800/674-7000.

AT&T: ☎ 999-9190 outside Guatemala City, 138-126 inside
Guatemala City. Check codes or for more information
☎ 800/288-2872.

Sprint FONCARD: ☎ 99-99-195. Check codes or for more
information ☎ 800/877-8000.

Canada Direct: ☎ 99-99-198. Check codes or for more information ☎ 800/561-8868.

Calling collect from Guatemala is very expensive, with rates starting at US $1 per minute. TELGUA has calling offices throughout the country (every village has one), where you can rent a booth with a phone and speak in relative privacy. The rates are slightly more expensive but the booths are quiet and usually air conditioned. You pay by the minute.

TRAVEL INFORMATION

◆ E-Mail

Every village, with the exception of remote spots, has an Internet café with e-mail capabilities. The cost is usually between Q5 and Q10 per hour, but it depends on whether the server is local or long distance. Those who must connect long distance will an have excruciatingly slow connection and, as a result, higher charges. If this is the case, consider waiting until you get to a larger village to check e-mail.

◆ Snail Mail

Regular mail is fairly reliable, although much slower than North American services. It can take up to three weeks for a letter to reach the US. Every village has a main post office (*Correo Central*) open daily from 8 am to 4 pm. Don't send anything of importance in the mail (including checks and credit cards numbers). If you want a letter to arrive quicker, pay a couple of extra quetzals and send it via "express" service. And if your mail is going out of the country, be sure to mark it as Airmail, *Correo Aereo*.

You can receive mail in any village. Have your letters addressed with your full name, followed by *Lista de Correo*, the village name, Guatemala, Central America. This system is most reliable in Guatemala City. Efficiency and swiftness is in direct proportion to the population and location of the village.

For very important documents, consider using a courier service. FEDEX and DHL both have offices in Guatemala City.

Fedex Guatemala, 14 avenida 7-12 zona 14, Bodega No. 20, ☎ 800/472-2222, fax 502/2-337-4900.

DHL S.A., 7 avenida 2-44, Zona 9, ☎ 502/2-379-1111.

Accommodations

◆ Considerations

There is an amazing range of accommodations in Guatemala. More expensive places list themselves as hotels, lodges and resorts, while budget hotels are the *pensiones*, *posadas* and *hospedajes*. By law, every hotel must post its rates, but this doesn't necessarily mean they will follow them. If you sign into their ledger, then a 20% tax will be added to your bill. Most budget hotels prefer to just take your money and give you a key. The more expensive hotels will ask you to register. All hotels must keep a comment book and make it available to any customer. The more reputable hotels will leave the book out for you to look through. Others keep it tucked away. Reading the comments can be a quick way to figure out the good, the bad and the ugly about your hotel.

Prices range from under US $10 to over US $150 per night. Rates quoted are per person. Rates are doubled for two people and are usually $10 or 15% more for a third person. The more tourists there are in the area, the higher the hotel prices.

Hot water is always a big problem. Budget hotels will advertise hot water, although they rarely provide water that is more than lukewarm. Moderate hotels usually have hot water, but you may have to ask the owner to turn the water heater on. High-end hotels have an endless supply.

◆ Tips for Budget Travelers

❖ Bring a lightweight sleeping bag for travel in remote areas. Often, budget hotels are the only option and they don't supply linens.

❖ Don't settle for the first budget hotel you see. Check out two or three and pick the best one. For a few dollars more you can always find something nicer.

❖ Always ask to see a couple of rooms.

❖ Check the bed before paying for the room. Sometimes the beds are done up nicely but are soft as butter or lumpy.

❖ Ask if there are specific times for hot water.

❖ Bring a small lock to put on your door. Budget hotels have pathetic locks that can be easily snapped off. If you are traveling with someone, share a combination lock so you don't have to worry about keys.

❖ Don't leave valuables in your room.

◆ Hotel Rates

Prices fluctuate. The smaller, more local places tend to post their rates in quetzals, while the more tourist-oriented hotels will post their prices in US dollars. When you see prices in US dollars, you can be almost certain that the prices are higher. The smaller hotels, especially those in the more remote areas, will only deal in local currency. They do no accept credit cards and if you insist on paying with American dollars your rate of exchange will be lousy. If

❖ HOTEL PRICING

Prices are per person.

$	Under $25
$$	$26 to $50
$$$	$51 to $85
$$$$	$86 to $125
$$$$$	over $125

you plan to travel to the more remote areas, bring small denominations of quetzals.

Reervations are not needed for the most part *unless* you are planning to travel during a very busy season such as to Antigua during Holy Week or to Esquipulas during the January dedications to the Black Christ. Hotels also fill up during the annual patron saint celebrations, so you should check to find out whether your intended village has anything happening before you head out.

Personal Safety

There's a new 24-hour **tourist hotline** that works from anywhere in the country: ☎ 502/2-421-2180.

The **Guatemala Tourist Board** (INGUAT(Instituto Guatemala de Turismo) has a new toll-free number: from the USA, ☎ 800-464-8281; within Guatemala, ☎ 801-464-8281.

◆ Theft

The US State Department (http://travel.state.gov/travel_warnings.html) has many warnings about the personal dangers of traveling in Guatemala. Although there are dangerous parts of Guatemala, many of the warnings are exaggerated. Robbery is a problem. This is an extremely poor country and every gringo looks wealthy. Your best bet is to leave at home anything you don't need, especially valuables. You won't worry about theft and will be able to enjoy a more relaxed trip.

Leave your **digital camera** and **video camera** at home. These are the most coveted items and they will be the first items stolen. Bring a cheap camera to use on your travels. Guatemala has many fine photographers selling beautiful postcards and prints.

Leave **gold** and **diamond** jewelry at home. Nothing displays your wealth so openly as gold jewelry. It's one of the first things thieves look for. There is no one to impress here.

Leave expensive **designer luggage** and **backpacks** at home. You may find yours missing, particularly if you are riding chicken buses. Choose a plain but sturdy bag instead.

Leave **designer sweatshirts**, **T-shirts** and **running shoes** at home, unless you would like to give them away as gifts. Making a fashion statement is a waste of time in Guatemala. The more discreet you look, the easier time you will have.

Take photocopies of your passports and other valuable documents and leave the originals in a hotel safe or other locked area.

◆ Feminism – A New Concept

Woman traveling should use tourist shuttles, travel in groups and not go out alone at night. They should *never* go into any of the bars or *cantinas* catering to men.

Rape is still not considered a crime here, and the woman is often blamed if such an event takes place. In smaller towns, act demurely and dress modestly. Maya women don't even show ankles; if you are dressed in the current American styles, you will be branded as a *puta* (whore). Usually, Maya men will avoid you, but *Ladino* men may think you are loose and make passes at you.

Never go **topless** anywhere, anytime. It's just not done in this conservative country.

Unfortunately, gringo women have the reputation of being loose. Blonde women are particularly prone to being harassed. In a land of jet-black hair, blonde is anyone with light to medium brown hair, and having a *rubio* girlfriend has become a potent sexual fantasy for many *Ladino* men. If you have a persistent admirer whom you need get rid of, tell him he must be more respectful because you're either a mother or not "THAT" kind of girl. It's an old-fashioned ploy, but it works. If you want to head off the beaten track, consider traveling with a companion.

> **AUTHOR TIP:** *The website www.journeywoman.com is an excellent resource if you are planning to travel solo.*

All these restrictions are frustrating, but the reality is that feminism hasn't made it this far south and women are still considered inferior. Save your breath; feminist rants will fall on deaf ears.

◆ Travel Warnings

Violence in Guatemala is sporadic. There are lots of rumors and exaggerations; the best source of information is your local embassy (they often exaggerate as well) or public bulletin boards that post warnings from other travelers. Talk to the ex-pats you meet or fellow travelers – they will know if there are any problem areas to avoid. The locals, including the INGUAT tourist board, often will not mention the problems for fear of chasing away much needed tourism.

See the Appendix, page 273, for a full list of Guatemalan embassies in the US and Canada.

Violent crimes involving physical harm seem to be restricted to Guatemala City and El Petén. Guatemala City has two million people and is like any other modern urban area. El Petén, however, is a special case. This area has lots of tourists who come to admire the many Maya ruins, including the famous Tikal. But it also has the largest population of desperately poor people. Most of them are honest and hard working; the robberies are usually committed by a handful of thugs. There is also spill-over crime from Belize, which is currently experiencing an epidemic of crimes against tourists. For that reason, Lívingston has become a hot spot for robberies.

In Antigua, Panajachel, Chichicastenango and Lake Atitlán, hotel robberies and pickpocketing are the biggest worries. The petty thieves won't hurt you if you just hand over the money and don't resist. Afterwards, go to the tourist police. They can be found at the local INGUAT office. Or the local police will refer you to the tourist police. They will be very sympathetic and will help you file a police report. Don't expect to get any of your valuables back. Don't take getting robbed personally and try to be forgiving. Most criminals here are desperately poor and angry about it.

Of the thousands of travelers who visit, only a small percentage have trouble. The majority of Guatemalans are kind, helpful and trustworthy. Don't be paranoid, just cautious.

Staying Healthy

A full range of modern medical care is available in Guatemala City, but medical care outside the city is limited. Most villages will have some kind of health clinic, sometimes without a doctor. For anything of a serious nature, you will have to go to Guatemala City. The state hospitals are extremely crowded and often suffer from a shortage of supplies and medicine. You will be better off in a private hospital. The care will be more than adequate for most common illnesses and injuries. However, doctors often expect to be paid upfront in cash before proceeding. Do not hesitate to contact your embassy to ask for their help in translating for you.

If you are planning to do any serious adventure activities you should have medical insurance with overseas coverage, including provision for medical evacuation. Check to see if your policy covers you.

◆ Private Hospitals in Guatemala City

Hospital Bella Aurora, 10 Calle 2-31, Zona 14, ☎ 502/2-368-1951, 2-337-3204, 2-337-3211.

Hospital Unversitario Esperanza, 6 Avenida 7-49, Zona 10, ☎ 502/2-339-3244 through 47.

Hospital Herrera Lllerandi, 6 Avenida 8-71, Zona 10, ☎ 502/2-334-5959.

Cedros de Libano, 8 Avenida 2-48, Zona 1, ☎ 502/2-230-6274.

Centro Medico, 6 Avenida 3-47, Zona 10, ☎ 502/2-332-3555.

Latino Americano, 7 Avenida A 7-50, Zona 2, ☎ 502/2-230-2396.

Nuestra Senora del Pilar, 3 Calle 10-71, Zona 15, Col Tecun Uman, ☎ 502/2-369-8088, 2-369-3249.

Roosevelt, Calzada Roosevelt 6-58, Zona 11, ☎ 502/2-471-3352, 2-471-1441.

◆ Public Hospitals

Hospital General San Juan de Dios, Av. Elena entre 9 y 10 Calle, Zona 1, ☎ 502/2-232-3741/44.

Hermeroteca Nacional, "Lic. Clemente Marroquin Rojas," 5 Av 7-26 Z-1 Niv 2, ☎ 502/2-232-7625.

Hospital de Gineco-Obstetrica, 14 Av y 4 C Zona 12 Col Colinas de Pamplona, Planta Telefónica, ☎ 502/2-471-0249.

Hospital de la Polcia Nacional, 11 Av 4-49 Zona 1, ☎ 502/2-232-7633.

Hospital de Rehabilitacion, 14 Av y 4 C Zona 12 Col Colinas de Pamplona, ☎ 502/2-472-1678.

Hospital de Salud Mental, Zona 18 Col Atlántida, ☎ 502/2-256-1486.

Hospital General de Accidentes, 13 Av y Calz, San Juan Zona 4 Mixco, ☎ 502/2-597-9626.

◆ Serious Ailments

Malaria

The **World Health Organization** (WHO), www.who.int, has issued malaria warnings for El Petén, Alta Verapaz, Baja Verapaz and San Marcos. There are moderate warnings for Escuintla, Huehuetenango, Izabal, Quiché, Retalhuleu, Suchitepequez and Zacapa. There is no risk in the highlands, Guatemala City, Antigua or Lake Atitlán, since all these places are above 4,921 feet (1,500 meters). Chloroquine, the recommended preventative medication, is usually taken once a week in a dosage of 500 mg. You must start one to two weeks before arrival and continue for four weeks after leaving. Many people suffer negative side-effects when taking chloroquine, including diarrhea, headache, dizziness, blurred vision and itching. Still, malaria is not something you want to experience. Bring your bug spray, wear long sleeves and pants to go into the jungle and invest in a mosquito net for your bed. Go indoors at dusk and make sure your hotel has got good screens.

Symptoms: Fever and flu-like illness, including shaking chills, headache, muscle aches, and tiredness. Nausea, vomiting, and diarrhea may also occur. Symptoms begin 10 days to four weeks after infection, although a person may feel ill as early as eight days or as late as one year afterward.

Treatment: Malaria can be cured with prescription drugs. The type of drugs and length of treatment depend on the type of malaria and the patient's condition.

Hepatitis A

Hepatitis A is not really a worry unless you are staying in filthy hotels and eating in dirty restaurants. Moderate hotels and family run restaurants are usually clean. While Hepatitis A is not dangerous or life threatening, it does make you sick for several weeks. Ask your doctor about getting a Hepatitis A vaccination.

Symptoms: Fever, malaise, anorexia, nausea, and abdominal discomfort, followed within a few days by jaundice. You can be asymptomatic or have a mild illness lasting one to two weeks, but for many this is a disabling disease lasting several months. There is no chronic infection and, once you have had hepatitis A, you cannot get it again. Some people experience a relapse within six to nine months after their initial exposure.

Treatment: Seek medical help immediately. Most people who have hepatitis A get well on their own after a few weeks, but you have to rest for several weeks under the care of a doctor. Medicine will be prescribed for your symptoms.

Hepatitis B

If you think you might have a romantic tryst with a local, consider getting a Hepatitis B vaccine. You can get this disease through sexual contact or a blood transfusion.

Symptoms: Jaundice, fatigue, abdominal pain, loss of appetite, nausea, vomiting, joint pain, bright yellow urine, yellow eyes, light-colored stools. About 30% of persons have no signs or symptoms and signs are less common in children.

Treatment: This is a serious disease that can cause permanent damage to the liver and you should seek medical attention immediately. The most commonly used drugs for treatment are adefovir dipivoxil, alpha interferon, and lamivudine. You can not drink any alcohol once you have had this disease.

Typhoid Fever

There is a risk of contracting typhoid fever in rural Guatemala, so you should speak with your doctor about vaccination. It can be given either by injection or as three pills taken every two days. Side-effects to the vaccine include abdominal discomfort, nausea, rash or hives. The vaccination is good for three years.

Symptoms: Sustained fever as high as 104° F (40° C), weakness, stomach pains, headache, loss of appetite, rash of flat, rose-colored spots. The only way to know for sure if an illness is typhoid fever is to have samples of stool or blood tested for the presence of *S. Typhi*.

Treatment: Seek medical treatment immediately. Three antibiotics are commonly prescribed: ampicillin, trimethoprim-sulfamethoxazole, and ciprofloxacin. Persons given antibiotics usually begin to feel better within two to three days, and deaths rarely occur.

Dengue Fever

This virus is also known as bone break fever because it feels as if your bones are being crushed. It's a virus transmitted through a bite from an infected mosquito. Fortunately, mosquitoes are rare in Guatemala because of the altitude. You will only have to worry about mosquitoes in the Izabal, Petén and Pacific regions.

Symptoms: High fever that lasts from two to seven days, severe headache, backache, joint pains, nausea and vomiting, eye pain, and rash. Generally, younger children have a milder illness than older children and adults.

Treatment: There is currently no medicine for this infection. Rest, drink plenty of fluids and take analgesics (pain relievers) with acetaminophen. Avoid aspirin. Consult a physician if the symptoms worsen.

Insect & Snake Bites

Most snakes in Guatemala are nocturnal and very timid, so the chances of a snake bite are slim. However, if you are traveling deep into the jungle make sure that one of your guides is carrying an anti-venom kit for snake bites. Wear long pants and hiking boots and stay on the trails. You will notice that most of the locals favor rubber boots that come up to their knees for walking in the jungle and they don't veer from the path. The two snakes to watch for are the **coral snake**, easily identified by its red, orange and black stripes and the yellow "**barba amarilla**" (yellow beard or fer-de-lance). This snake is known for attacking without provocation and should definitely be avoided.

Avoiding snakes is one of the primary reasons for hiring a guide.

There are only three types of spider bites that will need medical attention: **tarantula**, **black widow** (*latrodectus*) and **brown recluse** (*loxosceles*). The tarantula is known locally as the "araña de caballo" (horse spider) because they like to bite the hooves of horses and cows. They are sometimes found in banana trees as well. The bite resembles a bee sting, so if you are allergic to bees then you should seek medical attention.

The black widow spider likes to hide in dark places and its bite causes considerable pain and tissue damage. Although it is not life-threatening, you should have a doctor look at the area. Keep it clean and dry. The most serious bite is from the *Loxoceles reclusa*, the brown recluse spider or violin spider. In humans, their venom kills tissue surrounding the bite and then leaves a deep open sore that spreads. If you are bitten by a recluse spider, seek medical attention immediately and obtain medication to stop the tissue damage. Treatment includes cutting out the area that was bitten to prevent the spread of poison. These spiders are easily spotted by their light brown appearance with the dark shape of a violin on their head. Both the black widow and brown recluse like to nest in outhouses and latrines (the buttocks is the most common place for a bite). So check your outhouse with a flashlight before using it at night.

Fortunately, the **scorpions** in Guatemala are not fatal. Their bites can cause dizziness and numbness, especially in the mouth. Treatment involves rest and taking an antihistamine. Some people are more sensitive than others. Again, if you are allergic to bee stings you should seek medical attention immediately if bitten. The best treatment is prevention. Scorpions are shy creatures who like dark and damp places. To avoid getting bitten, don't walk outside in bare feet and check bags, shoes and backpacks before using them. Don't store any such items on the floor.

Watch out for the vicious **red ants** that will crawl up your pant legs and then bite all at once. The venom from their stings bubbles up into a small blister that itches for days. If bitten, ask for a cream for "hormigua roja" (red ant) at the local pharmacy. They will know what to give you.

Tourista

Tourista, or travelers' diarrhea, is the most common ailment. The usual culprit is the water. Always peel your fruits or vegetables before consumption or disinfect them using an iodine solution sold at the local grocery store. A pinch of chlorine in the water will do the trick as well. Locals avoid the water as well, so purified water is offered almost everywhere. If you are eating at a place that doesn't have electricity, avoid the meat and stick to things that have been boiled, like soup.

If you do come down with a bout of *tourista*, eat lightly. Rice, bananas and toast are good foods. Avoid dairy products, beans and meat. Drink plenty of fluids, including chamomile tea known locally as *manzana* tea. Only take Imodium if you need to travel, as this medicine will bind you up and it's best to let the bug out of your system. If you are still sick after three days, have bloody diarrhea, fever, shaking chills or marked abdominal pain, get yourself to a doctor immediately. The doctors in Guatemala are experts at dealing with this kind of thing and will prescribe something that gets you better immediately. Should you have stomach or bowel problems after you return home, tell your doctor you have been down south.

Dehydration/Altitude Sickness

Be sure to drink plenty of water to avoid dehydration while traveling in tropical regions. The first symptoms of dehydration are extreme fatigue and irritation. In the highlands, you may experience altitude sickness, which also will leave you feeling weak and tired. The only cure for this is to rest and get used to the climate. Drink plenty of water.

Medical Travel Insurance

No one plans to get sick or have an accident while on vacation but things don't also go according to plan. Check with your own medical insurance company to see if they cover you at all while out of the country. There are a number of companies offering travel insurance. Check the fine print and make sure you are fully covered including airlift costs before signing on the dotted line.

International SOS Assistance, Inc., Eight Neshaminy Interplex, Suite 207, Trevose, PA 19053-6956, ☎ 215/244-1500 or 800/523-8662, www.internationalsos.com.

Travel Insurance Services (Bertholon-Rowland Corporation), 2950 Camino Diablo, Suite 300, Walnut Creek, CA 94597-3991, ☎ toll-free US 800/937-1387, fax 925/932-0442, www.travelinsure.com.

Insurance Services of America, PO Box 1617, Chandler, AZ 85244, ☎ Canada/US toll free 800/647-4589, ☎ 480/821-9052 worldwide, fax 480/821-9297, www.worldwidemedical.com.

Canadian citizens may want to check out www.snowbirds.org to see how much of their medical expenses while traveling are covered by the health care system in each province. The official site for medical insurance is www.hc-sc.gc.ca.

❖ MOTHERLY TIPS ON STAYING HEALTHY

❖ Bring prescribed medication in its original packaging. Know the generic name (rather than the brand name) so a substitute can be found if needed.

❖ If you need syringes for medications, get a signed letter from your doctor stating they are a medical necessity. You may want to get the letter translated into Spanish.

❖ Bring an extra pair of glasses or contact lenses.

❖ Wear a medical alert bracelet if you have any allergies.

❖ Get adequate medical insurance, particularly if you are an adventure traveler. Make sure your insurance covers all your medical expenses abroad and will pay upfront for emergency evacuations.

❖ Avoid contact with stray dogs. Rabies is a major concern in Guatemala. If you get bitten, clean the wound thoroughly with hot water and soap. Contact the local health authorities immediately at the Centro de Salud or the local hospital. The police can also help. Very few dogs are vaccinated against rabies, so you will have to be closely monitored.

❖ Wear sun block, even in the highlands, where the sun is just as strong as on the beach.

❖ Always use a condom. Guatemala has AIDS as well.

❖ Leave motorcycles and scooters to the locals who are used to riding on cobblestone streets.

❖ Buy only bottled water and make sure the seal isn't broken.

❖ While on the road, avoid foods that you can't boil or peel.

❖ Get a good bug spray with 10% DEET.

❖ To avoid ticks, wear long sleeves, long pants, hats and shoes for tromping through the jungle.

❖ Be careful swimming off the Pacific coast, where rip-tides are dangerous.

Top 20 Attractions

Here are my favorite things to do and see, not in any particular order.

1. POPUL VUH & IXCHEL MUSEUMS, Guatemala City (page 57).

2. NUESTRA SENORA DE LA MERCED (Our Lady of Mercy Church), Antigua (page 78).

3. PACAYA VOLCANO, Escuintla (page 83).

4. SANTA MARIA VOLCANO/SANTIAGUITO, Quetzaltenango (page 132).

5. MONTERRICO NATURAL RESERVE/HAWAII NATIONAL PARK, Santa Rosa (page 250).

6. LAKE ATITLAN, at sunrise or sunset, visiting the villages, Sololá (pages 95, 96).

7. CHICHICASTENANGO THURSDAY MARKET, Quiché (page 152).

8. SEMUC CHAMPEY, Alta Verapaz (page 162).

9. MARIO DARY RIVERA BIOTOPO DEL QUETZAL, Baja Verapaz (page 169).

10. BOCAS DE POLOCHIC, Izabal (page 237).

11. RÍO DULCE CANYON, Izabal (page 221).

12. RUINS OF QUIRIGUA, Izabal (page 211).

13. TIKAL, El Petén (page 190).

14. IGLESIA Y MONASTERIO DE SAN FRANCISCO, La Antigua (page 79).

15. PALACIO NACIONAL, Guatemala City (page 52).

16. MARTYRS OF SANTIAGO ATITLAN CATHEDRAL, Santiago (page 120).

17. VISIT MAXIMON, Santiago (page 114, 120).

18. IGLESIA ZUNIL, Zunil (page 135).

19. CERRO CAHU, El Remate (page 185).

20. MACHAQUILA RUINS, LAS CONCHAS CAVE, Poptún (page 205)

Going Metric

GENERAL MEASUREMENTS

To make your travels a little easier, we have provided the following chart that shows metric equivalents for the measurements you are familiar with.

1 kilometer	=	.6124 miles
1 mile	=	1.6093 kilometers
1 foot	=	.304 meters
1 inch	=	2.54 centimeters
1 square mile	=	2.59 square kilometers
1 pound	=	.4536 kilograms
1 ounce	=	28.35 grams
1 imperial gallon	=	4.5459 liters
1 US gallon	=	3.7854 liters
1 quart	=	.94635 liters

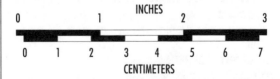

TEMPERATURES

For Farenheit: Multiply centigrade figure by 1.8 and add 32
For Centigrade: Subtract 32 from Farenheit figure and divide by 1.8.

Centigrade		Farenheit
40°	=	104°
35°	=	95°
30°	=	86°
25°	=	77°
20°	=	64°
15°	=	59°
10°	=	50°

Guatemala City

Guatemala City has been voted one of the ugliest cities in the world, and with good reason. It's a hideous mess of concrete, traffic and houses piled one on top of the other. Plenty of visitors skip this town, but since all transportation routes lead to *el capital* (as Guatemalans call it), you must make your peace with it. The visa extension office is located in the city.

It's not all horrible. The city has an active cultural life with incredible museums and excellent restaurants. Perhaps the best way to handle a visit is to take it in small doses. Pick a couple of sights close to one another and go from there. A good map will help. Guatemala City is divided up into zones and some are better than others. Most of the tourist sites are in Zona 1, Zona 4, Zona 10 and Zona 13. Only Zona 1 presents any serious problems with muggings or robberies.

Unlike other parts of Guatemala, budget travel is not really sensible here because it puts you in jeopardy. Plan on spending a bit more on transportation and accommodation.

History

Guatemala City was first a Maya city known as **Kaminal Juyú** that was settled in the Middle Preclassic period (1000-500 BC). Between AD 200 and 230, Kaminal Juyú became an ally of the powerful northern city El Mirador. Because of this partnership, it was able to control all trade routes and became a prosperous and powerful city-state. Later, during the Early Classic period (AD 200-500), it also developed ties with the invading Teotihuacán of Mexico. By AD 900, the city was deserted. Its buildings became hidden in the jungle, overlooked by all.

In 1620, the **Spanish** came into the area to build **La Ermita**, a small outpost designed to keep trade routes open. It remained a backwater for another 162 years before being chosen as the new capital. Actually, Guatemala City was not the first choice. The first capital was founded in 1520 near the Cakchiquel capital of Iximché. But the Spanish lieutenant in charge, Alvarado, was eventually driven out of the area – he fled to the Almononga Valley to build his second capital at the foot of the Agua Volcano. This was a bad choice. In 1531 the town was buried in a mudslide during a volcanic eruption. The capital was moved farther east into the

Panchoy Valley, between the three volcanoes – Agua, Fuego and de Acatenango. It became the city of Antigua. This third site was not a wise choice either. Antigua was continually being hit with earthquakes. The worst one, in 1773, left Antigua completely destroyed. The Governor had had enough and petitioned the King of Spain to move the capital. After some initial research, he settled on La Ermita. Permission was granted and, on January 1, 1776, **La Nueva Guatemala de la Asuncíon** became the new capital. There were high hopes for the city, which was designed to resemble a Spanish colonial city with a majestic Great Plaza, wide streets and neoclassic architecture. Estates close to the city center were given to wealthy citizens to replace the properties they left behind in Antigua. But money ran out, and many of the grand buildings were never completed.

To this day, Guatemala City is not as elegant as Antigua. By 1800 the population was up to 26,000 residents, but little work was done until the Conservative Government of 1855 began completing buildings and naming streets. The University of San Carlos de Guatemala, started in 1786, was finally completed between 1849 and 1855. A variety of churches were erected and the National Theater (*Teatro Nacional*) was built in 1958.

The Liberal government of 1873 opened the city and country to Europeans, who arrived in the city and began opening businesses. In order to develop properties for them, President Justo Rufino Barrios seized land from the church which, at that time, still owned 60% of the land. To organize the city he adopted the Byzantine street numbering system that's still in use today (see below, under *Adventures on Foot*). In 1890, the suburb of Exposicion was built in honor of the World Exhibition. The area became Zona 4.

The new liberal president **José María Reyna Barrios**, elected in 1892, decided to give the city a facelift. Using Paris as his role model, he ordered the creation of the wide Boulevard 30 de Junio, known today as Avenida La Reforma. A replica of the Eiffel Tower, botanical gardens and a temple to Minerva were also built at this time. Avenida 6 became Avenida Minerva and wealthy families fleeing Cobán after a 1902 earthquake settled into this area, known today as Zonas 9 and 10.

With a beautiful new look and established culture, Guatemala was set for a bright future. Then, in late 1917 a series of earthquakes hit the city. The tremors continued until early 1918 and, when the dust settled, the city was in ruins. President Ubico immediately started a reconstruction campaign. During this time the post office, the National Police Building, and the National Palace were built. But once again money ran out and when rural Guatemalans from all over the country began coming to the city looking for work, there was no place for them to live. They began building shanty towns in the nearby hills. The flow of people to the city increased during the turbulent years of 1954 to 1998, when the civil war displaced thousands of civilians. Again they landed in the surrounding hills. The problems were compounded by the 1976 earthquake, which reduced the city to rubble, killed 23,000 and injured another 75,000. Over one million were left homeless and rebuilt their house with any material available.

Guatemala City remains the commercial and administrative center of the country. Pollution, overcrowding and garbage continue to be its biggest environmental concerns. The more pressing issue, though, is poverty. There are over two million residents living in desperate poverty alongside the two percent of the population who are wealthy. The 21st century is going to be challenging.

Getting Here & Getting Around

A rriving and departing Guatemala City will probably be the simplest part of your trip. It's everything in between that is complicated.

◆ By Air

All international flights land at **La Aurora International Airport** in Zona 13, in the southeastern part of the city. Taxis wait outside the terminal on the Arrivals level. Catch a cab into town; the set prices are reasonable, running US $7 to Zona 9 or 10, US $10 for Zona 1. You can try negotiating, but be sure to settle on the price before getting into the cab. It takes about 10 minutes to reach the city.

Public buses offer service from the airport into the city. Tickets are Q15 (about $2) and it takes 45 minutes to reach the downtown core.

◆ By Bus

All the bus lines from around the country go directly to the capital – look for buses labeled GUATE. Bus terminals are located in Zona 4. This area is not the safest at night. If your bus arrives late, make sure you have hotel reservations already lined up. As soon are you are off the bus, call your hotel and ask them to send a cab for you.

Shuttle bus services offer the safest and most convenient way to arrive or depart from the city. Plenty of them operate between Antigua and Guatemala City, and all of the larger tourist centers have shuttle service into the capital. If you are coming from the east or the north, your service will be direct. If you are coming from the west then you will probably stop in Antigua first and may have to switch shuttles there. Rates start at US $7.

If there are no shuttle services, then travel on **first-class buses** into Guatemala City. You will be an easy target for thieves if you opt to make the trip on a chicken bus. First-class buses are also quicker, and should get you into the city at a decent hour. They leave from every village bus terminal.

Local bus service is a nightmare. Although frequent and cheap, the routes change on a daily basis in order to avoid traffic, so not even the locals know where the buses are going. That said, you can count on two main routes: buses from Zone 1 to Zone 10 down 10a Avenida and buses from Zone 10 to Zone 1 down either 6a Avenida or 7a Avenida, depending on the direction you are traveling. All public buses stop running at 9 pm and you will have to rely on private jitneys called **ruteleros**. These are best avoided. If you do need to use one, however, they can be flagged down on the main streets. The cost is under $1.

◆ By Taxi

Taxis are plentiful and the rates reasonable. Don't hail taxis off the street (many of those make a practice of robbing tourists); instead, call for one (**Amarillo Express**, ☎ 502/2-332-1515, or **Taxis Blanco y Azul**, ☎ 502/2-360-0903). Most taxis are metered, but if yours isn't, be sure to agree upon a price with the driver before jumping in. You should tip 5-10% of the fare.

Adventures on Foot

Finding an **address** can be a challenge here. The antiquated numbering system was implemented by an engineer in 1877. It was complicated back then and hasn't improved since. Streets are designed on the classic Spanish grid system. Avenidas (avenues) always run north to south. Calles (streets) always run east to west. Each municipal address has three numbers followed by its zone. The first number in the address is for the building, the second for the street, followed by the approximate distance (in meters) from the nearest cross street. For example, 3 Avenida17-05, Zona 14 would be read as #3, 17th Avenue, five meters from the cross street in Zone 14. Of course, these addresses don't really work and often additional instructions, such as the name of the building, are added. For example Edificio Casa Alta, Entre 6 y 7 Avenida, Local 5 would read as the Casa Alta Building, entrance on the corner of Avenues 6 and 7, in area 5 of that neighborhood. It takes some getting used to and most locals rely on landmarks for actual directions.

If the street numbering isn't confusing enough, the city has also been divided into **zones**. Main roads are used as the boundaries between each zone but otherwise there are no markers. Just because the zones are numbered does not mean they are in chronological order either. Look at a city map and you will notice that Zona 3 is beside Zona 7, which is beside Zona 19. Fortunately, as tourist, you need only concern yourself with Zonas, 1, 4, 10 and 13. Aside from Zona 13, these are in the center of the city.

> **AUTHOR WARNING:** *Walking around in Zona 10 is safe. However, be careful in Zona 1, as it can lead to some of the poorer neighborhoods where robberies are more likely to take place.*

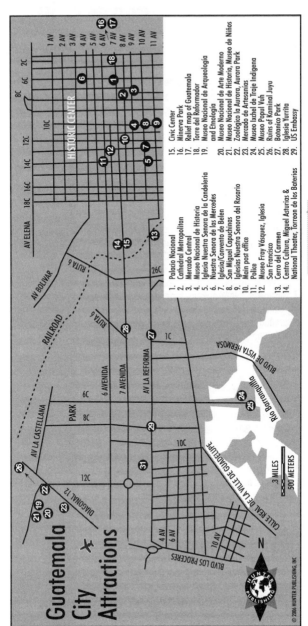

Guatemala City Attractions

GUATEMALA CITY

1. Palacio Nacional
2. Cathedral Metropolitan
3. Mercado Central
4. Museo Nacional de Historia
5. Iglesia Nuestra Senora de la Candelaria
6. Nuestra Senora de las Mercedes
7. Iglesia/Convento de Belen
8. San Miguel Capuchinos
9. Iglesias Nuestra Senora del Rosario
10. Main post office
11. Police
12. Museo Fray Vásquez, Iglesia
    San Francisco
13. Cerro del Carmen
14. Centro Cultura, Miguel Asturias &
    National Theater, Torreon de los Baterias
15. Civic Center
16. Minerva Park
17. Relief map of Guatemala
18. Torre del Reformador
19. Museo Nacional de Arqueologia
    and Ethnologia
20. Museo Nacional de Arte Moderno
21. Museo Nacional de Historia, Museo de Niños
22. Zoológico la Aurora, Aurora Park
23. Mercado de Artesanios
24. Museo Ixchel de Traje Indigena
25. Museo Popul Vuh
26. Ruins of Kaminal Juyu
27. Botanica Park
28. Iglesia Yurrita
29. US Embassy

© 2004 HUNTER PUBLISHING, INC.

◆ Walking Tour

Zona 1

Zona 1 is the city's historical section and it has the most attractions. It also has a red-light district right beside the attractions and this area should be avoided, especially after dark. Most of the city's cheap and mid-range hotels are in Zona 1. The best day to visit is Sunday, when the central plaza is full of families who come to enjoy all the action.

Plaza Mayor de la Constitución, 5a and 7a Avenida between 6a and 8a Calle. This plaza is the heart of the city and was one of the first places built in 1776. A large fountain stands in the middle of the plaza. Surrounding the park are other important historical monuments, such as the National Library (*Biblioteca Nacional*) and the Metropolitan Cathedral (*Catedral Metropolitana*). Plaza Mayor is also known as Plaza of the Arms (*Plaza de Armas*), one of its original names. On Sunday the plaza is filled with musicians, stalls selling crafts and small *comedores* (eateries).

Palacio Nacional, north side of Plaza Mayor, 6 Calle between Avenidas 6 and 7, ☎ /fax 502/2-221-4444. This is the former residence of General Jorge Ubico. It was built while he was in office between 1936 and 1943 and now houses the executive branch of the government. It is a rather eclectic blend of Renaissance, neoclassical and baroque styles using concrete, brick and granite. Many of Guatemala's foremost artists decorated the building and it is considered a museum because of their contribution. The 4,400-lb (2,000-kg) Bohemian-crystal chandelier should not be missed. On the second floor the reception room (*Salas de Recepion*) has a beautiful stained-glass window telling the story of Guatemala. Also look for **Kilometer Zero** (*kilometro cero*), the exact center of the country. Admission is free. Open 9 am to 5:30 pm, Monday to Friday, 8 am to 3 pm on weekends.

Catedral Metropolitana, west of Main Plaza, 7 Avenida 6 and 8 Calle, ☎ 502/2-232-7621. Also know as El Sagrario (The Most Sacred), this church is one of the few remaining 16th-century buildings in Guatemala City. There isn't much to see in this short, squat structure. Construction on the building was started in 1776 and finished in 1868. During the 1917 earthquake the baroque façade came crashing down and the cracked bell tower fell onto the altar below. The bell has been removed, but little else has been restored. Inside is the **Virgin of Perpetual Help** (*Virgén del Perpetuo Socorro*), Guatemala's oldest Christian image, which was brought over in 1522 by Hernan Cortes. Carved on the columns outside are the names of those killed during the civil war – a poignant reminder of the lives lost. The church is open daily. No admission fee.

Mercado Central, behind Palacio Nacional, 8 Avenida. The central market is one big hunk of concrete designed in reaction to the 1976 earthquake. It's the place to shop for handicrafts and you'll find goods from every region in the country. Hundreds of tiny booths sell everything from ceramics, sculptures and wooden masks to statues and leather goods – all at very low prices. If you can stand the crush of people, you can find some real bargains here. Beware of pickpockets in this market! Open 7 am to 6 pm, Monday to Saturday.

Pasaje Aycinena, 9 and 10 Calle between Avenidas 6 and 7. This cobblestone passageway used to link the houses on both sides of the street. All that is left is an arch with the name carved into the stone. The ground floors have been converted into shops and boutiques.

Palacio de Correos (Postal Palace), 7 Avenida and 12 Calle, ☎ 502/2-232-6101. This is a good example of the nationalistic colonial style created in Guatemala during the late 1930s. Started in 1937 and completed in 1940, the palace has two main buildings connected by an arched pedestrian walkway. The exterior walls are covered with national symbols in murals by local artists. In 1981, the palace was declared a national monument and it now serves as home to the National Department of Postal Services (*Dirección General de Correos y Telégrafos de Guatemala*). Open 8:30am-5:30pm, Monday-Friday; 9 am-1 pm, Saturday. Free.

Palacio de la Policía Nacional (Palace of the National Police), 6 Avenida 13-71, ☎ 502/2-232-0221. During the 1930s, Guatemala endured General Ubico, a dictator who believed he was the reincarnation of Napoleon. We have him to thank for this outlandish building that resembles a medieval castle complete with battlements. It's too hideous to miss and is a perfect headquarters for the Guatemalan police. Open daily.

Nuestra Señora de las Mercedes (Our Lady of Mercy), 5 Calle 11-67, ☎ 502/2-232-0631. Many of the images in this church were transported from Antigua when the capital was moved, and the building itself has survived numerous earthquakes. It features an extensive collection of baroque-style altarpieces, a large collection of colonial-era art and the second-largest organ in the country. The church was originally built by the Merced Order, but was taken over by the Jesuits in 1829. Outside, a stone façade is adorned with Greek columns and decorative scrolls. Open daily from 6 am until 6 pm. No admission.

Iglesia y Convento de Belén (Church and Convent of Belén), 10 Avenida y 13, ☎ 502/2-232-3605. At one time, this church and convent stretched for many city blocks. Brother Pedro San José de Betancourt of the Bethlehem Order built the baroque church and convent in 1776 and it housed many carved images of the Virgin Mary and Jesus. In 1813, pro-independence meetings were permitted to take place in the church and, as a result, President Barrios closed the convent and church and appropriated the land. All that remains is the small church. Today, the church has reopened and the convent has been converted to a girls' school. Open 6 am to 7 pm. Free admission.

Nuestra Señora de Candelaria (Our Lady of Candelaria), 13 Avenida 1-12, ☎ 502/2-253-6376. This beautiful little church took a long time to complete. Started in 1784 using salvage from a church in Antigua, it wasn't finished until 1867. Inside is the famous image of Jésus Nazareno de la Candelaria, brought from Antigua. In 1976, the church suffered severe earthquake damage and it has recently been restored.

Iglesia San Francisco, 6 Avenida y 13 Calle, ☎ 502/2-232-6325. Franciscan architects designed this baroque church in 1800 and completed the building in 1829. It's built in the shape of a crucifix with an altar 288 feet (88 meters) high and 39 feet (12 meters) wide in the center. Behind it are carved wooden statues of Jesus and one of the Immaculate Conception donated by King Carlos V of Spain. Open daily, 7 am to 5 pm.

San Miguel Capuchinas (St. Michael of the Capuchins), 10 Calle y 10 Avenida, ☎ 502/2-238-2126. This is one of the oldest surviving churches in the capital, inaugurated on August 7th, 1789. It has survived all the earthquakes fairly intact. It features a Mudejar-style roof, the first architectural style of the city (it was later abandoned for a more European look). Inside are several altarpieces with baroque paintings and carvings. Open 9 am to 10 pm daily, offering mass and confession.

Nuestra Señora del Rosario/Santo Domingo de Guzmán (Our Lady of the Rosary/St. Dominic of Guzmán), 12 Avenida 10-09, ☎ 502/2-232-2847. This is one of the most famous churches in Guatemala. It was built by the Dominicans in 1778 when they moved their order here from Antigua. The building was completed in 1804 and has many valuable pieces of colonial art. Unfortunately, it was severely damaged in 1917 and has been entirely rebuilt. Today it still contains one of the best collections of Dominican colonial art. Open daily, 6:30 am until 5 pm.

Torreón de las Baterias (Tower of the Battery), 24 Calle 3-81, Interior del Centro Cultural Miguel Angel Asturias, ☎ 502/2-253-5286. These are the remains of the San José fort which started as an artillery unit in 1876. The building was abandoned after the 1917 earthquake, when it was badly damaged. In 1994, during an uprising against the government, the fort was destroyed and all that remains is the main tower. For years, this section was used for various functions, including a circus and boxing ring. It was finally given to the Ministry of Defense, which turned the tower into the **Heraldic and Military Arms Museum of Guatemala** (*Museo Heraldico y de Armas del Ejército de Guatemala*). The museum has a collection of military objects and exhibits. Open 10 am to 5pm daily. Admission is Q5 for adults, Q2 for children.

Museo de Historiá, 9 Calle 9-70, ☎ 502/2-253-6149. This historical library and museum opened in 1974. It has a permanent collection of furniture and official documents that date back to 1821. The museum also offers ongoing cultural displays that change according to the seasons. A reference library is also open to the public. Museum is open 9 am to 5 pm, Monday to Friday. Admission is free.

Cerro del Carmen (Carmen Hill), end of 12 Avenida. At the top of this hill is a hermitage dating from 1620, donated to the city by the barefooted Carmelite congregation. Inside is a silver embossed image of the *Virgén del Carmen*. The view from here is quite lovely and many local families come here to enjoy a picnic. Don't come alone or at night.

Zona 2

This zone was built for the Maya Indians who left Antigua for the new capital in 1774. The area was gentrified during the 1940s, when the North Hippodrome neighborhood was added and wealthy families started building residences on Avenida del Hipódromo. It remains a lovely residential area. The park should be avoided after dark.

Parque Minerva – Mapa en Relieve (Minerva Park Relief Map), final de la Avenida Simeón Cañas, ☎/fax 502/2-254-1114. Minerva Park is not particularly nice but it does have a quirky relief map of Guatemala. Built in 1904, the map shows the geographical features of Guatemala such as mountain ranges, volcanoes, rivers, lakes, ports, roads and various districts and capitals. The whole thing covers 2,152 square yards (1,800 square meters). Its designer, Engineer Francisco Vela, traveled the whole country taking measurements and making calculations so the map would be accurate. You might even get lucky and be there when they turn on the water that makes the rivers flow. There is a small tourist shop nearby selling postcards and books about the map. This attraction is a big hit with kids. Avoid the area after sunset. Open 8 am until 6 pm daily. Admission is Q12.

Zone 4

This neighborhood was built in 1890 to house a special exhibit in honor of the Paris World Fair. Zona 4 is filled with various government buildings, as well as most bus terminals. Its notable feature is the Civic Center, with its marvelous murals. This is a safe zone, but steer clear of its southern end, as it approaches Zona 3.

Centro Cívico, 7a Avenida 1-17. The Civic Center is made up of a number of important structures built during the 1950s and 1960s, when civic pride was at an all-time high. Among the noteworthy buildings are the Supreme Court (*Corte Suprema de Justicia*), the Social Security Institute (*Instituto Guatemalteco de Seguridad Social*), the Guatemalan Tourist Board (*Instituto Guatemalteco de Turismo, INGUAT*), the Ministry of Finance (*Ministerio de Finanzas Publicas*) and the Bank of Guatemala (*el Banco de Guatemala*). These buildings are covered with incredible mosaics and murals created by Guatemala's foremost artists. The most impressive of these are the mosaic of Carlos Merida on the social security building and the relief murals of Dagoberto Vazquez on the Bank of Guatemala Building.

Iglesia de Yurrita, Ruta 6 8-52 Calle Mariscal Cruz, ☎ 502/2-312-5143. This little church is one of the most beautiful in the capital. It was named after its designer, Don Felipe de Yurrita, who owned the land from 1928 to 1941. To show his religious devotion, Yurrita built this small chapel dedicated to the Virgin Mary. It reveals an intricate and skillful mixture of Catalan art nouveau, neo-gothic and Mudejar styles. The façade uses cement, stone, tiles and bricks made from plaster, with obsidian, marble and tile accents. Inside are stained-glass windows, a carved marble altar and a painting of the Judgement of Christ in high relief. Open Saturdays from 6 pm until 9 pm and Sundays 8 am until 6 pm.

Zona 7

Zone 7 is a rather scrappy part of the city that includes a garbage dump, along with the ruins of an ancient Maya city.

Kaminal Juyú Ruins, Colonial Kaminal Juyú, 23 Avenida. This was once the largest Maya city in the Guatemalan highlands. It was built during the Middle Preclassic period (1000-500 BC) and grew into an important trade center. By AD 100, over 200 hundred pyramids had been constructed in the area, the largest reaching up to 59 feet (18 meters). Through a series of alliances with its powerful northern neighbor, El Mirador, Kaminal Juyú was able to develop into an important commercial center trading in jade and obsidian.

For many years it was thought that the existence of this city was a myth. Archeologists had come across references to it, but they had no physical proof. Its discovery was accidental; in the early 1970s the area was being bulldozed to make room for housing. Underneath were remains of Kaminal Juyú. The city contained some astonishing discoveries, including hieroglyphics that proved the Maya were literate much earlier than previously calculated, before even Tikal or Copán were built. In AD 400, the Teotihuacán from Central Mexico invaded the city and made it their regional capital. They soon controlled the region's jade and obsidian mines and their rulers constructed temples and buildings on top of the old.

Archeologists have now completed over 200 excavations and have found a variety of Maya ceramics, sculpture and architecture. Tombs contained corpses preserved with cinnabar and surrounded by sacred objects such as obsidian knives, stingray spines and quartz crystals. Many of the structures have been left underground in order to preserve them. To visit these ruins you need a special permit from the Anthropological & Historical Institute (*Instituto Guatemalteco de Antropología e Historiá*), IGAEH. You can obtain the permit at their office on 12 Avenida 11-65, Zone 1, ☎ 502/2-232-5571. Admission is Q10, which includes your permit

Zona 9

Avenida la Reforma separates Zone 10 and Zona 9, a wealthy residential area.

Torre del Reformador, 7 Avenida y 2 Calle. Although only 24 feet (75 meters) tall, this metallic structure is a replica of the Eiffel Tower. It was inaugurated on July 19, 1935 as a memorial to General Justo Rufino Barrios. On top of the tower is a bell donated by Belgium, as well as a beacon donated by American Airlines in 1994 to guide airplanes into Aurora International Airport. It's best seen during the day on foot or at night from a cab.

Zona 10/Zona Viva

Zona 10 is known as Zona Viva because of its nightlife. Many museums, hotels, restaurants and shops are located in this area. It's the safest zone in Guatemala City (and the most expensive) and you can feel secure going out at night here.

Museo Popul Vuh, 6 Calle Final, Universidad Francisco Marroquín, ☎ 502/2-361-2301, fax 502/2-361-2301. The private Popul Vuh Museum on the Marroquín University campus has an excellent collection of Maya relics, including polychrome incense burners, burial urns, carved wooden masks and traditional textiles of great historical and scientific value. In another room there is a collection of colonial art and silver objects.

There is also an accurate copy of the Dresden Codex – one of the few remaining Maya books. This was one of the first Mayan manuscripts brought back to Spain by Hernán Cortés in 1519. No one understood the language but the book was still considered a trophy and was given to a member of the Spanish royal family in Dresden. Thus the book became known as the Dresden Codex. It remains one of the few examples of Mayan literature. Most Mayan manuscripts were burned in 1562 by Fray Diego de Landa at his monastery in Man, Yucatán for being works of the Devil. This vicious destruction of the culture shocked even the Church and as penance Diego de Landa was instructed to write a book about the Maya. *Relación de las Cosas de Yucatán* (today entitled *Yucatán Before and After the Conquest,* Dover Press, 1978) was published in 1566 and is the most significant record we have of Mayan beliefs, customs and history. The museum offers a special tour for children which includes some quick lessons on how to decipher a few hieroglyphics in the Dresden Codex.

A gift shop sells books, magazines, posters, calendars and paintings about the Maya culture. Open 9 am to 5 pm, Monday to Friday, and 9 am to 1 pm on Saturdays. Admission is Q20 for adults, Q6 for children.

Museo Ixchel del Traje Indigena, end of 6 Calle, Campus de la Universidad Francisco Marroquín, ☎/fax 502/2-331-3638. This museum specializes in beautifully curated exhibits of Guatemalan textiles. Its permanent textile collection has samples from over 140 communities spanning several decades. It also runs several research and preservation programs dedicated to indigenous textiles. A permanent watercolor collection by Carmen L. Patterson depicts the various traditional Maya costumes, while paintings by Andres Curruchich document the daily life of the Kaqchiquel Maya.

The **Museum of Children and Young People** (*Museo de la Ninez y de la Juventud*) is part of the Textile Museum and offers children's programs in anything to do with textiles, including painting, embroidering, weaving and using natural inks. There is also a small café, art gallery, bookstore and gift shop. Open 9 am to 5 pm, Monday to Friday, and 9 am to 1 pm on Saturdays. Admission is Q20 for adults, Q6 for children.

Avenida La Reforma. This avenue runs along the boundary of Zones 9 and 10. Originally built in 1897 by President Barrios, who named it Boulevard 30 de Junio, its design was based on that of the Champs Elysées. The name was changed to Avenida La Reforma to honor Barrios, who was nicknamed The Reformer because of all the changes he brought to the country. Many historical monuments line this avenue and the whole street has been named a National Heritage Site. The avenue begins at Plaza Obelisco, where the eternal flame of Guatemala burns.

Zona 13

One of the newer and more modern zones in the city, Zona 13 is known for its beautiful museums and parks. Avenida de las Americás separates Zona 13 and 14. The International Airport is in Zona 13.

Museo Nacional de Arqueologiá y Etnologia, Finca La Aurora, ☎ 502/2-472-0478. Founded in 1945, the National Museum of Archaeology and Ethnology houses a collection of Maya jade, obsidian and pottery objects found in the royal tombs at Kaminal Juyú, Tikal and other ruins. Also included in the exhibit are stelae and carvings. Open 9 am to 4 pm, Tuesday to Friday, 9 am to noon, and 2 to 4 pm on Saturday. Admission is Q28.

Museo de Arte Moderno, Finca la Aurora, Local 6, ☎/fax 502/2-472-0467. The Museum of Modern Art was originally opened in Zona 1 in 1934; it was moved to its present location in 1968. The museum has a permanent collection of Guatemalan art and sculpture by the country's leading artists. Open 9 am to 4 pm, Tuesday to Friday, 9 am to noon and 2 to 4 pm on Saturday. Admission is Q9.

Museo de Historiá Natural, Finca la Aurora, ☎/fax 502/2-334-6055. The Museum of Natural History opened in 1950 with a small collection of animals that has grown steadily to include a large range of indigenous birds and mammals, as well as mineral and paleontological specimens. It features a butterfly pavilion and ecological library. The grounds include botanical gardens that focus on local and exotic plants, including many endangered species. Open 9 am to 4 pm, Tuesday to Friday, and 9 am to noon and 2 to 4 pm on Saturday. Admission is Q12.

Mercado de Artesanías, Finca la Aurora. Located by the museums is the official handicrafts market offering a variety of antiques, textiles, wooden carvings, ceramics and leather goods. Open 8 am to 6 pm, Monday to Saturday.

Zoológico La Aurora, Finca Nacional La Aurora, ☎ 502/2-472-0507, fax 502/2-471-5286. This zoo opened in 1925 with a selection of local animals. Since then it has been renovated to include a variety of species from around the world, all displayed in their natural habitat. It's a popular destination with local families, who also come for the interactive children's museum. Open 9 am to 5 pm, Tuesday to Sunday. Admission is Q10 for adults, Q5 for children.

Where to Stay

Guatemala City has a wide range of accommodations. There are plenty of large hotels offering all modern amenities (with prices to match). You can also find nice boutique hotels offering rooms with kitchens at reasonable prices. Most of the grand hotels are found in Zona 9, Zona 10 and Zona 13, while smaller hotels are found in Zona 4.

❖ HOTEL PRICING	
Prices are per person.	
$	Under $25
$$	$26 to $50
$$$	$51 to $85
$$$$	$86 to $125
$$$$$	over $125

All budget hotels are located in Zona 1. Be careful going the budget route, since many of these hotels are in areas that are not safe at night.

◆ Zona 1

Posada Belén, *13 Calle A 10-30, Zona 1, ☎ 502/2-253-4530 or 502/2-251-3478, www.guatemalaweb.com/posadabelen, 9 rooms, $$.* This museum hotel is an absolute oasis and one of the loveliest hotels in the city. Originally a colonial family home built in 1873, it has been operating as a hotel since 1972. It has an incredible garden and over 300 authentic Maya artifacts on display alongside antique handicrafts, furniture and paintings. Rooms are truly homey and welcoming, furnished with antiques and Guatemalan art. The common rooms and dining room are equally comfortable. The amiable Sanchinelli family, which owns and operates the hotel, will go out of their way to make your stay in the city safe and comfortable. It's small wonder that this is an extremely popular hotel.

Hotel Pan American, *9a Calle 5-63, Zona 1, ☎ 502/2-232-6807, fax 502/2-232-6402, www.hotelpanamerican.com, 52 rooms, $$.* The Pan American was built in 1942 and for years it served as Guatemala's finest hotel, attracting many return visitors. It's located in the heart of the historic center, just steps from the Palacio Nacional. Although a bit faded, it still retains an atmosphere of old-world elegance with its art deco furnishings and lovely Italian and Spanish Colonial antiques. Rooms are equally refined, with pleasant décor, private baths, fan and cable TV. The Pan American restaurant here has excellent food and the service is first class.

Hotel del Centro, *13 Calle 4-55, Zona 1, ☎ 502/2-253-3970, fax 502/2-230-0208, 55 rooms, $$.* This dependable hotel has a modern Spanish design and offers clean and comfortable rooms with spacious bathrooms, two double beds, a small refrigerator and cable TV. Some rooms face the street and can be noisy, so ask for a room at the back. Their restaurant has a lovely terrace with live music on the weekends.

Apart-Hotel Sanmari, *12 Calle A 3-38, Zona 1, ☎ 502/2-253-1474, fax 502/2-232-0135, www.quik.guate.com, 18 rooms, $$.* Tacky, yet clean and comfortable, this budget hotel is in the heart of the historic center.

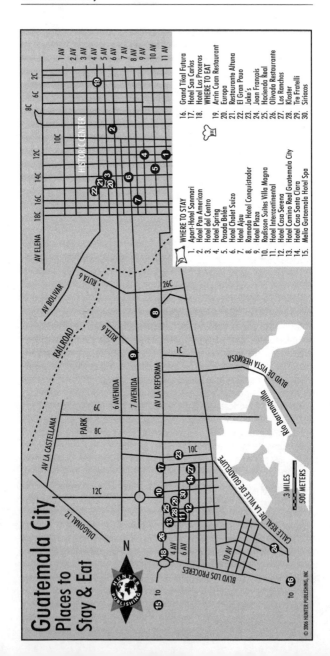

Guatemala City
Places to
Stay & Eat

© 2006 HUNTER PUBLISHING, INC

WHERE TO STAY
1. Aparr-Hotel Sonmari
2. Hotel Pan American
3. Hotel del Centro
4. Hotel Spring
5. Posada Belén
6. Hotel Chalet Suizo
7. Hotel Ajau
8. Ramada Hotel Conquistador
9. Hotel Plaza
10. Radisson Suites Villa Magna
11. Hotel Intercontinental
12. Hotel Casa Serena
13. Hotel Camino Real Guatemala City
14. Hotel Casa Santa Clara
15. Melia Guatemala Hotel Spa
16. Grand Tikal Futura
17. Hotel San Carlos
18. Hotel Los Proceros

WHERE TO EAT
19. Arrin Cuon Restaurant
20. Europa
21. Restaurante Altuna
22. El Gran Pavo
23. Jake's
24. Jean François
25. Hacienda Real
26. Olivada Restaurante
27. Los Ranchos
28. Kloster
29. Tre Fratelli
30. Siriacos

Rooms are equipped with one double bed (the flowered bedspreads are a hoot), small sitting rooms, cable TV and kitchenettes. A washer and dryer are also available.

Hotel Chatel Suizo, *14 Calle 6-82, Zona 1*, ☎ *502/2-251-3786, fax 502/2-232-0429, 51 rooms, $$.* Chalet Suizo is an airy hotel with a central courtyard that's filled with plants and flowers. The rooms are ultra-clean (in true Swiss tradition), with comfortable beds and cozy decorations. The cheapest rooms share a bath; rooms with private baths are double the price. This hotel fills up quickly and is popular with travelers from all over the globe.

Spring Hotel, *8a Avenida 12-65, Zona 1*, ☎ *502/2-232-6637, fax 502/2-232-0107, 18 rooms, $.* With a sunny location, cheery courtyard and reasonable prices, this hotel is the best of the budget places. Rooms are extremely basic, but clean and comfortable, with a shared bathroom and hot water (some rooms are available with a private bath). The cafeteria offers good food at economical prices. You can also do laundry here. Book ahead since this hotel fills up quickly.

Hotel Ajau, *8a Avenida 15-62, Zona 1*, ☎ *502/2-232-0488, fax 502/2-251-8097, 43 rooms, $.* This hotel is fairly comfortable and clean with very basic rooms. It's in a quieter section of the Zona 1. All rooms have TV and double beds. Ask for a room with a private bath; they are cleaner and, generally, more pleasant

◆ Zona 4

Ramada Hotel Conquistador, *Vía 5, 4-68, Zona 4*, ☎ *502/2-331-2222, fax 502/2-334-7245, 660 rooms, $$$$.* This colossal hotel was built in 1971 and offers ultra-modern rooms equipped with a refrigerator, cable TV, air conditioning and marble bathrooms. Balconies overlook the financial district. It has two restaurants, three bars, a swimming pool, sauna and gym. The hotel offers a complimentary shuttle service to the airport and can arrange tours of the city and surrounding areas. It's easy to get lost in the Conquistador.

Hotel Plaza, *Vía 7, 6-16, Zona 4*, ☎ *502/2-332-7626, fax 502/2-331-6824, 64 rooms, $$$.* The Plaza is a 15-minute walk from the Civic Center and central bus station. It's been designed in colonial style, with arches and a central landscaped garden. Fair-sized rooms are decorated with Guatemalan textiles and feature double beds, private baths and cable TV. The Plaza is a good choice if you need to catch an early morning bus or get into the city late.

◆ Zona 10

Hotel Westin Camino Real, *14 Calle 0-20, Zona 10*, ☎ *502/2-333-3000, fax 502/2-337-4313, www.caminoreal.com, 372 rooms, $$$$$.* You can't get more luxurious than this hotel. It oozes refined style with a lobby decked out in marble, glass, ceramics and flowers everywhere. The rooms are decorated in shades of pale cream and yellow, with matching furniture. The hotel has all the amenities you may wish for, and non-smoking and handicapped rooms are available. The bathrooms are posh, with marble floors, large bathtubs and plush towels. There are also three restaurants (the **Hacienda Real**, reviewed below, offers an excellent steak house menu), two heated pools, two tennis courts, Jacuzzis, a spa and 18-hole golf course nearby, as well as the largest convention center in Central America. Of course, you pay dearly for all this pampering.

Real Intercontinental, *14 Calle, between 2a y 3a, Zona 10,* ☎ *502/2-379-4444, fax 502/2-379-4445, www.intercontinental.com/index.shtml, 239 rooms, $$$$$.* This huge hotel is part of a business complex that includes shops, restaurants, government agencies and even a library. The lobby is positively palatial, featuring stately pillars and a sweeping staircase that leads to stylish accommodations. Rooms are decorated in warm earth tones and each has two king-size beds, elegant furniture and other amenities, including data port connections. Although geared toward the business traveler, it makes a good base for general travelers since it is within walking distance of everything Zona Viva has to offer. Rooms on higher floors have nice views of the city.

Radisson Hotel y Suites, *1a Avenida 12-46, Zona 10,* ☎ *502/421-5151, fax 502/2-232-9772, www.radisson.com, 100 rooms, $$$$$.* This is another luxury hotel. It features cozy rooms furnished with lovely mahogany furniture that feel more like luxury apartments. They have warm textiles, richly appointed bathrooms and small kitchenettes. The real draw is the incredible view of the city, mountains and volcanoes. A specially designed businesswomen's floor offers discounts on massage and spa services and provides guides for outings.

Hotel Casa Serena, *14 Calle 5-09, Zona 10,* ☎ *502/2-337-4089, fax 502/2-337-2972, 22 rooms, $$$$.* This small and graceful hotel, with its carved mahogany walls and soft lighting, is located along Avenida la Reforma within walking distance of Zona Viva. Rooms are set up like luxury apartments, with living-dining rooms, cable TV, private baths and fully equipped kitchens. Single Junior suites have only one bedroom, Double Juniors have two bedrooms, and Master Suites have three bathrooms and bedrooms. You may forget you are in Guatemala.

Hotel San Carlos, *Avenida la Reforma 7-89, Zona 10,* ☎ *502/2-362-9076, www.hotelsancarlos.com, 20 rooms, $$$$.* This colonial-style hotel has a yellow exterior and bright interior that is quite charming. Rooms have striped bedspreads, brightly colored floors and wooden furniture. The staff offers personable service that makes you feel right at home. Included in your room rate is 30 minutes of free Internet access every day and a breakfast buffet at the **Bon Vivant** restaurant. There's a swimming pool, business center and pub on site.

Hotel Casa Santa Clara, *12 Calle 4-51, Zona 10,* ☎ *502/2-339-1811, www.hotelcasasantaclara.com, 13 rooms, $$$.* This delightful small hotel offers a tranquil setting in the middle of the Zona Viva. Rooms are uncluttered and clean, with two double beds. The wooden furniture and floors combined with Guatemalan textiles and art give a warm ambience. The grounds feature a lovely tropical garden. A complimentary continental breakfast is included with your room. The service is impeccable in the hotel and at the on-site Middle Eastern restaurant, **Olivadda** (see *Where to Eat*, below).

Hotel Los Proceres, *Boulevard Los Proceres 14-53, Zona 10,* ☎ *502/2-368-1405, fax 502/2-363-0746s, 16 rooms, $$.* This is one of the few reasonably priced hotels in Zona 10. It has a tranquil setting surrounded by businesses and offices. Built in 1995, it has three floors, a bright and cheery lobby with a gift shop, a small restaurant and a bar. Rooms are basic, but nicely equipped with private baths, two double beds, cable TV and free newspapers.

◆ Zona 11

Hyatt Regency Guatemala, *Calzaz Roosevelt 22-43, Zona 11,* ☎ *502/2-440-1234, fax 502/2-440-4050, 205 rooms, $$$$.* Grand is a good word to use when describing this hotel, located just minutes from Aurora International Airport. It is part of the Tikal Futura Complex that has 140 shops, restaurants, offices and boutiques. Rooms are spacious, furnished with pastel rugs, blond furniture and white linens. Views of the city and mountains add to the ambience. The hotel also has a colossal swimming pool, fitness center, convention center and two restaurants.

◆ Zona 13

Melia Guatemala Hotel Spa & Convention Center, *Avenida Las Americás 9-08, Zona 13,* ☎ *502/2-339-0666, fax 502/2-339-0690, www. melia.com, 202 rooms, $$$$$.* This five-star hotel is just minutes from the airport and offers luxurious rooms furnished with a refrigerator, two king-size beds, cable TV and terraces that offer great views of the city. They also have fireplaces for those chilly evenings. The spa offers massages, body wraps and other European treatments that you can enjoy while looking out on an incredible view of the volcanoes. There's a pool and gymnasium. The convention center offers state-of-the-art technology, with video links, DVD and audio equipment.

Where to Eat

Guatemala City has some excellent restaurants and dining here is a real pleasure.

Reservations in the more touristed parts of Guatemala are a good idea. Restaurants in Guatemala City and Antigua take reservations but on a more casual basis than in North America. Don't get upset if your table is not ready immediately and you are asked to wait. Dining is more leisurely here and restaurants simply do not rush people out the door to make room for someone with reservations. In the smaller regions, reservations are not needed and the restaurants do not usually take them.

◆ Zona 1

Altuna, *5 Avenida 12-31, Zona 1*, ☎ *502/2-251-7185*. This Spanish restaurant in an old house has a private club ambience. Waiters are dressed in white jackets and offer discreet service. The main dining room looks out onto a courtyard. Private dining rooms are decorated with Iberian paintings, photographs and posters. Specialties include paella, filet mignon and calamari. US $7-15.

El Gran Pavo, *13 Calle 4-41, Zona 1*, ☎ *502/2-232-9912*. Just follow the neon sign to the bright pink building serving the best Mexican food in Guatemala. Inside is as flashy as outside, with lots of Mexican blankets and other trinkets on the walls. Enjoy tacos, enchiladas and *pollo con mole* (chicken in chocolate sauce), as well as dozens of other Mexican dishes. El Gran Pavo has Maríachi music and is open past midnight. US $6-12. Cash only.

Arrin Cuan, *5 Avenida 3-27, Zona 1*, ☎ 502/2-238-0242. Come to this restaurant for traditional Guatemalan food from the Cobán area, including dishes like *kak-ik* (a spicy turkey stew) and *gallo en chicha* (sweet chicken). Décor is traditional as well, featuring hand-woven fabrics, wooden masks and soda-bottle flower vases. On weekends there is live marimba music.

Europa Bar y Restaurante, *11 Calle 5-16, Zona 1*, ☎ *502/2-253-4929*. An American expatriate opened this friendly diner that serves American standards such as burgers, chili, mashed potatoes and large breakfasts with hash browns, bacon and eggs. The second floor is a bar where you can hang out, read, play board games or watch ESPN. US $3-6.

◆ Zona 10

Hacienda Real, *13 Calle 1-10, Zona 10*, ☎ *502/2-335-5409*. Located a block from the Camino Real Hotel, Hacienda Real has the best steak in town. Choose from platters of steak and pork loin served with fresh salsas and jalapeños. There is a good wine selection, and the tortillas are handmade. Try the caramel flan. US $12-20.

Jean Françoise, *Diagonal 6, 13-63, Zona 10*, ☎ *502/2-333-4785*. This restaurant doesn't have a sign out front, but then it doesn't need one since everyone flocks here. The ambience is incredible. You'll sit on embroidered chairs with stars above and cherubs gazing down on you while you enjoy the incredible Provençal menu. Try the shrimp soufflé; chicken ravioli or fettuccine with a mushroom-cream sauce. Look for the restaurant's whitewashed walls and enter through the passage to the right. US $10-16.

Los Ranchos, *2 Avenida 14-06, Zona 10*, ☎ *502/2-363-5028*. This is another great steak house with a colonial atmosphere. Specialties include rib eye and Châteaubriand, but its signature dish is *churrasco los ranchos*, a skirt steak recipe from Argentina. There are some excellent starters, such as the ultra-fattening fried pork rinds. An international wine list rounds it all out. US $12-20.

Olivadda, *12 Calle 4-21, Zona 10, ☎ 502/2-339-1811*. The cozy Hotel Casa Santa Clara is home to this Middle Eastern restaurant. Enjoy tabbouleh, baba ghanouj and falafel in a peaceful patio garden surrounded by flowers and hummingbirds. Other tasty menu items include *kafta* (beef in pita bread covered with tahini) and chicken with cumin dressing. US $4-6.

Siriacos, *1 Avenida 12-12, Zona 10, ☎ 502/2-334-6316*. This eatery has a dramatic art deco setting with black chairs and bright tables matching the modern art on the walls. The best offerings are fresh pasta and the large Caesar salad. The sunken dining room is fairly swank, with a skylight patio that creates a romantic nighttime atmosphere. US $25-20.

Kloster, *13 Calle 2-75, Zona 10, ☎ 502/2-334-7459*. The Kloster offers beer and fondue in a rustic setting. What more could you ask for? Chocolate, cheese and meat are among the most traditional fondues offered, but there are also more exotic ones, such as lobster, shrimp and seafood. Draft beer is sold by the yard and there's an extensive wine list. US $6-12.

Tre Fratelli, *2a Avenida 13-25, Zona 10, ☎ 502/2-366-2678*. Guatemala is gaining quite a reputation for its Italian restaurants, and this is one of the best. It has an intimate atmosphere and specializes in Northern Italian cuisine. The carpaccio and fresh fettuccine are excellent, as are the salads and soups. Fresh pastas are divine. The wines are from Italy or California. The service is as excellent as the food. US $12-15.

Jake's, *17 Calle 10-40, Zona 10, ☎ 502/2-368-0351*. Jake Denburg, a master chef, prepares innovative dishes such as smoked chicken tortellini with a homemade sauce. His best offerings feature seafood and fish, particularly *robálo* (sea bass). The converted farmhouse setting has lots of wood and tiles, as well as a great fireplace – quite romantic. Jake also has a good sense of humor. His tables are covered with paper and everyone is given crayons and encouraged to color the "tablecloths." US $12-25.

Nightlife

During the civil war, most places shut down after dark. Nightlife after 9 pm can be hard to find unless you know a local who can show you the current hot spots. Guatemala City does have a nightlife, but for safety's sake you should stick to Zona Viva or Zona 1 and not after midnight. Bars in the Zona 1 tend to focus on live music and poetry readings, while the bars in Zona 10 (Zona Viva) lean more toward discos. A new walking street, **4 Grados Norte** in Zona 4, has been opened up with a variety of clubs and bars.

Many visitors like to hang out in **Europa Bar**, 11 Calle 5-16, Zona 1, ☎ 502/2-253-4929 in the second-floor bar with its board games and ESPN. **La Bodeguita del Centro**, 2 Calle 3-55, Zona 1, ☎ 502/2-230-2976, has live poetry readings and music every evening. For some excellent jazz, check out **El Méson de Don Quijote**, 11 Calle 5-27, Zona 1 (☎ 502/2-232-1741), where the local musicians gather each evening. **Giuseppe Verde** is the upscale bar in Hotel Westin Camino Real, 14 alle 0-20, Zona 10, ☎ 502/2-333-3000, where many tourists like to dance and drink. You may want to check out **La Barraca de Don Pepe**, Ruta 5, 84-42, Zona 4, ☎ 502/2-660-2479, or **Estro Armonico**, 4, 4-36, ☎ 502/2-319-9240. Dance, classical music and cultural events can be enjoyed at **Centro Cultural Miguel Angel Asturias**, 24 Calle 3-81, Zona 4, ☎ 502/2-232-4041. The best (and safest) **movie theaters** are along Avenida 6 between Plaza Major and Parque Concordia in Zona 10.

Day-Trips from the City

Guatemala City is not considered a tourist destination since most of the attractions are outside of the city. But it is used as a starting-off point for the following tours. See the pages indicated for details.

❖   **San Pedro Volcano horseback tour**, page 102.
❖   **Whitewater rafting**, Río Cahabon, Alta Verapaz, page 158.

Shopping

Guatemala City is not known for its shops. There are the usual big chain outlets offering household goods and clothing but nothing that you won't find back at home. The best shopping for Guatemalan arts and crafts can be found at the **Mercado Central**. It's located behind Palacio Nacional, 8 avenida, with the entrance at 6 y 7 avenida. This market has hundreds of booths selling handicrafts from every region of the country. Open 7 am to 6 pm, Monday to Saturday. See page 52 for more details.

Central Highlands
~ The Gringo Trail ~

This area has been nicknamed the Gringo Trail because of the large numbers of tourists who come here. All of the country's most famous attractions are found in the area, including the historic city of Antigua, the celebrated Lake Atitlán and the world-renowned market at Chichicastenango. This region of the country welcomes tourists, with plenty of services and easy access.

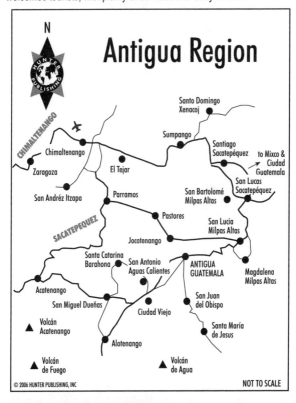

N

Antigua Region

HUNTER PUBLISHING

CHIMALTENANGO

Santo Domingo Xenacoj

Sumpango

Santiago Sacatepéquez

to Mixco & Ciudad Guatemala

Chimaltenango

El Tejar

Zaragoza

San Andréz Itzapa

Parramos

San Lucas Sacatepéquez

San Bartolomé Milpas Altas

SACATEPEQUEZ

Pastores

San Lucia Milpas Altas

Jocotenango

Santa Catarina Barahona

San Antonio Aguas Calientes

ANTIGUA GUATEMALA

Magdalena Milpas Altas

Acatenango

San Miguel Dueñas

Ciudad Viejo

San Juan del Obispo

Santa María de Jesus

▲ Volcán Acatenango

Alotenango

▲ Volcán de Agua

▲ Volcán de Fuego

© 2006 HUNTER PUBLISHING, INC

NOT TO SCALE

Department of Sacatepéquez

La Antigua

Antigua is in **Valle Panchoy** (Dry Lagoon), part of Guatemala's Central Highlands, 25 miles (40 km) northwest of Guatemala City.

Expect to be charmed, captivated and enchanted in La Antigua. This is one of the most beautiful colonial cities in the world and it has a fascinating Phoenix-like history. It has endured more earthquakes than any other city in Central America and has always been rebuilt – a testimony to how much its residents love their city.

Antigua is a city of religious architecture. At one point in time there were over 22 religious orders here and each built something to live in and something to worship in. Natural disasters may have blunted some of the original beauty, but there remains enough colonial architecture to make it one of the most beautiful cities in the Western Hemisphere.

Like any beautiful spot on earth, its popularity comes with all the associated evils. Hotels are overpriced, streets get crowded, there is just a little too much English spoken and the locals are bored with visitors. But that aside, Antigua remains one of the loveliest spots in Central America and it's well worth visiting.

◆ History

Antigua was the final attempt by **Pedro de Alvarado** to set up a royal capital in the Kingdom of Guatemala. His first capital was built in 1524 near the Maya site of Iximché, but the fierce Cakchiquel warriors chased him out of the region. His next choice was at the foot of the Agua Volcano in the Panchoy Valley. After establishing the new capital, Alvarado left for battle in Mexico, where he was promptly killed. His wife took over as governor and, just a few weeks later, the entire city was buried under an avalanche of lava, mud and rocks. On March 10, 1543, Antigua was selected as the location for another new capital. By royal decree, the official name was The Very Loyal and Very Noble City of the Knights of Saint James of Guatemala, *Muy Leal y Muy Noble Ciudad de Santiago de los Caballeros de Goathemala*. It was a rather pretentious title for a settlement built out of straw, bricks and mud.

Antigua grew into its name. Important architects and artists were invited to come and build in Antigua, and the capital grew as the **Spaniards** extended their kingdom from the north into Chiapas Mexico and down into Honduras and El Salvador. When the first printing press arrived in 1660, Antigua quickly became the kingdom's cultural center. At the same time, **Bishop Payo Enríquez** started the first publishing house that became famous for its literary achievements. One of its first books, *The True Story of the Conquest of New Spain*, written in 1670 by Bernal Diaz, is still in print today. In 1676 the first university in Central America was opened. The Royal and Pontifical University of San Carlos remains a prestigious university today.

The first series of **earthquakes** hit between 1651 to 1663, with a final devastating quake in 1666. But these were simply a warm up for the major earthquake of 1669 that destroyed most of the city. By then, Antigua was considered the heart and soul of the Guatemalan kingdom and rebuilding began immediately. The new construction was of a different nature, though. From 1699 to 1707, Antigua became a spiritual center, attracting a number of religious orders from Europe. Soon, friars, monks, priests and nuns arrived and began building cathedrals, churches and convents. **Diego de Porres**, a famous colonial architect, was hired to work on many of the buildings and his work transformed the mud-and-straw city into one of the most beautiful in Central America. A number of the churches and convents were finished just in time for the devastating earthquake of 1717 when, once again, Antigua was razed. And, once again, the citizens started rebuilding.

By 1770, in addition to a beautiful cathedral of ornate Spanish-baroque architecture and an impressive government palace, Antigua had over 30 churches, 18 convents and monasteries, 15 hermitages, 10 chapels, five hospitals, an orphanage, four parks and a university. There were municipal water and sewer systems too. Sadly, residents didn't have much time to enjoy the city's golden age.

On July 29, 1773 the savage Santa Marta earthquakes hit and the city was destroyed yet again. But this time city officials refused to rebuild and instead petitioned the King of Spain for permission to move the capital to the Ermita Valley. In 1776 La Nueva Guatemala de la Ascencion, known today as Guatemala City, became the country's new capital. Antigua gradually became a ghost town as government officials, wealthy families and all the religious orders abandoned the city in favor of the new capital. Only the very poor were left behind and, to survive, these *Antigüeños* moved into the ruined houses and churches left behind. In 1779, to add insult to injury, Antigua was officially demoted and became merely the capital of the Sacatepéquez Department.

During the 18th century, Antigua was largely ignored. Some restoration work was done on the cathedral and university, but the majority of the city buildings were left alone. But being overlooked actually saved Antigua. Its buildings were not torn down or replaced by more modern buildings, as happened in Guatemala City. In 1944, President Jorge Ubico declared Antigua a **National Monument**, ending almost 165 years of benign neglect. Restoration began on the city and, in 1965, the Pan American Institute of Geography and History named it the "Monumental City of the Americas."

In 1969 La Antigua and the National Council for the Protection of Antigua Guatemala (*Consejo Nacional para la Protección de Antigua*

CENTRAL HIGHLANDS

Guatemala) was established to oversee restoration work. Antigua passed through the 1976 earthquake with very little damage, while other parts of the country, including the capital, were severely hit. In 1979, UNESCO chose Antigua as a **Cultural Heritage of Mankind Site**.

This was all the recognition the city needed to blossom into a major tourist attraction. Ironically, Guatemala City has never achieved the same splendor as Antigua and is actually considered to be one of the ugliest capitals in the world. Religious celebrations remain the focus in Antigua. Semana Santa (Easter Week) attracts visitors from all over the globe, who come to witness the most colorful celebration of Easter in the Western Hemisphere. (Read more about this festival on page 22.)

◆ Getting Here & Getting Around

The city's close proximity to the capital and its popularity ensure easy access.

By Air

There are no direct flights into Antigua, national or international. All flights land at La Aurora International Airport in Guatemala City, an hour away by car. A cab ride from the city to Antigua will cost about US $40. A much cheaper option is to take one of the many tourist shuttles that leave the airport regularly. They cost between US $8 and $15. You can also take a city bus to the bus terminal and grab a second-class bus to Antigua for US $1.75. Local buses leave Guatemalsa City every five minutes.

By Bus

You have to go to Guatemala City and then switch to a local bus heading to Antigua. A more comfortable, but more expensive, alternative is to use a tourist shuttle operated by a travel agency. Most offer direct routes to and from Antigua from all the major tourist spots. On the whole, these vans are faster and safer than buses.

> #### ❖ SHUTTLE SERVICES
>
> A number of companies offer shuttle services in and around Guatemala City, Copán Honduras, Panajachel, Chichicastenango and the surrounding areas.
>
> **Adventure Travel Center Viareal, SA**, 5a Avenida Norte #25B, ☎/fax 502/7-832-0162, viareal@guate.net.
>
> **Atitrans**, 6a Avenida Sur #8, ☎ 502/7-832-1381, 502/7-832-0644.
>
> **Monarca Travel**, Calzana Santa Lucia Norte #17, ☎/fax 502/7-832-1939, monarcas@conexion.com.gt. This company also offers shuttle service from San Cristóbal de las Casas, Chiapas, Mexico to Antigua Guatemala. Tickets

start at US $40 per person and include help with border crossings.

Rain Forest, 4ta Avenida Norte #4A, ☎ 502/7-832-5670, fax 502/832-6299, www.rainforest.guate.com.

Sin Fronteras, 5a Avenida Norte #15A, ☎ 502/7-832-1017, fax 502/832-8453, www.sinfront.com.

Turansa, 9a Calle (inside Hotel Villa Antigua), ☎ 502/7-832-2928, fax 502/832-4692, www.turansa.com.

Rainbow Travel, Avenida Sur #8, ☎/fax 502/7-832-4202.

Antigua's main public bus terminal is located behind the municipal market, a 10-minute walk from downtown. Buses to Guatemala City, Panajchel, Chichicastenango or Sololá are frequent and cheap. The public buses are often crowded and run infrequently. Tickets are Q3. Tourist shuttles usually leave from the Main Plaza, although you can also arrange to be picked up from your hotel.

Once in the city, you can walk to almost all sights and attractions.

> ❖ **INSIDER TIP: CHICKEN BUS TRAVEL**
>
> If you decide to ride the chicken buses, leave your passport, large amounts of cash, credit cards and jewelry in a lock-up at your hotel. Instead, carry a photocopy of your documents. If you bring anything of value, including money, use a money pouch and wear it next to your skin, i.e., under your clothing. Thieves like to target tourists riding the chicken buses and usually do that buy slicing the lining of your bag and removing its contents. You don't realize anything is missing until you open your bag.

By Car

Cars are a nuisance in Antigua. The cobblestone streets make for bumpy rides and parking is scarce. Robberies are also a big problem. Don't leave your car parked on the street, even during the day. Car alarms provide no security whatsoever. The only safe alternative is a private parking lot (*parqueo*) with a security guard. They cost between Q40 and 60 per night. Some people hire the local street kids to watch their car, but sometimes these are the very people robbing the cars.

CAR RENTALS

If you can, rent a car at the airport or in Guatemala City, where rates tend to be lower. Among the car rental agencies in town:

Dollar Rent a Car, 5ta Avenida Norte Casa No.15, ☎ 502/5-219-6848, www.dollarguatemala.com.

Tabarini Rentals, 6a Avenida Sur #22, ☎ 502/7-832-8107, www.tabarini.com.

The highway outside of Antigua is single lane and mountainous, with many twists and turns. Add diesel trucks, tourist vans, chicken buses and other drivers and you have stressful driving conditions. Drive slowly, get insurance and never drive at night – not only do you run the risk of an accident, you are also prey for robbers.

Walking

The city is easy to navigate. It's laid out in a classic colonial grid. Streets running west and east are called Calles (Streets). West of the main plaza, they are Calle Poniente (West Street) and east of the plaza they are always Calle Oriente (East Street). This applies even if the street is continuous. For example, 5a Calle Poniente (5th Street West) becomes 5a Calle Oriente (5th Street East) when it passes the plaza.

Streets running north-south are called Avenidas (Avenues). Avenues south of the main plaza are called Avenida Sur (South Avenue) and those running north of the plaza are Avenida Norte (North Avenue). This applies even if the street is continuous. For example, 1 Avenida Sur (South Avenue 1) becomes 1 Avenida Norte (North Avenue 1) as soon as it passes the plaza.

The exception to this rule are streets with names, rather than numbers, but these are usually very short and run only a few blocks.

◆ Spanish Language Education

Antigua is famous for its Spanish language schools, which are big business here. Rates are incredibly reasonable: US $150-200 per week for room and board with a Guatemalan family and four to five hours per day of one-on-one private instruction. The schools usually plan sightseeing trips in the afternoon, while evenings are dedicated to practicing *Español* with other gringos in one of the many bars or restaurants in downtown Antigua. This is a fun way to learn Spanish. Keep in mind that lots of English is spoken in Antigua, so your course will not be a full immersion unless you avoid English speakers.

❖ SPANISH 101

Use the following tips to get the most out of your language school session.

❖ Visit several schools before choosing one.

❖ Ask for references and speak with other graduates.

❖ Is your teacher experienced; does he/she have a university degree?

❖ Do you like your teacher? There's no point in studying with someone you don't connect with – you're going to be spending a lot of time together.

❖ Don't sign up for too many hours. Four to five hours per day of learning is all most people can absorb. Any more is a waste of time and money.

❖ Bring materials, such as workbooks, paper, pencils and dictionaries, with you, since training material is limited in Guatemala.

❖ Agree only to one week of study at a time. That way, if things don't work out you are free to go elsewhere.

❖ Choose a school that treats its teachers humanely and pays properly. There are more teachers than jobs in Guatemala so competition is fierce. Some unscrupulous schools exploit the situation by offering low salaries and long hours. It's no fun learning with a cranky, underpaid teacher.

Spanish Schools

Although you can find a list of recognized schools in the INGUAT office, it's rather a lackluster affair. Many of those listed have paid to be included. The most reputable schools in Antigua are:

Academia de Español Guatemala, 7a Calle Lote 15, ☎ 502/7-832-5057, fax 502/7-832-5058, aegnow@guate. net.

Academia de Español Sevilla, 1a Avenida Sur 8, ☎ 502/7-832-5101, www.sevillantigua.com.

Academia de Español Tecún Umán, 6a Calle Poniente 34, ☎ 502/7-832-2792, http://tecununam.centroamerica. com.

Centro Lingüístico La Unión, 1a Avenida Sur 21, ☎/fax 502/7-832-7337, www.launion.conexion.com.

Centro Lingüístico Maya, 5a Calle Pte 20, ☎ 502/7-832-5492.

Escuela de Español San José el Viejo, 5a Avenida Sur 34, ☎ 502/7-832-3028, fax 502/832-3029, www.guate.net/spanish.

Proyecto Lingüístico Francisco Marroquín, 7a Calle Pte 31, ☎/fax 502/7-832-2886, in the US 800/552-2051, info@langlink.com.

◆ Sightseeing

Jade Factory, 4a Calle Oriente No 34, ☎ 502/7-832-3841, fax 502/832-2755. The ancient Maya revered jade and used it to create sacred objects for their religious rituals. Excavations at a number of Maya ruins, such as Palenque, Chichen Itzá and Tikal, revealed tombs filled with jade death masks, jewelry, nose plugs, statues and other objects. The natural source of Maya jade was lost for centuries and many people dismissed the possibility that mines existed as myth, until **Mary Lou Ridinger** came along. This intrepid archeologist defied popular sentiment and, using old records made by Spanish Conquistadors, identified the source of Maya jade mines in the remote jungles of the Sierra de las Minas Mountains and Motagua Valley. During the 1960s she began her search and by 1975 had reopened the jade mines. She started Jade SA, the largest jade factory in Central America to revive the lost art of jade carving.

Today, Jades SA employs more than 50 lapidaries who have created a fantastic collection of masks, sculptures and jewelry available for sale. At the factory, located downtown, you can see how the jewelry is made. The showroom has a collection of replica death masks, including the famous mask found on King Pakal of Palenque, Mexico. The factory tour also includes a demonstration of the equipment and techniques used to work with jade. An outdoor courtyard has restaurants, cafés and craft shops. Tours are offered from 9 am to 6.30 pm, daily. Call ahead for free pickup from your hotel. No admission fee.

You can take a bike tour offered by **Old Town Outfitters** (5A Avenida Sur #12, ☎ 502/2-399-0440, www.bikeguatemala.com).

Ik'Bolay Serpentarium, Calle de los Duelos #4. This miniature zoo is a 10-minute walk from downtown. It has a fascinating display of over 110 species of reptiles, amphibians, bats and hummingbirds indigenous to Guatemala. Learn how to identify venomous snakes (a handy thing to know if you plan any wilderness hiking) and the first-aid treatment if you do get bitten. You can visit with cute vampire bats or go into the aviary to watch various Guatemalan hummingbirds, known locally as "garden jewels." The zoo guides share popular Guatemalan legends and discuss ongoing conservation issues, This is a popular tour for families – but only if your kids like snakes! Open 9 am to 4:30 pm, daily except on Tuesdays. Q7 per person.

◆ Adventures on Foot

Historic Buildings

Historical Antigua, Hotel Casa Santo Domingo, 3a Calle Oriente #28, ☎/fax 502/7-820-1220, www.antiguatours.net. Antigua is a city filled with many historical buildings, each with a tale to tell. Elizabeth Bell, one of Antigua's foremost historians, offers a fascinating city tour that focuses on the folklore, history and architecture of colonial buildings. The tour also visits sites currently under restoration. The tour is an excellent way to get your bearings and learn more about the history of Antigua. It departs from the Fountain of the Sirens (*La Fuente De Las Sirenas*) in the main plaza. Reservations by phone or e-mail are appreciated. The three-hour tours start at 9:30 am, Tuesday, Wednesday, Friday and Saturday. US $18.

Plaza Major (main plaza, center of Antigua between 5a Calle Poniente and 4a Calle Poniente. The main plaza is also known as Plaza Armas,

Antigua Attractions

218 FEET
200 METERS

© 2006 HUNTER PUBLISHING, INC

✝ CHURCHES

1. La Merced
2. Recolección (Ruins)
3. San Jerónimo
4. Las Capuchinas
5. Santo Domingo
6. El Carmen
7. Santa Clara
8. San Francisco
9. Santa Catarina
10. Cathedral

🏛 HISTORIC SIGHTS

11. Palacio de Ayuntamiento;
    Museo de Santiago;
    Museo del Libro Antiguo
12. Museo de Arte Colonial;
    Universidad de San Carlos
13. Casa Popenoe

✍ LANGUAGE SCHOOLS

14. Academía de Español Seville
15. La Unión
16. Academía de Español
    Guatemala
17. Español Tecún Uman
18. Idiomas San José El Viejo
19. Proyecto Linguistico
    Fransisco Marroquín
20. Centro Linguistico Maya

due to its history as a meeting place of the army, or Parque Central. It spans a whole city block and is surrounded by buildings on all sides: south is the Palace of the Captain's Generals (*Palacio de Los Capitanes Generales*); on the east side is the *Catedral Metropolitana*; to the north is City Hall (*Ayuntamiento*); and on the west side is the old Trade Arcade building. The famous Spanish architect **Juan Bautista Antonelli** designed the plaza in 1543; it was renovated in 1704. The famous **Fountain of the Sirens** (*La Fuente de las Sirenas*), designed by Miguel de Porres in 1739, sits in the plaza's center. The original fountain once served as a water supply until it was destroyed in the 1773 earthquakes. It was reconstructed in 1936 using stones from the original fountain. This area is a focal point in the city. In the evenings, locals gather here to stroll, talk and generally socialize. During New Year celebrations and Holy Week, many festivities are held in the square.

Palacio de los Capitanes Generales (Palace of the Captain's Generals), 5 Calle Poniente, south side of the plaza. This building is easily recognized by its 26 stately arches. Originally constructed in 1549 and finished in 1558, the palace has been rebuilt several times since then. The beautiful arches spanning more than 330 feet (100 meters) were added in 1735 when the building was used to house the Royal Mint and the royal colonial officers. The arches are the only original pieces to survive the devastation of the 1773 earthquakes (the building was damaged again in the 1976 earthquake). Today, the palace serves as the headquarters for INGUAT (Guatemala's Tourist Office), as well as other government departments. Open 9 am to 5 pm weekdays. The office has many good maps and brochures on Antigua.

Catedral Metropolitana (Main Cathedral), 4 Avenida Norte, east side of the main plaza. This beautiful cathedral has a modern church, as well as an old church that's currently undergoing restoration. The foundations of the old church were laid in 1542 using the rubble from Ciudad Vieja, the first capital that was buried in a mudslide. Construction was delayed as the building was ruined in the earthquakes of 1651, 1663 and 1666. It was finally inaugurated in 1680, only to be destroyed by another earthquake. A second cathedral was built in its place and was finished in 1743. Decorated with sculptures, painting and silver created by the artisans of that era, it was considered the most beautiful cathedral in Central America. Tragically, that too was destroyed in 1773 during the Santa Marta earthquakes. As you wander the ruins, you can still see the elaborately sculpted domes, columns and pillars. Two of the entrances to the chapels remain intact. They were restored in the 18th century and are known today known as the Ogles de San José.

Many famous people are buried at the original cathedral, including the notorious Spanish Conquistadors Bernal Diaz del Castillo and Don Pedro de Alvarado, Conqueror of Guatemala. The present-day church is an 1820 reconstruction of a small portion of the original cathedral. It has only one nave (instead of the original five) and a beautiful façade decorated with impressive statues and carvings closely resembling the original. Open 9 am to 5 pm, daily. Q4 admission to the old cathedral.

Palacio de Ayuntamiento (City Hall or Palace of the Noble City), 4 Calle Poniente, north side of the plaza. Antigua's City Hall was officially inaugurated in 1743 and its double-arch façade with columns of solid stone and sculpted rock walls proved to be quite strong – most of the original building survived the devastation of 1773 and 1976. For over two hundred years it was the seat of the city council and it still houses the offices of the municipal government and the Guatemala Ministry of Tourism. It also has two lovely museums: the **St. James Museum** (*Museo de Santiago*) and the **Antique Book Museum** (*Museo del Libro Antiguo*). City Hall is open 9 am to 5 pm, weekdays.

Museo de Santiago (St. James Museum), Palacio de Ayuntamiento, 4 Calle Poniente, ☎ 502/7-832-2868. This museum has displays of weapons, sculpture and furniture dating to the 1600s. Among its collection are famous portraits of the founding members of the city, including one of Pedro de Alvarado. Open 9 am to 4 pm, Tuesday-Friday; 9 am to noon and 2 to 4 pm on weekends. Q5.

Museo del Libro Antiguo (Antique Book Museum), Palacio de Ayuntamiento, 4 Calle Poniente. This tiny, delightful museum is set on the original location of the first printing press in Central America, established in 1660. (A replica of the original press is one of the displays.) It houses a fascinating collection of antique books from the 16th and 17th centuries. The bronze cannons outside were used by the Spanish Conquistadors to fend off rebellious Indians. Open 9 am to 4 pm, daily. Q12.

Museo de Arte Colonial (Colonial Art Museum), Calle de la Universidad and 4 Avenida Sur, ☎ 502/7-832-0429. This graceful colonial museum is on the former grounds of the Universidad de San Carlos, across from the ruins of the cathedral. The university, the first in Central America, was founded on January 31, 1676 by royal decree of his majesty King Charles III. It survived all the earthquakes, including the major ones in 1773. One of the last museums to leave the old capital, it did not move here until 1832. The buildings have since been renovated and turned into a public school. The colonial interior remains intact and the courtyard features a lovely fountain with Moorish arches. Today, the museum displays an excellent collection of 17th-century religious paintings and statues commissioned by Spanish royalty. It also has a permanent photography collection of Holy Week celebrations in Antigua. Open 9 am-4 pm, Tuesday-Friday; 2-4 pm on weekends. Q28.

Casa Popenoe (Dr Popenoe's house), corner of 1 Avenida at 5 Calle Oriente. This beautiful colonial house was built at the turn of the 18th century for Don Luis de las Infantas y Mendoza, a Spanish judge in the Royal Court. Like many other city homes, it was damaged in the devastating earthquakes of 1717 and 1773, and was finally abandoned in 1774. It stayed empty until 1931 when an employee of the United Fruit Company bought the house. Dr Wilson Popenoe and his wife, Dorothy, restored the house and filled it with period antiques and colonial art collected over the years. While the outside of the building is unimpressive, the interior is magnificent, with beautiful flowered patios linked by a series of arched passageways. The kitchen, bedrooms, bath and gardens are just like homes typically built for the Spanish elite. The Popenoe family still lives in the house and keeps it open to the public. Open 2 pm to 4 pm, weekdays. Q14.

Mercado Central (Central Market), between Calle de Santa Lucía and Calle Sucia. Antigua's central market is a labyrinth filled with vendors selling fresh flowers, fruits, vegetables, meat, woven baskets, ceramics, textiles, pots and pans alongside live chickens. On Saturdays, merchants from surrounding areas open booths outside the permanent stalls, covering the whole area behind the market. It's colorful, chaotic and shouldn't be missed, especially if you are a bargain hunter. Open 8 am to 5 pm, daily.

Churches & Convents

Nuestra Señora de La Merced (Our Lady of Mercy), Alameda de las Rosas, corner of 1 Calle Poniente and 6 Avenida Norte. This church is one of the most famous landmarks in Antigua. The Mercedarian order of monks was established in Guatemala in 1538 and immediately began building a church and monastery in Ciudad Vieja. Both were completed in 1546, only to be destroyed in the 1565 earthquake that buried Ciudad Vieja. They moved to the current location and built a new church and monastery, which had rooms for over 100 monks and an impressive library alongside the largest (at that time) fountain in Central America. Unfortunately, both the cloister and church were destroyed in the 1717 earthquake. All you can see today are the remains of the 80-foot-wide (24-meter) Fountain of Fish (*Fuente de Pescados*), named for the fish-breeding experiments done by the Mercedarian brothers. However, the church was rebuilt and work was completed in 1767. It survived the 1773 earthquakes thanks to the sturdy design by architect Juan Luis de Dios Estrada. Estrada made the church rather squat, with thick walls and small, high windows. The white stucco façade on a yellow background is the building's most striking feature. It has three large naves filled with imposing statues, a majestic cupola and elaborate baroque decorations.

When Antigua was abandoned as the capital in 1774, the La Merced order was moved, but the church remained open since Nuestra Señora de la Merced is the patron saint of Antigua. It remains a popular place of worship and is the starting and finishing point for the famous Good Friday procession during Holy Week. The monastery is open 9 am to noon and 3 to 6 pm, daily; church hours are dawn until dusk. Admission to monastery is Q4.

Iglesia y Convento de la Recolección (Church and Convent of the Recollection), 1 Calle Poniente at Calle de la Recolección; the unmarked ruins are across the street. Construction of this impressive monastery began in 1701 by the great architect of Antigua, Diego de Porres, and was completed by his son José de Porres in 1717 – just in time for the earthquake, which it survived with some damage. But the luck didn't last. The church and convent were completely razed in the 1976 earthquake. All that remains is a graceful stone arch over a stairway surrounded by the nave's crumbling walls. The monastery ruins have beautiful arches covering thick walls centered around a spacious courtyard. Open 9 am to 5 pm, daily. Q12.

Iglesia y Convento de Santo Domingo (St. Dominic Church and Convent), 3 Calle Oriente 28, ☎ 502/832-0140, fax 502/832-0102. The Dominican Order came to Central America in 1538 and its missionaries began a humble convent in Ciudad Vieja. Its founder, Fray Bartolomé de Las Casas, became known as the "protector of the Indians." Ironically, the order grew into the wealthiest one in Antigua, owning a substantial chunk of the city. In 1701, the Dominicans began building a more impressive convent and church. The original church had two towers with 10 bells. One of the towers had Antigua's first public clock. Both the church and monastery were filled with artistic treasures. There was even an artificial lake for fishing (boats are available on the grounds) and a famous octagonal fountain. The monks then started the College of St. Thomas of Aquinas (*Colegio Santo Tomás de Aquino*), a predecessor of the University of San Carlos. Unfortunately, the church and convent were totally destroyed in 1773 and never rebuilt. The ruins have been incorporated into Hotel Casa Santo Domingo. Open daily.

Iglesia y Monasterio de San Francisco (St. Francis Church and Monastery), 7 Calle Oriente and 1 Avenida Sur. The Franciscans began their order in 1525 with five monks and a simple monastery in Ciudad Vieja. Like everyone else, they moved to the new capital and began building. By 1689 there were 80 monks. They commissioned Diego de Porres to build them a church, which was completed in 1702. Its high ceilings and curved columns were built in Spanish-American baroque style. The monastery included a lovely chapel and housing for the monks, as well as a hospital, clinic and a complete library, publishing house and the famous San Buenaventura School of Theology and Philosophy. Unfortunately, most of the monastery was destroyed in 1773 and there are now only modeled stuccos and traces of painted murals. The chapel survived and is the burial site of Hermano Pedro de Betancur (Brother Peter of Betancur). It was restored in the early 1800s amid much controversy. Many felt the restoration was not true to the original architecture. The current church has 16 vaulted niches, each containing a statue of a saint or a friar. Several richly decorated altarpieces have paintings and sculptures created by contemporary Guatemalan artists. This church sees a good number of pilgrims who come to ask their Hermano Pedro for help. In fact, many miracles have been attributed to Friar Pedro and in 1980 he was beatified. His tomb is covered with letters, photos and plaques attesting to his many miracles. Open 9 am to 5 pm, daily. Q4 for the museum, church is free.

Colegio de San Jerónimo (St Jerome College), Alameda de Santa Lucía at 1a Calle Poniente. This college was built by the Order of

Mercedarians in 1757 and operated as a renegade school until it was closed in 1761 by King Carlos III. He ordered the building to be torn down, but locals felt it was too beautiful to destroy. Instead, it became the Royal Custom House run by Capitan General Fernández de Heredia – a famous figure in Guatemalan history. Unfortunately, most of the building was destroyed in 1773, but it is currently being restored by the The National Council for the Protection of Antigua Guatemala (*Consejo Nacional para la Protección de Antigua Guatemala*), which now controls development in Antigua and oversees all restoration work. Open 9 am to 5 pm daily. Q7.

El Convento de Nuestra Señora del Pilar de Zaragoza, 3 Avenida Norte, between 1a Calle Oriente and 2a Calle Oriente. In 1725, the Capuchin nuns of Madrid petitioned the royal courts for permission to open a convent in Antigua, even though locals opposed it. They were granted permission with the stipulation that they would have only 25 nuns and charge no dowry fees to join (as other convents did). The nuns took it one step further and became famous for their services toward destitute women. The convent (nicknamed Convento las Capuchinas, or Convent of the Brown Hoods) was completed in 1736 under the direction of Diego de Porres. It was spacious, offering many rooms, a large courtyard, garden, orchards and fountains. It also had the only circular cloister in existence, known as The Tower of Retreat for the Novices (*La Torre de retirada por las Novicios*), which remains the only tower of its kind in the world. Both the church and convent were abandoned after the 1773 earthquakes that damaged both buildings. The ruined sections include the Tower of Retreat and are worth visiting if only to see the 14 bedrooms, all of which had their own bathrooms with running water and bathtubs. Below the tower is a series of underground chambers that resonate only when certain notes are sung; no one knows the original purpose of these chambers, but many legends have grown up around this cloister. The Capuchin nuns were an order that followed St. Francis de Assis. They were thought to have special abilities to predict the future and to heal people. The myth dates back to the 13th century when Francis de Assis was said to have cured the war hero Bonaventure. It was thought that the underground chambers were used for mystical practices that enabled the Capuchins to health the sick.

The chapel has the remains of a 120-foot-long (36-meter) nave that can be viewed from the second floor choir loft. Also visible from that spot are the twin volcanoes, Fuego and Acatenango. Both the convent and church were sold in 1850 to a family who tore down the tiled roofs in order to dry coffee beans. Ironically, this saved both structures from further decay because it allowed them to dry out, thereby preventing rot and mildew. Today, the convent houses a museum as well as the offices of the National Council for the Protection of Antigua Guatemala. Open 9 am to 5 pm daily. Q10.

Iglesia y Convento de Santa Clara (St. Claire's Church and Convent), 2 Avenida Sur at 6 Calle Oriente, ☎ 502/832-3185. Santa Clara convent was founded in 1699 by a group of nuns from Puebla, Mexico. The convent's first church was completed in 1705 and was destroyed shortly afterwards in the 1717 earthquake. A new convent and church was built in 1723 and finished in 1734. It featured a large cloister surrounded by a two-storied arcade with 46 cells, a hospital (with a ward for the insane), rooms for novices, a sacristy, and a dining room with adjoining kitchen. Both the church and cloister were severely damaged in 1773 and eventually abandoned in 1774. All that remains of the church are some rather gloomy vaults that you should explore only with the aid of a flashlight. There is also a series of corridors and stairwells still intact. At the south side of the church you can see some well-preserved frescoes. The most beautiful part is the cloister, which has a two-tiered arcade on half-circle arches and hidden passages leading to underground rooms. The grounds have been landscaped with flowering trees and shrubs around a large fountain, making this a very romantic setting. Open 9 am to 5 pm, daily. Q12.

Convento y Arco de Santa Catalina (St. Catherine's Church and Arch), Calle de Arco, between 5 Avenida Norte and 2 Calle Poniente. The cloistered order of Santa Catalina began in Antigua in 1613. Their church and convent was completed in 1647, but by 1694 the order was so large it was forced to expand across the street. The graceful yellow arch was constructed so the nuns could pass unseen into the orchid gardens in the original location. The arch is the only part left of the original buildings – the rest was destroyed in the Santa Marta earthquakes of 1773. A hotel was built over the remains of the convent, but the church ruins remain untouched. Today, the arc has become an icon of Antigua and is, without a doubt, the most photographed landmark in the city. This area is often referred to as *Calle del Arco* (Street of the Arch) and many local events take place here.

Iglesia del Carmen (Church of the Carmens), 4 Av. Norte y 4a Calle Oriente. This church first housed the Capuchin nuns when they arrived in 1726. It was completed in 1728, but sustained damage in 1773. The main façade of the church has an ornate baroque style, with triple pairs of columns instead of the usual niches found at other churches. The interior of the nave is just under 150 feet (45 meters) long. There is now a private home where the original convent used to be. 9 am to 5 pm, daily.

◆ Adventures on Horseback

Cerro de la Cruz (Hill of the Cross), northeast of downtown. The Hill of the Cross overlooks the city. At its foot is the original site of the Hermitage of Santa Cruz (*La Ermita de la Santa Cruz*), built in 1749 for the sole purpose of conducting masses. To mark the spot, a giant cross was erected, hence the name. Today, the park is filled with monuments to Guatemalan war heroes. It has an incredible view of the city with the two volcanoes – Acatenango and Fuego – in the background. In years past, the park developed a notorious reputation due to a series of armed robberies targeted at tourists, but it is now heavily patrolled by both the regular and tourist police and is safe to visit during the day. It should still be avoided at dusk or at night.

You can get to the hill on a bicycle or by taxi, and some choose to arrive on horseback. It's about 10 minutes from downtown by car.

◆ Adventures on Wheels

The **Almolonga Valley** is west of Antigua, nestled between Agua, Fuego and Acatenango volcanoes. The village of Ciudad Vieja is thought to be the location of the original Santiago de los Caballeros, which was buried under a mudslide when the volcano erupted in 1541. There is no trace of the old city left and some people dispute the claim. This bicycle tour travels through the valley to Ciudad Vieja to visit the lovely 18th-century cathedral and plaza. It also stops off at the Valhalla Macadamia Plantation and visits the weavers in San Antonio Aguas Caliente.

❖ OUTFITTER

Old Town Outfitters offers this route as an easy, full-day tour. Contact them at 5a Avenida Sur #12, ☎ 502/2-399-0440, www.bikeguatemala.com. The cost is US $25 per person.

◆ Day & Overnight Trips

Antigua is surrounded by volcanoes and a number of agencies offer day and overnight trips to four volcanoes. Day-trips usually head either to Pacaya or Agua. Most of the overnight camping trips go to Fuego or Acatenango. Day tours leave from Parque Central at 8 am and return by 5 pm. Costs for day-trips to Pacaya and Agua are usually US $7 per person; to Acatenango or Fuego they run about US $25 per person. Overnight camping trips start at US $50 per person. Depending on the agency, you may need to bring your own tent and sleeping bag. Tours depart Antigua at 6 am and return the following day at 3 pm. See below for a list of operators offering volcano tours.

Agua Volcano

Originally known as Hunapú after the Maya sun god, Volcán Agua (Volcano of Water) was renamed after the 16th-century explosion that buried the original capital (now known as Ciudad Vieja de Antigua). This volcano is currently inactive. Located just south of modern Antigua, it is 12,478 feet (3,750 meters) above sea level, making it the fifth-highest volcano in Guatemala. It is also the most perfectly shaped volcano. Day hiking tours start at the Santa María de Jésus Village and take about five hours to reach the summit (see *Recommended Tour Agencies*, below). Unfortunately, there are a number of communication antennae at the summit, so you hike as high as you can to get a good picture of Antigua and the Valley of Panchoy. If you choose to hike independently, hire a local guide. Don't attempt to climb alone – it's too easy to get lost on the trail.

Pacaya Volcano

Pacaya is located south of Antigua on the highway to Esquintla, about a mile before the village of Palín in the Cerro Grande-Pacaya-Cerro Chino volcanic complex. It's the most active volcano in Guatemala. Easy access and spectacular views make it one of the most popular volcanoes to visit. Pacaya reaches 8,366 feet (2,550 meters) and has gas and lava eruptions that are spectacular in the early evening. In recognition of its importance, Pacaya Volcano was declared a national park in June 2001. Visitors now enter the park through the village of San Francisco de Sales and pay an admission fee of Q25 (children are admitted free of charge).

The main **hiking** trail begins behind the visitor center. It has *guardabosques* (rangers) patrolling the trail, rest areas, signs and bathrooms. The hike itself is not particularly demanding, but it does take over two hours to reach the volcano from the visitor center. Those severely affected by the elevation (asthma sufferers seem to be hit the worst) can hire horses (see below) to take them up the trail as far as the volcano for about US $10.

For your final ascent, you must hike about 500 feet (150 meters) up a mountain of charcoal – some of it smoldering. This final jaunt can take between 45 minutes and one hour, depending on your stamina.

You will soon forget your aches and pains once you reach the summit and look down on the tops of mountains and bottoms of valleys surrounded by Lake Amatitlán. In the distance is Guatemala City as well as three other volcanoes – Agua, Fuego and Acatenango – partially covered by clouds. The most thrilling part is standing on the edge of Pacaya and looking down into the red-hot lava pit while surrounded by clouds of sulfur. Don't be surprised to find yourself thinking about hell and damnation while gazing into the blazing inferno.

The descent is much easier. You can take the trail or hold onto your guide's arm and ski down the hill. It will probably be the most fun you've had in ages. Be careful though – it's a long fall to the bottom. Always take a guided tour using one of the licensed tour operators. Do not attempt any deserted trails, no matter how tempting; tourists have been robbed at knifepoint on these trails and many get lost. It's also a good idea to bring only a small amount of money and leave valuables at your hotel. Keep an eye on your camera equipment and leave your watch behind (volcanic ash only ruins delicate mechanisms). Wear good hiking boots and a raincoat, and bring a flashlight.

Pacaya Volcano is active, so check conditions before booking a tour. The latest volcanic activities can be found at the INGUAT office in Antigua's main plaza or at any of the travel agencies.

Acatenango Volcano

Acatenango, one hour southeast of Antigua, is the third-tallest peak in Guatemala at 13,121 feet (3,976 meters). Although last active in 1924, it still has a few craters emitting sulfur fumes. This volcano has two peaks: Pico Mayor (Greater Peak) is the tallest at 13,044 feet (3,976 meters), followed by Yepocaya or Tres Marías (Three Marys) at 12,000 feet (3,820 meters).

Acatenango is almost identical to Fuego Volcano and, in fact, the two are connected by a passage called La Horqueta (Forked Passage). It takes about one hour of hiking to reach the first lookout at 8,000 feet (2,400 meters) and another 1½ hours to Tres Marías summit. From there, you can continue up for a half-hour to Pico Mayor, where the view is spectacular. Camping is usually done right at the summit, but is dependent upon the weather. The best spot is inside one of the craters at the summit of Yepocaya's peak or in the Conejera (Rabbit), a flat plateau in the middle of a beautiful pine forest. The route to Acatenango begins in the village of La Soledad and it takes four hours to hike to the top.

> ❖   **INSIDER TIP: VOLCANO SAFETY**
>
> Don't attempt to climb any of the volcanoes alone. If you want to visit independently, hire a local guide from one of the nearby villages. Solo tourists usually end up lost on the trail and get stranded overnight or longer.

Fuego Volcano

Fuego is also known as *Chigag* (Where the Fire is). At 12,345 feet (3,763 meters), it is the highest active volcano in the country and it has been erupting steadily since 1524. This volcano is usually admired from afar and El Mirador (the lookout, halfway up) is a good place to see Fuego's hunchback summit. This is also a place for camping. A hike to this volcano is usually combined with a visit to Acatenango since the two are connected. To reach Fuego, first take the route starting at the village of Alotenango. To reach the summit of Acatenango, start at Fuego and take the route starting at La Soledad. Visiting both volcanoes is known as La Ruta la Doble (the Double Route). There is a tremendous amount of sand and ash in this area, so reaching the summit can take between four and five hours.

> ❖   **VOLCANOES – RECOMMENDED TOUR AGENCIES**
>
> A number of travel agencies offer **volcano tours**. Day-trips from Antigua are run by:
>
> **Adventure Travel Center**, Viareal, SA, 5a Avenida Norte #25B, ☎/fax 502/7-832-0162.
>
> **Rainbow Travel**, 7 Avenida Sur #8, ☎/fax 502/7-832-4202.

Gran Jaguar, Calzada Santa Lucía Sur #3, ☎/fax 502/7-832-3149, 832-4574.

Mundo Guatemala, 4a Avenida Sur #1, ☎/fax 502/7- 832-3896 or 832-9134, www.mundo-guatemala.com.

Biking trips are available through:

Guatemala Ventures/Mayan Bike Tours, 1ra. Avenida Sur # 15, ☎ 502/7-832-3383, fax 502/7-832-5836, www.guatemalaventures.com.

Old Town Outfitters, 5a Avenida Sur #12, ☎ 502/2-399-0440, www.bikeguatemala.com. This company offers biking trips and overnight camping to all four volcanoes for US $50-$85 per person. Ticket price includes all gear, guide and food.

Copán Ruins, Honduras

The ruins at Copán are widely considered the most beautiful of all Maya ruins and the site has been dubbed the "Paris of the Maya World." Copán was blessed with a long line of rulers who kept building on their predecessors' visions of the city. The most famous king, 18-Rabbit, also known as Ruler 13 (AD 695-738), was responsible for many of the carved stelae, altars and sculptures found here.

The most famous structure is the 30-foot-wide (nine-meter) **Hieroglyphic Stairway**, created with 1,250 glyph blocks put together to form the 60-foot-high (18-meter) stairs. The carvings tell the story of the ruling dynasty from AD 426 to 755. Unfortunately, by the time the stairway was discovered it had already been dismantled and piecing it back together has been a life-long puzzle for many researchers. Also of note are the 3-D carved stelae found only at Copán and the neighboring ruins of Quirigia. These unique stelae depict the rulers of Copán dressed in royal garb. A series of tunnels underneath the city lead to older temples. The Maya often buried their temples to preserve them and this is a prime example of that practice. The Rosalila tunnel leads to an incredible temple with its original colors and carvings still intact, while the Jaguars tunnel is 2,100 feet (640 meters) of carved façades, staircases, an aqueduct system and an ancient bathroom.

The excellent on-site museum houses the most delicate stelae, as well as an exact replica of the Roaslila temple. The one drawback is the expensive entrance fees: $10 per person for entry to the grounds, $5 for the museum, $12 for the tunnels.

Copán can be reached in five to six hours by signing up for one of the many tours offered by companies in Antigua. Going with a group usually costs more than traveling independently, but it's certainly more convenient. Transportation to the ruins costs US $50 per person and overnight trips run between US $150 and $250.

CENTRAL HIGHLANDS

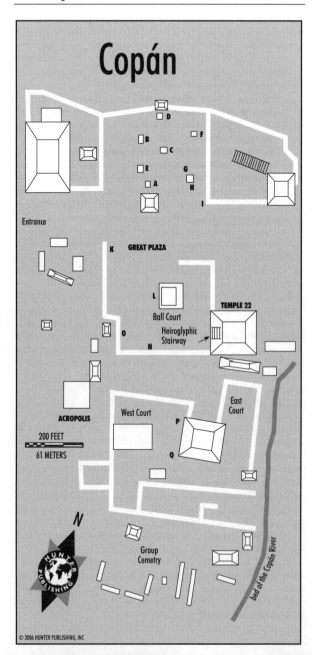

Copán

Entrance

K **GREAT PLAZA**

D
B
F
C
E
G
A
H
I

L

Ball Court

TEMPLE 22

Heiroglyphic
Stairway

O

N

West Court

East Court

ACROPOLIS

P

Q

200 FEET
61 METERS

N

HUNTER
PUBLISHING

Group
Cemetry

bed of the Copán River

© 2006 HUNTER PUBLISHING, INC

A number of agencies offer trips to Copán from Antigua. The following have the best schedules and prices.

Horizontes Travel, 6ta. Avenida Sur #10, ☎ 502/7-832-1530, fax 502/7-832-0926.

Sin Fronteras, 5a Avenida Norte #15A, ☎ 502/7-832-1017, fax 502/7-832-8453.

Monarca Travel, Calzada Santa Lucia Norte #17, ☎/fax 502/7-832-1939, monarcas@conexion.com.gt.

Plantation Tours

Finca Los Nietos Coffee Plantation Tour, San Lorenzo El Cubo, ☎ 502/7-831-5438, losnietos@conexion.com.gt. Due to its rich volcanic soil, Guatemala produces some of the best coffee in the world. Antigua has a number of plantations on private country estates, known as *fincas* (farms). In the past, these *fincas* had a reputation for brutality toward their workers. Today, most are locally owned collectives that grow organic coffee and work toward making the industry more profitable, with better working conditions. Finca Los Nietos (the Grandchildren's farm), started in 1991, is one of these collectives. It offers a one-hour guided tour of the operation starting at a spectacular point where over 1,000 coffee trees overlook Agua Volcano. Your tour then follows the entire process from tree stage to *oro* (gold) stage – so-called because the coffee bean is now ready to be sold. Seeing the entire labor-intensive process is a real eye-opener and will make you truly appreciate your next cup of java. The two-to three-hour tours start at 8 am and 11 am on weekdays and reservations are required. There's a minimum of two people per tour. Q40 per person.

Finca Los Nietos is four miles (seven km) southeast of Antigua. Take the bus from downtown Antigua to San Lorenzo El Cubo. Go through the town to the crossroads just before the road turns downhill to San Antonio. Walk south (right) toward the volcano for three blocks. Finca Los Nietos is on the right corner. Look for the gray wall covered with bougainvillea and ring the bell.

Capeuleu Finaco Coffee Tour, San Miguel Dueñas, ☎ 502/385-4116 ext 20, offers a similar tour of its larger and more commercial plantation. It doesn't have the same charm of Los Nietos and is farther (19 miles/ 32 km) from Antiguas. The one bonus is the pickup and drop-off shuttle service that's included in your entrance fee of Q140. This tour takes 1½ hours.

❖ **PLANTATION TOUR COMPANIES & OUTFITTERS**

Rainbow Travel, 7 Avenida Sur #8, ☎/fax 502/7-832-4202, also offers a variety of coffee plantation tours along with a visit to San Antonio for US $30.

Old Town Outfitters offers a half-day mountain bike tour of the nearby coffee plantations. You bike on country roads into the small villages including San Antonio Aguas Caliente. It's an easy ride. Price includes mountain bike, drinks and guide. Contact Old Town Outfitters, 5 Avenida Sur #1, ☎ 502/2-399-0440, www.bikeguatemala.com. US $ 25 per person.

Macadamia Plantation Tour, c/o The Valhalla Project, Km 52.5 a San Miguel Duenas, ☎ 502/7-831-5799, fax 502/7-831-5799, www.exvalhalla.com. The macadamia nut is delicious and its oil is the key ingredient to all those over-priced anti-aging creams sold by large cosmetics companies. It's an expensive nut because the only source is in the islands of Hawaii. The Valhalla Experimental Agricultural Station was started by Lorenzo and Emilia Gottschamer, who have been experimenting for 20 years with a variety of macadamia trees. They have developed a high-quality, high-yield macadamia tree that is starting to bear fruit and will make Guatemala the second largest producer of the nut. The two-hour tour of their Valhalla operation includes a free facial with pure organic macadamia oil (most creams use diluted oil), a sample of nut butters and chocolate-coated macadamia nuts. You can buy their 100% pure macadamia oils and creams, as well as the nuts, at the gift shop. Tours run from 7 am to 5 pm, daily. Q40.

The plantation is three miles (five km) east of Antigua, close to San Miguel Village. You can catch a local bus to the village and ask the driver to let you off at Valhalla.

◆ Where to Stay

There are plenty of hotels in Antigua. Some are quite swanky and cater to the celebrity crowd, while others are simple, family-run hotels. There are rooms to suit every budget.

> **AUTHOR TIP:** *Be sure to check the room before signing in and don't rent a room where the locks don't look and feel secure. Those are the rooms that get robbed. Second-floor rooms are usually quieter and more secure.*

Casa Santo Domingo, 3 Calle Oriente #28, ☎ 502/7-832-1220, fax 502/7-820-1221, www.casasantodomingo.com.gt, 97 rooms, $$$$$. This very elegant hotel is built around the ruins of the Santo Domingo monastery. Long passageways lead to romantic gardens filled with flowers and fountains. The rooms have yellow walls and are furnished with antique carved furniture, iron candlesticks and 17th-century colonial paintings. They also have antique fireplaces – perfect for chilly nights. Casa Santo Domingo, located just steps from all the downtown shops and restaurants, has two muse-

❖ HOTEL PRICING	
Prices are per person.	
$	Under $25
$$	$26 to $50
$$$	$51 to $85
$$$$	$86 to $125
$$$$$	over $125

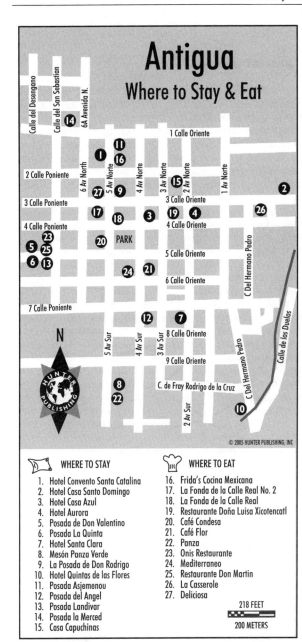

Antigua
Where to Stay & Eat

Calle del Desengano
Calle del San Sebastian
6A Avenida N.

14

1 Calle Oriente

1
11
16

2 Calle Poniente

6 Av North
5 Av Norte
4 Av Norte
3 Av Norte
2 Av Norte
1 Av Norte

2

27
9

3 Calle Poniente

15

3 Calle Oriente

26

17
18
3

19
4

4 Calle Poniente

4 Calle Oriente

23
20

PARK

5 Calle Oriente

5
25

6
13

24
21

6 Calle Oriente

C Del Hermano Pedro

7 Calle Poniente

12
7

N

5 Av Sur
4 Av Sur
3 Av Sur

8 Calle Oriente

9 Calle Oriente

8
22

C. de Fray Rodrigo de la Cruz

2 Av Sur

C Del Hermano Pedro

Calle de los Duelos

10

© 2005 HUNTER PUBLISHING, INC

CENTRAL HIGHLANDS

WHERE TO STAY

1. Hotel Convento Santa Catalina
2. Hotel Casa Santo Domingo
3. Hotel Casa Azul
4. Hotel Aurora
5. Posada de Don Valentino
6. Posada La Quinta
7. Hotel Santa Clara
8. Mesón Panza Verde
9. La Posada de Don Rodrigo
10. Hotel Quintas de las Flores
11. Posada Asjemenou
12. Posada del Angel
13. Posada Landivar
14. Posada la Merced
15. Casa Capuchinas

WHERE TO EAT

16. Frida's Cocina Mexicana
17. La Fonda de la Calle Real No. 2
18. La Fonda de la Calle Real
19. Restaurante Doña Luisa Xicotencatl
20. Café Condesa
21. Café Flor
22. Panza
23. Onis Restaurante
24. Mediterraneo
25. Restaurante Don Martin
26. La Casserole
27. Deliciosa

218 FEET
200 METERS

ums. The Spanish Colonial Art Museum displays 16th- and 17th-century art and artifacts, and the pre-Columbian Museum exhibits ancient Maya artifacts.

Posada del Angel, *4 Avenida Sur #24a*, ☎ *502/7-832-5303, 800/934-0065, fax 502/7-832- 0260, www.posadadelangel.com, 5 rooms, $$$$.* Despite the weather-beaten entrance, this supremely discreet hotel oozes polish and good taste. Quite a few celebrity guests have graced its rooms, including Bill Clinton (sans Monica or Hillary). Mere mortals are still welcomed. You can stay in one of the luxurious rooms decorated with colonial art and antiques and furnished with a fireplace and ornate beds complete with large fluffy pillows and duvets. An elegant sitting room looks out onto a pool and garden, which leads to a restaurant, bar and library. The service is impeccable, leading many to claim this is *the* perfect hotel.

Casa Azul, *4 Avenida Norte #5*, ☎ *502/7-832-0961 or 0962, fax 502/7-832-0944, www.casazul.guate.com, 12 rooms, $$$$.* This serene and attractive hotel is located in the heart of downtown Antigua, just steps away from the plaza. Although the building is modern, it uses colonial architectural styles of the 17th and 18th centuries, with sitting rooms that open into a courtyard and garden. Rooms are decorated in washes of red and blue and furnished with comfortable upholstered chairs and couches, wooden tables and bureaus. Decorative touches, such as ceramic tiles and copper lamps, create a calm ambience. The second-floor rooms have spectacular volcano views (and cost more than rooms on the first floor).

Mesón Panza Verde, *5a Avenida Sur #19*, ☎ *502/7-832-2925, www.panzaverde.com, 3 rooms, 9 suites, $$$.* The name refers to those *Antigüeños* left behind when the city was abandoned in 1774. They were so poor they had to subsist on avocados, which gave them *panza verde*, or green belly. This hotel's handsome entrance features a long fountain flanked by a carved wall on one side and verdant gardens on the other. The rooms are elegantly furnished with antiques, colorful bedspreads and huge windows with wrought-iron edges that give maximum light. Ground-floor rooms open onto a small garden, and second-floor suites have a private patio equipped with hammocks and chairs. Suites are also equipped with four-poster beds and down duvets. An upstairs terrace on the third floor offers spectacular sunset views. It's a bit of a jaunt to downtown, but you may not even want to leave such a cultivated atmosphere, especially since the restaurant serves such excellent food (see review on page 92).

Hotel Posada de Don Rodrigo, *5 Avenida Norte #17*, ☎ *502/7-832-0291, fax 502/7-832-0387, www.guatemalatravelmall.com/index.html, 35 rooms, $$$.* Once upon time, in 1707, there was a comely mansion called Casa de los Leones (House of the Lions), named for the noble stone lions that lined its entrance. The lions are long gone – victims of the 1717 earthquake – and the home has been converted into this gorgeous hotel. Much of the original wood remains, including baroque carvings, shutters and doors. Rooms feature original tiles and fireplaces and are furnished with antique armoires, dressers and tables. All open onto a lush patio overlooking a central garden and fountain. Every effort has been made to maintain the original colonial flavor and the effect is both romantic and elegant.

Hotel Aurora, *4 Calle Oriente #16,* ☎ *502/7-832-5155, fax 502/7-832-0217, www.hotel-aurora-antigua-guatemala.com/reservations.htm, 15 rooms, $$$.* This family hotel has been in operation since 1923. The wood and rattan furniture, giant armoires and claw-foot bathtubs help maintain its old-fashioned genteel air. The plumbing, however, is thoroughly modern. All rooms face a large, lush garden that surrounds a tiled portico. You are welcome to sit in a chair and enjoy the garden. Breakfast is included. The Aurora is steps away from all the restaurants, shops and attractions.

Hotel Quintas de las Flores, *Calle del Hermano Pedro 6,* ☎ *502/7-832-3721, fax 502/7-832-3726, 14 rooms, $$$$$.* The lovely gardens here have gorgeous fountains and benches where you can sit and relax. The large, luxurious rooms have cozy beds and linens, fireplaces and lovely garden views. There is a terrific little restaurant that serves Guatemalan food. Also available are fully equipped private houses that can sleep up to five people.

Hotel Convento Santa Catalina, *Calle del Arco #28, Antigua, Guatemala,* ☎ *502/7-832-3080, fax 502/7-832-3079, www.convento.com, 18 rooms, $$.* This lovely hotel is set among the ruins of a 1647 church built for the cloistered order of Santa Catalina. The only part of the cloister left is the beautiful yellow arch just outside the hotel, which is the most famous landmark in Antigua. Front rooms are decorated with hand-woven Guatemalan textiles and local art. Most open up into the lush courtyard with a central fountain. The more modern rooms are brighter, have a kitchenette, and are located in the back annex.

Casa Capuchinas B & B, *2a Avenida Norte #7,* ☎ *502/7-832-0121, www.guatemalatravelmall.com, 5 rooms, $$.* This delightful colonial home turned B&B is across the street from the La Capuchinas ruins. Each room is individually decorated with local textiles and handicrafts and furnished with antiques and a fireplace. The colonial-style windows overlook the garden on the first floor or offer scenic views of the volcanoes from the second floor. Owners Alejandro and Fátima Rayo are happy to offer travel advice or recommend the best restaurants and shops in Antigua. A full breakfast is included in the price of your room.

Posada La Merced y Posada Landivar, *Posada la Merced, 7a Avenida Norte #43,* ☎ *502/7-832-3197 or 3301 and Posada Landivar, 5a Calle Poniente #23,* ☎ *502/7-832-2962, 32 rooms in each hotel, $.* These sister hotels are within walking distance of each other. They offer affordable, comfortable clean rooms with nice views of the city right downtown. Since they offer single, double or triple rooms, sharing with someone can make this quite a bargain. Not all rooms have private bathrooms. A kitchen is available for guest use. The staff is super helpful, willing to arrange shuttles, tours or Spanish lessons. Children are heartily welcomed at both places. Cash only.

Posada Asjemenou, *5a Calle Poniente #4,* ☎ *502/7-832-2670, 12 rooms, $.* This lovely and economical hotel is a converted colonial mansion with clean, comfortable rooms furnished with just a few pieces. The staff is friendly and helpful. A small café serves breakfasts and snacks, or you can walk over to the Posada Asjemenou restaurant (just off Plaza Major) for something more filling. Some rooms have shared bathrooms. Reservations are recommended – Asjemenou is usually full. Cash only.

Hotel Santa Clara, *2a Avenida Sur #20,* ☎ *504/7-832-0342, 14 rooms, $.* Rooms at this small colonial home-turned-hotel are clean, cozy and quite a bargain. It's a bit off the beaten track – about four blocks from downtown. However, it is close to a number of Spanish schools, has a lovely garden and most of the rooms are set up for students, with small desks and chairs alongside the double bed. Some rooms even have their own private bathrooms. Those with shared baths rent for as little as US $5 per night. The staff is very friendly and will help you with your Spanish. Cash only.

Posada de Don Valentino, *5a Calle Poniente 28,* ☎ *502/7-832-0384, 14 rooms, $.* This is a very nice budget hotel with spacious rooms that feature double beds and large bathrooms. There is also a pretty patio and dining room, as well as an Internet café. Don Valentino is within walking distance of the bus terminal and downtown. It tends to attract the noisy backpacker crowd because of its location. Cash only.

◆ Where to Eat

EL Restaurante de Don Martin, *4 Avenida Norte #16,* ☎ *502/7-832-1063.* This posh restaurant is set in a restored colonial home. Ring the bell at the entrance and you'll be led to your table on the garden courtyard or in a private room with its own fireplace. The menu is classic Guatemalan cuisine and includes a variety of grilled meats (the steak and sausage are outstanding). Fresh fish dishes often use snook or grouper. For a real treat, try the succulent venison. The service is as flawless as the décor. Leave the kiddies back at the hotel. US $12-20.

Mesón Panza Verde, *5a Avenida Sur #19,* ☎ *502/7-832-2925, www. panzaverde.com.* This restaurant is part of the classy Panza Verde hotel (see review above). Like the hotel, the restaurant is tranquil and classy. Specialties include *lomito* (thinly sliced beef), escargot, salads, fresh fish and grilled meats. Both the dessert menu and wine list are outstanding. This is an excellent choice for a romantic dinner. Reservations are a must. US $15-25.

Café Condesa, *5 Avenida Sur,* ☎ *502/7-832-0038.* This house has a fascinating history. It was built in 1549 for the royal Count of Gomera. A long line of royal tenants followed the count. Amazingly, the house withstood the earthquakes of 1669, 1717 and 1773, but was abandoned when the capital was moved to Guatemala in 1774. Popular folklore claims the body of a servant was buried in the house, apparently killed by a count who returned home earlier than expected and found his naked wife in the arms of her butler. The myth turned out to be true when, during the clean up after the 1976 earthquake, an upright skeleton was found behind a pantry wall. The skeleton has been removed and this house is now a pleasant restaurant serving tasty meals and an all-day breakfast. Vegetable omelets, fresh fruit drinks, quiche, salads and cheese plates are some of the highlights. The homemade pies, pastries, bread and excellent coffee make this place really stand out. You can dine inside or out on the patio. If you are in a hurry, get a take out at the Café Condesa Express next door. US $4-6.

La Casserole, *Callejón de la Concepción #7*, ☎ *502/7-832-0219*. This small restaurant is beautifully decorated with peach and gold walls. The windows look out over a central garden with a fountain. Local artists and photographers regularly display their work here, which adds to the artistic atmosphere. The food is French with Guatemalan influences and is extremely innovative. The menu changes every 10 days and it's always a delightful surprise. Specialties include a seafood bouillabaisse cooked in a spicy tomato sauce and the chiltepe chicken, flavored with a large dried and smoked jalapeño chile pepper. This is a popular place with gourmands. US $12-15.

Café Flor, *4 Avenida Sur 1*, ☎ *502/7-832-5274*. This place is so trendy it may give you a rash. But if you can ignore the pretentious service and illegible blackboard menu, you will be able to enjoy some excellent Indian and Chinese food. On weekends, the restaurant is open late. Reservations are not required. US $5-8 per person.

El Meditteraneo, *6 Calle Poniente #6A*, ☎ *502/7-832-7180*. This tiny eatery is a slice of Northern Italy in Antigua, with the best Italian in the area. Try the homemade pastas accompanied by one of their many sauces. There's an excellent selection of wines. The atmosphere is one of casual elegance. US $6-12.

Doña Luisa Xicotencatl, *4 Calle Oriente #12*, ☎ *502/7-832-2578*. Doña Luisa was the Indian mistress of the notorious Spanish Conquistador Pedro Alvarado. She would be pleased with this popular restaurant named in her honor – it has become a local landmark famous for both its food and art. Come early to get a table either on the balcony, terrace or inside. Early morning treats include freshly baked bread, pancakes, French toast, fruit salad and egg dishes. Sandwiches, soups and salads are offered on the lunch menu. Downstairs at the bakery, a community bulletin board used by ex-pats and tourists is an excellent resource. US $3-5. Cash only.

Frida's Cocina Mexicana, *5 Avenida Norte #25, near the arch, Antigua, Guatemala*, ☎ *502/7-832-0504*. Named after the famous Mexican artist, Frida Kahlo, this restaurant/bar serves classic Mexican food in a lively cantina setting. Standards include *taquitos* (fried, stuffed tacos), enchiladas, guacamole and *burros con frijoles* (tortillas with beans). This is a popular watering hole for gringo tourists and at night you'll see more beer and margaritas than food. US $3-6 per person (for food).

CENTRAL HIGHLANDS

Fonda de la Calle Real, *5a Avenida Norte #5*, ☎ *502/7-832-0721;* **La Fonda de "a la vuleta,"** *3a Calle Poniente #7*, ☎ *502/7-832-0507, fax 502/7-832-0721.* These two restaurants have the same owner and same menu. Both are extremely popular with Guatemalans from the capital. The original location (Calle Real) is just off Plaza Major on the second floor of a colonial building with picturesque views of the square. The newer restaurant is just around the corner on the first floor of a restored colonial mansion. The menus feature Guatemalan and Mexican cuisine. Mexican specialties include *queso fundido* (tortillas with melted cheese), *caldo real* (hearty chicken soup); Guatemalan dishes include the famous *Antigüeño* grilled sausage and *pollo pepián* (fiesta chicken). The newer restaurant has live music on the weekends. Both are extremely busy on Sundays when residents of Guatemala City come here to eat. US $6-12.

Deliciosa, *3a Calle Poniente #2*, ☎ *502/7-832-6500.* This is a great delicatessen with incredible sandwiches to go. You can also buy cold cuts, cheese, prepared food, dips, fresh bread, pastries, take-out pasta – everything you need for a gourmet picnic lunch. They will also deliver to your hotel. US $3-6. Cash only.

Onis Restaurante, *7a Avenida Norte #2 Local 1.* This little café has a nice view of the San Agustín Ruins by the local bus station. It offers simple meals of sandwiches, salads and fresh pastas. The meals are hearty, delicious and cheap. Happy hour is from 7-10 pm every day. US $2-5. Cash only.

◆ Nightlife

Bars & Discos

Anitgua is the exception in Guatemala for nightlife. There is plenty to do here and the bars tend to stay open later than in other cities. **Monoloco**, 5a Avenida sur #6, ☎ 502/7-832-4235, has a cool bar with satellite TV tuned to all the sports. **Frida's Bar**, 5a Ave Norte #25, ☎ 502/7-832-0504, has a free pool table and a regular happy hour. **Macondo Pub**, 5 Avenida Norte, under the arch, no phone, gets very lively and is a popular meeting place for gringos in town. **Al Afro**, 6 Calle Poniente 9, ☎ 502/7-832-3138, has live salsa and Latin jazz during its happy hour. **La Casbah**, 5a Avenida Nte 30, ☎ 502/7-832-2640, is open from Wednesday to Saturday, 7 pm to 1 am. It's the most popular disco in town.

Movies

There are no movie theaters in town but there are plenty of video houses showing a wide variety of international films for around US $1.50. The most popular are:

Cine Café, 7a Calle, Pte 22.

Cinema Bistro, 5a Avenida Sur 14.

Cinema Tecún Umán, 6a Calle Pte 34A.

Cultural Events

Proyecto Cultural El Sitio, 5a Calle Pts 34A, ☎ 502/832 3037 presents a variety of cultural events that include theater, concerts, poetry readings and art exhibitions. They post a weekly schedule.

Department of Sololá

The department of Sololá is bordered to the north by the departments of Totonicapán and Quiché; to the east by Chimaltenango; to the southwest by Suchitepequez; and to the west by Quezaltenango. It has the largest and most varied Maya population with the highest number of indigenous languages still in use. It covers 19 municipalities in total, although most tourists usually visit only Lake Atitlán.

This department remains primarily agricultural, cultivating corn, beans, squash and some fruit. Weaving is the second major industry and almost every village has its own techniques for creating highly stylized shirts, trousers, huipils, skirts, blouses, sashes, purses and fabrics. It is one of the most popular destinations in Guatemala.

Lake Atitlán, a deep, wide lake surrounded by volcanoes, is probably the most famous place in Guatemala and it has been attracting visitors for hundreds of years. They are drawn by the panorama of the lake, sky and volcanoes. Located in the Western Highlands, which is often called the heart of the Maya world, Lake Atitlán sits 5,128 feet (1,563 meters) above sea level. It is wide and deep, covering 49.3 square miles (127 sq km) and reaching down 1,049 feet (320 meters). Along the south shore are three enormous volcanoes – **Atitlán** at 11,670 feet (3,557 meters), **Tolimán** at 10,361 feet (3,158 meters) and **San Pedro** at 9,908 feet (3,020 meters).

Surrounding the lake are many small indigenous villages where natives still wear traditional dress and continue a traditional way of life without much Western influence. **Panajachel** is the exception. It has a large international community and makes a good base for exploring the other villages around the lake, such as Santiago Atitlán, San Pedro, San Juan la Laguna and Sololá.

You will read many quotes about how Lake Atitlán is considered one of the most beautiful places on earth – in case you can't figure this out on your own.

Getting Here & Getting Around

Most of the Sololá buses and shuttles head for Panajachel. Although many of the villages around the lake have roads to them, it is still faster and more comfortable to reach them by boat from Panajachel.

Sololá

With a population of 9,000, Sololá is one of the largest Maya cities in Guatemala. It sits 1,968 feet (600 meters) above the lake and offers incredible views of the area. Originally known as Cakhay, Sololá was built 19.6 miles (six km) from Iximché, the capital of the Cakchiquel Maya. In 1517, the city was captured by Lahuh Nor, the ruler of Iximché, and came under that city's rule. Around 1541 the village was moved to its present site and named Tecpan Atitlán. In 1547, the Spanish friars arrived and baptized the population. To celebrate, they renamed the city Nuestra Senora de la Asuncion de Sololá (Our Lady of the Assumption of Sololá). Only Sololá stuck.

◆ History

This is one of the most traditional cities in the area with the town divided into the same clans that existed before the conquest. Their native garb is quite colorful. The women wear skirts and blouses made of red striped cloth and the men wear flamboyant cowboy shirts with embroidered trousers. A highly stylized bat, the symbol of Maya royal house of Xahil, is worn on the back of their shiny jackets. The Xahil were rulers of the Cakchiquel at the time of the conquest.

◆ Getting Here

Sololá is extremely easy to reach because it is on the same road as Panajachel and all buses going there must pass through the town. The road to Sololá/Panajachel starts a few miles west of the traffic hub Los Encuentros on the Pan-American Highway. Buses depart from Guatemala City and Antigua every half-hour; shuttles also bring you to Sololá.

◆ Attractions

The best day to come to Sololá is Friday, when the **market** is in full swing. Hundreds of people come down from the highlands dressed in their finery to buy and sell. This is a more authentic market than the one in Panajachel and it's not as crowded as Chichicastenango's market. But the selection here is limited, since space is dedicated to selling practical things needed by the locals. The market takes place along the cathedral and central plaza, which was renovated in 2001 (locals are quite proud of the results). On non-market days, this town is pretty sleepy and the central square is almost deserted. But it makes for a pleasant visit away from the bustle of Panajachel.

Sunday is also a big day in Sololá, when the elders of the religious brotherhoods, known as *confradías*, have a **procession** through the streets to the cathedral. Although this is a solemn and dignified affair, it's certainly worth seeing.

> ❖ **INSIDER TIP: KEEPING THE PEACE**
>
> Keep your camera tucked away. Picture-taking is not appreciated during the ceremony.

Another extremely picturesque place is the **cemetery**, just off the highway down to Lake Atitlán. It has the best view of the lake. The graves here have been painted bright colors and are decorated with an assortment of angels, flowers and plaques. Opulent family crypts are also the norm and some mausoleums are small masterpieces. Naturally, this is a very tranquil place and the only other people you will run into are those visiting their family or checking out their own plot.

◆ Where to Stay & Eat

The few hotels and restaurants are very basic. No credit cards are accepted at any of the hotels or restaurants. If you're looking for cheap food, head to one of the *comedores* around the central plaza. They serve tortillas, rice, bean and chicken.

Hotel y Restaurant Belén, *10a Calle 4-36, Zona 1*, ☎ *502/7-762-3105, 8 rooms, $.* This hotel is a block uphill from the central plaza and has a small, pleasant courtyard. Rooms have one double bed, overhead fan and private bathrooms. Hot water is sometimes available, but don't count on it.

    Posada Café Vista Hermosa Solala, *Calzada Venancio Barrios 0-85, Zona 2*, ☎ *502/7-762-3576, 4 rooms, $.* This small guesthouse is attached to a residence. The rooms are tiny, but clean, with one double bed, private bath with hot water, and parking. It offers some nice views of the central plaza and surrounding streets but, unfortunately, not many of the lake. The restaurant serves daily specials that include chicken, soup, beef and sometimes fresh fish.

Panajachel

Once upon a time Panajachel was a little village settled by the Cakchiquel Indians after the Spanish chased them away from Iximché. Like other fishing villages, it led a quiet life until one day some flower children arrived from the States. They fell in love with place and called it paradise. They told their friends, and their friends told their friends. Soon, Panajachel was famous. The flower children opened small restaurants and hotels and woke up one day to find that Panajachel was now a major tourist attraction. Then it was time for private lakeside villas and exclusive hotels to be built. Once the new-age healers and spiritual groups conducting energy workshops settled in, the transition was complete. Panajachel had become **Gringotenango** (Place of the Foreigners).

You can still find Cakchiquel and Tz'utuhil Maya here, but they are difficult to meet since most are busy making a living and have little time for tourists.

> ❖   **INSIDER TIP: GETTING TO KNOW YOU**
>
> You should consider taking a language course or participating in one of the community projects to experience daily life in Panajachel.

The worst things in Panajachel are the crowds and the street vendors, who are very aggressive and will test your patience. But keep in mind that development has created a have/have-not situation, with most of the Maya being the have-nots. At times, resentment runs high. Robberies are on the increase, so protect your valuables.

When the hassles become too much, head down to the serene lake. It will remind you of the real reason people are drawn to Gringotenango.

With no ruins and little cultural life, most of the activities in Panajachel are centered around shopping or outdoor activities. Terrific hiking and biking trails lead to nearby villages. There are also horseback riding tours and a variety of watersports, such as kayaking, sailing and scuba diving.

◆ Getting Here

Panajachel, or Pana as the locals refer to it, is very easy to reach. Numerous shuttle services in every major city are eager to whisk you off to the lake. Public buses leave several times a day from Guatemala City and other locations. The shuttle services are even more convenient – they take half the time, but are more expensive (US $7-12 per person, one way). **Atitrans** Guatemala, 13 Calle 1-51, Zona 10 Local 22, Edificio Santa Clara II, ☎ 502/2-331-8181, fax 502/2-332-5788, www.atitransguate.com, offers the best shuttle service from either Guatemala City, Antigua or Quetzaltenango. The main bus stop in town is at the corner of Calle Santander and Calle Real, across from the Banco Mercantil.

◆ Getting Around

Everything is within walking distance in Panajachel, so you won't need to take taxis.

Public ferries offer rides to nearby villages. The boat to San Pedro leaves from the end of Calle Embarcadero, west of the main street, Calle Santander. All other boats leave from Calle del Balneario at the end of Calle Santander. Always check for the departure times at the main kiosk on the dock. The average ride on the ferry boat is Q10.

You can buy a round-trip ticket for Q20, but this really isn't convenient because it means you must return on the same boat that you came on.

Murphy's Law dictates that another boat will be returning when you want to head back. Also, some local boatmen will let you onto the boat knowing you have the wrong ticket. Once you are halfway across the lake, they tell you that you must buy another ticket since you are on the wrong boat. Just refuse. They won't push it.

Most boats returning to Panajachel from the other villages leave at 3 pm. For this reason, most people decide to stay overnight. If you do want to go back to Pana and have missed your ferry, you can hire a private boat for Q200 to take you back across the lake. You can also take the public bus from any of the villages back to Pana, although this is a long way back and some villages don't have buses.

> ❖ **INSIDER TIP: FERRY ALERT**
>
> Be wary of the *lancheros* (boatmen), who will approach you trying to sell rides. They will outright lie to you and tell you certain ferries are no longer running, running late or leaving at an inconvenient time. This is just a ploy to sell you a ticket on their boat for 150% more than the public ferry.

◆ Spanish Language Education

Panajachel has several Spanish schools offering full-time courses at reasonable prices. Courses usually are a week long, with four to five hours of one-on-one teaching. For complete immersion you should consider living with a local family. It's a win-win situation – you will learn the language much more quickly and a local family is provided with some income. Prices for the school start at US $65 for classes only and US $120 for classes plus room and board for one week.

The most established schools in Panajachel are:

Jabel Tinamit, Calle Santander, ☎ 502/7-762-0238, www.jabeltinamit.com.

Pana Atitlán Language School, Calle de la Navidad, 0-40 Zona 1, ☎ 502/7-762-1196. This school will also send teachers out to the smaller villages for you to study there.

◆ Adventures on Foot

Reserva Natural Atitlán (Atitlán Nature Reserve), one mile (two km) west of Panajachel, on the main highway, next to Hotel Atitlán, ☎ 502/7-762-2656. This is probably the simplest tour to organize in the Panajachel area. The reserve is within walking distance of town, or you can opt to take a free ride on the reserve's catamaran which leaves from the dock at the end of Calle Embarcadero, west of Calle Santander.

The reserve has a nature trail that leads across a suspended bridge over a small river canyon and continues to a small waterfall. Along the trail are spider monkey and coatimundi enclosures, and past the waterfall is a butterfly preserve and herb garden. The visitor center has an observation deck and a private beach where you can swim. This makes a lovely and relaxing day-trip for the whole family. Open daily from 8 am until 5 pm. US $7 for adults, $3.50 for students and children.

The simplest and cheapest way to tour the area is to stroll along the road that makes its way around **Lake Atitlán**. The walk east from Panajachel to Santa Catarina takes about one hour and continues on to San Antonio, another 45 minutes away. With the lake and volcanoes to admire, the route is very picturesque. Sunset is particularly spectacular, but you shouldn't be too far from your hotel at this time as it gets dark quickly after the sun dips below the horizon. There are several spots to swim, but be aware that winds pick up in the afternoon, making the water choppy. The lake also gets deep very quickly. If you are tired and don't want to walk back, catch a boat back to Panajachel.

Santa Cruz to San Marcos Hike. This full-day excursion starts with a ferry ride across to Santa Cruz. You then take the trail that connects that village with Jaibalito, Tzununa and San Marcos. You return from San Marcos to Panajachel by boat. The trail is moderately difficult, with some climbing and slopes along the lake. Price is US $36 per person and in-cludes a packed lunch, drinking water and the boat ride. There's also a **full Lake Trek**. This tour follows the old footpaths that criss-cross all around the lake. It includes visits to nearby villages and other stops along the way. You have the option to camp out or to stay in a rustic hotel.

❖ HIKING OUTFITTER

Richard Morgan, **Adventures in Education**, Posada Los Encuentros, Callejon Chotzar 0-41, Jucanya ☎ 502/7-762-2093, fax 502/7-762-1309, www.adventure- study.com.

◆ Adventures on Wheels

Touring **Lake Atitlán** by bike is a pleasant way to visit. The road is not too hilly and the ride is relatively easy (although the return trip seems to be harder!). Depending on your level of fitness, the ride can take between four and six hours. Be sure to bring a hat and lots of water. If you don't feel like biking back, you can put your bicycle on one of the boats returning to Panajachel or try to get a ride on one of the small mini-vans that go from village to village (you may have to pay extra to put your bike on top).

❖ BICYCLE RENTALS & OUTFITTERS

A number of places rent bicycles in Panajachel. Most of the shops are located along Calle Santander. Prices start at US $4 per day, per bike.

Maco Rent, Calle Santander, ☎/fax 502/7-762-0883.

Emanuel's Moto & Bike Rentals, Calle 14 de Febrero, ☎ 502/7-762-1336.

If you would like to do an organized **mountain bike tour**, contact **La Vía Maya**, Boulevard Liberación 6-31, Zona 9, Guatemala City, ☎ 502/339-3601, fax 502/339-3608, www.laviamaya.com. This company offers a bike tour that starts off at the ancient capital of Iximché (see page 150) and follows country paths to El Mirador (The Lookout). The ride continues with several other stops along the way. Total distance is 30 miles (50 km) with only five miles of uphill biking. You can extend this trip into a three-day tour that combines other adventures such as climbing a volcano, horseback riding, sailing, kayaking or high-altitude scuba diving. Contact the company for prices and dates.

> ❖   **INSIDER TIP: SMART BIKING**
>
> Inspect your bike before you head out. Some places offer some real clunkers that probably shouldn't be on the road.

Old Town Outfitters, 5a Avenida Sur #12, ☎ 502/2-399-0440, www. bikeguatemala.com, offers a wonderful combination bike/kayak tour. Their "Paddle and Pedal" starts off with a bike ride on a cliffside trail with panoramic views that leads down to the lake where kayaks await. You kayak across the lake to their "secret" swim hole for some cliffside diving and a visit to a nearby hotel. You can add a third day to the trip and try rock climbing, rappelling or hiking up the San Pedro volcano. Prices include all gear, food, accommodations, guides and equipment. Fees are US $140 per person for two-day tour; US $175 per person for a three-day tour (two-person minimum).

◆ Adventures on Water

ATI Divers offer **scuba diving** as well as PADI training courses. Although they have an office in Panajachel on Calle Santander, the actual school is in Santa Cruz at the La Iguana Perdida hotel. See that listing, page 112, for more information.

Take a **boat tour** of Lake Atitlán. Head down to the main dock in town at the foot of Calle Balneario, where most of the boats are kept. The boatmen will approach you and quote a ridiculously high sum. You are expected to barter and get it down to the reasonable Q70 per person, depending on how many people are in your group (the more people, the lower the fare). You can ask for stopovers at villages along the way. If negotiating with the boatmen seems too daunting, contact a tour agency. **Servicios Turístico Mundo Nueva**, Avenida Santanda 4-26, Zona 2, ☎ 502/7-761-0818, offers tours starting at US $25 per person; fees include a trip to San Pedro, Santiago and San Antonio Palopó. You stop in each village for one hour. Price includes transportation to the public dock, boat tickets, guide and a box lunch. The boat departs at 8:30 am or 9:30 am and returns at 4 pm.

> **AUTHOR NOTE:** *If you prefer independent travel, forego the lunch and guide and simply buy a boat ticket.*

◆ Volcano Adventures

San Pedro Volcano

Volcán San Pedro is on the south side of the lake and rises to 9,908 feet (3,020 meters). The base of the volcano is covered by coffee plantations that eventually give way to pine and deciduous forests. The trees here are tall and wide, so you don't have a view of the lake or the neighboring volcanoes until you reach the top. It takes three or four hours to climb along the trail as it passes through corn and coffee fields. It becomes steeper and more arduous the closer you get to the summit.

If you are not taking an organized tour, hire a local guide. Finding one is easy enough – in fact, when you step off the boat in the village of San Pedro La Laguna, you will be approached by a number of people. If you don't make arrangements there, ask at Nick's Restaurant in town. The going rate is Q100; make the price clear before heading out. Bring plenty of water and snacks for both you and your guide, and be sure you have a sweater or jacket for the cooler air once you reach the summit. See the San Pedro section below, page 117, for a list of hotels in this area.

AUTHOR WARNING: *Don't do this trek alone – it's very easy to get lost on the trails and you may be stranded for several days.*

❖ TOURS OF SAN PEDRO VOLCANO

SAN PEDRO VOLCANO & THREE VILLAGE TOUR: This two-day hike starts in Panajachel and travels by boat to Santa Cruz for a half-day hike to San Marcos. After lunch in San Marcos, the tour continues to San Pedro de la Laguna for an overnight stay. In the morning, get your boots on for the climb to summit of San Pedro. This is a moderate-to-difficult hike. Contact Richard Morgan, **Adventures in Education**, Posada Los Encuentros, Callejon Chotzar 0-41, Jucanya, ☎ 502/7-762-2093, fax 502/7-762-1309, www. adventurestudy.com.

HORSEBACK TOUR: This two-day/one-night tour starts in Guatemala City. The first day includes a sailing tour of the lake, a visit to the Atitlán Nature Reserve & Butterfly Farm and shopping for handicrafts. You stay overnight in Panajachel. The next day you cross the lake to San Pedro la Laguna, where your horses are waiting. Lunch is on the trail in a wood cabin. Along the way, the guide will stop for birding and to point out the local flora and fauna. The price of $175 per person includes all transportation, meals, one night's accommodation, guides and horses. Contact **Maya Expeditions**, 15 Calle 1-91, Zona 10, local 104. Guatemala City, ☎ 502/363-4955, fax 502/337-4660, www.maya expeditions.com, for more information and prices.

◆ Shopping

Panajachel has one of the largest outdoor handicraft markets in Guatemala. Dozens of stalls sell a myriad different crafts such as beaded purses, necklaces, textiles, ceramics, leather goods and clothing. Street vendors also wander this area. The market, Comericales de Artesanías Tipicas Tinamit Maya, stretches the full length of Calle Santander down to the public docks.

There are lots of bargains to be found here, but be sure to barter. Prices are automatically doubled or even tripled because the vendors expect you to barter. Start by offering half of what you are willing to pay and move up from there. Halfway through the negotiations, pretend to become disgusted with the prices being offered and walk away. The vendor will call you back and negotiations can start again. Eventually, you will settle on a price (usually half of what is being asked) and everyone leaves happy. (Bartering is not done in the stores.)

❖ DEALING WITH STREET VENDORS

You will be approached by many street vendors. At first, buying from them may be fun. Some of the children are pretty cute. But after a few days of constant badgering and having things shoved under your nose while you are trying to eat, the charm of vendors can wear thin. Most are from the school of nag-'em-til-they-buy-something. You will hear over and over: *Una para ti, bueno color para ti, por favor, una, una para ti* (here is one for you, it's a good color for you, one, please, just one, for you). They will also give you a story about needing to sell something in order to buy tortillas. Keep in mind that most of the street vendors in Panajachel are doing okay (the poorer vendors work in the smaller villages). The more aggressive ones will drape their goods around your shoulders and then refuse to take their sample back and demand you pay for what you have taken. Ignore them and hand back their goods.

Some tourists think they will buy just one thing to show they have already spent their money. This doesn't work and the vendors will suggest you need another *por una amiga* (for a friend). Unless you want to end up owning a small truckload of bracelets or be pestered to the point of insanity, you must learn how to deal with them. The best – albeit the rudest way – is not to respond to them. Most take a *no, gracias* to mean they can wear you down. But if you don't respond at all they will eventually leave. This is difficult to do without feeling like a heartless human being. (Canadians may find this strategy impossible.)

◆ Where to Stay

There is a vast assortment of hotels in Panajachel ranging from the budget digs to very exclusive resorts. While seemingly a bargain, many of the budget hotels are nasty, overpriced and unsafe. The mid-range hotels are much safer. Whatever your budget, check your room before you pay.

❖ HOTEL PRICING

Prices are per person.

$	Under $25
$$	$26 to $50
$$$	$51 to $85
$$$$	$86 to $125
$$$$$	over $125

> **AUTHOR TIP:** *Smaller hotels use a padlock system for securing doors. There is a latch and bolt attached to the door and frame that you put a lock through. Usually this works quite well, unless the screws holding the bolt are loose and the whole lock can be easily removed. Robbers have the system down and can clean you out in 15 minutes. Check the security of your hotel. Most mid-range hotels have on-site security and safes for guests to lock up valuables.*

Hotel Atitlán, *Finca San Buenaventura, one mile (two km) west of Panajachel, on the lake,* ☎ *502/2-360-8405, fax 502/2-334-0640, www. hotelatitlan.com, 64 rooms, $$$$.* This luxury hotel in a quiet cove is the best in Panajachel. It has a Spanish hacienda building style and décor, with rooms centered around a pool and garden. Rooms are richly appointed, with two wrought-iron queen-size beds, colorful linens, tile floors, antique wooden furniture, private bathrooms and a balcony or patio with a lake view. The grounds are quite spectacular and feature sculpted trees and bushes accented by flowers and shrubs. On the premises are a restaurant, tennis courts, pool, bar and shop. The long, lovely beach borders the Atitlán Nature Reserve. Even if you are not staying here, stop by the restaurant for a drink or meal and watch the sunset over the lake (see *Where to Eat*, below, for complete restaurant review).

Barceló del Lago, *2a Avenida 6-17, Zona 2,* ☎ *502/7-762-1555, fax 502/7-762-1562, 100 rooms, $$$$.* Large, gaudy and very modern, this hotel offers maximum comfort with very little style. It's conveniently located in the middle of town. Rooms have wall-to-wall carpet and all amenities, including cable TV, air conditioning and large bathrooms. All have first-class views of the lake. There is a restaurant, pool, gym, spa and bar on-site. The service is wonderful. See *Where to Eat*, below, for restaurant review.

Hotel Posada de Don Rodrigo, *Calle Santander and Calle de las Buenas Nuevas,* ☎ *502/7-762-2326, fax 502/7-762-2329, 30 rooms, $$$.* This small luxury hotel has easy access to the lake. The rooms are large and tastefully decorated with local textiles, dark wood furniture and lovely rugs. The showers are divine (plenty of water pressure and hot water). Out back, the grounds have hammocks and chairs, while in front is the lakeside restaurant with a pool and water slide. There is also a sauna and a squash court.

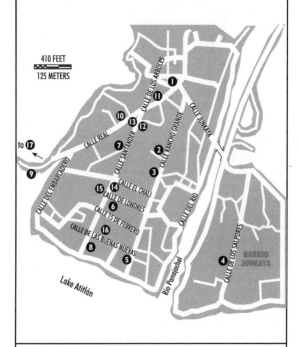

Panajachel

410 FEET
125 METERS

to 17

CENTRAL HIGHLANDS

BARRIO JUNKAYA

Lake Atitlán

Río Panajachel

CALLE DE LOS ÁRBOLES
CALLE JUNKAYA
CALLE RANCHO GRANDE
CALLE REAL
CALLE SANTANDER
CALLE DEL EMBARCADERO
CALLE EL CHALÍ
CALLE DE LONDRES
CALLE 15 DE FEBRERO
CALLE DE LAS BUENAS NUEVAS
CALLE DEL RÍO
CALLE DE LOS SALPORES

WHERE TO STAY & EAT

1. Hotel Maya Kanek
2. Mullers Guest House
3. Rancho Grande Inn
4. Posada Los Encuentros
5. Hotel/Restaurant Barceló del Lago
6. Hotel Dos Mundos
7. Hotel/Restaurant Cacique
8. Hotel/Restaurant Posada de Don Rodrigo
9. Hotel Tzanjuyú
10. Casablanca Restaurant
11. Bombay Pub
12. La Terraza
13. El Patio
14. Pana Rock
15. Orale!
16. El Bistro
17. San Buenaventura de Atitlán Hotel/Restaurant

N

© 2006 HUNTER PUBLISHING, INC

Hotel Cacique Inn, *Calle del Embarcadero*, ☎ *502/7-762-1205, 34 rooms, $$$*. This hotel is actually several buildings tucked away from the main street. It doesn't have a lake view, but it does have a lovely private garden and swimming pool surrounded by a wall. The rooms are well decorated, with wooden furniture and tile floors, but the best features are the fireplaces and doors that open onto the garden. The restaurant is excellent (see page 107).

Hotel Dos Mundos, *Calle Santander 4-72*, ☎ *502/7-762-2078, fax 502/7-762-0127, 21 rooms, $$-$$$*. Dos Mundos refers to the two worlds brought together in this hotel. The owner has combined Guatemalan and Italian décor to create a classy hotel at a reasonable price. The palapa-roofed bungalows are casually styled with wooden furniture and splashes of color. Most open onto the immaculate pool and tropical gardens that lead up to the fantastic restaurant, La Tanerna, which serves the best Italian food in the area.

Rancho Grande Inn, *Calle Rancho Grande*, ☎ *502/7-762-2255, fax 502/7-762-2247, 11 bungalows, $$*. This was one of the first hotels in Panajachel, opened in 1940 by a German woman who became famous for her hospitality. Her legacy has continued with Marlita Hannstein, who now operates this country inn combining European and Guatemalan styles. Each bungalow has been decorated individually with woven rugs and bedspreads. All have wonderfully comfortable king-size beds, wood ceilings, white stucco walls and tile floors. Private porches look out onto well-tended flower gardens and a hearty family-style breakfast is included in your room rate. It's one of the best deals in town and fills up quickly. Reservations are a must.

Posada Los Encuentros, *Callejon Chotzar 0-41, Jucanya*, ☎ *502/7-762-2093, fax 502/7-762-1309, www.atitlan.com/encuentros, 5 rooms, $$*. This is one of the newer hotels in town and it feels more like a private home. It's open, airy and gracefully decorated with Guatemalan art, sculpture, throw rugs, animal masks and ceramic tiles. The living room, located next to a small gym, is filled with cozy sofas and a fireplace. Rooms are simple and elegant, with a large king-size bed, wooden furniture and lovely wall art. The food is healthy and delicious, though the restaurant is for guests only. The owners offer a number of interesting workshops in yoga, meditation and nutrition, as well as tours in the area.

Hotel Tzanjuyú, *San Buenaventura Road on the way to Hotel Atitlán*, ☎ *502/7-762-1317, 32 rooms, $$*. You can't beat the location of this hotel. It's tucked away on an eastern corner of the lake and rooms have a balcony and windows that give panoramic views. The hotel is a bit weather-beaten (almost bordering on decrepit), but this seems to add to its appeal as a true lakeside resort. The room décor is nonexistent and the floors are in bad shape, but the beds are quite comfortable and the showers are decent. A pleasing floral garden leads to a small lakeside pool.

Müller's Guest House, *Calle Rancho Grande 1-82*, ☎ *502/7-762-2442. 3 rooms, 1 bungalow, $$*. This is another guest house opened by a European and it closely resembles a B&B. All rooms open onto a sweet flowering garden. Rooms are decorated in pastel colors with blond furniture and floors. Breakfasts are served in a cozy nook and there are snacks of wine and cheese in the afternoon. Everyone enjoys this tranquil guest-house and it fills up quickly. Make sure you have a reservation.

Hotel Maya Kanek, *Calle Principal*, ☎ *502/7-762-1104, fax 502/7-762-0084, 20 rooms, $*. The owner is very welcoming and helpful. The hotel is on the edge of the older part of town, which means its quiet. There isn't much ambience and the sparsely decorated rooms are centered around a parking lot. However, everything is very clean, very quiet and very cheap. Most of the rooms have private baths, although hot water is available only in the mornings and evenings. No credit cards.

◆ Where to Eat

Hotel Atitlán Restaurant, *Finca San Buenaventura, one mile (two km) west of Panajachel, on the lake*, ☎ *502/360-8405, fax 502/334-0640, www.hotelatitlan.com*. The food here is reliably good, but the real draw is the phenomenal ambience and first-class service. The restaurant overlooks the lake and offers views of the fantastic sunsets. Good dishes include roast chicken, porterhouse steak, Caesar salad and wonderful desserts. You have access to the pool and beach while at the restaurant. If you're not up for dinner, stop by for a cocktail as the sun goes down. US $12-25.

Barceló del Lago, *2a Avenida 6-17, Zona 2*, ☎ *502/7-762-1555, fax 502/7-762-1562*. During high season this hotel puts on an incredible Sunday brunch and dinner buffet. There are plenty of delicious French, Italian and Guatemalan dishes from which to choose. Come early and come hungry. US $7-13.

Cacique Inn Restaurant, *Calle del Embarcadero*, ☎ *502/7-762-1205*. This quaint hotel restaurant serves delicious traditional dishes. Try the red pepper soup, chorizos (spicy sausage), *chiles rellenos* (stuffed peppers) or *pepian de pollo* (spicy chicken in pumpkin and sesame sauce). International dishes includes shrimp ceviche, *robálo* (fish) and fresh pasta. It's all terrific. US $12-20.

La Terrraza, *end of Calle Santander above the IGUAT office*, ☎ *502/7-761-0041*. This unassuming restaurant is one of the best in the Lake Atitlán area. It has a nicely decorated open-air terrace and an eclectic menu featuring European and Asian cuisine. Try the Niçoise salad or spring rolls for starters, followed by steak tartare or Veracruzana fish (served in a tomato, olive and onion sauce). The menu changes frequently to make use of the freshest ingredients. Ask about the wonderful daily specials. US $8-15.

Hotel Posada de Don Rodrigo Restaurant, *Calle Santander and Calle de las Buenas Nuevas*, ☎ *502/7-762-2326, fax 502/7-762-2329*. The food is very good, especially the handmade tortillas, fish dishes and fresh pastas. But the best thing about this restaurant is the romantic setting. Terrace tables overlook a courtyard with a beautiful tiled fountain and lovely garden that are both lighted at night. Live marimba music completes the experience. US $12-20.

Casablanca, *Calle Prinsipal 0-93*, ☎ *502/7-762-1015*. This is one terrific little restaurant. It has a warm décor with white walls that are trimmed with wood and decorated with bright Guatemalan artwork. The windows open up onto the street so you can watch people go by. Specialties are fish and seafood dishes. Try the grilled lake fish, served in a bed of steamed rice. Pasta options are quite good, too. US $6-$12.

El Bistro, *end of Calle Santander*, ☎ *502/7-762-0508*. A cozy restaurant suitable for a romantic dinner either inside by candlelight or outside with the garden lights. The menu is Italian – and what food it is! The bruschetta is incredible, as are the fresh pastas (try the fettuccine), antipasto and green salads. I especially liked the steak au poivre (pepper steak). El Bistro is a bit hidden. Look for the iron gate beside a low wall just where the road hits the lake. US $8-15.

El Patio, *halfway down Calle Santander*, ☎ *502/7-762-2041*. The décor is rather non-specific, but this restaurant has an incredible menu. Enjoy such classics as Virginia baked ham, goulash, roast beef, filet mignon and chicken à la king. It also serves a terrific breakfast with pancakes, egg dishes and great coffee. Their Sunday barbecue is popular with the expatriate crowd. US $6-10.

Bombay, *Calle de kis Arboles*, ☎ *502/7-762-0611*. Despite the name, this restaurant does not serve Indian food. It does, however, have wonderful Middle Eastern dishes such as falafel and pita bread sandwiches. There are also vegetarian specials and fresh fruit drinks. US $2-6. No credit cards.

Pana Rock, *Calle Santander past the main bank*, ☎ *502/7-762-2121*. This is an excellent Italian restaurant run by an Italian expatriate who came to Pana six years ago. It offers terrific pizza, pastas and other Tex-Mex specialties. The bar is well stocked and there is live music almost every evening. It's open until the wee hours and is a good place to catch a late-night snack. Avoid the copycat restaurant upstairs, which has really terrible and overpriced food. US $4-7.

¡Orale!, *Calle Santander 4-29, Zona 2*, ☎ *502/7-762-0017*. This is the home of the US $2 breakfast as well as cheap and filling tacos. More expensive dishes are also offered – such as steak and grilled meat – but the best meals remain the breakfasts. It's got good beer prices. US $1-6.

Villages of Lake Atitlán

The villages around Lake Atitlán are populated with a variety of Maya tribes who have kept their colorful clothing and traditional way of life. Each village has something different to offer, and each has accommodations so overnight stays are relatively easy. These are the places where you come to enjoy markets, natural wonders and Maya culture. Although some of the communities can be reached by road, the simplest and most comfortable way to visit is by boat from Panajachel.

Eastern Lake Atitlán

◆ Santa Catarina Palopó

This small village is only 13 miles (four km) east of Panajachel. It used to be a fishing village until the introduction of black bass, which promptly ate all the other fish. Today, residents support themselves by growing coffee and selling their distinctive weaving with its bold zigzags. It's a charming place, with narrow cobblestone streets and adobe houses. Sadly, it's difficult to enjoy the shoreline since it has been filled with exclusive private villas and posh hotels. Other than enjoying the beautiful views, there is not much to do here.

Where to Stay

Casa Palopó, *Km 6.8*, ☎ *502/7-762-2270, www.casapalopo.com, 7 rooms, $$$$$*. This exclusive and gorgeous private villa is on the shores of Lake Atitlán. Rooms are done up with cushy king-size beds, wooden floors, exposed ceilings and walls painted lovely shades of blue to match the beautiful linens. All rooms open up onto a small terrace that overlooks the lake and volcanoes. The sitting areas have fireplaces, wooden floors, throw rugs, soft upholstered chairs and Maya art. A full breakfast, served on the terrace overlooking the lake, is included in your room rate. There is an elegant pool and cute dining room. The hotel offers a shuttle service, helicopter pick-up, a business center and tours to anywhere in Guatemala. All this luxury just might give you a nosebleed. It's far too posh for children, who are not welcome.

Villa Santa Catarina, *8a Calle 1-75, Zona 10*, ☎ *502/7-5-334-8136, 31 rooms, $$$*. This is an adobe-style two-story hotel with a lovely tile roof and yellow walls. The rooms are snug, with hardwood floors, exposed beams, pastel colors and Guatemalan bedspreads. Each has a private balcony with a lake view. There are also two nice lakeside pools (one for children) and a tennis court. The restaurant here serves excellent local dishes, including *pepian de pollo* (chicken in a spicy pumpkin sauce) and grilled fish.

◆ San Antonio Palopó

Another 3.1 miles (five km) past San Catarina is San Antonio Palopó, a traditional small village where most of the men and women dress in their characteristic purple clothing. The village is set on a cliff overlooking the lake. Irrigated terraces have been built and it's here that locals grow vege-

CENTRAL HIGHLANDS

tables that they sell at various markets. There is little to do here but enjoy the quite pace of life, walk the trails around the village and just relax.

Where to Stay

Terrazas del Lago, *Calle de la Playa*, ☎ *502/7-762-0037, 12 rooms, $$*. This dear little hotel overlooks the town's public beach, which offers excellent swimming. The entire hotel, including the bedrooms, is decorated in floral-pattern tiles. Rooms are huge, with comfortable wooden tables, candles and other nice accents. Ask for a front room; they have a patio that overlooks the lake with the volcanoes in the background. The rooftop restaurant serves good simple meals. Breakfast is particularly pleasant here.

> **NOTE: You** *can take either a bus or boat from Panajachel to reach both Santa Catarina and San Antonio. Sometimes the bus is faster – it's also cheaper.*

◆ San Lucas Tolimán

This village on the far southeast corner of the lake is primarily a coffee-growing area with a *Ladino* population. Tolimán Volcano looms in the background. The Friday market here is large and colorful, but it's not geared toward tourists and sells mostly produce and practical goods. The town church, Iglesia San Lucas in the central plaza, dates back to the 1600s and is worth visiting. As you walk through town, you will see traditional homes made from bamboo. Because this village is a transportation hub for the Pacific departments and Guatemala City, there is quite a lot of traffic.

Where to Stay

Hotel Toliman, *Calle Principal*, ☎ *502/7-206-7561, www.atitlan.com/ toliman.htm, 20 rooms, $$$*. This tranquil hotel has been done up like a traditional Guatemalan ranch with historic d furnishing, colorful ceramics and indigenous art and is reminiscent of the 17th century coffee plantations that use to dominate this area. All rooms have private bathrooms with hot water and there are nine suites with private verandas. The grounds are filled with trees, flowers and the view of the lake is really spectacular. There is a complementary traditional Guatemalan breakfast that is a great way to start the day. Hosts Eduardo and Yara Olivero provide special attention to make sure your visit is stress free.

Hotel y Restaurante Brisas del Lago, *Calle Principal*, ☎ *502/7-762-0102, 8 rooms, $*. Decidedly less upscale than its graceful neighbor, this small village hotel is still pleasant. Rooms are large and clean, with private baths and hot water. Some of them offer pleasing views of the church and lake; ask to see before accepting one. The restaurant serves basic Guatemalan fare – roast chicken and fish are the staples. No credit cards.

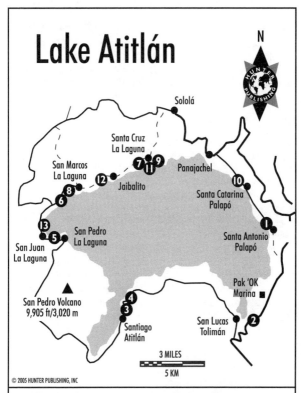

Lake Atitlán

Sololá

Santa Cruz
La Laguna

San Marcos
La Laguna

Panajachel

Jaibalito

Santa Catarina
Palapó

San Pedro
La Laguna

San Juan
La Laguna

Santa Antonio
Palapó

Pak 'OK
Marina

▲
San Pedro Volcano
9,905 ft/3,020 m

Santiago
Atitlán

San Lucas
Tolimán

3 MILES

5 KM

© 2005 HUNTER PUBLISHING, INC

1. Hotel Terrazas del Lago
2. Hotel Toliman
3. Hotel Posada de Santiago
4. Hotel El Bambú
5. Hotel Casa San Pedro/Ti'kaaj/
   Sakcari/Trippy's
6. Posada Schuman
7. Hotel/Restaurante Arca de Noe
8. Centro de Meditación Las Piramides/
   Hotel Jinava
9. Hotel La Iguana Perdida
10. Hotel Villa Santa Catarina
11. Villa Sumaya
12. Jaibalito Casa del Mundo/Vulcano Lodge
13. Ulaxbil

Western Lake Atitlán

◆ Santa Cruz La Laguna

Santa Cruz La Laguna is the nearest village to the west of Panajachel and one of the largest on the western shore. It sits on a cliff overlooking the lake and has some wonderful walking trails that lead alongside the lake to either Panajachel or San Marcos. Lake Atitlán's only scuba school is located here.

ATI Divers is located next to La Iguana Perdida hotel. They offer a variety of courses, including open-water certification (US $175) and PADI high-altitude diving. A two-tank dive costs US $45. They maintain an office in Panajachel on Calle Santander. ATI recommends that you dive between May and October, when the lake water is at its clearest. Contact them at ☎ 502/762-2646, fax 762-1196, santacruz@guate.net.

Where to Stay

La Iguana Perdida, *main dock, ☎ 502/7-762-2621, 3 dorm-style rooms with shared bath, 3 cabins with private bath. $.* This is a back-to-nature hotel with little in the way of electricity or hot water. The thatched bungalows come with kerosene lamps and dorm-style rooms that will remind you of summer camp. The restaurant serves excellent vegetarian food and there is a nice sauna on site. Most of the people are here for the ATI diving courses and you may feel out of place if you are not taking a course. No credit cards.

Arca de Noe, *main dock, ☎ 502/5-515-3712, 10 rooms, 6 with private baths. $.* This is another rustic hotel with small bungalows set alongside the lake. The small, neat rooms are furnished with local textiles and have light (from solar power), but no hot water. Delicious meals of fresh vegetables and baked bread are served in the main house. It's a very congenial and tranquil atmosphere. Bring your bug repellent. No credit cards.

Villa Sumaya, *down from the main dock, ☎ 502/5-617-1209, www. villasumaya.com, 7 rooms, $$.* This is a small, private villa offering creative workshops and meditation retreats along the shores of Lake Atitlán. Rooms are in palapa-roof bungalows with ceramic tile floors, wooden furniture and crisp linens in coordinated brown and sienna colors. A long veranda has rocking chairs and hammocks where you can enjoy the view. There is also a hot tub, meditation corner and reading room. Meals are made with organic fruits, vegetables and meat, along with freshly baked bread. Kayaks, yoga, massage and Spanish lessons are also available. The hotel will pick you up from Panajachel. No credit cards.

◆ Jabalito

This tiny village has no roads and is accessible only by boat. Ancient trails, some leading all the way to Sololá, criss-cross the area. This is the place to come for adventurous treks. You can catch a boat from Panajachel directly here, but a more scenic route is to get off at Santa Cruz and walk the cliffside trail for 45 minutes to reach Jabalito. It's an astonishing hike, with views of the lake and volcanoes – worth the effort.

Where to Stay

Casa del Mundo, *Jaibalito dock,* ☎ *502/5-218-5332, www.lacasa delmundo.com, 8 rooms, 4 with baths, $$.* Many promise but few deliver. This hotel, built on a sheer cliff, really does have the best view of Lake Atitlán. The view from every room is so breathtaking that you barely notice the décor, which is a shame because it is lovely. Rooms are decorated with wood-beam ceilings, red-tile floors, stucco walls and great Maya art. The restaurant has large windows too, and serves delicious meals of fresh fish and assorted Guatemalan specialties. The verdant gardens are alongside an outdoor hot tub. Brave souls may want to try the nine-foot (15-meter) cliff jump into a pristine pool. Quieter types may prefer to rent one of the boats and head out on the lake.

Vulcano Lodge, *four minutes from Jabalito dock,* ☎ *502/5-410-2237, 54 rooms, $$.* This cute hotel is set amid a coffee plantation away from the lake. The gardens have fruit trees, flowering bushes, flowers, orchids and a variety of other plants. Rooms are small, with private patios, nice bathrooms and firm beds. Beautiful artwork by local artists is displayed throughout the house. The food is a gourmet blend of European cooking with Guatemalan overtones. Everything combines to offer a tranquil resort – you don't even miss the lake after the first day. The lodge attracts an international crowd of sophisticated travelers. They have no phone. The only contact is through their website at www.atitlan.com/vulcano/reservations.htm.

◆ San Marcos La Laguna

San Marcos has become a gathering spot for the New Age element in Lake Atitlán. The village itself is tiny, with only a few houses set among fruit trees and coffee plantations and a small church built by the Franciscans in 1584. There isn't much to do here unless you are having your aura balanced or taking a meditation workshop (see *Las Piramides,* below). The shore is quite rocky, so you will have to swim off the docks in town.

Solar Pools is run by a German lady, Marty Bischoff, who offers small Jacuzzi pools on her property where you can soak as the evening chill settles over the area. It's only Q15 per person for an unlimited time. Marty also runs a wonderful bakery and local women sell her bread in town. It's the best bread in the area.

Where to Stay

Las Piramides, *inland from dock,* ☎ *502/2-205-7151, 7 pyramids, $ (meals are extra).* Every building on this property is in the shape of a pyramid, including the guesthouse. The design helps facilitate a number of New Age courses taught here, such as channeling, tarot card reading, yoga and inner peace. They offer a lunar meditation course that starts at the full moon and lasts four weeks (the last week involves fasting and silence so this may not be for everyone). Accommodations are in dormitory-style pyramids that are Zen-like in their simplicity. The food is strictly vegetarian. Visitors are welcome to join the hathayoga sessions.

Posada Schumann, *lakeside, just past the main dock*, ☎ *502/5-202-2216, fax 502/5-474-7017, 4 rooms with shared bath, 3 private bungalows, $.* This is a pleasing European-style hotel with a great lakeside location. The bungalows are rustic and feature lovely stonework, wood panels and bright Guatemalan textiles. They are equipped with a kitchen and private bath. The restaurant serves simple, tasty meals. There is even a private dock for those arriving by boat. Ask your boatman to drop you off here.

Hotel Jinava, *by main dock, www.hoteljinava.com, 5 bungalows, $$, no credit cards.* The rustic but comfortable rooms at this relaxed hotel are shaded by avocado and papaya trees. Balconies overlook the lake, there is a sauna on the beach and plenty of hot water. The owner does massage and is rumored to be the best on the lake). The waterfront restaurant serves up a truly delicious menu of international dishes. Excursions to the volcanoes are held every few days – if you can tear yourself away from the serenity.

Unicorno Rooms, *main dock, no phone, 3 bungalows, $, no credit cards.* This is another communal hotel with three small palapa-roofed bungalows with shared bath. There is no hot water or electricity, but there is a sauna and great garden. It's affiliated with the San Marcos Holistic Centre (www.sanmholisticcentre.com) that offers professional therapies and training courses in a variety of natural healing techniques.

◆ San Juan La Laguna

This Maya community is set along a large bay with lovely beaches and, in the near distance, San Pedro Volcano. Most of its 3,500 inhabitants work on local coffee farms, but a number of them also produce *petates*, delicate mats woven from the reeds that grow along the banks of the bay. There is also a small community of painters producing naïve art. Not many tourists come here, which leads to a very relaxed atmosphere. You can hike the volcano or follow the path along the shore to neighboring San Pedro. One popular trail leads to the beautiful Las Cristilinas mountains. You should hire a guide for this trip (ask at the ferry docks). Fishing is also good in this area.

San Pedro is also home to the Maya god, Maximón. The town has a low-key shrine (as opposed to Santiago Atitlán, where it has become a major tourist attraction). If you want to pay your respects to Maximón without a lot of hoopla, then this is the place to visit. See page 120 for more details about Maximón.

Where to Stay

Uxlabil EcoHotel, *6 blocks from village, ℅ 502/5-366-9555, www.uxlabil. com, 10 rooms, $$.* Uxlabil is Mayan for "breath." This enchanting eco-hotel opened in February 2002. As one of its community projects it hired the stone carvers of San Juan to construct most of the hotel. The gesture helped keep this ancient trade alive; the few artisans here are some of the last carvers in the world practicing this ancient craft. As a result of their hard work, the hotel is quite distinctive. Surrounded by two acres of land covered with coffee plantations, it offers a sweeping view of the lake. The hotel is done in a colonial hacienda style, while the restaurant and reception area is built like a colonial church. Rooms have stone walls, carved stone headboards and *petates*, woven mats, covering the ceilings and walls. A wonderful 147-foot (45-meter) dock is used for swimming and fishing. The hotel will pick you up in Panajachel. Tours to the volcanoes and other eco-tours are offered. The restaurant, run by a local Maya family, serves fish and crab from the lake along with other Maya dishes. Meals are an additional US $16 per day for all three meals and morning coffee. No credit cards.

◆ San Pedro La Laguna

This is the naughty village on the lake. While other communities are meditating or communing with nature, San Pedro is growing pot and partying every night. It makes no bones about being the marijuana capital of Atitlán and you will be offered herb as soon as you step off the boat. However, there is more to do here than get high.

This quirky village isn't as polished as the other villages in the area. It has no official streets, just cobblestone paths that are sometimes strewn with garbage. Everything seems to cost US $2 and there is a disproportionate number of Evangelical churches. There are lovely hot springs about town but, oddly, no hot water in most of the hotels. Added to the general milieu are the very eccentric foreigners who have settled here. Despite all these drawbacks, there is something pulling it all together and eventually San Pedro grows on you. So much so that some visitors never leave.

Getting Around

The main road is called Calle del Embarcadero a Panajachel, but directions are given with reference to the two main docks. The south dock is for boats to Santiago Atitlán, while the north dock is for boats to Pana. Walk straight ahead from either dock, uphill, to the center of town or follow the paths to the right or left to the various hotels. It doesn't matter which way you go – the village is too small to get lost.

There is no telephone service in the village, so none of the hotels have land phones, although a few have cell phones. Everyone uses the community telephone at the Telgua Office (Guatemala's phone company) in town, which is ☎ 502/7-762-2486.

CENTRAL HIGHLANDS

Spanish Language Education

There are two excellent Spanish schools in San Pedro. **Escuela de Español Casa Rosario**, the first school in town, has been operating for eight years. The owners, Vicente and Samuel Cumes, are considered the best teachers in the area. They offer 20 hours of instruction for just US $90, which includes a host family, but no meals. They encourage contact between the teachers and students and offer some interesting tours, including visits to nearby villages. You have the option of renting an apartment in the school building if you do not want to board with a family. The school doesn't have a phone, but it does have an excellent website, www.casarosario.com.

Co-operative of Guatemalan Spanish Teachers, www.atitlanonline.com/cooperativa, is the new kid on the block. The cost for 20 hours of instruction per week is US $90, including the host family of Tz'utujil Mayas (they, too, offers tours). You can also combine your classes with some volunteer work teaching English at the school, which is a great way to meet non-gringo members of the community.

Local Artisans

Café Arte, Calle del embarcadero a Santiago just past Hotel San Pedro, is a combination art gallery displaying the works of two of San Pedros famous primitive painters. Rafael Gonzalez y Gonzalez and Pedro Rafael Gonzalez Chavajay are both internationally recognized artists. They paint the local landscapes and people using print colors and simple designs. The gallery displays their work as well as paintings from other family members. For more information visit www.artemaya.com.

Situated in the Hotel San Pedro is the **Museo Maya Tz'Utujil**, which displays rare photographs of the Tz'Utujil Maya alongside textile exhibits and archaeological exhibits. The museum holds folkloric activities like traditional music and dance. Artwork is also for sale. Open Mon-Fri, 8 am-noon and 2-6 pm.

Walking Tours

A number of terrific scenic trails lead from San Pedro to the neighboring communities of San Juan and San Pablo. There are some great spots for swimming along the way, particularly as you get close to San Juan. The whole hike takes about three hours. If you are feeling really ambitious, try the southern trail that leads to Santiago Atitlán, which takes about four hours. This, too, offers some great views of the lake.

Although the San Pedro Volcano is in the backyard of San Pedro, no official tours run from the village; most of the tours leave from either Pana or Guatemala City (see page 66). Things are more casual here, and local guides take people up the volcano. The going rate is Q100 per person, less if you have a group. Your tour will start in the coffee plantations, ascending the forest trail and, eventually, the summit. Bring bug repellant, water, snacks and warm clothes (it's chilly at the top). Ask around town and people will point out the reliable guides.

> **AUTHOR WARNING:** *Don't do this trek alone. It's very easy to get lost on the trails or run into other trouble if you are alone. There have been reports of robberies.*

Where to Stay

There are lots of budget hotels. In fact, San Pedro offers *only* budget hotels. None accept credit cards. Cleanliness and comfort vary, although most places are decent.

❖ HOTEL PRICING
Prices are per person.
$ . . . . Under $25
$$ . . . . $26 to $50
$$$ . . . . $51 to $85
$$$$ . . . . $86 to $125
$$$$$ . . . . over $125

Hotel Casa San Pedro, *Calle del Embarcadero a Santiago*, ☎ *502/5-515-9174, www.hotelcasasanpedro.com, 10 rooms, $$.* Without a doubt, this is the most luxurious hotel in San Pedro. Spacious rooms overlook the mountains and lakes and have been decorated in bright colors with Maya art as accents. On the ground floor is the sauna, gym, private garden, restaurant and living room with a huge CD collection for guests to enjoy. You can rent kayaks to explore the lake and there are regular tours to the volcanoes.

Hotel Ti'Kaaj, *first street right off Calle del Embarcadero a Santiago,* ☎ *502/5-219-2225, 5 rooms, $.* The best thing about this hotel are the hammocks set up in the spectacular garden filled with tropical flowers, trees and birds. The rooms are fairly spartan, but they are comfortable and clean. There are two private rooms with their own bathroom, the other rooms share a bath. A restaurant across the street serves good pasta dishes and pizza.

Hotelito Sak'cari y el Amanecer, *first street right off Calle del Embarcadero a Santiago,* ☎ *502/5-812-1113, 10 rooms, $.* This hotel has really pleasing, very clean rooms that are comfortable. Their private baths have lots of hot water. All rooms have a view of either the lake or the surrounding mountains. It's within walking distance of all the great restaurants in town.

Trippy's Hostel, *first street right off Calle del Embarcadero a Santiago (turn left at the docks, look for signs), 30 beds, $.* This hostel has co-ed or women's only dorms with a shared bathroom and kitchen. There are also some private rooms with private baths. There is a lovely garden here and the atmosphere is congenial. Not much privacy but lots of socializing.

Where to Eat

There are plenty of restaurants in San Pedro, and almost all of them offer a meal for about US $2. Few have telephones.

Nick's Place is the first place you will see when you step off the ferry from Panajachel. This is one of the most popular places to hang out. Enjoy grilled chicken, fish soup, guacamole and great dessert while watch-

CENTRAL HIGHLANDS

ing all the action on the lake. People in town comes for Nick's video evening and to drink beer. US $2-6.

Chile's, Calle del Embarcadero a Panajachel (just up from the docks), ☎ 502/5-594-6194. This cheery restaurant is open early and closes late. It serves a variety of hamburgers and pastas, along with typical Guatemala fare. It has the best stocked bar in town, making it a popular party place. There is live music on Saturday evening and free salsa lessons every Tuesday and Friday. US $2-7.

Restaurant Pinocchio, Calle del Embarcadero a Santiago is straight up from the Santiago Pier and has super food. There are homemade pastas, good burgers, excellent salads and great cakes. Breakfast here is the best meal offered and is huge but economical. The wine list is surprisingly good.

Freedom, first street left of Calle del embarcadero a Panajachel. This is pleasant lakeside restaurant serves up a variety of Ecuadorean specialties, soups, salads, smoothies and other vegetarian fare. In the evenings, there are often bonfires that everyone is welcome to attend.

Café San Pedro, first street left Calle del Embarcadero a Panajachel, ☎ 502/5-563-3867. Get your Strabucks fix at this café with an incredible view of the lake. Owner Violeta offers capuccino, moccachino, expresso, café-au-lait and accompanying pastries. The perfect place to get your caffeine buzz.

The cheapest places to eat in town are the *comedores* that set up along the Santiago Pier. They offer typical tasty fare, such as rice and beans, tortillas, *chile enchiladas*, fruit *licuados* and fried plantains.

◆ Santiago Atitlán

This village is on the far end of the lake and takes 45 minutes to reach from Panajachel by ferry. After Pana, it receives the most tourists, but has managed to maintain its old way of life. Everyone wears colorful native garb and participates in native traditions. The *huipiles* worn here are famous and often feature intricate embroidered patterns such as birds and flowers. The women wear *toyacal* headdresses made from 10 meters of brilliant red cloth wrapped in a coil; the women of Santiago are some of the most photographed Maya in Guatemala. The *toyacal* is featured on the 25 *centavo* coin. Farming and fishing used to be the main industries, but they are now practiced only on a small scale. Locals make their living from coffee and selling their weaving.

Try to visit on a market day when there are more local vendors with their wares – Friday, Sunday or Tuesday. A permanent handicrafts market starts at the dock and goes all the way up Calle Principal. The vendors here a bit more laid back than in Panajachel and other villages. They take no for an answer after the third time.

❖ **THE QUETZAL KID DILEMMA**

There are lots of "quetzal" kids in the villages that get a lot of tourist traffic, especially Santiago and Panajachel. They run up and ask for a quetzal, usually to spend on candy. Locals are trying to encourage these children to stay in school and not pass their childhood on the streets, but the lure of quetzals and candy is too strong. It's hard to say no to them, but when you give them money, remember that you are encouraging them to beg in the streets and lose out on their education. Your one quetzal can do a lot of damage. If you feel inspired to help them, make a donation to one of the charitable organizations that focus on this problem. You will be contributing toward the community in a more positive way. See the *Appendix*, page 269, for a list of organizations that are helping.

History

Santiago was the original capital of the **Tz'utujil Maya**. They settled here in the late Post Classic period (AD 900-1400) and shortly after started skirmishes with nearby tribes. When the **Spanish** arrived in 1524, the Tz'utujil were having a bloody war with the **Cakchiquel Maya**. After Alvarado did his trademark divide-and-conquer routine, the **Catholic Church** was left in charge. It set about building a cathedral and baptizing all natives. Fortunately, none of the priests quite got the hang of the Tz'utujil language and, since none of the Tz'utujil would learn Spanish, they were left alone to develop their own brand of Christianity. They have managed to keep their Maya shamans and gods alongside the Christian saints.

From 1980 until 1990, Santiago was targeted for the "scorched-earth" campaign waged by the Guatemalan army. Torching of homes, threats, beatings and assassinations of suspected communists became quite common. Ironically, the same institution that took away many of their rights fought the hardest for the Tz'utujil during this dark period. Father Stanley Rother opened the cathedral as a refuge for many of the targeted families and brought international attention to their plight. He had been working in the area for 13 years building clinics and schools and was already branded a communist when, on July 28, 1981, he was murdered in his rectory while sleeping. Santiago rose up in protest and the campaign to purge the army from its region lasted for nine years. When 13 people were gunned down on December 2, 1990 outside the town of Panabaj, over 20,000 people protested and the army was finally forced to leave the area. At that time, the elders in Santiago also kicked out the local police force and have been running things themselves with few problems. The village has become a role model for other Indian villages along the lake who want the army gone.

CENTRAL HIGHLANDS

Sightseeing

The **cathedral** (The Martyrs of Santiago Atitlán) in Santiago is one the oldest buildings in the area. Franciscans arrived in 1538 and began construction in 1571. The building was completed in 1582. It survived several earthquakes, but was severely damaged in the 1976 quake. It has since been restored, including the original bell tower. Inside the church are wooden statues of saints dressed in clothing made by the local woman. Every year the saints get a change of clothes. The devotion shown to these doll saints is touching. The pulpit and altar are intricately carved with pictures of quetzals and corn (the Maya believe men were made from corn). There are several renditions of Yum-Kaz, the Maya god of corn. Under the west arch are three plaques denoting the **Martyrs of Santiago Atitlán Monument**. The plaques honor Father Stanley Rother and other church members killed by the army. When Rother was killed, the villagers requested that his heart remain in the church and built this plaque to indicate its final resting spot. Each December they hold a week-long festival in his honor. The rectory next door has been turned into a shrine with an exhibit of Rother's personal belongings and a bible. On the floor where he died locals maintain a permanent candlelight vigil. This is a very moving place to visit

Maximón, the mischievous scoundrel, is popular in Santiago, but there is a controversy over his presence. The more right-wing Christian Evangelists are trying to get him banned, since they believe he is a heretic. But Maximón remains as part of the great trickster tradition found in many indigenous religions and to his loyal followers he is an integral part of their lives. Maximón is the one who answers their prayers and helps them in their hour of need. The fact that he smokes, drinks and enjoys the occasional romp only makes him more real. Many locals have been upset by his expulsion from the church and exclusion in the Holy Week celebrations. Without a permanent home, Maximón resides in one of the local houses. He is moved every so often by one of the elders. If you would like to visit this Maya saint, ask one of the local boys to bring you to "La Casa de San Simón." They will charge you Q10 to act as your guide. You will have to pay an additional Q10 to see the saint and even more to take his picture. Bring along a candle, cigar or some liquor if you want Maximón to be agreeable.

Where to Stay & Eat

The two best hotels and restaurants are actually just outside of Santiago. In the downtown area, there isn't much selection.

DOWNTOWN

Hotel Tzutuhil Atitlán, *three blocks uphill on Calle Principal*, ☎ *502/7-721-7174, 26 rooms, $*. You can't miss this bright pink five-story hotel; it's the only modern building in town. Rooms are large, with good views and double beds. Ask for one with a private bath and cable TV for US $2 more

– they are much nicer and considerably cleaner. The rooftop terrace is a wonderful place to watch the sun set over the lake. A downstairs restaurant serves decent food such as roast chicken, fried fish and pasta. No credit cards.

Restaurante Brisas del Lago, *just down from central plaza*. This is another simple café with nice wooden tables and chairs. It has fairly decent fruit salads, sandwiches, fried chicken and French fries. It's also the cheapest place in town. Q3-10. No credit cards.

OUTSKIRTS OF TOWN

Posada de Santiago, *a half-mile south of town on the road to San Pedro,* ☎ *502/7-721-7167, fax 502/7-721-7365, www.posadadesantiago.com, 12 rooms, $$*. Surrounded by an avocado grove and coffee plantation, this hotel offers rustic stone-walled cottages with all the comforts of home. Each has a comfortable bed, fireplace and balcony with views of the garden and lake. Local artwork from neighboring villages is displayed throughout. An excellent restaurant serves gourmet food. Bread and pastries are baked daily, and marinated fish, fowl and meat are prepared in their special steam-smoker. The ice cream is homemade and the coffee organic. Canoe and mountain bikes are available for all guests.

Bambú, *a half-mile east of town on the road to San Lucas Tolimán,* ☎ *502/7-721-7332, fax 502/7-721-7197, www.atitlan.com, 5 bungalows, $$*. The gardens and restaurant here are first rate. Bright bungalows are carefully arranged in a garden that has been organized according to plant type. Stone pathways connect each bungalow to the garden. Rooms are neat and elegant, with red tile floors and balconies offering views of the garden. The restaurant is in an A-frame dining room with a fireplace and exposed beams that overlooks the lake. The menu features mostly Spanish food cuisine, and most of the fruits and vegetables served come from their own gardens. This is a lovely oasis.

CENTRAL HIGHLANDS

Los Altos Region

Santa Eulalia

N

MEXICO

Todos Santos
Cuchumatán

HUEHUETENANGO

Zaculeu

Tacaná Volcano

Tajumulco Volcano

Momostenango

TOTONICAPAN

San Francisco El Alto

San Andrés Xecul

Salcajá

SAN MARCOS

Zunil

QUETZALTENANGO

Tecún
Uman

Santa María
Volcano

© 2006 HUNTER PUBLISHING, INC

Los Altos

The region of Guatemala referred to as Los Altos is made up of four departments: **Quetzaltenango**, **Totonicapán**, **San Marcos** and **Huehuetenango**. The region is known for its indigenous villages wedged between volcanoes and the tallest mountain range in Cen-

tral America, the **Sierra de los Cuchumatánes**. These mountains reach upwards to 13,123 feet (4,000 meters) and the dramatic landscape is wild and intensely beautiful. Few tourists make it as far north as Los Altos, but those who do will experience the very heart of Guatemala.

History

Los Altos has always been a fiercely independent part of Guatemala and never quite joined the rest of the country. On February 2, 1820, the departments of Quetzaltenango, Totonicapán, Sololá, San Marcos, Quiché, Retalhuleu and Suchitepequez formed the **Republic of Los Altos** and demanded recognition from the Supreme Court of the newly formed Guatemala. The lack of response didn't stop the leaders of the new state; they held elections for a provisional government that declared Quetzaltenango the capital. When Los Altos tried to secede from Guatemala in 1948, **President Carrera** brought in the army to squelch the uprising. The area was able to retain some of its autonomy simply because of its distance from the capital and for a while Los Altos was an economic and cultural force. The glory days ended in 1902, when the region was hit with an earthquake and volcanic eruption.

Life remains hard in Los Altos with many people struggling to make a living from growing coffee, maize, apples, rice and cardamom. Cattle and sheep ranches, as well as factories, play an important role in the economy.

The area is famous for its weavers. Tourists come to experience the indigenous culture, study Spanish at excellent schools, and explore the volcanoes, mountains, hot springs and lagoons.

Department of Quetzaltenango

The department of Quetzaltenango is west of Lake Atitlán and rests in a large basin on the southern side of the Cuchumatánes Mountains. Because it has the most fertile land in Los Altos, many people have made their homes here. It was originally settled by the **Quiché Maya** in the Early Classic period (AD 200-500), and was ruled by Zaculeu in the north, now the site of Huehuetenango. The Quiché invaded the area in AD 1400 and ruled it until 1524 when the **Spanish** arrived. The Dominicans and Franciscans spent many years trying to convert the Quiché to Christianity, but for the most part the Quiché resisted assimilation. During the 1900s, Quetzaltenango began developing into an economic stronghold. Today, it is the largest city in the region, followed by the textile centers of Salcaja and Zunil.

Quetzaltenango/Xela

The capital city of Quetzaltenango is called by its Quiché name, Xela (SHAY-la), a shortened version of Xelajú which translates as "beneath the 10 gods." The 10 gods are the volcanoes surrounding the city. The two names are interchangeable. Quetzaltenango is the official name used on maps, buses and the like, but all the locals refer to the city as Xela – the Maya name. The city itself is 7,654 feet (2,333 meters) above sea level.

Although it is Guatemala's second-largest city, Xela doesn't see the same numbers of tourists as other parts of the country. It's considered the capital of the modern Quiché Maya and is a city focused on commerce and trade. It prides itself on being "La Cuna de la Cultura" (The Cradle of the Culture), and has produced many of Guatemala's best writers, musicians and politicians. It has a large student population, with three universities and dozens of music schools.

Xela is gaining an international reputation for its **Spanish schools** and it has dozens of them. There is almost no English spoken in Xela, so it can offer a total immersion experience. The city is quite active during the day, but as the evening turns cool, things begin to close down.

This is a lovely city with cobblestone streets that wind past neoclassical architecture, lovely parks and colorful markets. It's a perfect base for exploring the smaller villages in Los Altos, whether on day-trips (you can reach hot springs and volcanoes) or on longer journeys.

◆ History

Xelajú was part of the **Quiché Maya** kingdom ruled by **King Gucumatz**, who brought the Western Highlands under his control in AD 1400. The

Quiché kept control of the area until **Alvarado** arrived in 1524. **Tecún Umán** was king at this time and was fighting with many of the other tribes who wanted their freedom. By pitting the tribes against one another, Alvarado was able to take control of the area quickly. But Tecún Umán refused to surrender and he met Alvarado in hand-to-hand combat just outside Xela on February 15, 1524. Legend tells of Alvarado gazing down upon the slain king dressed in his quetzal feathers and commenting on how he had never seen a more beautiful warrior. His Nahuatl allies renamed the city **Quetzaltenango**, or Land of the Quetzals.

Under colonial rule Xela prospered. It had fertile farmlands and served as a connection to the Pacific coast and its agricultural goods. In 1820, when Los Altos broke away from the newly formed Guatemala Republic, Xela was named its capital and there was a flurry of construction. The new city was built in the style of a Greek city state. When the independence movement was squashed in 1948, the city settled into the role of an economic force in the north, as a coffee-broker and storage center. It also established its excellent universities during this period and became so successful that it was considered a rival of Guatemala City. Its golden era ended on October 25, 1902, when Santa María Volcano erupted, triggered by a series of earthquakes. Over 5,000 people were killed and the city was completely destroyed buried under a mountain of volcanic ash. But rebuilding began promptly and by 1928 the city was operating well enough to install a new electric railroad that ran to the Pacific city of Retalhuleu. Xela never regained its former glory, but it has grown into a prosperous provincial city with a healthy economy.

Xela is currently experiencing rapid growth with a sprawling population that has taken over outlying farms and left many *campesinos* homeless. Unemployment is becoming an issue and many children are being sent out to work washing cars or shining shoes. Dozens of agencies here run volunteer programs that work to solve the problems and the city's future certainly seems brighter than that of Guatemala City.

◆ Getting Here & Getting Around

Xela is well connected to the rest of Guatemala by bus service. Most western cities have direct buses to Xela. The run from Guatemala City takes about 4½ hours; from Panajachel it's just under two hours. If you are coming from the east you will have to go to transfer in Guatemala City.

Xela does not have a central bus station. Buses from other departments come into the largest bus terminal, **Parque Minerva**, on the western side of town in Zone 3. Local buses heading for smaller outlying villages leave from the terminal on the eastern side of the city on 7a Av Calzada Independencia, Zone 2, near the **Monumento a la Marimba** (Marimba monument). First-class buses coming from Guatemala City will drop you off either at this terminal or at their downtown offices.

To get downtown from the Parque Minerva terminal, walk through the market and park and catch a bus to **Mercado Democracia**. That will drop

LOS ALTOS

you off and you will then have to walk 10 minutes downhill to the city center. Due to a dispute over fares, no local buses are allowed in the downtown core. You can take a cab into the downtown core for about Q30.

Driving a car is not practical in this city due to the many one-way cobblestone streets, lack of parking and horrendous traffic. Most hotels and restaurants are located within walking distance of the central plaza and taxis are cheap and plentiful.

◆ Schools

Spanish Language

Spanish language schools have become big business in Xela and there are dozens of them. Originally, most offered participation in volunteer programs as part of the curriculum. The idea was to use part of the tuition fee to help finance the organization, while helping students learn Spanish by participating in community building. It was a win-win situation for all, but greed took over and some of the larger schools began asking a finder's fee from the organizations or used the students to work on their own farms. Donations started going missing as well. If you are interested in helping the community as you study, we recommend that you contact the organizations below directly.

Social Organizations

There are a number of local organizations always in need of a helping hand.

> **CPD - Centro Pluricultural Para la Democracia,** Calle "A" 23-84 Zona 1, ☎/fax: 502/7-761-0067 or 502/7-765-1655. This NGO is helping with the Guatemalan Peace Progress through educational programs for rural families throughout northern Guatemala.

> **Habitat for Humanity** (Habitat para la Humandidad), Ave de las Americas, 950 Supercom Delco, 2nd nivel oficina 9, ☎ 502/7-763-5308, www.habitguate.org.

> **ICA Friends Project Reforestation** (ICA Amigos Proyecto de Reforestación), 1a calle 16-93 Zona 1, ☎ 502/7-763-1871.

The Coordinating Association of Spanish Schools of Quetzaltenango, **ACEEQ** (*Asociación de Eescuelas de Español de Quetzaltenango*), insures that language schools listed with them offer 20 hours a week of one-on-one training with a university-trained teacher, as well as day-trips, cultural outings and proper diplomas. It also began monitoring the volunteer programs, home stays and teacher working conditions. It established guidelines for payment of US $100-120 per student, per week. You can find more information on Xela's Spanish schools at www.xelapages.com (keep in mind these schools have paid a fee to be listed). You can also get some sound consumer protection advice at Alert Xela at www. transformart.com/xela/index.htm.

The schools listed here area all members of ACEEQ:

> **Celas Maya**, 6ta Calle 14-55, Zona 1, ☎/fax 502/7-761-4342, www.xelapages.com/celasmaya.
>
> **Juan Sisay**, 15 Avenida 8-38, Zona 1, ☎/fax 502/7-765-1318, fax 502/763-2104, www.xelapages.com/juansisay.
>
> **Miguel Angel Asturias**, 8a Calle 16-23, Zona 1, ☎ 502/7-767-4427, www.spanishschool.com/xelapages.
>
> **Minerva Intensive**, 24 Avenida 4-39, Zone 3, Colonia Minerva, ☎/fax 502/767-4427, www.xelapages.com/minerva/index.htm.
>
> **Proyecto Lingüístico Santa María**, 5 CAlle 2-40, Zona 1, ☎/fax 502/7-763-1061, spanishgua@c.net.gt.
>
> **Ulew Tinimit**, 7a. Avenida 3-18, Zona 1, Apartado 346, ☎/fax 502/7-761-6242, www.xelapages.com/ulewtinimit/index.htm.

Weaving School

The highlands are famous for their flawless handwoven textiles that are made by using unique techniques. Learning Guatemalan weaving has become a popular pastime with tourists and Xela now has a several weaving schools run by local women. The best school of the bunch is run by the **Association of Women Weavers** (TRAMA, *Asociación de Mujeres Tejedoras*) at 12 Avenida 3-39, Zona 1, ☎ 502/7-763-0823, fax 502/5-614-0178, www.xelapages.com/asotrama/weavingschool.htm. TRAMA is a collective of 350 backstrap weavers that are Mam, Ixil, Cakchiquel, T'zutuhil and Quiché Maya women. The purpose of the group was to guarantee fair wages for the women weavers whose goods are sold in the markets throughout Guatemala. Profits, particularly from the tourist markets, very often don't make it back to these women. TRAMA's prices are little higher than those you will find in the markets, but the proceeds do go directly to the women and their families.

The school offers several excellent courses where you learn the different techniques, the history of weaving, how to select the best materials and how to combine different weaves. Prices range from US $50-115 per person for 40 to 60 hours of instruction. Accommodations with local families can also be arranged for a nominal fee. Non-students can visit the store which sells high quality, 100% cotton, pre-washed, preshrunk, and color fast materials, shawls, place mats and other goods.

◆ Sightseeing

Parque Centramerica, between 5a Avenida Sur and 4a Avenida Norte, Zona 1. This park was constructed by the famed Latin architect Rafaél Perez de Leon between 1935 and 1942 and is considered one of the loveliest parks in Central America. Perez adorned the park with lampposts built like Greek columns and neoclassical monuments. There are plenty of benches beneath the giant trees and usually a vendor or two. On Sundays, the park hosts an excellent market where many locals from outlying villages come to sell their wares. Sundays are also celebrated with live marimba music and dancing.

Museo Quezaltenango, 7 Calle 11-09, Zona 1, ☎ 502/7-761-6427. This eclectic museum at the south end of the park is in the Casa del Cultura del Occidente building, which resembles a Greek temple with bold columns and a sweeping staircase. On the ground floor a historical museum displays documents from the revolution of the State of Los Altos. Next door is the marimba museum, showing how the instrument is made. Upstairs is the Natural History Museum (*Museo de Historiá Natural*), which has displays of Maya artifacts, samples of local costumes and stuffed animals. There is also a collection of antique soda bottles. It's a weird mix, but fun to visit. Open 8 am-12 pm and from 2-6 pm, Monday to Friday, and 9 am-1 pm, Saturday. Admission is Q7.

Museo de Ferrocarril de los Altos, 12a Avenida at 7 Calle, Zona 1, no phone. This museum is dedicated to the railroad that once connected Xela to Retalhuleu. It has old photos, displays and historical records. Upstairs is the Jésus Castillo of Quetzaltenengo National School of Music (*Escuela Nacional de Musica Jésus Castillo de Quetzaltenango*). Founded in 1948 to honor one of Guatemala's foremost composers, the school offers a variety of musical degrees, including marimba. Its graduates include many famous Guatemalan musicians, earning the school an international reputation. Admission is Q7.

Palacio Municipal, 4a Avenida Norte, Zona 1. This grand 1897 building has a neoclassical style with decorated Corinthian pillars and intricate stone carvings. It serves as the town hall but at one point was a mansion for the governor. The grounds are built around a palm tree with the state flag depicted with plants and flowers. On each side are Greek columns and a monument to President Barrios, who ruled from 1873 to 1885. Open daily, 8 am-7 pm. No admission charge.

Metropolitan Cathedral, 4a Avenida Norte, Zona 1. This large cathedral was built in 1879. It has a baroque façade and niches that hold life-size sculptures of various saints. Unfortunately, the church was severely damaged in the earthquake of 1902 – the only thing that survived was the façade. In back is a large, modern concrete church that doesn't have much character.

Pasaje Enriquez, 5a Avenida Sur, Zona 1. This passageway was built in 1900 by the architect Alberto Porta and decorated by the sculptor Luis Liutti. The passageway has combined elements of Greek, Moorish and baroque design and features an elegant glass archway. Liutti sculpted the front and floor with beautiful designs. Unfortunately, the upscale restaurant and shops never opened and the passage remains almost deserted. It is being restored and has been adopted as an icon for the city.

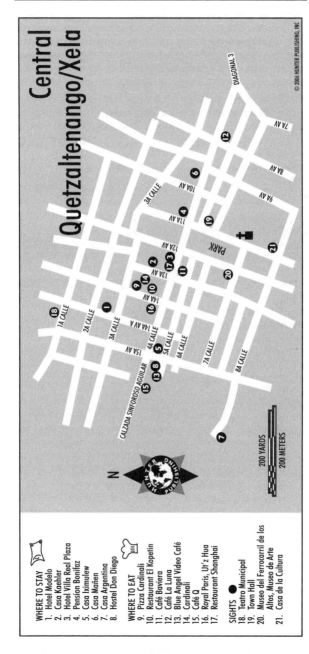

Central
Quetzaltenango/Xela

© 2006 HUNTER PUBLISHING, INC.

LOS ALTOS

WHERE TO STAY
1. Hotel Modelo
2. Casa Kaehler
3. Hotel Villa Real Plaza
4. Pension Bonifaz
5. Casa Iximulew
6. Casa Mañen
7. Casa Argentina
8. Hostel Don Diego

WHERE TO EAT
9. Pizza Cardinali
10. Restaurant El Kopetin
11. Café Baviera
12. Café La Luna
13. Blue Angel Video Café
14. Cardinali
15. Café Q
16. Royal Paris, Ut'z Hua
17. Restaurant Shanghai

SIGHTS
18. Teatro Municipal
19. Town Hall
20. Museo del Ferrocarril de los Altos, Museo de Arte
21. Casa de la Cultura

Teatro Municipal, 14a Avenida at 1a Calle, Zona 1, ☎ 502/7-761-6427 or 761-2218. Xela takes pride in its role as the cultural center for the Western Highlands. In 1884, the city commissioned a group of artists and architects to build a Greco-Roman style theater. The results are a rather imposing building with large pillars holding up a vaulted roof over arched doorways. A wide staircase leads to a plaza that's decorated with busts of local artists, including Guatemala's first poet laureate, Osmundo Arriola (1886-1958), and great marimba composer and defender of Maya music, Jésus Castillo (1877-1949). The tiered box seats set over three levels resemble those found in the grand opera houses of Europe. The theater offers many excellent concerts and recitals.

Mercado Democracia, 15 Avenida at 2 Calle, Zona 3. This is a huge market with a labyrinth of stalls selling almost everything you could find in Guatemala. It's geared for the locals and there aren't many handicrafts, but it's worth a visit to see the hustle and bustle.

Iglesia San Nicolas, 4 Calle at 15 Avenida, Zona 1. This monstrous neo-Gothic church was built in the late 19th century. Its imposing front features sharp arches and a tall, lean steeple. Take a look at the ornate stained-glass windows and neo-Gothic artwork inside. Behind the church is a large domed building that serves as a school.

Parque a Benito Juárez, 15 Avenida at Calle 3, Zona 3. This park used to be known as La Democracia, but changed its name in honor of Benito Juárez, the Mexican revolutionary in recognition of Xela's Mexican community. It hosts a long and loud Independence Day party every September 15th. See *Festivals*, page 22.

Templo Minerva y Mercado, 6a Calle, Zona 3. This replica of a Greek temple was built in honor of President Barrios, who was a great supporter of education. Minerva was the goddess of knowledge and learning, and it was hoped the building would inspire the youth of Xela. Today, they use it as a place to hang out and watch the cars whizzing by on both sides of the temple (urban expansion has placed the temple in the middle of a busy intersection). Beside the temple is a little zoo with a rather sad collection of animals. The gigantic Minerva Market is the economic heart of the city, where you will see Indian traders from all over Los Altos doing business. It's colorful and very hectic. The bus terminal is also located here, so you'll no doubt find yourself in the market at some point during your travels.

Puente de Los Chocoyos, 15 Avenida at diagonal 11. Every rainy season during the 19th century, a river flowed down Calles los Choyocos, now 15 Avenida, and people were unable to get from one side of the street to the other. So the city set about building a bridge. On December 23rd, 1883, Puente de los Choyocos (Choyocos Bridge) was unveiled. It cost Q700, about US $100 – a small fortune at the time – because it had a wood base, a body of lime slate and two lovely staircases, one on either end. Although esthetically pleasing, the construction was not stable and by 1893 the bridge needed major repairs. The money was raised and Puente de los Chocoyos was rebuilt, but after the 1908 eruption it almost collapsed. All the wood was replaced with steel, but even that did not make the bridge stable. In 1928 the municipality completely rebuilt the bridge, keeping the original design. Today, the river no longer flows down this street so the bridge is simply a beautiful landmark.

◆ Adventures on Foot

Highland Trek

Quetzaltrekkers, Casa Argentina, diagonal 12, 8-37, Zona 1 ☎ 502/7-761-2470, www.quetzaltrekkers.org, offers an incredible highland trek leaving from Xela and traveling to San Pedro La Laguna on Lake Atitlán. The tour begins just outside of town and travels from the valley up to the cloud rainforest. It passes through remote mountain villages along an incredibly scenic trail. On day one you travel to the small village of Xetinamit and set up camp for the evening. On day two you hike to the village of Santa María Visitacion, 1,312 feet (400 meters) above the lake where there is another campground. Day three is a hike to San Pedro for a swim in Lake Atitlán. You return to Xela by bus that afternoon. The San Pedro Trek is usually offered every weekend, but the company will run a week-day trip for groups of four people or more. The cost is US $65 per person, which includes all transportation, vegetarian meals, camping equipment and a professional mountain guide. All the proceeds from this tour go to the Escuela de la Calle (EDELAC) to help the street children of Xela.

◆ Volcano Adventures

Chicabel Lake & Volcano

Volcán Chicabel is 10 miles (16 km) from Xela and spans across the San Marcos and Sacatepéquez department. This dormant volcano reaches 9,514 feet (2,900 meters) and has a well-formed cone at 8,897 feet (2,712 meters). Inside the cone is a 1,640-foot-wide (500-meter) lagoon with emerald water. The whole area around the lake is shrouded in a mist created as the hot volcanic water comes into contact with the cool mountain air. The local Quiché and Mam believe this lagoon is a sacred place and come here to burn copal and candles while making offerings to the gods for rain and good harvests. They place wooden crosses with prayers on them throughout the woods. On May 3, the Maya New Year, shamans from the various tribes meet here to conduct rituals.

This is a nesting ground for the quetzal bird and several other species, so birding is excellent when the skies are clear. From the volcano's summit you can see the lake and surrounding forests. Swimming or camping in this area is not permitted.

▶▶ *GETTING HERE: Take a bus from Xela to San Martin, Sacatepéquez. It's a 1.86-mile (three-km) hike from San Martin to the volcano, but there are usually pickup trucks along the highway giving rides for a few quet-zals. The hike up to the lagoon takes 45 minutes along a well-cleared path that begins at the foot of the volcano. There are no services in the area, so bring food and water.*

❖   **CHICABEL LAKE TOUR COMPANIES**

Adrenalina Tours, Pasaje Enriquez, 5a Avenida Sur, Zona 1, ☎ 502/7-761-4509 or 502/4-214-1293, www.adrenalina tours.com, offers daily tours to the lagoon for US $18 per person (US $13 for groups of four or more). Price includes transportation, a guide and drink.

Santa María Volcano & Santiaguito

Volcán Santa María dominates the landscape around Xela. It is part of a larger volcanic system that includes Siete Orejas (Seven Ears) and Chicabel volcanoes. Locals call this volcano *Gagxanul*, which means "naked mountain" – it has more rock surface than trees. Santa María reaches 12,275 feet (3,772 meters) and is one of the tallest volcanoes in the region. It was dormant for over 1,000 years until October 24, 1902, when it erupted with lava flows that reached over five miles (8.6 km), burying Xela under ash. The skies around the city were darkened for days and volcanic ash was found as far north as San Francisco in the US. It is considered to have been the largest and most explosive eruption of the 20th century and was great enough to blow a crater in the side of Santa María. Twenty years later, this crater gave birth to a small lava dome named Santiaguito. This is the newest volcano on the continent and it remains active, with lava eruptions every half-hour. From the Santa María summit you can see lava flowing from Santiaguito's crater. The incredible view also extends as far west as the Pacific Ocean and Tajumulco Volcano.

▶▶   *GETTING HERE: To get to Santa María you must first take a 20-minute bus ride to the village of Llano del Pinal, where a dirt trail leads up to the summit. The trail quickly becomes rocky and steep as it climbs from 8,202 to 12,371 feet (2,500 to 3,773 meters). Watch for the painted arrows that mark the way along the trail and keep an eye out for signs that say "NO" when you are heading off in the wrong direction. It takes between three and five hours to reach the top, depending on your physical condition. It's best to do this climb early in the morning when visibility is good. Afternoons here are often cloudy and rainy.*

❖   **SANTA MARIA TOUR COMPANIES**

Several companies offer guided tours to Santa María. The best trek is with the non-profit organization **Quetzal-t rekkers**, Casa Argentina, diagonal 12, 8-37, Zona 1, ☎ 502/7-761-2470, www.quetzaltrekkers.org. Cost is Q75 per person and includes your transportation and guide. All the proceeds from this tour go to the Escuela de la Calle (EDELAC), which helps the street children of Xela.

Adrenalina Tours, Pasaje Enriquez, 5a Avenida Sur, Zona 1, ☎ 502/7-761-4509, 502/5-214-1293, www.adrenalina tours.com, offers daily trips for $18 per person.

LOCAL SPANISH SCHOOL: *Proyecto Lingüístico Quetzalteco de Español (PLQE) has opened the **Escuela de la Montaña** in the rural community of Nueva San José, near Colomba at the foot of the volcano.*

Querro Quemado/Los Vahos

Querro Quemado (Burned Hill) is an active volcano just 1.86 miles (three km) outside of Xela that rises to 10,489 feet (3,197 meters) above sea level. The natives call it *Catinocjuyup*, which means "fire underneath fire." This volcano last erupted in 1888, but it continues to belch gas and steam through several vents. Los Vahos (The Vapors) are the natural steam bath at the foot of the volcano. You can reach Los Vahos via several paths that lead up to the steam baths and go on to the summit. It's Q15 for a sauna/steam bath.

Los Vahos is a two-mile (3½-km) hike from Parque Centroamérica in Xela. The route is scenic as it passes by the mountains. Start off for the baths at 12a Avenida and walk uphill for half a mile (.8 km) to the trailhead. It's 1.4 miles (2.3 km) from there to the steam baths. Allow 1½ hours to reach Los Vahos.

▶▶ *GETTING HERE: You can hike from town in about two hours (see above), or take any local bus going to the village of Almolonga and ask to be let off at the Los Vahos. Look for a tiny sign pointing to the path.*

❖   QUERRO QUEMADO TOUR COMPANIES

Adrenalina Tours, Pasaje Enriquez, 5a Avenida Sur, Zona 1, ☎ 502/7-761-4509 or 502/5-214-1293, www.adrenalina tours.com, offers daily trips for $18 per person. Your fee includes a tour of the volcano and the lava tunnel, geographical information and a visit to the steam baths.

Tajumulco Volcano

Tajumulco, in the department of San Marcos, is the tallest volcano in Central America. It has two separate peaks, the tallest reaching 13,845 feet (4,200 meters) with a 160-foot-wide (50-meter) crater on top. The lower peak is 13,451 feet (4,100 meters). This is one of the coldest places in Guatemala because of the elevation. Although the summit trail is relatively easy, with some very picturesque parts through pine glens, not many people hike here. The final ascent is the hardest part as the trail gets very steep just before it reaches the cone. Once at the summit, you can see Tacana on the Mexican border, the Pacific coast, Lake Atitlán, Xela, seven volcanoes around Antigua and the eruptions of Santiaguito.

LOS ALTOS

▶▶   *GETTING HERE: You shouldn't climb this volcano on your own as the high altitude can cause breathing problems if you're not acclimatized. Sign on for a guided tour.*

❖   TAJUMULCO TOUR COMPANY

The best tour is with **Quetzaltrekkers**, Casa Argentina, Diagonal 12, 8-37, Zona 1 ☎ 502/7-761-2470, www. quetzaltrekkers.org. You leave early Saturday morning for the village of Tuichan, where the trail begins. You spend Saturday night camping at the lower summit here. Just before dawn on Sunday you begin the ascent to the summit to watch the sunrise. The rest of the day is spent hiking back down. The cost is US $40 per person, including all transportation, vegetarian meals, camping equipment and a professional mountain guide. All the proceeds from this tour go to the Escuela de la Calle (EDELAC) to help the street children of Xela.

◆ Day-Trips

Thermal Baths of Almolonga

Almolonga is a small rural community just 1.86 miles (three km) from Xela; it was originally founded in 1839. It's quite a prosperous village, with most of the Indians owning their own land and participating in a lucrative vegetable export business. The village market held on Wednesday and Saturday is quite intense as people come to haggle for the best deals on vegetables and flowers. While the women of Almolonga still wear orange *huipiles* and woven headbands, the village has abandoned its religious traditions in favor of Evangelism. There are more than 25 Evangelist churches in the area, and residents attend services at least once a day. The new religion is credited for lowering the rate of alcoholism, as well as for the area's bountiful crops.

On the outskirts of the Almolonga are **Los Baños**, a series of steam baths heated by the thermal waters from Querro Quemado. It is believed these waters have curative powers and many locals bathe in them. Several companies offer private sunken bathtubs where you can enjoy the hot waters. Cost is Q10. Keep in mind that these baths are 100 years old and not very elegant.

Nearby is **Los Chorros**, a series of swimming pools also fed by the underground thermal waters. Both baths are open from 5 am to 10 pm daily.

▶▶   *GETTING HERE: Local buses leave from Xela and head to the baths every half-hour. Just ask to be let off at Los Baños just past the city. The last bus from Los Baños to Xela leaves at 7 pm.*

Glass Factory at Cantel

Originally known as Chuijllub (on the hill), Cantel is an industrial village located between Almolonga and Zunil, about eight miles (12 km) from Xela. The town's Cantel Fabrica is the huge factory that produces 25% of Guatemala's textiles. There is also a small glass factory run by a group of artists. Founded in 1976, Cooperativa Artesania de Vidrios (COPAVIC) uses a variety of glass-blowing techniques to create unique pitchers, glasses, dishes, statuettes, ash trays, candleholders and vases. The glass they start with is recycled. COPAVIC offers tours of its factory and also has a wholesale store that will ship purchases internationally. For more information, contact COPAVIC, Carretera al Pacífico Km 217.5, Canton Pasac II, Cantel, Quetzaltenango, ☎ 502/7-763-8038, 502/7-753-8131, www.copavic.com.

▶▶ *GETTING HERE: Catch a local bus from Xela to either Almolonga or Zunil and ask to be let off at the factory. Cantel is just past the Las Rosas junction on the main highway.*

Zunil

Six miles (10 km) outside of Xela is the colonial town of Zunil. When it was founded in 1529 it was known as Santa Catarina Zunil, but over the years the name has been shortened. This is an attractive village set in a lush valley at the foot of Zunil Volcano. Many of the houses have red tile roofs offsetting the white cathedral.

The beautiful Río Samala runs through the village, dividing it in two: on one side is the center core, on the other the Chacap neighborhood.

The indoor **market**, on Tuesdays only, is particularly colorful, with everyone dressed in flamboyant traditional dress. Unlike its neighbor Cantel, Zunil has retained its indigenous religion and remains loyal to the Mayan Saint **Maximón**, also known as San Simón (see page 120 for more information). If you would like to visit this rascal saint to present him with a cigar or swig of liquor, ask one of the local children to take you to "La Casa de San Simón." They will ask you for a small tip. Q5 is plenty.

Iglesia Zunil in the center of town is worth a visit. It was built in the mid-16th century and has eight pairs of ornately carved serpentine columns matching the silver altar inside. The altar is now behind a locked gate to protect it from thieves but you can still enjoy the intricate work. Open daily.

Zunil is famous for its beautiful textiles. **Cooperativa Santa Ana** offers individual weaving classes on the waistloom and footloom taught by local members. This cooperative was founded in 1970 and has 550 members. It sells 100% cotton handwoven clothes, purses, linens and shawls. Prices are quite reasonable, if a little more than you would pay in the market, but all proceeds go directly to the women. Open daily, 6:30 am to 7 pm. For information on classes, contact Cooperativa Integral de Produccion Artesanal Santa Ana R.L., 5a Avenida 6-15, Zona 1, Canton Xesiguan, Zunil, Quetzaltenango, ☎ 502/7-765-5379, coop_santa_ana @yahoo.com.

LOS ALTOS

Fuentes Georginas Hot Springs

In the hills above Zunil are the splendid Fuentes Georginas hot springs, probably the most beautiful natural spa in the country. Amid lush jungle and tropical flowers is a series of thermal pools all with different temperatures. Guatemalans from across the country come to sit in the waters, which are said to have curative powers. The spa was built during the 1930s and named after the dictator Jorge Ubico, who apparently visited regularly. Despite the heat, everything remains fresh, cooled by mountain air. There's an excellent restaurant and a pleasant outdoor area equipped with picnic tables and a grill. The hot springs are very popular with local families on the weekends. Open daily, 8 am-6 pm. Admission is Q15 per person. You must wear a bathing suit in the baths – bathing in clothes is not allowed.

If you would like to stay over and do some night bathing, there is just one hotel. **Turicentro Fuentes Georginas**, *located just on the hill below the hot springs, 10 bungalows, $.* There are 10 rustic bungalows, each with a bathtub, fireplace, two double beds and outdoor patio. The rooms are very basic, but still quite charming, and resemble a family cottage. Ask for enough wood to keep the fire stoked all night; it gets really chilly in the mountains at night. The hotel offers special packages that include your room, day-pass to the springs and access for nighttime bathing. The restaurant, serving traditional Guatemalan dishes, is good.

▶▶ *GETTING HERE: Buses to Zunil leave from Xela every half-hour or so. The church, market, weaving school and Maximón are all within walking distance in the village. Fuentes Georgina is four miles (eight km) from Zunil. You can walk there in just over three hours along a scenic uphill trail. Alternately, hire a pick-up truck at the central plaza in Zunil. Prices run from Q30 to Q70 for a return trip. Be sure to arrange a pick-up time or you will end up walking back to Zunil.*

Salcaja

Just seven miles (11 km) northwest of Xela is the colonial city of Salcaja, one of Guatemala's main textile centers. Weavers here produce huge quantities of material used in traditional Maya clothing. You can see the fabric stretched out to dry on oversized looms in the streets. Although there isn't any historical evidence, Salcaja claims to be the first Spanish settlement in the country with the first Catholic church. The San Jacinto church certainly is a beautiful example of early Spanish colonial architecture.

The town produces a drink known as *caldo de frutas*, or *rompopo*, a fermented fruit liquor that carries quite a punch.

The best day to come is **market** day, Tuesday, when the streets are filled with activity.

▶▶ *GETTING HERE: Most northbound buses leaving Xela stop off at Salcaja. Just be sure to get off before the Cuatro Caminos junction. Direct buses do leave Xela twice a day, but they don't have a regular schedule. The village has no tourist services, so you will have to return to Xela at the end of the day. The last bus leaves at 3 pm.*

◆ Where to Stay

Nights in Xela can be get very chilly and most buildings don't have central heating, so look for beds with plenty of blankets, windows that close properly and showers with hot water. Hotels with fireplaces are simply the best.

❖ HOTEL PRICING

Prices are per person.

$	Under $25
$$	$26 to $50
$$$	$51 to $85
$$$$	$86 to $125
$$$$$	over $125

Hotel Villa Real Plaza, *4 Calle 12-22, Zona 1*, ☎ *502/7-761-6270, fax 502/7-761-6180, 50 rooms, $$$.* This is one of the largest hotels in the city and it comes with all modern conveniences. Rooms are huge, with wall-to-wall carpet, double beds, cable TV, private bath and fireplaces. A covered courtyard with skylights houses a popular restaurant and bar. It can be noisy, so ask for a room at the back.

Casa Mañen, *9 Avenida 4-11, Zona 1*, ☎ *502/7-765-0786, fax 502/7-765-0678, www.comeseeit.com, 9 rooms, $$$.* This delightful B&B is furnished with hand-carved furniture, beautiful wall hangings and rugs. Everything has been put together tastefully and the effect is romantic and comfortable. Bedrooms are large and bright, with lovely homey touches such as rocking chairs and pillows. Each has a private bath, cable TV and a balcony with a view. Several rooms also have fireplaces. Breakfast is served in the small dining room downstairs, or you can wander up to the rooftop terrace with a stunning view of the city.

Pension Bonifáz, *4 Calle 10-50, Zona 1*, ☎ *502/7-761-2279, fax 502/7-761-2850, www.quetzalnet.com/QuetzalNET/bonifaz, 75 rooms, $$$.* This is the most famous hotel in Xela. Señor Bonifáz first opened this elegant colonial home in 1935 and the place quickly became popular with both local and foreign travelers. Rooms have wall-to-wall carpeting, private bathroom, hot water and cable TV. Some of the older rooms have marvelous old-fashioned bathtubs. There is a refined (and somewhat stuffy) dining room serving international fare, an indoor pool with Jacuzzi and a lovely rooftop garden.

Hotel Modelo, *14 Avenida A 2-31, Zona 1*, ☎ *502/7-761-4396 or 2959, 22 rooms, $$.* This distinguished hotel opened in 1883. Most of the original furniture is still in the hotel, which gives it a lovely old-world flavor. The charming rooms have wooden floors and walls decorated with local textiles, and most open up onto small courtyards. Ask for a room with a fireplace for even more atmosphere. The restaurant here serves an excellent breakfast and lunch. If the hotel is full, ask about the annex across the street. It has another nine rooms that are in the $ range.

Casa Ixlueu, *15 Avenida at 5 Calle, Zona 1*, ☎ *502/7-765-1308, fax 502/7-765-2584, www.xelapages.com/iximulew/accommodations.htm, 4 rooms, $.* This budget hotel offers clean but rather bare rooms with a B&B

option. Rooms have private baths, double beds and small tables. For longer stays, ask about their fully equipped apartments that sleep two. They have a kitchen, living room, courtyard and cable TV. Unfurnished apartments are also available. Minimum rental for the apartments is one month. No credit cards.

Casa Argentina, *diagonal 12, 8-37, Zona 1 (Barrio Las Flores)*, ☎ 502/7-761-2470, 20 rooms, $. This friendly hotel has a family atmosphere, making it a favorite with budget travelers. The rooms are clean and comfortable and have two double beds and shared baths. Three communal kitchens have purified water supplied. The owner, Doña Argentina Villaseca, is very helpful. Quetzaltrekkers has an office here, so planning a hiking trip is easy. Casa Argentina also offers long-term rentals. No credit cards.

Casa Kaehler, *13 Avenida 3-33, Zona 1*, ☎ 502/7-761-2091, 7 rooms, $. This old-style European pension is just a few blocks from the central plaza. It has an odd assortment of different-sized rooms facing a small courtyard crammed with flowers and plants. Rooms are very basic. They have a double bed and are very clean and comfortable. The bathroom is shared, although one room does have a private bath (of course, it's more expensive). A common area is used by guests to relax. No credit cards.

Hotel Río Azul, *2a Calle 12-15, Zona 1*, ☎ 502/7-761-4396, www.xelapages.com/rioazul, 19 rooms, $. This is a comfortable, clean family-run hotel within walking distance of the central plaza. Rooms have two single beds, private baths with hot water and cable TV. No credit cards.

Hostal Don Diego, *7a Calle 15-20, Zona 1*, ☎ 502/7-761-6497, 6 rooms, $. Xela's newest hotel is run by a young Guatemalan who renovated this abandoned colonial and made it into a very pleasant and homey B&B. The basic rooms have two single beds and a table. Bathrooms are all shared and, unfortunately, there is only lukewarm water. A pleasant courtyard is where you'll be served a fantastic breakfast. In the afternoons, you can take salsa dance lessons there. No credit cards.

◆ Where to Eat

Xela has many restaurants and the majority of them offer the same menu of bad pizza, fries and burgers. Luckily, there are some wonderful alternatives that have terrific menus. Xela also has a vast selection of cafés that offer excellent food.

Royal Paris, *Calle 14A 3-06*, ☎ 502/7-761-1942. This is absolutely the best restaurant in Xela. It resembles a French bistro, complete with artwork and jazz, and has a wide selection of innovative dishes. The curries and various chicken and fish dinners are all excellent, as are their salads, soups and sandwiches. An extensive wine list complements the food and a selection of European magazines is available for light reading. It's open late and usually filled with an international crowd. Q50-100.

Cardinali, *14 Avenida 3-25, Zona 1*, ☎ 502/7-761-0922. Benny Cardinali is a transplanted Italian who runs the best Italian restaurant in the region. Cardinali offers huge portions at reasonable prices. The homemade pastafs and breads, soups, salad and, of course, pizza are all superb. There's an excellent wine list and the service is relaxed and personable. Q 42-70.

El Kopetin, *14 Avenida 3-51,* ☎ *502/7-761-8381.* This tiny restaurant has wood paneling, small tables and a bar. It feels like someone's living room. The home cooking incorporates lots of meat and seafood smothered in fattening sauces. Locals love this place, so it gets really crowded in the evenings. Q35-60. No credit cards.

Shai Long Restaurant Lounge, *18 Avenida 4-44, Zona 3,* ☎ *502/7-767-4396.* This place has absolutely no atmosphere, but it does serve excellent Chinese food in huge portions. The orange duck, chow mein, sweet and sour chicken and shrimp fried rice are especially tasty. Swill it down with lots of beer or a glass of wine. Q35-80.

Café Q, *diagonal 12-4-46, Zona 1,* ☎ *502/7-761-1636.* A cute jazz café that serves fantastic vegetarian food. Try the tomato omelet or vegetable curries, soy burgers, salads, soups and home-baked breads. Café Q is a great place to hang out, drink coffee and people-watch. Q15-45. No credit cards.

Blue Angel Video Café, *7a Calle 15-22, Zona 1, no phone.* This place offers great food at reasonable prices and is usually packed. Pasta dishes are the best options, but there are also great sandwiches and soups and plenty on the menu for vegetarians. In the back, a video room shows popular movies every evening. This is a great spot to network and meet other travelers. Q20-50. No credit cards.

Ut'z Hua, *12 Avenida 3-02, Zona 1, no phone.* This is the best place in Xela to try out typical Xela food. The *pollo en mole* (chicken in a chocolate sauce) should be first on your list. Adventurous eaters might enjoy *pollo jocón* (chicken with fresh coriander) or *pache*, a tamale prepared with mashed potato filling. Vegetarian plates are available upon request. Q20-50. No credit cards.

Café Baviera, *5a Calle 13-14, Zona 1,* ☎ *502/7-761-1855.* A European-style café with good coffee roasted on the premises and served with terrific pastries and desserts. There is also a light lunch menu of sandwiches and other snacks. Q10-35. No credit cards.

La Luna, *corner of 8 Avenida at 4 Calle,* ☎ *502/7-761-2242.* This sinful little café is also a chocolate museum. Trace 100 years of chocolate history and then pick out some to eat from their huge selection. You will get the best cup of hot chocolate here, which you can enjoy with glorious desserts. The coffee is also heavenly. A great place to hang out. Q15-50. No credit cards.

Department of Huehuetenango

Huehuetenango is Guatemala's most northern department, sharing an eastern border with Mexico, southern borders with San Marcos, Quetzaltenango and Totonicapán, and a western border with Quiché. This area is dominated by the rugged **Cuchumatánes Mountains** and is a place of jagged peaks and deep valleys. Villages are located on a limestone plateau in the west and there's dense rainforest to the north. The traditional ways have been preserved and there are seven Mayan dialects spoken: Mam, Teko, Awakateko, Akateko, Chuj, Popta and Q'anjob'al. Spanish is a second language and English isn't heard.

The capital city of **Huehuetenango** is easily accessible and makes a good base for exploring the more remote regions such as Todos Santos. The most significant ruins in the area are found at **Zaculeu**.

History

Fossils and hunting tools have been found in the area, indicating that it was first settled during the Paleo-Indian period. Over 140 archeological sites have been located in the Cuchumatánes Mountains, attesting to over 1,000 years of occupation by the Maya. The **Olmec** were the first to settle in around 1500 BC. The sites of Santo, Chaculá and Libertad are similar to those Olmec sites found in Mexico. During the Early Classic period (AD 200-400) the **Mam Maya** began settling the area and developing the agricultural centers of Cambote, Pucal and Cucal. The largest site uncovered so far is **Zaculeu**, near the capital city Huehuetenango. During the Classic period (AD 600-900), the **Toltec** began invading the area, followed by the **Nahuatl** in the Post Classic period (AD 900-1500).

By the time **Spanish Conquistadors** made their way north in 1524, Zaculeu was an important trade center with many silver mines. The Spanish immediately took control of the silver mines, ran them empty, and quickly lost interest. They left the area in the control of Franciscans, who had little success in converting the people to Christianity and eventually withdrew down to Quetzaltenango. From 1820 until 1840, Huehuetenango was part of the Los Altos territory and remained independent of Guatemala City. However, when the independence movement was crushed, the area came under the control of the Guatemalan government who encouraged settlers to set up sugar and coffee plantations. The area was officially recognized as a department in 1877.

As the area opened up, many *Ladinos* came to work on the farms and settled throughout the region, making it one of the more heavily populated areas in Los Altos. Today, coffee, sugar, corn, beans, asparagus and broccoli grow alongside sheep that graze in ranches. Some of the mines are still productive and light manufacturing has also become an important part of the economy. The roads remain primitive, despite all the progress.

Getting Here & Getting Around

The capital, Huehuetenango – also referred to as Hue-Hue – is the first city most people stop in when coming from Mexico. There are regular buses to the Mexican border town of La Mesilla/Ciudad Cuauhtemoc, as well as direct bus service from Quetzaltenango and Guatemala City. To visit any of the local villages around here you will have to take one of the chicken buses that leave from Hue-Hue.

Huehuetenango

Huehuetenango is a dusty town whose streets are usually filled with huge trucks. It has a mixed population of *Ladino* and Maya. The town has two distinct personalities. The center is pretty sedate, with most commerce being done at one of the 40 banks lining the streets. A few blocks away is the huge Indian market, where the streets are crowded with people dealing and trading. The main bus terminal is located here.

There is very little to see in Hue-Hue, but it makes a good base for exploring the region and has a number of decent hotels and restaurants. The main attractions are the giant **relief map** built in 1880 in the Central Plaza and the large **neoclassical church** with Doric pillars and Grecian urns on its façade. Off the central plaza is the local **tourist office**, PROCUCH, ☎ 502/771-8139, that can help you to organize trips to the more remote areas.

◆ Spanish Education

Several schools in Hue-Hue teach both Spanish and Mam. They offer the usual 20 hours a week of one-on-one instruction combined with social and cultural activities. The cost is US $120-140 per person and includes accommodations with a local family. The schools will also help you make arrangements for visiting other parts of Huehuetenango.

> **Academia de Español Fundacións 23**, 6a Avenida 6-126, Zona 1, ☎ 502/7-964-1478.

> **Spanish Academy "Xinabajul,"** 6a Avenida 0-69, Zona 1, ☎/fax 502/7-764-1518.

LOS ALTOS

◆ Sightseeing

Chiantla

The small village of Chiantla is four miles (seven km) north of Hue-Hue. Its church, **Virgén del Rosario**, houses a silver statue of the Virgin given by a rich Spaniard who owned a local silver mine. The statue is believed to have miraculous powers to heal the sick and grant wishes, and people from all over Guatemala travel to the shrine to ask help from the great *madre* (mother). The church itself was built by Dominican friars and has interior murals, painted in 1950 by Carlos Rigalt, showing Indians toiling in the mines and seeing God. The largest pilgrimage to the church is on the feast day for the Virgin of the Rosary, February 2. See *Holidays & Festivals*, page 22.

Another 2½ miles (four km) from town is **El Mirador**, where the plateau of the Cuchumatánes begins to climb to more than 9,842 feet (3,000 meters) above sea level. The view of the Huehuetenango Valley and surrounding mountains is extremely beautiful. A monument here was built to resemble a Maya temple and a plaque is inscribed with the famous poem, *A Los Cuchumatánes*. The poem was written by the Guatemalan poet Juan Diéguez Olaverri after he was exiled in Chiapas for his participation in the failed Los Altos revolution.

▶▶ *GETTING HERE: Buses leave Hue-Hue from 1 Avenida and 1 Calle every 20 minutes. From Chiantla you can walk the remaining distance to El Mirador or grab any bus heading north to Todos Santos.*

◆ Adventures on Horseback

Unicornio Azul (Blue Unicorn), Hacienda Casco Chancol, Chiantla Chancol, ☎ 502/7-205-9328, fax 502/7-205-9089. Unicornio Azul is a horse ranch set at the foot of the Cuchumatánes Mountains. It was started in 1998 by a Guatemala-French couple, Fernando Mejia and Pauline Decamps, who offer horseback rides into the mountains that last anywhere from one to nine days. The ranch also serves as an equestrian training center and, on longer journeys, each rider takes over the care and feeding of their equine friend. From November to May, trips head to Todos Santos, Laguna Magdalena and the surrounding areas; in March and April the rides go to the Ixil Triangle; and from June to August they are limited to the Huehuetenango plateau. You can also build your own itinerary. Rates are US $13 per hour, US $73 per day (five to six hours, including lunch, accommodation and guides).

You can opt to stay over at the ranch's hacienda-style hotel, which has an adobe roof and inner courtyard. Rooms have private baths, comfortable beds and spectacular views of the mountains. A full breakfast is included. *5 rooms. $.*

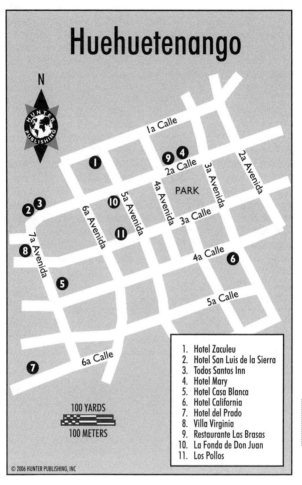

Huehuetenango

N

1a Calle

9 4

2a Calle

3a Avenida

2a Avenida

1

5a Avenida

4a Avenida

PARK

2 3

6a Avenida

10

3a Calle

8

7a Avenida

11

4a Calle

6

5

4a Calle

5a Calle

7

6a Calle

100 YARDS

100 METERS

1. Hotel Zaculeu
2. Hotel San Luis de la Sierra
3. Todos Santos Inn
4. Hotel Mary
5. Hotel Casa Blanca
6. Hotel California
7. Hotel del Prado
8. Villa Virginia
9. Restaurante Las Brasas
10. La Fonda de Don Juan
11. Los Pollos

© 2006 HUNTER PUBLISHING, INC

LOS ALTOS

◆ Maya Ruins

Zaculeu Ruins

These ruins are eight miles (five km) west of town. Zaculeu means "white earth" in Quiché Mayan and refers to the white limestone plaster used by the Mam on all their buildings. The Mam first settled here during the Classic period from AD 300-900. They chose the site for its natural barriers – two ravines and a river. This naturally fortified area quickly became the

Mam's capital and the people developed links to Kaminal Juyu and El Tajin. Some of Zaculeu's architecture is similar to that of those two cities and points to a Toltec influence. Zaculeu soon controlled the trade routes that extended as far north as Todos Santos and along the Selegua and Cuilco valleys. Around 1250, the Mam began enhancing the ravines around the city.

HISTORY

According to the Popul Vuh book of the Quiché, Zaculeu was brought under their rule between 1400 and 1475. When Quicab, king of the Quiché, died in 1475, the Mam rose up in rebellion and demanded their freedom. But it didn't last long. The Spanish showed up in 1525, led by Gonzalo de Alvarado, Pedro's little brother, who brought his Quiché and Cakchiquel as allies. Alvarado was looking for revenge after being told that the plot to kill him at Utalan was the work of the Mam leader Caibal Balam. Five thousand Mam warriors met 8,000 Spanish just outside the village of Malacatancito. Seeing that he was outnumbered, Caibal Balam quickly withdrew to Zaculeu and held out against the Spanish for six weeks. But the natural fortification meant they were boxed in and the Mam started to starve. Caibal tried to surrender, but Gonzalo allowed the Mam to live only if they converted to Christianity. Caibal agreed, and the captives were divided into religious congregations that eventually evolved into the various municipalities throughout the department. The city fell into disuse and became overgrown by jungle. During his epic journey of 1840, John Stephens rediscovered the ruins and wrote about them in his book, *Incidents of Travel in Central America, Chiapas and Yucatán*. Sylvanus Morley and Edwin Shook mapped the area in the early 1930s.

EXPLORING THE RUINS

The Zaculeu ruins remained untouched until 1946, when the notorious United Fruit Company decided to restore them. In typical UFC style, the ruins were reconstructed with a heavy hand and, consequently, have become the poster child for bad archeological "restorations." Several large temples, plazas and the ball court have all been slathered with thick white plaster. No roof combs, carvings, stucco or moldings were preserved. In a few places the original stone work and traces of paint can be seen. The difference is obvious. The most interesting finds were the burial sites, with bodies crammed into great urns or laid out in vaults. Alongside the bodies were pyrite plaques, carved jade, jewelry and ceramics. These items are displayed at a small on-site museum.

Close by, in Chivacabé Village, is the **Cave of the Mammoth** (*Cueva el Mamut*). Inside this cave bones of a giant mastodon were found alongside fossils dating back to the Paleo-Indian period (13000-7900 BC).

▶▶ *GETTING HERE: The ruins are only 2½ miles (four km) north of Hue-Hue and are easily accessed by bus. Ruta 3 buses leave downtown Hue-Hue from 7a Avenida, between Calles 3 and 4. The ruins are open daily from 8 am to 5 pm. Admission is free.*

◆ Where to Stay

Hotel Casa Blanca, *7 Avenida 3-41*, ☎ / *fax 502/7-769-0777, 5 rooms, $$*. This is the nicest hotel in town and is an unexpected surprise in an otherwise noisy and dusty downtown. The rooms are huge and have great views of the mountains, particularly those on the third floor. All rooms have private baths (with plenty of hot water), cozy beds and cable TV.

❖ HOTEL PRICING
Prices are per person.
$ . . . . Under $25
$$ . . . . $26 to $50
$$$ . . . . $51 to $85
$$$$ . . . . $86 to $125
$$$$$ . . . . over $125

There are two excellent restaurants and a fireplace, and the central courtyard has a lovely garden. Service is excellent.

Hotel Zaculeu, *5 Avenida 1-14*, ☎ *502/7-764-1086, fax 502/7-764-1575, 38 rooms, $$*. This 1885 hotel is a landmark in the city and has the most character of all the hotels. It features colonial architecture and layout, with the rooms built around a courtyard and lovely garden filled with very old trees. Ask for a room in the older section, as the newer rooms in the back are more expensive and lack charm. All rooms have double beds, private baths with hot water and cable TV. There is an excellent laundry service and a dining room.

Hotel California, *3a Avenida 4-25, Zona 5*, ☎ *502/7-769-0500, fax 502/7-764-1941, 40 rooms, $$*. This modern hotel looks more like an office building than a hotel, but inside it is quite pleasing. The lobby is set up like a living room and the rooms have lovely blond-wood furniture, double beds and brightly colored walls. All have private baths with plenty of hot water, cable TV and small terraces that overlook the central plaza. A dining room serves decent daily specials.

Hotel Villa Virginia, *3a Calle La Terminal, Zona 5*, ☎ *502/7-764-2744, 11 rooms, $*. This is one of the nicest hotels in Hue-Hue. It's set in a renovated colonial house and has a lovely garden around which the accommodations are arranged. Rooms have wooden furniture, double beds, throw rugs, private baths and a working fireplace.

Hotel Mary, *2 Calle 3-52, Zona 1*, ☎ *502/7-764-1618, 35 rooms, $*. This is a good budget hotel that's both clean and comfortable. The décor includes some nice homey touches, such as the throw rugs and nice bedspreads, but it's on the plain side. Rooms have private baths with limited hot water, cable TV and decent furniture. If you don't like the first room you are shown, ask to see a better one.

◆ Where to Eat

Café Jardin, *4 Calle and 6 Avenida, Zona 1*, ☎ *502/7-769-0769*. This bright and cheery restaurant serves good food. It's popular with locals and gets full very quickly. Café Jardin opens early for breakfast, the best meal of the day – try the pancakes and milkshakes. Lunch and dinner are beef and chicken dishes. Q10-40. No credit cards.

Las Brasas, *2 Calle 1-55, Zona 1,* ☎ *502/7-764-2339.* HueHue's best restaurant is this unassuming steakhouse with red checkered tablecloths and wooden interior. The house specialty is grilled steak, but other choices include Chinese and vegetarian dishes. A full meal with ample servings is Q70. No credit cards.

Hotel Casa Blanca, *7 Avenida 3-41,* ☎ *fax 502/7-769-0775.* The two restaurants in this lovely hotel serve excellent breakfasts with fresh juice, eggs, pancakes and coffee. The lunch menu includes soup, sandwiches and burgers – all very good. For dinner, try the grilled steak or chicken. The service is excellent. Q21-70.

Las Fonda de Don Juan, *2a Calle, 5-35, no phone.* This little place, just off the central plaza, serves excellent pizza and pasta. It's clean and pleasant. Q21-45. No credit cards.

Department of San Marcos

San Marcos is a remote rural area known for its sugar, maize, beans, wheat, barley, rice, bananas, cane, cacao and cattle ranches. Furniture, cotton and wool are also produced in this area. With the notable exception of Tajumulco Volcano, there are few tourist attractions in this department and, consequently, no tourist services. If you want to visit the volcano, it's best to book a trip with a tour company such as **Quetzaltrekkers**, Casa Argentina, diagonal 12, 8-37, Zona 1, ☎ 502/761-5865, www.quetzaltrekkers.org.

Tecún Umán

If you are coming from or going to any of the southern states in Mexico (such as Oaxaca or southern Chiapas), you will probably pass through the border town of Tecún Umán. Like most border towns, it's not particularly pleasant and parts of the city are unsafe. The smartest plan is to be at the border early and catch the first bus out of town. Several bus companies offer direct rides from Mexico to Guatemala City.

◆ Transportation Services

Shuttles from Antigua to Mexico

Monarca Travel, Calzada Santa Lucia Norte #17, ☎/fax 502/832-1939, monarcas@conexion.com.gt. This company also offers shuttle service from San Cristobal de las Casas, Chiapas, Mexico to Antigua Guatemala. Tickets start at $40 per person and include help with border crossings.

Sin Fronteras, 5a Avenida Norte#15A, ☎ 502/7-832-1017, fax 502/7-832-8453, www.sinfront.com, offers a special bus pass to and from Mexico for up to 14 days starting at $94.

Public Buses from Guatemala City to the Mexican Border

Public buses leave regularly from the Mexican border in Tecun Umán, San Marcos, to Guatemala. The bus companies Galgos, Fortalezas, Rapidos del Sur, Rutas Lima, Transportes Marquensita all have buses leaving on the hour.

Buses from Chiapas, Mexico to La Mesilla, Huehuetenango

UNO, ☎ 52/51-55-533-2424 or toll free throughout Mexico 80/702-8000, www.uno.com.mx.

Colon Cristobal, toll free in Mexico ☎ 800/849-6136, www.cristobalcolon.com.mx.

ADO, ☎ 51-55-533-2424 or toll free in Mexico, 01 800 702 8000, www.ado.com.mx.

Prices will vary according to the bus line, but tickets usually start at around $30 to get to the border. Your seat is guaranteed when you buy a ticket and reservations can be made online.

Watch out at the border for the sleazy border help. If you get stuck for whatever reason, get to **Hotel Don José**, Calle Real del Comercio, ☎ 502/7-776-8164. This semi-decent hotel has 18 rooms and is, at least, safe. Don't go out wandering at night in this city.

LOS ALTOS

Northern Highlands

The Northern Highlands, also known as **Los Altiplanos**, consist of three departments: **Quiché**, **Alta Verapaz** and **Baja Verapaz**. This is an area of immense beauty and isolation inhabited by traditional Cakchiquel, Achi' Q'eqchí and Pokomam Maya.

Department of Quiché

The department of Quiché shares a northern border with Mexico, an eastern border with Alta and Baja Verapaces, a southern border with Chimaltenango and a western border with Totonicapán and Huehuetenango. The most visited place in this department is the village of **Chichicastenango**, but there are also some incredible areas to explore farther north where **Sierra de Chuacús** mountain range joins the Cuchumatánes mountains and gives way to the virgin rainforests of the **Ixcán**.

History

This department is named after the greatest of the Maya tribes, the **Quiché**. From their capital city of **Utatlán**, the Quiché were a powerful force that controlled most of the highlands and ruled over many other tribes. At first, the Quiché were able to stop the advance of the Conquistadors, but were defeated when **Avlarado** made alliances with the other tribes that had been under their rule. The remoteness of the area soon proved to be too much for the Spanish, who left shortly after the conquest realizing there was little for them to plunder. Quiché was left on its own until the 1800s, when large-scale commercial farms began visiting the area to recruit workers. Quiché became a source of cheap labor and the Quiché Maya were virtual slaves working in harsh conditions for very little money. This went on for 200 years until the population was so fed up they eagerly supported the rebels in the civil war. The region suffered for this support.

Today, Quiché is primarily rural, producing corn, beans, wheat, potatoes and, on a lesser scale, coffee, sugar, rice and tobacco. It is famous for its cotton and wool textiles, pottery, weaving and fireworks.

Chichicastenango

Chichicastenango is a Nahuatl word meaning, "place of the nettles." Today, a more apt description would be "place of the bargains." Chichi (as locals call it) has one of the most famous markets in the world. It attracts all the Indian weavers from across the highlands and from other parts to sell their wares in the market. Its close proximity to Guatemala City, Antigua and Panajachel make it a favorite day-trip for tourists. After Tikal and Antigua, Chichicastenango is the most visited place in Guatemala.

But Chichi is more than just a market. It is also the cultural and religious center for the local highland Maya, with a parallel Indian and *Ladino* government. Important religious shrines here are still used by the Maya in their ceremonies.

▸▸ *GETTING HERE: Dozens of shuttles serve Chichi from Guatemala City, Antigua and Panajachel. There are also five major bus companies with regularly scheduled service, but the routes are not as direct. Riding the chicken bus is a harrowing experience because of the sheer volume of people and the hairpin curves on this mountainous road often taken at breakneck speeds. Shuttles are comfortable and cost just a little more (the average ticket runs US $9-18).*

Most people come just for the day, arriving early in the morning and leaving by late afternoon. This may be too rushed if you want to explore the area farther. Chichi has a number of good hotels and restaurants.

◆ History

The **Cakchiquel Maya** first settled the area and established a market in AD 1200. But they left in 1470 after repeated skirmishes with the Quiché, settling nearby in their capital of **Iximché**, where they mounted campaign after campaign against the Quiché. The Quiché finally abandoned the area in favor of their capital K'umarcaaj, later known as Utatlán. In 1524, the **Spanish** built up Chichi as a refuge city for the survivors of Utatlán after it was burned down by Alvarado. The Conquistadors left shortly afterwards. The priests left in charge were very tolerant toward the Quiché, allowing them to keep their religion and gods and combining them with Catholicism. Some of the rituals are still used today. During the 1800s the church also protected many of the residents from inscription into the slave labor camps. Unfortunately, the protection didn't last long enough and the area suffered during the civil war.

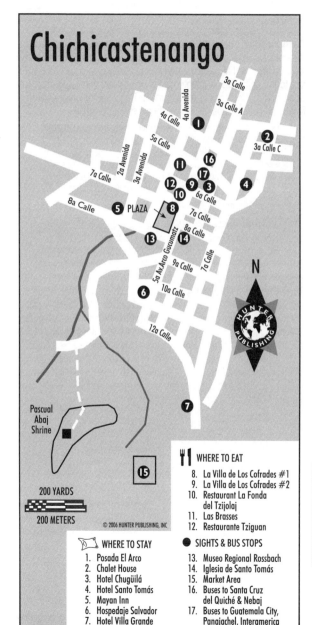

Chichicastenango

Streets labeled on map: 3a Calle, 3a Calle A, 4a Avenida, 4a Calle, 5a Calle, 3a Calle C, 2a Avenida, 3a Avenida, 7a Calle, 8a Calle, 6a Calle, 7a Calle, 8a Calle, 5a Av. Arco Gucumatz, 9a Calle, 10a Calle, 12a Calle, 7a Calle

PLAZA

N

HUNTER PUBLISHING

Pascual Abaj Shrine

200 YARDS
200 METERS

© 2006 HUNTER PUBLISHING, INC.

WHERE TO STAY

1. Posada El Arco
2. Chalet House
3. Hotel Chugüilá
4. Hotel Santo Tomás
5. Mayan Inn
6. Hospedaje Salvador
7. Hotel Villa Grande

WHERE TO EAT

8. La Villa de Los Cofrades #1
9. La Villa de Los Cofrades #2
10. Restaurant La Fonda del Tzijolaj
11. Las Brasses
12. Restaurante Tziguan

SIGHTS & BUS STOPS

13. Museo Regional Rossbach
14. Iglesia de Santo Tomás
15. Market Area
16. Buses to Santa Cruz del Quiché & Nebaj
17. Buses to Guatemala City, Panajachel, Interamerica

◆ Sightseeing

The big **market** is held on Sunday, and there's a smaller one on Thursday. Streets are lined with stalls and packed with people. The selection is endless. Be prepared to wade through a lot of trashy tourist stuff before getting to the gold. Tourist-oriented stalls usually sell masks, embroidered cloth, clothing, tablecloths and tapestries. Be aware that all prices are inflated and you must barter in order to get even a fair deal.

> **❖ INSIDER TIP: BARGAINING SAVVY**
>
> Don't touch anything until you are ready to haggle. Touching denotes you are interested in buying and will start the bartering process. The best time to get bargains is in the morning before 10 am (when the tour buses arrive) and after 4 pm (when the buses have left).

AUTHOR WARNING: *Watch your belongings in the market. Pickpockets love this place and are very good at what they do. Bring the money you plan to spend and leave the rest, along with your documents, in a safe place.*

Iglesias de Santo Tomás. This lovely whitewashed church on the central plaza was built in 1540 on the site of a Maya altar. It has been rebuilt and restored several times, and much of the original structure remains. Maya Indians began worshipping here in earnest from 1701 to 1703, when Friar Francisco Ximenez began using their bible, the Popul Vuh, as the church text. This book is the most famous piece of Maya literature (see page 57) and outlines the cosmology and myths of the Quiché. It is one of the only remaining written works; most were burned by zealous monks. Ximenez made a copy of the Popul Vuh. The copy now resides in the Newberry Library of Chicago and the original has been lost.

Santo Tomás is still a place of worship for the Quiché, so be extremely respectful when visiting. Put away your camera and don't walk up the steps of the church. They are considered sacred ground and are usually being blessed by one of the elders, since everyone must ask permission to enter. Usually permission is sought by burning copal incense. Gringos must use the side door to enter.

Inside, the faithful worship on their knees in front of candles offered to their ancestors and various saints. Each saint has their place in the church, and you will see the Maya gods alongside Catholic saints. Different sections of the church are devoted to specific blessings. There is one area for children, another for marriage, etc.

AUTHOR TIP: *Don't try to sneak any photos or you will be tossed out on your ear. Stay quiet. This is the only church in Chichi that permits foreigners.*

Rossbach Museum Regional Museum. This is just outside of town. Ildefonso Rossbach was a Franciscan priest who served in Chichi from

1894 until 1944. This museum houses his collection of pre-Colombian jade and copper jewelry, along with obsidian spearheads and arrowheads found in the area. The collection also includes clay figurines, ancient pots and ceramic pieces dating as far back as 1200 BC: Rossbach received many of these articles as gifts from the local Quiché families he helped over the years. Open 8 am to noon and 2 to 5 pm daily, except Tuesdays.

Shrine of Pascual Abaj. The Pascual Abaj, or Sacrifice Stone, is a shrine to the Maya earth god and it draws many Maya, who come to worship and give offerings. Should you be at the shrine during one of their rituals, keep a respectful distance and put away your camera. The shrine is actually several small altars surrounding a pre-Columbian sculpture of a man's face. It is similar to the Olmec heads in Mexico, only much smaller. Time and weather have worn down the features. In 1957, newly baptized Catholics smashed the statue, but it was rebuilt by locals using the old pieces reinforced with cement and steel. In 1999, a visiting museum tried to move the statue in order to examine it more closely. They managed to snap off the nose and have not yet repaired the damage. Still, the Quiché continue to gather here and worship with offerings of flowers, incense and alcohol.

> ❖ **INSIDER TIP: STEPPING SAFELY**
>
> Don't visit this shrine on your own. It's in a deserted location where numerous tourists have been robbed. Even the locals will warn you not to go. The safest way to visit is in a group with a hired guide. You won't have any trouble finding someone to take you; there is an enclave of village lads all eager to show you the way. You should tip them Q5 for their efforts.

◆ Where to Stay

The town tends to fill up in anticipation of the market, so either have a reservation or come early to get a room on Wednesdays and Saturdays. The rest of the week you will have no problem getting a room.

> ❖ **INSIDER TIP: HOTEL RUSE**
>
> Ignore the local children who tell you that your hotel of choice is closed. It's a ruse to get you to a hotel that pays them a kickback fee for bringing you in.

Mayan Inn, *3 Avenida at 8 Calle*, ☎ *502/7-756-1176, fax 502/7-756-1212, 30 rooms, $$$$.* Built in 1932 by the Clark family of Clark Tours, this hotel oozes class and style. The original building is genuine adobe complete with the original woodwork. The other buildings are restored colonial houses.

❖ **HOTEL PRICING**

Prices are per person.

$	Under $25
$$	$26 to $50
$$$	$51 to $85
$$$$	$86 to $125
$$$$$	over $125

Rooms have fireplaces, antique furniture (including carved headboards and side tables), private baths and colorful decorative art as accents. All look out onto the beautifully maintained flower gardens or the hills beyond. Meals are in a majestic dining room with a fireplace; the menu changes daily. The service here is first-class.

Hotel Santo Tomás, *7 Avenida 5-32, ☎ 502/7-756-1316, fax 502/7-756-1306, 43 rooms, $$$*. Combining colonial architecture with modern conveniences, this hotel is fquite side
popular with tourists. Outdoor passageways lead from the bedrooms to a beautiful courtyard filled with flowers and fountains. Rooms are large and decorated with local textiles and wooden furniture. Back rooms have views of the country, while the front rooms look out onto town. There's a pool, gym, hot tub, sauna and restaurant.

Hotel Villa Grande, *Canton Pachoj Alto, Km 144 on road to Antigua, ☎ 502/7-756-1053, fax 502/7-756-1140, 67 rooms, $$$*. It's large, it's luxurious and it's bland. What a shame the buildings are so ugly because the view is incredible. Guest rooms are painted peach and beds have embroidered spreads made locally. The more spacious rooms have fireplaces. There is a restaurant, pool, hot tub and bar. The hotel can arrange a shuttle to town.

Hotel Chugüila, *5 Avenida 5-24 ☎ 502/7-756-1134, fax 756-1279, 31 rooms, $$*. This is a pleasant hotel with good rates. Rooms are furnished with a wooden table and chairs and are centered around a cobblestone courtyard that also acts as the parking lot. The more expensive rooms have fireplaces. The dining room is the hotel's best feature; you can look out at the courtyard or watch all the action on the main street. The restaurant serves hamburgers, pasta, pizza and sandwiches.

Hotel Chalet, *3 Calle C 7-44, ☎ 502/7-756-1793, 7 rooms, $$*. A friendly couple runs this cozy little hotel on a quiet side street. It has cheery yellow walls decorated with masks and Guatemalan handicrafts. The rooms are tidy and have nice bathrooms. Breakfasts are quite pleasant, with a good menu, amiable service and a great atmosphere.

Hospedaje Salvador, *10 Calle at 5 Avenida, 502/7-756-1329, 46 rooms, $*. This hodgepodge of a hotel has lots of character. Rooms are tucked away in nooks and crannies that you find hidden along passages and staircases. These walkways all seem to lead to the main courtyard, which displays a giant statue of the Virgin Mary alongside a Maya god. Potted plants are the main décor. Rooms are basic and clean, but the beds are soft. No credit cards.

Posada El Arco, *4 Calle 4-36, ☎ 502/7-756-1255, 7 rooms, $*. The best of the budget hotels in Chichi, Posada El Arco has 1950s décor that creates a homey ambience. Spacious rooms have wood-frame beds, fireplaces and bathrooms with lots of hot water. There is a laundry service. This place fills up fast, so arrive early. No credit cards.

◆ Where to Eat

On market days a number of excellent *comedores* set up in the market area. The rest of the week, try the *comedores* by the post office. The two posh hotels, **Maya Inn** and **Hotel Santo Thomàs** (above), have restaurants that have great décor but only so-so food. They are usually packed with tour groups.

La Villa de los Cofrades #1 y #2. This is actually two sister restaurants. The smaller café is located on the central plaza near Centro Commercial. Terrific breakfasts with great coffee and delicious waffles are served on a small patio where you can watch all the action. The other restaurant, located at the corner of 6a Calle and 5a Avenida, is on the second floor and is more tranquil. The lunch and dinner menus are the same at both places and consist of fish, chicken, and beef. A few vegetarian dishes are offered. The service is slow here. Q16-48. No credit cards.

La Fonda el Tzijolaj, *Centro Commercial, north side*, ☎ *502/7-756-1013*. Located on the second floor, this restaurant overlooks the market and is a great place to watch the whole thing unfold. It serves traditional Guatemalan meals along with pizza and pasta (which is really excellent). Prices are low and the meals come with soup, salad and a drink. Q24-48. No credit cards.

Las Brasses, *6 Calle 4-52, above Hotel Girón*, ☎ *502/7-756-2226*. This restaurant is nicely decorated with pine boughs and textiles. Its specialty is steak, which it does well, but there are also terrific egg dishes and vegetarian meals. Try the local *longaniza* (a spicy sausage) – it's very good here. There is a full bar and many people come only for a drink. Q32-64.

Restaurante Tziguan Tinamit, *6 Calle and 5a Avenida*. Tziguan Tinamit is the Quiché name for Chichicastenango. Since this eatery is located right in the middle of the market, it's popular with tour groups. The fare is uninspiring – pizza, pastas, hamburgers, French fries and the occasional decent soup. The waitstaff, however, is charming and the beer prices low. Q32-56.

Departments of Las Verapaces

These two sister departments, **Alta Verapaz** and **Baja Verapaz**, share a similar history and together make up the final section of Los Altiplanos. Physically, they are quite different. The more southerly Baja Verapaz sits in the flat-bottomed Salamá Valley with rivers and lush forests. It is sparsely populated with **Achi' Maya**. Alta Verapaz is home to the **Q'ekchí** (or K'ekchí) and, to a lesser extent, the **Poqomchi' Maya**. All three tribes are often referred to as the **Rabinal Maya**. Since Alta Verapaz is on higher grounds, a continuous light rain, known as *chipi-chipi*, falls here year-round. This area is becoming very popular with eco-tourists.

> **AUTHOR NOTE:** *Two of Guatemala's national symbols are found in Alta Verapaz: the* **monja blanca orchid** *and the resplendent* **quetzal bird**.

Las Verapaces Region

© 2006 HUNTER PUBLISHING, INC

History

The fierce **Q'ekchí** once ruled this part of the highlands. They were considered the most bloodthirsty of all the Maya and were feared by many. They were the only tribe that the Conquistadors were unable to tame. **Alvarado** arrived here in 1520; by 1530 he had withdrawn his men and named the area **Tezulutlan-Tierra de Guerra** (Land of War.)

The great scholar and humanist **Fray Bartolomé de las Casas** asked the king to let him try and convert the Indians to Christianity. Since de las Casas had successfully brought about a peace accord with the Indians of Chiapas, Mexico, the Spanish government agreed to his proposal and decreed that no Spanish soldiers were allowed into the area. De las Casas arrived with some Indian musicians from Chiapas and a handful of Dominican friars. The brothers set about learning the Q'ekchí language and translated several verses of the bible, setting them to song. They taught these songs to the traders and gave them a variety of goods to sell.

The Q'ekchí chieftain, **Juan Matalbatz**, heard the songs and became curious about this Conquistador who wore robes instead of armor and was not interested in gold. The traders arranged for the two men to meet. Shortly afterwards, Matalbatz converted to Christianity. In 1548, the Q'ekchí became Spanish citizens and King Carlos V renamed the area **Las Verapaces** (True Peace). As Spanish citizens, the Q'ekchí were allowed to keep their language and customs.

Sadly, peace did not last. De las Casas died in 1576 and the Spanish colonial government took control. The soldiers sent into the area were convinced there was hidden gold and ended up looting the villages and killing many of the locals. When nothing was found, the soldiers left, but the damage was done. Las Verapaces became a backwater community and it continued to be overlooked even after Guatemala became independent 1821.

In 1870, **President Barrios** invited German immigrants to develop the region. They were given huge tracts of land on which they built coffee plantations. The Germans quickly took control, but never really assimilated. They kept their German passports, spoke their own language and had their own schools. In the 1930s, most of the Guatemalan Germans actively supported Hitler and when the United States declared war on Germany in 1941, Guatemala was pressured into "containing the enemy presence." The government responded by deporting all Germans and confiscating their property. But the coffee plantations remained and Las Verapaces remains one of the largest producers of coffee. In the last few years, cardamom has also become an important export. Germans first planted this spice as a hobby, but it has become the country's second-largest export and La Verapaces is now the largest producer of cardamom in the world.

Getting Here & Getting Around

Only one main road leads through Las Verapaces, so it's hard to get lost. At the junction of El Rancho, Carretera Atlántico (CA-9) branches off north to CA-14. This road climbs through the foothills of the Sierra de las Miñas before heading down into the Salamá Valley to Baja Verapaz and then ascending to Alta Verapaz.

Since Cobán is the main tourist destination, all tourist shuttles go there from Antigua, Guatemala City, Río Dulce and Flores. Fares vary. Shuttles are the most comfortable and quickest way to travel. From Cobán, you can take local chicken buses to visit the villages.

Public buses service Las Verapaces region. Depending on the bus company, you may have to change at El Rancho junction on CA-9.

Cobán

A lta Verapaz is the largest of the two departments. Its capital city is Cobán, located at the end of the highway. There are a number of remote and hard-to-access villages in the departments northern reaches. The area is part of a large watershed that originates in Mexico and is filled with rivers and lakes. The mighty **Río Cahabon** and **Río Polochíc** flow through this department, are fed by the Chioxy-Usumacinta river system that start in the Gulf of Mexico. The Cahabon and Polochíc empty into **Lake Izabal** and **Río Dulce**, which flows out to the Caribbean Sea.

Cobán rests 5,000 feet (4,316 meters) above sea level and has a surprisingly large population – 70,000. It is the principal city in the region and one of the largest in the country.

◆ History

Cobán was founded in 1543 by **Fray Bartolomé de las Casas** when he came to convert the Q'ekchí to god-fearing Christians. Shortly afterward, King Carlos V declared Cobán an Imperial City. This didn't amount to much since Cobán remained isolated for hundreds of years, allowing the Rabinal Maya to preserve their language and culture.

The city grew extensively during the 1870s when German immigrants came. They found the area with its mild temperatures and annual rainfall of 70 inches had the perfect conditions for growing coffee and they began building huge *fincas*. Other Germans followed, opening up silver mines, restaurants and hotels. Eventually, they controlled most of Cobán and it became known as the German Capital of Central America. In order to get their coffee to market they built a railway that extended down from Cobán to Lake Izabal.

When the Germans were deported in 1941, Cobán continued growing and exporting coffee. It remains the largest producer of Guatemala's gourmet coffees, and is also becoming a major tourist destination, serving as the jumping-off point for explorations into the incredible natural wonders in the area.

◆ Getting Here & Getting Around

Buses and shuttles offer direct service to Cobán. The city's hotels, restaurants and shops are located within walking distance of the main square so you won't need transportation in town. If you do want to get to other sites outside of the downtown core, taxis are cheap and plentiful. The average ride costs Q10.

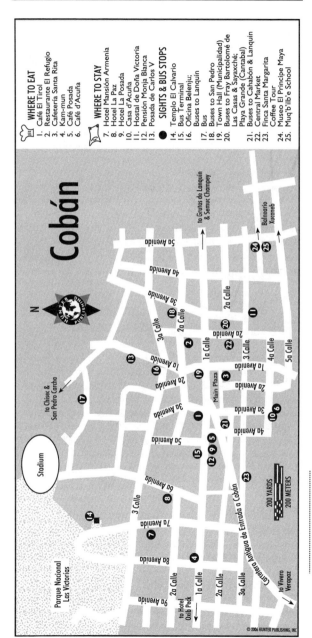

Cobán

WHERE TO EAT
1. Café El Tirol
2. Restaurante El Refugio
3. Cafetería Santa Rita
4. Kam-mun
5. Café Posada
6. Café d'Acuña

WHERE TO STAY
7. Hotel Mansión Armenia
8. Hotel La Paz
9. Hotel La Posada
10. Casa d'Acuña
11. Hostal de Doña Victoria
12. Pensión Monja Blanca
13. Posada de Carlos V

SIGHTS & BUS STOPS
14. Templo El Calvario
15. Bus Terminal
16. Oficina Belenju; Buses to Lanquín
17. Bus
18. Buses to San Pedro
19. Town Hall (Municipalidad)
20. Buses to Fray Bartolomé de Las Casas & Sayaxché; Playa Grande (Cantabal)
21. Buses to Cahabón & Lanquín
22. Central Market
23. Finca Santa Margarita Coffee Tour
24. Museo El Príncipe Maya
25. Muq'b'lib'e School

to Grutas de Lanquín & Semuc Champey

Parque Nacional Las Victorias

Stadium

to Chisec & San Pedro Carchá

Main Plaza

Balneario Xucaneb

to Hotel Onib Peck

to Vivero Verapaz

Carretera Antigua de Entrada a Cobán

200 YARDS
200 METERS

© 2006 HUNTER PUBLISHING, INC

NORTHERN HIGHLANDS

Getting to some of the outlying attractions can be difficult. The roads outside of the city are terrible and, although buses are frequent, they often don't leave until they are full. You have to be patient and allow for extra traveling time. Some travel agencies offer shuttle service to Cobán at reasonable rates. However, most official tours are terribly overpriced.

AUTHOR TIP: *See page 70 for a list of companies offering shuttle services.*

There are two "main" bus terminals. The newer terminal services buses heading to northern cities. It is located near Parque Nacional Las Victorias on Calle 3a. The older bus terminal serves buses coming from the south. It's located down the hill behind City Hall on 2a Avenida between 1a Calle and 3a Calle.

Local buses leave from various corners around the city and there is no way to figure out the routes. The best strategy is to ask at your hotel and be pointed to the appropriate street corner. You can also ask the taxi drivers in the main plaza, although they will try to convince you that you need to take a taxi to get the bus stop.

◆ Study Spanish, Q'ekchí

Very little English is spoken in Cobán, which makes it an excellent place to study Spanish. You'll learn quickly in this total-immersion environment. There are three language schools in town.

School of Arts and Language, Finca Tzalampec, 16 Avenida 2-50, Zona 1, no phone. Located on a small *finca* outside Cobán, this school offers one-on-one Spanish lessons. They allow only one student per host family. The school itself is new, but the director has many years of teaching Spanish in Guatemala and El Salvador. After-school activities include a workshop in marimba playing, weaving and cooking. Cost is US $110 per week, including room, board and all Spanish lessons.

Active Spanish School, 3 Calle 6-12, Zona 1, ☎ 502/7-951-1432. This is a lively school with lessons in a private home. Outings include trips to *fincas*, parks and clubs, where you will learn more about the social scene in Cobán. The school also offers classes in Q'ekchí. Cost for a 20-hour week of lessons with a host family is US $90.

◆ Sightseeing

The **Central Plaza** is a reminder of the German heyday in Cobán. It features a number of statues set alongside trees and benches. To the north is the large **Metropolitan Cathedrale**, with its original bell dating back to 1548.

Calle Diagonal 4 divides the plaza and on the southern side is a small area with a bulletin board posting bus schedules, maps and other information. This serves as the official **tourist office**. Behind the other end of the plaza is the rather dignified **City Hall**. Across the street, in another colonial building, is the local **market**, which sells lots of good handicrafts. It's open every day. In the evenings when the market has closed, street vendors take over selling food. Most festivities take place in the Central Plaza.

Principe Maya Museum, 6a Avenida 4-26, Zona 3, ☎ 502/7-952-1541. This small museum has an excellent collection of Maya and pre-Columbian artifacts found in the area. Jade pieces, obsidian arrowheads, work tools, ceremonial objects and polychromatic pottery are on display alongside hieroglyphic panels, a replica of a Maya tomb and a collection of clay figurines representing warriors wearing animal masks. The museum is officially open from 9 am to 6 pm, Monday to Saturday, but call ahead since the posted hours are sometimes ignored. Admission is Q10.

Iglesia Calvario, 7a Avenida, Zona 1, take staircase. The Calvario is a focal point for many religious ceremonies practiced in Cobán throughout the year. Small worship altars have been built in front of the church. Los Tigrillos Altare is used for requests for help and wishes. Farther up the hill is San Salvador, the altar for help with love and relationships. The altar closest to the church, La Calavera, is for good health. The 1810 church itself is very simple, with whitewashed walls and little adornment. Candles are found on every surface and you will see devout Q'eqchí on their knees whispering prayers. Don't disturb them and don't take pictures. The panoramic view shows the whole of the city with the mountains in the distance. You can walk around the church to get into Parque Nacional Las Victorias (see below). It's best not to come to the church very early in the morning or at night. Robberies do occur.

Parque Nacional Las Victorias (Victoria Park, named for the victory of independence), 9a Avenida and 3a Calle, Zona 1. This large park is located in the north end of Cobán. It features four nature trails that lead to different areas of the park. The longest and most difficult is four miles (7½ km) and takes up to four hours to complete. The park's forest supports a variety of orchids and other flowers, birds and butterflies and an ornamental garden has medicinal plants. The park is ideal for children and has a playground, picnic tables, barbecue grills and small snack shop. Camping is permitted, but you must get permission from the tourist office in town. Open 8 am-4 pm, daily. Admission is Q5 for adults, Q2 for children.

Vivero Verapaz Orchid Nursery, Carretera Antigua, 18 miles (three km) from town center, ☎ 502/7-952-1133 or 951-4202. This Garden of Eden has 60,00 orchids from 750 species on display. The nursery was the life work of Otto Mittelstaedt who originally came to Cobán as a coffee farmer. His widow now runs the nursery. Be sure to see the collection of 200 miniature orchids – the best in the world. Some are so tiny they can be seen only with a magnifying glass. There are also many examples of the *monja blanca* orchid, Guatemala's national flower.

The plants are spread out on three levels and interspersed with other flowering shrubs and plants, including coffee. This is a nice way to spend an afternoon. Open 9 am-noon and 2-5 pm, Monday to Saturday. Admission is Q10 per person and includes a guided tour in English, German or Spanish.

▶▶ *GETTING HERE: You can walk from town along the highway, but it's not very pleasant or safe. Take a taxi from the Central Plaza for Q10.*

Finca Margarita, 3a Calle 4-12, Zone 2, ☎ 502/7-951-3067. In 1888 Erwin Paul Dieseldorff came to Cobán and bought land a few blocks from the Central Plaza. While he was building his coffee plantation, he lived with the Rabinal Maya and learned their languages and customs. Over time, he became an expert on Maya archeology, folklore and herbal medicine and gathered an incredible number of Maya artifacts. His collection is now on display in Guatemala City in the National Museum of Archeology & History. Dieseldorff ran his plantations on the feudal system of debt patronage that kept many of his Indian friends virtual slaves. When he died, his son took over the business and it remains a working *finca*, albeit with better working conditions. The downtown *finca* offers a one-hour tour that winds through the farm and shows all the stages of coffee production. At the end, gourmet coffee is offered in fine china and you can purchase a pound or two at wholesale prices. This is a delightful way to pass a few hours and the Maya tour guides are charming. Open 8 am-12:30 and 1:30-5 pm, Monday to Friday; mornings only on Saturdays. Admission is Q15.

◆ Adventures on Foot

Lanquín National Park/Grottoes

Lanquín is a small town 40 miles (64 km) west of Cobán. It has a lovely church built in 1602 that features its original silver altar and many religious relics dating back to the colonial period. The Río Lanquín flows nearby and just outside town is a series of subterranean caves that have a series of incredible stalactite and stalagmite formations. Inside one of the caves are some ancient Mayan altars that are still used today. Go into the caves at dusk and you will see bats assembling for their night visit to the river (a good swimming spot) – it's an impressive sight. Open 8 am-4 pm, but you can request that the caves stay open to see the bats. Admission is Q10. Camping is permitted here for an additional Q10 fee.

> **AUTHOR NOTE:** *The caves have some lights, but electricity is unreliable so bring your own flashlight. Don't go too far in unless you are an experienced spelunker – these caves haven't been fully explored.*

About six miles (10 km) southeast of Lanquín is **Semuc Champey** (Q'eqchí for "Sacred Waters"), a 984-foot (300-meter) natural limestone bridge created by Río Cahabon thundering into a cave and passing out the other side. As the calcium carbonate-rich water surges past the rocks, it leaves deposits that, over time, build up. A natural staircase has formed and the water flowing over the steps forms pools and waterfalls that cascade into the river below. The effect is quite extraordinary. Many consider this the country's most beautiful tourist attraction and locals refer to it as the eighth wonder of the world. There are many idyllic spots along here to swim or relax by the river. The site is really breathtaking and worth the dreary haul to get there. Admission to the park is Q20.

AUTHOR NOTE: *If you walk along the bridge to look down into the pools, be careful not to slip. Wear shoes with a good grip.*

> #### ❖   INSIDER TIP: THEFT ALERT
>
> Don't leave any belongings unattended at Semuc. Local gangs of boys have been known to wait in hiding until you are in the water to come out and steal your belongings. Don't bring valuables. If you are camping, ask if you can leave your possessions at a nearby hotel. Your tent will likely be searched when you are not in it.

▶▶   *GETTING HERE: On a normal road this trip would take about 1½ hours, but this road is such a mess and the potholes are so large that it takes over five hours to travel the 38 miles (62 km) from Cobán. It matters little whether you go via shuttle service or bus – the ride is simply miserable. Day tours from Cobán start at US $40. Let your tour guide know if you want to stay overnight, which gives you a more leisurely visit and a chance to recover from the journey. To reach the caves from the lagoons, you must hitchhike. There is plenty of truck traffic on the highway and catching a ride isn't difficult. You can also take a taxi or rent a truck in Lanquín for about Q120.*

There are a few places to stay near Lanquín National Park.

El Centro, *north of the central plaza, 6 rooms $.* Another bare-bones hotel with rooms that have a double bed and fan. The big sell is hot water. Sometimes this hotel is not clean. No credit cards.

El Recreo Hotel, *highway between caves and Semuc.* ☎ *502/7-952-2180, 25 rooms, $$-$.* This is the largest hotel in the area. It has more amenities than others, but is overpriced. Rooms are large, with two double beds and private baths without hot water. There is a swimming pool and restaurant on site. Do a walk-through here before taking a room – it goes through cycles of being neglected and can be really dirty. No credit cards.

El Retiro, *1,640 feet (500 meters) outside Lanquín on the way to Cahabon, 4 rooms, $.* Not only is this the cheapest guesthouse in the area, it is also the nicest and sits right by the river. You can easily pass several days lounging in a hammock. El Retiro is popular with backpackers and gets full quickly. If you are alone, you will have to share a room. The hotel offers free tubes for floating down Río Cahabon. No credit cards.

❖   **LANQUIN TOUR COMPANIES**

A number of companies in Cobán offer either transportation services or guided tours to Lanquín.

Aventuras Turisticas3 Calle 2-38, Zona 1, ☎ 502/7-952-2213, has a two-day/one-night tour for US $40, which includes transportation, camping equipment, food, guides and entrance fees.

Hostal d'Acuña, Calle 4 3-17, Zona 2, ☎ 502/7-952-1547, offers a two-day/one-night tour for US $35. The trip includes an overnight stay in the hotel, transportation to and from Semuc Champey, guide, lunch and entrance fees.

◆ Cultural Adventures – Traditional Maya Villages

San Cristóbal Verapaz

San Cristóbal, 12.4 miles (20 km) west of Cobán, is a traditional rural Pokomchí village on the banks of Chichoj Lake. It's surrounded by fields of coffee and sugar cane. You can take a tour of the local miramba (shoe factory), or visit with local woman as they create hammocks, bags and mats from the maguey plant.

The Pokomchí have a strong tradition of **massage and sauna** using aromatic herbs in combination with *temascal*, a sauna used to purify both body and soul. To have a session with one of the local healers, contact Lourdes Coy, ☎ 502/7-950-4130, for an appointment.

The nearby village of **Pan Kinich** is the spiritual center of the Pokomchí and many **religious ceremonies** are performed there. You can participate in a ceremony honoring Father Sun, Mother Earth and the Seven Brothers of the Stars. Contact Oscar Capriel, ☎ 502/7-650-4654, to find out more.

Museum Katinamit, Calle de Calvario, ☎ 502/7-950-4039. This darling little museum is set in an old adobe house. It has re-created a typical Pokomchí house with typical household items and products. An interesting side trip. Open 8 am-5 pm, Monday-Saturday; 9 am-noon, Sunday. Admission is Q5.

El Calvario Church, Central Plaza. This is one of the tallest churches in Las Verapaces, and from it there's an incredible view of the surrounding area all the way over to Chichoj Lake. The church has been decorated entirely by local artisans and is a good example of the blend of Maya pagan beliefs with Christianity. During Holy Week a sawdust prayer mat is created that extends down the .62-mile (one km) road to the center of town.

Balneario Cecilinda/Grutas Rey Marcos, 3.7 miles (six km) from San Juan Chamelco on the road to Chamil. Balneario Cecilinda is a privately owned park set at the foot of a mountain. At its side, a stream pours down into a series of pools and waterfalls. This is a great place to go for a swim, take a nature hike on the scenic mountain trail or enjoy an afternoon picnic. A nature trail leads up the mountains where you'll find picnic tables, a children's swimming pool and a weekend-only restaurant. This is a popular spot with locals. Entrance fee is Q10.

Nearby are the **King Mark Caves** (*Grutas Rey Marco*), which were discovered by a local walking his dog on the nature trail above the stream. To enter the cave you must first crawl through the 12-foot entrance tunnel that deliver you into a tall cave. A river runs through the cave and translucent stalagmites reveal elaborate natural designs. Many of the locals believe this is a magical place and that the gods respect all wishes made in the cave. The park and caves are open on the weekends from 8 am to 5 pm and throughout the week by appointment only. Contact Aventuras Turisticas or Don Jerónimos, below. Entry fee to the caves is Q15, which includes a helmet. Bring a flashlight and wear sturdy shoes.

▶▶ *GETTING HERE: The easiest way to reach the caves is on a local tour that offers pickup and dropoff at your hotel (see below). The absolute cheapest way to get to the park and caves is on a public bus, but it's a complicated time-consuming journey. First, catch a bus to San Juan Chamelco at the corner of 5 Avenida and 4 Calle, Zona 3 in Cobán. Tickets are Q1. Transfer to the Chamil bus at the corner of 0 Calle and 0 Avenida in Chamelco and ask the bus driver to let you off at the park. Follow the signs. To get back, wait for a bus (there's no fixed schedule) or hitch a ride. You can also hire a taxi to bring you out to the park for Q60. Guides can be hired at the entrance.*

❖ **BALNEARIO CECILINDA OUTFITTER**

Aventuras Turisticas, 3 Calle 2-38, Zona 1, ☎ 502/7-952-2213, offers the best tour for US $12 per person. The price includes transportation, entrance fees to the park and caves and a guide.

◆ Where to Stay

There are plenty of budget hotels in Cobán, but watch out for damp and cold in the low-budget hotels. Many incredible mid-range hotels have a great atmosphere and character.

<table>
<tr><td colspan="2">❖ HOTEL PRICING</td></tr>
<tr><td colspan="2">Prices are per person.</td></tr>
<tr><td>$ . . . .</td><td>Under $25</td></tr>
<tr><td>$$ . . . .</td><td>$26 to $50</td></tr>
<tr><td>$$$ . . . .</td><td>$51 to $85</td></tr>
<tr><td>$$$$ . . . .</td><td>$86 to $125</td></tr>
<tr><td>$$$$$ . . . .</td><td>over $125</td></tr>
</table>

Hotel La Posada, *Calle 4-12, Zona 2,* ☎ *502/7-952-1495, fax 502/7-951-0646, 14 rooms, $$.* This is the most artistic hotel in Cobán. The converted colonial home is furnished with lovely antiques and Guatemalan art. Rooms have four-poster beds, fireplaces and private baths and are set around two courtyards filled with flowers and little nooks with chairs and hammocks. The atmosphere is both luxurious and relaxed. There is an excellent restaurant and café, Café Posada (see page 242).

Pension Monja Blanca, *1C 2-33, Zona 4,* ☎ *502/7-952-1712, $$.* This is another colonial home converted into a guesthouse. Its rooms are charmingly old-fashioned and have good beds, antique furniture and private baths. A courtyard is filled with many kinds of flowers and trees. The pension is a quiet oasis in the center of town.

Hotel Doña Victoria, *3 Calle 2-38, Zona 3,* ☎ *502/7-951-4213, 8 rooms, $$.* This hotel oozes historical charm. Over 400 years old, it was one of the first buildings in Cobán built by Dominican monks for their cloistered nuns. The old tunnel that connected the convent to the church is now a bar. A wealthy family bought the property as a bridal home for their daughter. Unfortunately, she was jilted at the altar and withdrew from society. For over 20 years she ran a candle factory inside her home and customers came to pick up their orders. The garden here is over 200 years old and has banana trees, coffee plants and tropical flowers. The bright rooms have their original furniture from the 18th century and are simply furnished with double or single beds. Be sure to try the restaurant (see below). An excellent travel agency, **Aventuras Turisticas**, ☎ *502/7-951-1358,* has its office here.

Hostal Acuña, *4a Calle 3-11, Zona 2,* ☎ *502/7-7951-0482, fax 502/7-952-1547, 7 rooms, $.* This lovely European-style pension is located down the steep hill in town. Rooms have bunk beds with a shared bath, so there isn't much privacy. There is one private room. La Casa has a great restaurant and a wonderful bulletin board with tons of valuable information. The hotel offers a variety of tours, including one to Semuc Champey and another to the Candelería caves.

Hotel de Don Juan Matalbatz, *3a Calle 1-46, Zona 1,* ☎/fax *502/7-952-1599, 15 rooms, $.* Rooms are large, clean and come with cable TV and private baths with hot water. Shared rooms are also available and have little balconies with street views. The courtyard is pleasing. Check your room before signing in since some smell like mildew. Hotel de Don Juan features a large on-site pool table and a good restaurant. No credit cards.

Hotel La Paz, *6 Avenida 2-19,* ☎ *502/7-952-1358, 28 rooms, $.* La Paz is cheap and cheerful. Rooms are clean and airy and all baths are shared (hot water runs out quickly). There is parking and a good cafeteria next door. No credit cards.

Hotel Oxib Peck, *3a Calle 12-11, Zona 1,* ☎ *502/7-952-1039, fax 502/7-951-3224, 13 rooms, $.* Set 20 minutes from downtown and closer to Parque Victorias, this hotel has a nice courtyard with a small aviary that houses some cheeky parrots. Rooms are clean and agreeable with double beds, private baths and TV.

Hotel Mansion Armenia, *7a Avenida 2-18, Zona 1,* ☎ *502/7-952-2284, 23 rooms, $.* Another hotel tucked away from downtown, Armenia is close to El Calvario and Parque Victorias. It's clean, quiet and modern.

Rooms have private baths and cable TV, and there's parking and a cafeteria. No credit cards.

Hotel Posada de Carlos V, *1a Avenida 3-44, Zona 1,* ☎ *502/7-951-3502, fax 502/7-952-1780, 14 rooms, $.* A long name for a small hotel. The building has a chalet style, with lots of pine trim and crisp décor. Rooms are clean and functional, with private baths and cable TV. The lobby has some great photos of the old Cobán. No credit cards.

Don Jerónimo's, *Km 5.3 Carretera Chamil,* ☎ *502/7-301-3191, www. dearbrutus.com/donjeronimo, 5 bungalows, $$.* This resort is located on a blueberry/medicinal plant farm by Río Sotzil. It's operated by Bob Maransky, known locally as Don Jerónimo. Comfortable and rustic private bungalows are equipped with kitchens and private baths. All have wooden floors and furniture with woven mats and textiles for decoration. Private porches overlook the mountains, forest and river. The price of a room includes three vegetarian meals a day and all recreational activities, such as swimming, tubing and hiking. Ask Don Jerónimo to share some of his local ghost stories with you.

To get here, follow the directions for the Rey Marcos Cave (above), but ask the bus driver to let you off at Don Jerónimo's by Aldea village. Cross the river at the bridge. A cab out here will run Q70.

◆ Where to Eat

Cobán has a wonderful mixture of basic *comedores* and European-style cafés. Nothing is outrageously expensive. For a bargain meal, check out the street vendors that come out after the market closes. They sell great steamed corn, tortillas and barbecued meats.

Café d'Acuña, *4a Calle 3-11, Zona 2,* ☎ *502/7-7951-0482, fax 502/7-952-1547.* Café d'Acuña is, without a doubt, the best restaurant in Cobán. Set in a lovely colonial courtyard, the café offers crisp delicious salads, tasty quiches, fresh pasta dishes and excellent daily specials that include soup and salad. Save room for something from the cake cabinet, full of sinfully delicious cakes and pastries. US $3-9.

Hostal Doña Victoria, *3 Calle 2-38, Zona 3,* ☎ *502/7-951-4213.* The restaurant in this historical home looks out onto a 200-year-old courtyard garden. The menu offers good chicken dishes along with fresh pastas and salads. The bar is really cool – it used to be the tunnel used by the nuns for going over to the church. Q15-35.

Café Posada, *located in Hotel La Posada, Calle 4-12, Zona 2,* ☎ *502/7-952-1495, fax 502/7-951-0646.* This is actually two restaurants. The café outside overlooks the plaza and serves coffees, teas and pastries. You can eat your meal in one of the sitting rooms that have couches and fireplaces. The main dining room is very refined and decorated with art to the point of distraction. The menu includes meat, chicken, fish, pizza and pasta. It's a tad overpriced, but the atmosphere can't be beat. Q25-95.

Café Tirol, *1a Calle 3-13, Zona 1,* ☎ *502/7-951-4042.* Café Tirol offers over 22 different kinds of coffee, so it's hard to make a decision. The pastries are good, and light breakfasts and lunches include pancakes, eggs and sandwiches. Q7-14. No credit cards.

La Esperanza Restaurante, *Calle 1, Zona 1*, ☎ *502/7-952-1495*. This is *the* place to come for breakfast. Downstairs there is a bakery and upstairs is where you go to enjoy the goodies. There are several good breakfasts offered and the coffee is heavenly. Breakfast finishes at 10:30 am, so come early. Q7-20. No credit cards.

El Refugio, *2a Calle y 2 Avenida, Zona 4.* Set on a hilltop overlooking the street and with plenty of rustic décor, this restaurant serves wonderful steaks and fresh game, such as veal and fish. The soups are excellent (but avoid the turtle soup, since turtles are on the endangered species list). Q15-35. No credit cards.

Café Santa Rita, *south side of the park.* This little café serves bang-up breakfasts. You have plenty of choices. Have some eggs served with beans and coffee. Or try the *mosh*, a spiced oatmeal with cream. Lunch and dinner dishes are traditional, such as *chile rellano* (stuffed chiles) or *tortas*. They have good desserts and coffee, too. Q4-9. No credit cards.

Kam-mun, *1a Calle 8- 2, Zona 2.* This large restaurant has an outside patio. It serves yummy Chinese food in large portions. The egg rolls, sweet and sour chicken and won-ton soup are delicious. Portions are large, presumably to justify the slightly high prices. Q42-70. No credit cards.

Salamá

Baja Verapaz is the much smaller department in Las Verapaces. It has remote Achi Maya villages. Sections of the region are dry and flat and form part of the Salamá Valley, but the department does eventually become mountainous and there are some incredible mountain trails to explore, along with caves and the wonderful **Quetzal Biotope**. Since it is so lush and green, producing some of the country's best fruit, the area has been dubbed the Green Heart of Guatemala (*la Corazón Verde de Guatemala*).

Salamá, the capital of Baja Verapaz, is a prosperous village with a mostly *Ladino* population. You will see little traditional dress. There isn't much to do in the village, but the Sunday **market** is worth a look since it does carry some of the famous Rabinal pottery.

The colonial **church** dating back to the 16th century is also worth a visit. It faces a lovely main plaza with sculptured trees. The church has a simple façade and a gold-leafed altar and a pulpit with Rococo carvings. The only other pulpit like this in Latin America is in Lima, Peru. A life-size statue shows Jesus lying in his satin-lined coffin with his wounds bandaged.

West of the city the highway ends and a dirt road its climb into the mountains where the traditional villages of San Miguel Chicaj, Rabinal and Cubulco are found.

◆ Purulha/Cloud Forest Treks

Purulha is a small rural village that grows the plant Xate, commonly used in North American floral arrangements. You'll see the plant on hills, covered in large black plastic tarps for protection. There are no services at all in this town, but it is the jumping-off point for visits to the surrounding cloud forests.

Mario Dary Rivera Biotópo del Quetzal

This famous and popular reserve covers 2,500 acres (11 square km) of tropical cloud forest. The University of San Carlos manages the biotope and has opened a small section to the public. The high humidity has created a dense jungle of great beauty. Two trails wind through the misty forest, past ancient trees, orchids, red flowering bromeliads, mosses and ferns. Parts of the trail overlook the mountains, which are usually shrouded in clouds. The aguacatillo tree grows in abundance and is the favorite tree of the quetzal, the national bird. Although there is a high population of quetzals in the park, they are surprisingly difficult to spot because they can remain motionless for hours and their feathers blend with the surrounding flowers. The best time to spot the birds is at the crack of dawn, when they come to feed in the trees close to the highway.

The easier trail, Senderos Helecho (Path of the Ferns) is 1.2 miles (2 km) long and takes 1½ hours to complete, depending on your fitness level. The more challenging Senderos los Musgos (Path of the Mosses) is 2.4 miles (four km) and takes between 2½ and 4½ hours to complete. Both trails pass by waterfalls and lagoons where you can stop and swim in the pure mountain water. At the entrance to the park are rangers, a small natural museum with photos of quetzals and a small store that sells snacks, drinks and some souvenirs. Camping is no longer permitted in the park, despite what people will tell you. Open daily, 7 am-4 pm. Admission is Q20.

▸▸ *GETTING HERE: You can easily do this tour on your own as a day-trip. The biotope is located right on the Guatemala-Cobán highway at Km 160, four km south of Purulha village. Whether you are coming from Guatemala or Cobán, just ask the driver to let you off Biotope del Quetzal. To return, simply hail one of the many colectivos and buses that pass by every 15-30 minutes.*

There are several excellent hotels close by the reserve (see *Places to Stay*, below).

◆ Where to Stay

Purulha

Country Delight Reserve, *Km 166.5, Purulha*, ☎ *502/7-709-1149, 2 rooms & 2 bungalows. $$.* This working farm is a member of the Association of Guatemalan Private Natural Reserves (*La Asociación de Reservas Naturales Privadas de Guatemala*). Farm owners belonging to this organization have set

❖ HOTEL PRICING
Prices are per person.
$ . . . . Under $25
$$ . . . . $26 to $50
$$$ . . . . $51 to $85
$$$$ . . . . $86 to $125
$$$$$ . . . . over $125

aside a portion of their land as a reserve with lodging and hiking trails. Country Delight is located at the edge of the Biotope and quetzals come to roost in the trees at dawn and at dusk. There are two rooms and two bungalows on the Swiss chalet-style property. The bungalows can sleep up to four people and are suitable for families. All accommodations are furnished in bright textiles and have incredibly cozy beds. The restaurant serves homemade bread and traditional specialties using produce and including organic chickens from their farm. Meals are enjoyed in front of a roaring fire. There are horses, a small pond with fish and nature trails.

Ram Tzul Eco-Lodge, *Km 158, Carreterra Guatemala-Cobán*, ☎ *502/7-335-1805, ramtzul@internet.net.gt, 8 rooms, 5 cabañas, $$.* Ram-Tzul (Spirit of the Mountain) is a private ecological park located between the Sierra de las Minas Reserve and the Biotope Quetzal in an area known as Ram Tzul. The forests here are a mixture of cypress and pine and the eco-lodge was created to blend into these surroundings. Bamboo walls and natural stone floors are covered with palapa roofs. Private rooms are equipped with two double beds, mosquito nets and have views of the forests. Bathrooms are shared. Cabañas resemble small cottages and have private balconies overlooking the mountains as well as private bathrooms. There's an information center and a small restaurant.

A nature trail leads from Ram Tzul to a large waterfall that cascades down the mountain to the lagoon and several swimming spots. Other trails lead through the forest and offer great birding. The resort has a reforestation program and has replanted over 21 different species of pine and registered the surrounding area as a protected zone.

El Petén

El Petén is considered Guatemala's last wilderness frontier, an area famous for lost Maya cities and impenetrable forests. It is a vast region encompassing rainforests, savannas and wetlands. But like many wilderness areas, El Petén is under threat and is rapidly being deforested by a growing population and logging companies. Various multinationals have their eye on the oil and other natural resources, while conservation organizations are working hard to

save the area. Eco-tourism is seen as a viable alternative for the region.

Most of the settlers in El Petén are of mixed blood, or *Ladino*, and there is little of the indigenous culture found in other parts of the country.

History

Once inhabited by several million people, **El Petén Valley** was the center of the **Maya** civilization for centuries. Researchers believe this area, known as the southern Maya lowlands (now Belize, northern Guatemala and eastern Mexico), had the densest population. It reached its golden era during the Late Classic period (AD 600-900). Between AD 650 and 930, various city-states, such as El Mirador, Tikal, Dos Pilas, Ceibal and Yaxhá, emerged from the jungle as mighty forces whose influence was felt as far north as Chichén Itzá in Mexico's Yucatán. The struggle for power spawned many wars and the chronicles of victories and defeat are recorded in the stelae on buildings, pyramids and staircases. Yet for all its power and wealth, the southern Maya lowlands area was deserted by AD 930. Theories continue to evolve with each new discovery and researchers believe this area may hold the answer to the mysterious disappearance of this great civilization.

Overlooked for centuries, El Petén holds a lost kingdom that is only starting to come to light. During the 18th century, both **Spain** and **Britain** attempted logging in the Petén, but the remoteness and lack of roads made any real development difficult to maintain. Ninety percent of virgin rainforest remained until 1970. The civil war that raged from 1960 until 1996 actually helped preserve the area, since the rebels set up base camps in the Petén and discouraged anyone else from settling there. During the 1980s, the Guatemala government decided the Petén was the solution for the many displaced survivors of the war and encouraged homesteading by selling parcels of land for as little as Q175 (US $25). At the same time it allowed oil and logging companies to start building roads through forests. As a result, over 400,000 misplaced Guatemalans arrived to claim their piece of land. Today, half of the rainforest has now been cut down by either logging companies, cattle barons or by settlers practicing slash-and-burn agriculture. All are devastating to the area. And this has not turned out to be the Promised Land for settlers – the poor soil quality forces residents to hunt for survival. The end result has been a drastically reduced wildlife population. White-tailed deer, tepezcuintle (an agouti paca), jaguars and ocellated turkey are in danger of disappearing from El Petén.

In 1990, Mexico, Guatemala and Belize created the **Maya Biosphere Reserve**. Its five million acres include most of the northern Petén as well as the **Mexican Calakmul Biosphere** and the **Río Bravo Conservation Area** in Belize. In Guatemala, the Maya Biosphere is divided into three zones. The Core Zone Area is 4.7 million acres under absolute protection with no human settlements allowed. Visitors are permitted to visit only for eco-tours or to conduct research. Surrounding the Core Zone is the Multiple Use Zone, which allows the use of natural resources by oil and timber companies, as well as the local population. A nine-mile Buffer Zone separates the biosphere from the southern Petén. Most of the settlements, industry and agriculture are located in the Multiple Use Zone or Buffer Zone. The 1996 peace accord allowed the Guatemalan government to start focusing on conservation and **CONAP** (Consejo Nacional de Areas Protegidas – National Council of Protected Areas) was established to oversee the Maya Biosphere Reserve.

CONAP helped create an international conservation team known as Projecto Peténero para un Bosque Sostenible (ProPetén). Its main focus is working with local forest communities to develop cottage industries and eco-tours that bring income to the area. It is hoped these programs will reduce the locals' need to hunt or practice slash-and-burn farming. The success of the Scarlet Macaw Trail (page 190) and other trails has encouraged locals to start up other eco-businesses. The revenue from park admission, guide fees, restaurants, eco-lodges and other services is starting to make a difference.

So, while El Petén still has a long way to go with some complex problems to be solved, the future looks promising.

Flora & Fauna

The region is considered subtropical with a warm and humid climate. Rainy season begins in May and lasts well into December with at least

150 days of rain during those months. Over 2,000 plant species have been identified here, along with six species of cedar and four species of palm trees. Fifty-four mammal species include the howler monkey, spider monkey, anteater, three-toed sloth, armadillo, brown coati, paca, ocelot, jaguarundi, jaguar, Baird's tapir, white-lipped peccary and white-tailed deer. Over 350 species of birds have been identified, among them the red macaw, scarlet macaw, jaribu stork, crested eagle, and ocellated turkey. There are nine families of amphibian, six of turtles, and 38 species of non-poisonous and poisonous snakes.

There is so much offered in the Petén that you could easily spend a few months exploring the whole region. Visiting involves sacrificing some of the luxuries, but the effort is worth it as this is a chance to explore true wilderness, see fantastic Maya ruins and meet some hardy pioneers.

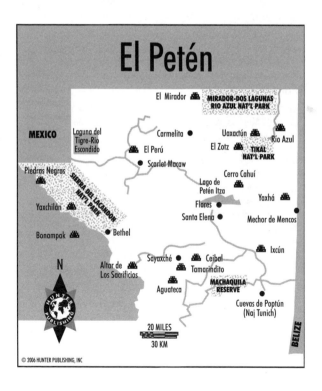

Melchor de Mencos

Melchor de Mencos is an unattractive, chaotic border town with little to offer the visitor. Its main highlight is the stelae from the ruins of El Naranjo on display in the central plaza. Melchor makes a poor introduction or exit to Guatemala and most tourists don't linger. Everyone makes sure their transportation is arranged to bypass the town once their business at the Guatemala-Belize border is finished.

It's unfortunate the introduction to this area is unpleasant. Away from the town are some fascinating ruins to explore, and the lush jungle offers excellent birdwatching and hiking. However, it is difficult to explore this area on your own, since most of the ruins are remote and require a guide. If you prefer to travel solo, take a trip to Yaxhá, just one hour from Melchor.

◆ Getting Here & Getting Around

By Bus

If you are coming from Belize you will cross over from Benque Viejo into Melchor de Mencos. You will first have to pass through the Belizean customs, pay your US $10 exit fee and US $7.50 conservation tax before going through Guatemalan customs. Once you have finished at Guatemala customs, you get back on board your bus and continue across the bridge. Sometimes the bus is stopped and everyone is asked to pay a Q10 municipal tax. If you are crossing on foot you may be asked to pay more: some enterprising officials were charging US $10 fee. Watch your belongings when crossing the bridge, and be prepared to be approached by hordes of people who want to sell you something under the guise of being helpful.

Coming from the interior of Guatemala, you must first take a bus to Flores and then catch a local bus to Melchor. Buses leave every hour from Flores. Bus lines are Pinita Bus, leaving at 5, 8 and 10 am; and Rosita, leaving at 11 am, 3 and 6 pm. If you have four or more people you could also consider hiring a taxi. The cost would be Q300-400. Most tourist areas have a shuttle service that whisks you from Guatemala into Belize with no stopover in Melchor.

Lake Petén Itzá

Lago de Petén Itzá is the largest lake in the Petén and it has a number of communities on its shores. The largest is **Flores**, followed by its sister

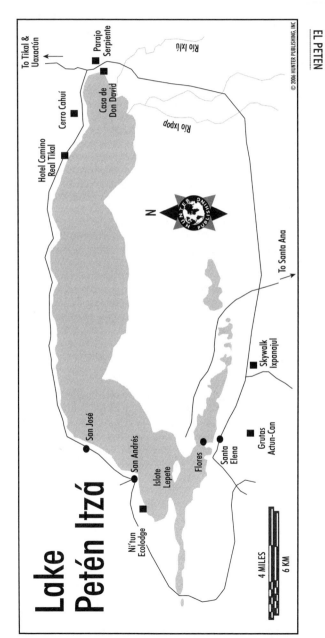

city of **Santa Elena**. You will find the most services, hotels and restaurants here. San Andrés and San José are two smaller communities close to Flores, while El Remate is on the other side of the lake.

Flores

◆ History

Once the ancient Maya city of **Tayasal**, Flores is now the capital of El Petén with a population of 2,200. There is little to see of the original city since most of it is underwater, but Tayasal remains historically important. When the Itzá were forced to abandon their cities up north, including Chichén Itzá, they took refuge in the jungles of the Petén, founding Noh-Petén (Tayasal) on the island of Chal Tun Ha (Lake Petén).

Their first contact with the **Spanish** was in 1541 when Hernan Cortes visited on his way to Honduras. He left behind a giant white horse that was too sick to continue the journey, promising to return. He never did. In 1618 when two Franciscan friars arrived they found the Itzá worshipping a large sculpture of a white horse they had named "Thunder Horse." Outraged, the friars smashed the idol and fled the island. In retaliation, the Itzá chief invited 20 conquistadors to Tayasal and promptly sacrificed them to the horse god. This earned the Itzá a reputation as cruel barbarians and made the Spanish even more eager to conquer them, but each of their many attempts ended in failure. It wasn't until 1697 that an army led by Martín de Ursua y Arismendi managed to overtake the city. However, the Spanish victory was based more on deception than military skill. One of the brothers, Fray Andrés de Avendaño, was fluent in the Itzá language. He noted a prophecy in their holy book about the surrender of the city on the same day as the arrival of the Spanish. The conquistadors used this to their advantage and the Itzá handed over Tayasal. The Spanish then swarmed through Tayasal smashing everything in sight. The Itzá may have surrendered the city, but they refused to live under Spanish rule and fled to the nearby jungle and established a new city. Their community has grown to be San José.

In 1698, the Spanish turned the island into a penal colony and Flores was founded two years later. It quickly became a commercial center for chicle, hardwoods, rubber and sugarcane, but as each of those markets slowed down the city was forgotten. In 1970, the Guatemalan government began promoting Flores as a tourist gateway to Tikal. Today the city is a charming island town with historical buildings lined up along cobblestone streets. At the top of the summit are the main square and a lovely cathedral. There are plenty of hotels, restaurants, shops and services here. Flores is connected to its sister communities of Santa Elena and San Benito by a manmade causeway.

Whatever charm the area holds quickly evaporates once you cross over to the mainland. **Santa Elena** and **San Benito** are a chaotic mix of unpaved one-way streets snarled with traffic and lined with scrappy shops, restaurants and budget hotels crammed one on top of the other. Locals refer to Santa Elena as *un disastero* (a disaster) and barely acknowledge San Benito. There are several good hotels on the shores of Santa Elena, but neither city is recommended, especially at night.

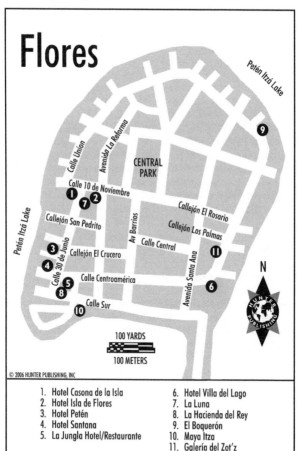

Flores

© 2006 HUNTER PUBLISHING, INC

1. Hotel Casona de la Isla
2. Hotel Isla de Flores
3. Hotel Petén
4. Hotel Santana
5. La Jungla Hotel/Restaurante
6. Hotel Villa del Lago
7. La Luna
8. La Hacienda del Rey
9. El Boquerón
10. Maya Itza
11. Galería del Zot'z

◆ Getting Here & Getting Around

By Bus

There is one main route to Flores, CA-13, a well-maintained highway that starts outside of Guatemala City, passing through the departments of El Progresso, Zacapa and Izabal before turning north to El Petén. If you are coming west from the Highlands or Antigua, you will have to transfer in Guatemala City. If you are coming from the Verapaces Departments, you will change buses at El Rancho along CA-13. **Río Dulce** in Izabal has regular buses several times a day to Flores.

Many tourists use the **shuttles** that are available in most of the tourist areas (see page 70). They are more expensive than public buses, but are far more comfortable and convenient. Shuttle services operate between Panajchel, Antigua, Guatemala City, Cobán and Río Dulce.

It's a long haul from Guatemala City to Flores, 12-15 hours covering 344 miles (554 km). Many people prefer to break up the trip by passing a few days in Río Dulce or Poptún.

Once in Flores, you will have to walk across the causeway since most of the bus lines stop in Santa Elena. Cabs can take you over for Q10 and are readily available. Everything is in walking distance in both Flores and Santa Elena. Flores is a pleasant place to stroll, but Santa Elena is more like a strenuous game of dodge-that-diesel-bus-and-try-not-to-fall-into-a-pothole.

LEAVING FLORES: Trying to figure out which line goes where can be confusing. The best approach is to choose your destination and then ask for directions to the bus line (most are found in Santa Elena). The **INGUAT** office in the main square in Flores has a current bus schedule but you should still double-check since times change regularly. Public bus lines include **Transportes Pinita, Transportes María Elena, Fuentes del Norte, Linea Dorado, Autobuses Máxima** and **Transportes Rosío**. These all offer second-class service except for Linea Dorado, which runs a marvelous luxury bus from Guate to Flores.

TO TIKAL: Local buses leave from the end of the causeway every half-hour or so. Tourist minibuses will pick you up at your hotel or from the airport with advance arrangements (see page 28). The trip from Flores to Tikal takes about 1½ hours and you can come back the same day. If you decide to stay over at the ruins, let the driver know so he can reserve a seat for you the next day. The round-trip fare is Q42.

By Car

Most of the rental car companies are located at the airport and have a good selection of cars, 4WD trucks and minivans. Prices start at US $50 and usually have some kind of distance allowance known as *kilometraje*. Read the small print in your contract carefully and check the car for damage before signing anything. The cars all have standard gears. If automatic gears are important to you, make your request ahead of time. The largest rental company is **Koka Rent Autos**, ☎ 502/7-926-1233.

By Plane

Many visitors choose to fly to Flores from Guatemala City. The Flores International airport is actually 1.8 miles east of Santa Elena on the mainland.

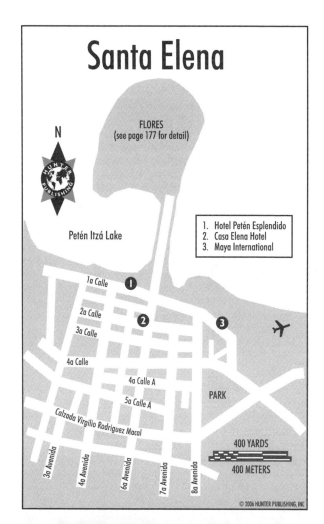

Santa Elena

N

FLORES
(see page 177 for detail)

Petén Itzá Lake

1. Hotel Petén Esplendido
2. Casa Elena Hotel
3. Maya International

1a Calle

2a Calle

3a Calle

4a Calle

4a Calle A

5a Calle A

Calzada Virgilio Rodriguez Macal

PARK

400 YARDS

400 METERS

3a Avenida

4a Avenida

6a Avenida

7a Avenida

8a Avenida

© 2006 HUNTER PUBLISHING, INC

❖ **AIRLINES SERVICING TIKAL**

Most of the domestic airlines offer flights to Tikal that leave from Guatemala. Some are more reliable than others. Rates start at about US $80 and can go as high as US $175 per person for a one-way ticket. Keep in mind these flights are often cancelled, delayed or overbooked. You must check directly with the airline to get their current schedule. Leave enough time to catch your international flight. All these domestic airlines have offices at the Aurora Airport in Guatemala City.

Aeroquetzal . . . . ☎ 502/2-334-7689
Aviateca . . . . ☎ 502/2-470-8222
Racsa, SA . . . . ☎ 502/2-361-7056
Taca . . . . ☎ 502/2-470-8222
Tikal Airlines . . . . ☎ 502/7-926-3823

> **AUTHOR TIP:** *Tickets for trips from Flores to Guatemala are less expensive if bought directly from the airline as the local agencies tend to overcharge.*

There is no direct local buses from the airport to Flores, but there are plenty of tourist shuttle buses and taxis. The fare should be about Q14, one way.

By Boat

You can take a local motor launch (known as a *lanchas colectivo*) to the neighboring towns of San Andrés, San José or El Remate. Launches depart on the west side of Santa Elena near San Benito and also from Hotel Santana in Flores. Tickets are Q4. You must wait for the launch to show up, or you can hire a private boat for Q100. *Lanchas* may also be rented to tour the lake for between Q70 and Q200, depending on the number of people and length of the tour.

> **AUTHOR TIP:** *Bargain hard, since the lancheros (boatmen) tend to overcharge. And don't buy the expensive guided tour to Tayasal – most of the ruins are underwater. Instead, rent a pedal boat from Hotel Petén and explore the lake on your own.*

◆ Adventures on Foot

Actuncan Cave

This limestone cave is located one mile (1.6 km) west from Flores. It's also known as La Cueva de la Serpiente (Cave of the Serpent) after a large snake that used to live there (it hasn't been spotted in years). Inside are tall caverns between 10-20 feet (three to six meters) high with giant stalactites and stalagmites. The formations are famous for their shapes resembling animals and human faces. If the guide is around, get him to point out some of the more bizarre formations. Inside is adequately lit, but you may want to bring a flashlight with you. Be sure to wear sturdy shoes since the clay floor is wet and slippery. The tour takes about 45 minutes to complete. Entrance fee is Q14. You can walk from Flores, but taking a taxi for about Q14 is probably easier.

> **AUTHOR TIP:** *Stay on the path. The cave is large and un-mapped – not the kind of place to get lost in.*

Tayasal

There is little to see of this once grand city since the Spanish destroyed most if it, and the remains are now underwater or covered with jungle. But there is a wonderful lookout at the top of the hill that offers a spectacular view of Lake Petén. It's especially lovely at sunset. And it's a great place for a picnic or swim.

Petencito Island

This tiny little island is popular with local families who like to come for picnics and swimming. The nature area includes a nice sand beach, picnic tables and a small wooden dock. There are well-maintained nature trails through the forest reaching a look out. There is also a humble little zoo with Guatemalan wildlife such as a jaguar, spider monkeys, armadillos, crocodiles, deer and coatimundi. The animals are well looked after, but their cages are not exactly luxurious, so heavy-duty animal lovers may want to stay away.

>> *GETTING HERE: Colectivos leave from the same dock as those heading for San Jose and San Andres. You can also hire a private lancha, which will be more expensive. Rates vary from Q100 to Q300, so negotiate skillfully.*

Skyway Ixpanpajul

Located just four miles south from the airport, this park has nature trails joined together by hanging bridges. As you hike along you will be able to see the trees, flowers and plants up close or look down over the canopy of trees. Depending on the time of day, you may even spot some howler monkeys and other wildlife. All trails meet at the top of **Cerro Miramás** (See More Mountain), where you can see miles of jungle as well as Lake Petén Itzá. The park also offers horses for a trek through the surrounding jungle, bicycles for the trails and tractor rides. ☎ 502/7-863-1317. Open 6 am-6 pm, Monday to Friday. Q35.

◆ Where to Stay

Flores

Hotel Isla de Flores, *Avenida La Reforma,* ☎ *502/7-926-0614, fax 502/ 926-0053, 18 rooms, $$.* This hotel has medium-sized rooms with two double beds, air conditioning and cable TV. Small balconies open up to the street. The lobby is bright and nicely furnished in rattan furniture. It is a bit overpriced.

Hotel La Casona de la Isla, *Calle 30 de Junio*, ☎ *502/7-926-0692, 926-0593, lacasona@gua.net, 27 rooms, $$.* This appealing three-story hotel has 27 attractive rooms with all the usual amenities. But it is the private balconies with their sunset views and the lakeside Jacuzzi, pool and restaurant that really make this hotel stand out.

> **❖ HOTEL PRICING**
>
> Prices are per person.
>
> $ . . . . Under $25
> $$ . . . . $26 to $50
> $$$ . . . . $51 to $85
> $$$$ . . . . $86 to $125
> $$$$$ . . . . over $125

Hotel Petén, *Calle 30 de Junio*, ☎ *502/926-1692, fax 502/926-0662, 21 rooms, $$.* This is one of the town's first hotels. Inside, a smart courtyard leads to an indoor pool and restaurant. Just outside is the lakeside cafe with a great view. Unfortunately, the food is dreadful and the service only vaguely polite. The rooms are lovely though, with nice decorations, air conditioning and private bath. Ask for a room on the top floor, since the view of the lake from up there is spectacular.

Hotel y Restaurante Santana, *corner of Calle 30 de Junio and Calle Centroamérica*, ☎ *502/7-926-0662, www.santanapeten.com, 32 rooms, $$.* This was one of the first hotels in Flores and has a great location on the end of the island. All three floors were renovated in 1999 so the rooms are modern and clean (first-floor rooms even have their own patios that face the lake). There is also a pool and restaurant by the lake. The nearby dock is the place to catch the boat heading out to the other villages.

Hotel Villa de Lago, *corner of Calle Centroamérica and Calle 15 September*, ☎ *502/7-926-0508, 15 rooms, $.* The outside of this hotel is rather ugly, but the inside is quite decent. Rooms are tiny and basic, but cozy and tidy. There are some bigger (and more expensive) rooms with private bathrooms and cable TV. The hotel offers a great breakfast for Q14 and has an excellent laundry service. No credit cards.

Hotel la Jungla, *corner of Calle 30 Junio and Calle Centroamérica*, ☎ *502/7-926-0634, 16 rooms, $.* This budget hotel offers good value with homey rooms with private bathrooms and plenty of hot water. The rooms have either a view of the lake or town. There is also an excellent little restaurant. No credit cards.

Santa Elena

Petén Esplendido Hotel and Conference Center, *1a Calle 5-01, Zona 1*, ☎ *502/7-926-0880, fax 502/7-926-0866, www.petenesplendido.com, 62 rooms, $$$.* This luxury hotel is just three minutes from the Flores International Airport on the lake in front of Flores. It has all the usual luxuries, including air conditioning, cable TV, a large swimming pool and a posh restaurant and bar. Each room has a small balcony with a view of the lake.

Hotel Maya Internacional, *Lago Petén Itzá, ☎ 502/7-926-1276, www. villasdeguatemala.com, 30 rooms, $$$.* This is a quiet hotel tucked away on the lake. The rooms open up onto balconies facing the lake and are furnished with wooden furniture and ceiling fans. There is a pleasant bar and lakeside pool. The hotel's main draw is the tranquil location.

Casa Elena Hotel, *6 Avenida at 4 Calle Principal, ☎ 502/7-926-2238, fax 502/926-0097, 28 rooms, $$.* Casa Elena is situated right on the causeway just steps from the bus stop. It doesn't have much character, but it is extremely clean, comfortable and quiet. Rooms are on the small side, but come with new beds and terrific water pressure in the bathrooms. The restaurant has a decent menu and there's also a nice pool.

◆ Where to Eat

Flores

There are plenty of restaurants in both Flores and Santa Elena. Unfortunately, most suffer from the copycat syndrome and serve the same menu of hamburgers, chicken and pizza. Thankfully, there are some gems here as well.

La Luna, *corner Calle 10 de Noviembre and Calle 30 de Junio. ☎ 502/ 926-0357.* This is, without a doubt, the best restaurant in Flores and the surrounding area. The menu is fresh and original, with delectable dishes such as pork medallions in a pineapple sauce or Cordon Bleu, mixed salads and fresh pasta. The charming décor adds to the whole dining experience. Prices range from Q49 to Q26.

La Casona de la Isla, *Calle 30 de Junio, ☎ 502/7-926-0692, 7-926-0593.* This restaurant, part of the comely La Casona Hotel, is an excellent place for lunch. Offerings include fresh salads, pastas and chicken specials from Q48 to Q27. Relax and watch local traffic from their terrace.

Café la Galeria de Zotz, *Calle 15 de Septiembre. No phone.* Enjoy the local art in this funky yet elegant cafe-bistro that serves up lots of exotic cocktails from a well-stocked bar. Drinks are between Q11 to Q20. Recommended dishes are the chicken curry and chef salad. Q25-40. No credit cards.

El Boquerón Restaurante, *Calle 15 de Septiembre, ☎ 502/7-926-3429.* Vegetarians rejoice. There is a place for you. It serves fresh and delicious wholewheat bread, veggie casseroles, fruit salads and green salads, as well as soy products that are difficult to find elsewhere. Prices range from Q10 to Q30. No credit cards.

San Andrés & San José

The small town of San Andrés sits on the northeast shore of Lake Petén and has a small Maya community.

◆ Getting Here

The most pleasant way to reach either village is by **boat** from Flores. It's a half-hour ride to San Andrés and 45 minutes to San José. The cheapest option is via the public *lanchas* that leave whenever they are full and cost between five and seven quetzals. If you are in a hurry, negotiate the fare for a private boat. Rates start at Q250.

Buses leave twice a day from Santa Elena, one in the morning, one in the afternoon. But the road is bumpy, dusty and the bus usually crowded.

◆ Sightseeing

There isn't much in the way of hotels and restaurants, but there are two excellent Spanish schools. Eco-Escuela combines Spanish-language in-struction with ecological activities such as helping out local conservation-ists build the Sacbaquecan Interpretative Trail or working on the Ixcalapa Reforestation Area. Local outings include visits to the Macantun Public Beach. One-on-one lessons are tailored to the needs of each student. Ac-commodations are with local Maya families who also provide all the meals. The course is US $175 per person and includes 20 hour of instruc-tion, three meals a day and lodging. Classes begin every Monday. For fur-ther information, contact **EcoMaya**, Eco-Escuela de Español, Flores, Petén, ☎ 502/7-926-4981, www.ecomaya.com.

Picturesque San José village overlooks a lovely bay on the lake. Origi-nally, San José was the village created by the Itzá when they were finally forced out of Tayasal (now known as Flores). For many years the only lan-guage spoken was Itzá. However, when the area opened up, the number of villagers speaking Itzá dwindled to a handful. In the early 1990s the community began a campaign to revive the language and it is now taught in all the schools in this region. La Academia de las Lenguas Mayas de Guatemala (Academy of the Mayan Languages of Guatemala) even of-fers a program to promote the use of Itzá.

Also in the area is an interpretative **medicine trail** and center for **me-dicinal plants** run by the Bio-Itzá's Women's Group of San José. Stu-dents at the Escuela Bio-Itzá de San José are welcome to participate in both organizations. Classes are four to six hours a day and fees include lodging with a local Itzá family and three meals a day. For a small addi-tional fee, you can also arrange outings to the Bio-Itzá Reserve, a cultural and ethno-botanical area located 14 miles north in virgin jungle. Cost for the language course is US $175 per person, per week. For more details, contact EcoMaya, Eco-Escuela de Español, Flores, Petén. ☎ 502/7-926-3202, www.ecomaya.com.

◆ Where to Stay

Ni'tun Eco-Lodge, *northeast shore of Lake Petén*, ☎ 501/7-926-0493, *4 cabins. $$, meals included.* Bernie Mittelstaedt and Lore Castillo have created a enchanting hotel on their giant lakefront property just a few miles from San Andrés. Four stone and wood cabins with thatched roofs are furnished with comely Guatemalan textiles, furniture and art. All the cabins have a view of the lake and are spaced far enough away to offer maximum privacy. The on-site restaurant has an amazing ambience and the food served is excellent. If available, be sure to try their *chiclero* chicken that uses herbs and spices from the rainforest. Bernie also owns Monkey Eco Tours and is considered one of the best tour guides in the area. He offers a number of excellent excursions to remote sites. The best way to communicate with the lodge is through their website at www.nitun. com.

El Remate

◆ History

El Remate is a small village community on the east end of the lake. It's also on the same road as Tikal, which makes it a good place to stay if you are planning to visit the ruins. It is generally more tranquil and cleaner than Flores, with nicer hotels and restaurants at half the price. The Cerro Cehaui Biosphere, just outside of town, offer spectacular hiking and nature trails. This side of the lake is also cleaner, making swimming more pleasant. Fishing and kayaking trips are also available (see below).

◆ Getting Here

Public **buses** leave from Santa Elena several times a day, while *colectivos* (minivans) leave hourly from both Santa Elena and the international airport. **Taxis** can be hired for about Q100. The ride takes about 20 minutes, depending on traffic. If you are coming from Belize you will probably be dropped off in El Cruce Ixlu and from there you can either walk the remaining 1.5 miles or take a bus or taxi.

◆ Adventures on Foot

Hiking in Biotope Cerro Cahu

Cerro Cahui means giant crocodile in Mayan. Originally created in 1981 by Guatemala's University of San Carlos for the purpose of studying local flora and fauna, this 1,608-acre (650.73-hectare) reserve has more than six miles (9.65 km) of well-maintained hiking trails. It covers lakeshore, ponds and mature forest and is home to more than 60 species of trees, 28 species of mammals and 300 species of birds. Two trails lead to the top of **Cerro Cahui Mountain** to lookout points (*miradors*). From atop you can see the whole of Lake Petén Izta, as well as two smaller lakes nearby,

Macanche and Sal Itzá. Río Ixpot and Río Ixlu flow through the reserve, along with two smaller streams, El Tigre (tiger) and El Pollo (chicken). Both trails take three or four hours to complete.

The dock at the entrance to the park is an excellent place to swim and enjoy a picnic. English-speaking guides are available for about Q200 and offer a three-four-hour trip with explanation on the plants and animals. If you want to trek deeper into the jungle, visiting a gorge, the rivers and other areas of the mountain, check with **Santiago Billy** at the Mon Ami Hotel & Restaurant. He offers tours starting at Q150.

The park entrance fee is US $2.50. Open hours are 6:30 am until dusk. It's a 30-minute drive from the Flores Airport or a one-mile (1.5-km) walk from El Remate along a road that follows the lake. You can also hire a *lancha* (boat) for Q350-500 from Flores to take you across the lake to Cerro Cahui.

> **TAKE NOTE:** *In the past, robberies on the trails were a problem. However, the community of El Remate hired a special tourist police force to patrol the area and the trails are now quite safe.*

◆ Adventures in Nature

Birdwatching in Biotope Cerro Cahu

Biotope Cerro Cahu (above) is home to more than 60 species of trees, 28 species of mammals and 300 species of birds, including toucans, parrots, hummingbirds, woodpeckers, owls, ocellated turkeys, red macaws, jaribu storks and crested eagles. You may also see spider and howler monkeys in the trees above.

Several rivers drain into the lake and are favorite nesting spots for many birds, including the jabiru stork. The **Río Ixpop** has some of the best birding in the region. Francisco from La Casa de Doña Tonita offers a two-hour birdwatching tour via the lake to the river nesting area. There's a minimum of two people and the cost is Q120 per person. You can also arrange a tour at La Casa de Don David (page 188) for the same fee.

◆ Adventures on Wheels

Biking Around the Lake

The road around the lake is a decent unpaved country road. Other than some dust from the speeding shuttle bus on its way to the Camino Real (a major bone of contention with locals), the route is pleasant for biking. An excellent day-trip is to follow the road all the way around the lake, visiting San Andrés and San José, and ending in Flores. You can return on the local bus to El Remate. Biking along the main highway is not recommended since there is no shoulder and everyone speeds. Bicycles are complimentary for guests of La Casa de Don David and Casa Roja Eco-Lodge (see pages 188 and 189). There are rumors of a bicycle rental place opening up in the village, so ask around.

◆ Adventures on Horseback

A three-hour horseback ride with a local guide should cost between Q70 and Q105. You can choose where to go, but popular trails include those in the Cerro Cehai and surrounding areas. The best place to organize a tour is through La Casa de Don David (page 188).

◆ Adventures on Water

Crocodile Tour

Lake Petén is home to the endangered Moreletti's crocodile that, fortunately, doesn't hang about the shores of El Remate. Instead, it prefers its own company and that of the lake fish to tourists. A two-hour tour can be arranged with La Casa de Don David (page 188) or La Casa de Doña Tonita with Francisco. On the trip, you visit nearby rivers where the crocodiles make their home. There's a minimum of two people and the cost is Q150 per person. Advance notice is appreciated.

Kayaking

The tranquil waters of Lake Petén are perfect for kayaking. Mornings, when the temperature is much cooler, is the best time. Several of the local hotels rent kayaks at very reasonable prices that run about Q10 per hour (less on longer rentals). Check with La Casa de Doña Tonita and La Casa de Don David (see page 188).

◆ Where to Stay

El Remate has an abundance of pleasant and economical hotels ranging from $ for a basic bed to $$$ for fancier digs. Most of them don't have a phone and reservations are usually not needed. If one hotel is full they will recommend another hotel and point you in the right direction.

❖ HOTEL PRICING
Prices are per person.
$ . . . . Under $25
$$ . . . . $26 to $50
$$$ . . . . $51 to $85
$$$$ . . . . $86 to $125
$$$$$ . . . . over $125

Camino Real, *Lake Petén Road*, ☎ /fax 502/2-337-0009, *www.caminoreal.com*, *72 rooms*, *$$$$*. This fancy hotel is located within the Biotope Cerro Cahui on the outskirts of town. Rooms are spread among seven pyramid-shaped buildings. Ground-level units have garden views, while those on the middle and top floors have a view of the lake. The rooms are rather generic, with cable TV, comfortable beds and luxurious bathrooms. You may forget you are in the jungle. Included are use of kayaks, a pool, windsurf boards, sailing, fishing and daily excursions into the reserve. Two **restaurants** serve decent food and there's also a bar. The electricity here is from a generator that can be quite loud – check the noise level in your room.

La Casa de Don David, ☎ *502/7-928-8469, www.lacasadedondavid. com, 9 rooms, $$, meals average US $4.50.* This comfortable and welcoming hotel is a landmark in the village. Don David, one of the original settlers, has 25 years of experience in the area and graciously shares his knowledge. Rooms are homey, with lots of hot water (it costs a little extra) crisp linens and good beds. All guests have access to a beautiful garden that faces the lake. In the main building is their excellent restaurant, which serves good home-cooked meals and daily specials. The wide open-air terrace also overlooks the lake and is a popular spot with locals and tourists alike. You can book tours here, buy bus tickets and exchange money.

Hotel le Mansion del Parajo Serpiente (House of the Serpent Bird), on the Main Hill, ☎/fax *502/7-926-4246 in Flores, 10 rooms, 1 bungalow. US $20 per person, US $75 for bungalow.* This idyllic oasis is tucked away on a cliff overlooking the lake. The views are incredible and the higher you go the more breathtaking it gets. Each room has been elegantly decorated with handwoven bedspreads, rugs and locally crafted furniture. A verdant tropical garden filled with butterflies and orchids alongside a pool offers the perfect setting for a Garden of Eden vacation. For true romance, book the top bungalow and its outside Jacuzzi facing the lake. Meals are served on a charming open-air terrace. Owner Nancy Salazar is a pioneer and, if you are lucky, you may hear some of her tales about opening up the first hotel in Tikal and raising three children in the jungle.

La Lancha Village, *Lake Petén Itzá, past Camino Real.* ☎ *502/7-928-8331, www.lalanchavillage.com, 6 bungalows, $$.* This engaging eco-hotel is set on a hilltop overlooking Lake Petén about half an hour from El Remate. Six simple but chic bungalows are scattered throughout the property and each offers two double beds, overhead fans, private bathroom and a balcony with a lake view. There is a lovely pool set in the jungle and the main lobby has an open-air restaurant overlooking the property. The French owners have created a delicious and varied international menu. Swimming, lounging or going for jungle walks are the preferred activities at this tranquil hotel. Tours to the various ruins, including Tikal, Uaxactún and Ceibal, are offered at reasonable prices for guests.

There are several good budget hotels right on the main strip. None have phones or take credit cards.

Posada Ixchel, has three simple but clean rooms. $.

Hotel Bruno has comfortable rooms with shared baths for Q25. They also serve an early breakfast if you book one day ahead. $.

Lakeside

Farther down on the road that follows the lake are some funky hotels with great lake views.

Next door is **La Casa de Doña Tonita**, with five thatched-roofed rooms that feature double beds set out in dormitory style. A small restaurant serves basic breakfasts and lunch. This hotel has the largest dock and is the best place for swimming. A variety of excellent tours are offered. Doña Tonita is very popular with backpackers and fills up quickly. *15 beds. $.*

◆ Where to Eat

Restaurante Mon Ami, ☎ *502/7-928-8413, www.monami.com*, down the road from Casa de Don David on the way to Camino Real. This is an attractive restaurant located right by the lake so each table has a view. Owner Santiago Billy is usually on site overseeing the meals. The menu offers delicious fresh pastas with a variety of sauces, such as pesto, tomato or garlic. The salads and bruschetta are also excellent. Behind the restaurant are some nice bungalows for rent at US $20. Menu prices range from Q18 to 75.

La Casa Roja Eco-Lodge, no phone, has terrific vegetarian meals that include soups, salads and sandwiches all starting at Q10.

Maya Biosphere

The Maya Biosphere Reserve is an ecosystem of more than 6,000 square miles in northern El Petén. It encompasses the largest area of wetlands in Central America as well as the largest intact rainforest. Included in the Biosphere are five national parks: Tikal, El Mirador, Rio Azul, Laguna Del Tigre and Sierra Lacandón. There are also three wildlife reserves, also known as biotopes: El Zotz, Dos Lagunas and Laguna Del Tigre. Within these parks and reserves are an amazing array of wildlife that includes such endangered species as the jaguar, scarlet macaw, spider monkey and harpy eagle.

The most famous area in the Biosphere is Tikal. As the southernmost part of the park, it is also the most accessible. Close to Tikal are the ruins of Uaxactun and Biotope El Zotz.

North of Tikal, at the top of the Biosphere, are two more national parks: El Mirador in the west and Río Azul/Rio Bravo in the East. In between these two is the Dos Lagunas Biotope.

El Mirador National Park shares a border with the Calakmul Biosphere in the state of Campeche, Mexico, and the ruins of El Mirador are found here. Río Azul National Park, shares its border with the Río Bravo National Park in Belize and the ruins of Río Azul and Kinal are found here. No permanent residents live within either park and visitors are permitted for only short periods of time. Tours to this area are a combination of birdwatching, jungle trekking and horseback riding. You should be in excellent physical condition to visit this area.

The westernmost section of the Biosphere also shares a border with Mexico. The Laguna Del Tigre National Park encompasses the Laguna del Tigre Wildlife Reserve. Most of this reserve is closed to the public, but there an excellent tour along the Scarlet Macaw Trail. Directly below Del Tigre is the newest national park, Sierra Lacandón that joins onto the Parque Nacional Sierra del Lacandon in Mexico. Several famous ruins are found in this area, including Piedras Negras. It is also the entry point for exploring the Mexican ruins of Yaxchilán and Bonampak.

Tikal National Park

Tikal translates to "Where Spirit Voices are Heard." This famous ruin is located in the middle of Tikal National Park that is part of the Maya Biosphere Reserve. Here, magnificent jungle and wildlife can still be found. Amid the ceiba, zapote and mahogany trees are over 285 species of birds, troops of spider and howler monkeys, jaguars, pumas, ocelots, pecarry, small deer and other rare animals. Tikal is considered one of the most important Maya cities, as well as one of the largest. It is vast and has over 3,000 structures within a six-square-mile (9.65-square-km) radius. These include ball courts, palaces, streets, plazas, temples, baths and terraces, in addition to great pyramids. At least 14 different rulers from AD 320 to 869 have structures dedicated to them.

◆ Getting Here

BY BUS: There are no direct public buses to Tikal. You will need to reach Flores first, then catch one of the local **shuttles** that leave from the causeway every half-hour or so. Round-trip fare is Q42. If you are staying in El Remate, you can flag one of the tourist shuttles down coming from Flores or have your hotel arrange a taxi for you.

BY PLANE: There are no longer any direct flights into Tikal. You must first fly into the Flores International Airport and take a tourist shuttle from there (see the Flores section for more information on flights and ticket prices).

◆ History

Tikal appears to have been founded in 700 BC, although construction started as early as 500 BC. The pyramids in the Great Plaza were mostly completed by 100 BC. In its beginning, the city remained under control of **El Mirador**, its larger northern neighbor. At the same time it competed with its sister city, **Uaxactún**, for trade routes and territory. When **King Yax Moxh Xoc** ascended the throne around AD 230, the power of El Mirador had faded and he began building up Tikal. The dynasty Yax Moxh Xoc founded continued for decades. A series of brilliant leaders, all part of the great Jaguar clan, turned Tikal into the most powerful political and religious center in the Maya world. Great Jaguar created a powerful alliance with other cities in the highlands, including **Kaminaliju**. This alliance allowed Tikal to finally overtake Uaxactún. Soon after, it dominated trade routes north to the Yucatán Peninsula, west to Yaxchilán in Chiapas, Mexico, and south to Copán, Honduras. It would control these areas for over 1,500 years.

Tikal remained unchallenged until AD 456 when the city of **Calakmul** (now in Campeche, Mexico) attacked. This inspired other cities to rebel and began 137 years of battles that Linda Schele referred to as "Star Wars" in her book *A Forest of Kings*. In AD 562, Ah Ha (Lord Water) of **Caracol** attacked Tikal and brought the great city to its knees. Tikal remained crippled until **Hasaw Chan K'awil** or Ah Cacau (Lord Chocolate) ascended the throne in AD 682. Under his kingship the city experienced a renaissance. Lord Chocolate refurbished the main ceremonial areas and started building the famous twin pyramids Temple I and II. His son **Yik'in Chan K'awil** finished those temples and started Temple IV.

Tikal was abandoned in AD 900 and what brought about its downfall remains one of the greatest mysteries surrounding the Maya.

The jungle swallowed Tikal and it was forgotten for almost a thousand years. **Friar Andres de Avendano** is thought to be the first white man to see Tikal. His chronicle about his 1696 escape from Tayasal (now Flores) described passing through an ancient city filled with large white buildings and temples.

In 1848, a *chiclero* by the name of Ambrosio Tut showed Modesto Mendéz, the Governor and Magistrate of El Petén, the ancient city. Their report attracted a gaggle of explorers to the area. Serious investigation of Tikal began in 1881 when the famous archeologist **Alfred P. Maudslay** arrived. **Teobert Mahler** mapped the city from 1895 to 1904, but it was **Alfred Tozzer** who eventually completed the mapping. He worked at the site until his death in 1954. **Sylvanus Griswold Morley** also investigated the ruins from 1914 to 1937.

The ruins were first declared a national monument is 1931 and became a national park on May 26, 1955. The following year excavations began when the University of Pennsylvania and Guatemala government began the 14-year **Tikal Project**. In 1979, Proyecto Nacional Tikal continued their work unearthing hundreds of buildings including the Lost World Complex. That same year, Tikal was named an UNESCO World Heritage Site. In 1991 Guatemala and Spain began work to restore Temples I and V. Work was completed early in 2001.

Tikal remains one of the most famous Maya sites ever discovered and it attracts visitors from around the world.

❖ FAMOUS TIKAL EXPLORERS

❖ **ANDRES DE AVENDANO:** Considered the first white man to visit Tikal. In 1695, Avendano had been living with the Itzá when he discovered a plot to have him sacrificed by the seeming friendly King Canek. He fled the area and inadvertently stumbled onto Tikal while trying to make his way back to Merida in Mexico's Yucatán Peninsula. In his chronicles, he mentions passing through a city filled with grand white buildings.

❖ **AMBROSIO TUT & MODESTO MENDEZ:** Ambrosio Tut, a *chiclero*, rediscovered the ruins while in the jungles gathering the sap of sapodilla trees. He reported his finding to Modesto Mendéz, the Governor and Magistrate of El Petén. Together, Mendéz and Tut wrote a report for the Guatemalan government which was published by the *La Gaceta* newspaper. They employed Eusebio Lara to draw their discoveries. In 1853, the report was published in the Berlin Academy of Sciences' Magazine, introducing Tikal to European and American treasure hunters and scientists.

❖ **GUSTAVE BERNOUILLI:** In 1877 Gustave Bernouilli, a botanist from Switzerland, removed several lintels from Temples IV and I during his expedition. They are now on display at the Völker Kunde Museum in Basel, Switzerland. Unfortunately, he did this without permission from the Guatemalan government.

❖ **SIR ALFRED PERCIVAL MAUDSLAY:** Maudslay was the first to map and take photos of Tikal (the camera had just been invented during his visit in 1881-82). He was the first to start excavations by removing the 1,000-year-old vegetation from the Grand Plaza. He lived in the Five Story Palace in the Central Acropolis while working on the site. He spread awareness about the Maya civilization, publishing over 87 volumes. Maudslay is considered the father of Maya archeology.

❖ **TEOBERT MAHLER:** Mahler arrived in 1895 to draw a map commissioned by Harvard University's Peabody Museum. He worked on the map until 1904, but never turned it in. Although a respected German scholar, he thought nothing of drawing graffiti on one of the ancient walls where he was living. You can see his artwork in the Mahler Palace, located in the Central Acropolis.

❖ **ALFRED TOZZER:** Tozzer was sent by Harvard to complete Mahler's job in 1910. He took many photos and worked extensively at the ruins until his death in 1954.

❖ **SYLVANUS GRISWOLD MORLEY:** This famous scientist from the Carnegie Institution worked at Tikal from 1914 until 1937. He was instrumental in deciphering many of the Maya hieroglyphics inscribed on monuments. A small museum in the park is named for him and contains many artifacts found during the 1956 dig by the University of Pennsylvania.

The **Museo Sylvanus G. Morley**, a small museum, is found at the entrance to the ruins. It has an interesting collection of ceramics and artifacts found during various excavations at the ruins. There is an excellent stele of King Stormy Sky and a re-creation of Lord Chocolate's tomb with the original bones, seashells, pearls and ceramics found during the dig in 1957. Other items on display include an incense burner, ceramic platter and a miniature jade carving of a jaguar.

The **Stele Museum** houses the most important Tikal stelae. Many were suffering from erosion before being placed in the museum. Alongside the carvings is an exhibit showing how the Maya may have erected these huge stones. A second display, Called the Era of Exploration, was done by the Pennsylvania University and outlines all the digs at the ruins.

Nearby is the **Visitors Center** with a relief map of the ruins. There is also a restaurant, bathroom and gift shop. The center has an excellent map of the park for sale, as well as guidebooks and souvenirs. You can arrange for a guide here too, though guides aren't necessary to enjoy the ruins.

◆ Exploring the Ruins

COMPLEX Q & COMPLEX R

This is the first set of buildings you will find just off the entrance. Complex Q is a twin pyramid complex with some excellent Late Classic sculpture. Stele 22 shows Lord Chi'taam scattering corn and the glyphs give a detailed description of his life. On Altar 10 there is a carving showing a bound prisoner captured by Lord Chi'taam. It's only a short walk from here to the Great Plaza.

THE GREAT PLAZA

The Great Plaza is probably the most spectacular part of Tikal, surrounded by stelae, carved altars, ceremonial buildings, palaces and a ball court. It contains the famous twin pyramids, Temples I and II. Both are majestic examples of Late Classical architecture. It is thought that The Great Plaza was the focus of sociopolitical life at Tikal; various causeways connect each of the temples to each other and the Great Plaza.

TEMPLE I: Located at the east end of the Great Plaza facing the setting sun, Grand Jaguar Temple I was built in AD 734 to honor Lord Chocolate. Rising 155 feet, this pyramid contained a vaulted tomb with the remains of Lord Chocolate resting alongside 180 jade artifacts, 90 bones carved with hieroglyphics, shells, stingray spines and other sacred objects. At the top is a temple with three rooms and a corbel arch. In 1877 Gustave Bernouilli removed a carved wooden lintel showing a jaguar from this temple, along with a wooden lintel from Temple IV depicting Lord Chocolate with his son Yiki'in. Both are still on display in Basel, Switzerland's Völkerkunde Museum. Unfortunately, you can no longer climb Temple I – it's been closed for years because several people tumbled to their deaths.

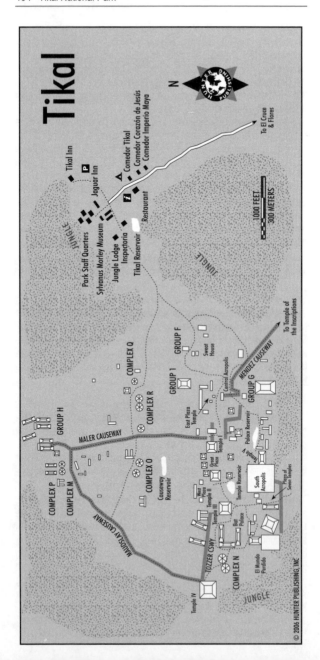

TEMPLE II: Built on the west end of the Great Plaza, Temple II faces the rising sun. It was the first temple to be completed by Lord Chocolate and appears to be a monument to his wife, Lady Twelve Macaw. It stands 122 feet (37 m) tall, shorter than its twin Temple I because of the missing roof-comb. You can still climb this pyramid for some impressive views of the city and surrounding jungle.

TEMPLE III: The Temple of the Jaguar Priest, or Temple III, was constructed in AD 810 and rises to 180 feet (55 m). The lintels here are the most intact of all those found at Tikal. Carved from the hard wood of the sapodilla tree (the same tree that produced sap for Chiclets gum) one lintel depicts a rather portly king dressed in jaguar skins. In front of the temple, resting by a stele with carvings of the water god Chaac, is a stone altar. Archeologists believe it may hold the remains of Lord Chi'taam, Tikal's final ruler. This was quite possibly the last great temple to be erected before its fall.

BAT PALACE: Near Temple III is the Bat Palace, also known as Structure 5C-13. This two-story palace is filled with stepped vaults and interconnecting rooms that have built-in benches and beds. Next door is Complex N, where Altar 5 and Stele 16 were found virtually intact. The originals are now in the visitor's center. The Tozzer causeway leading to Temple IV starts here.

TEMPLE IV: Temple IV, also known as Temple of the Double Headed Serpent, is Tikal's tallest pyramid standing 229 feet high (69 m). It was built in AD 740 by Lord Chocolate's son, Ah Yik'in Chan K'awil, and is considered his most ambitious construction project built to commemorate his father. The base of the pyramid is quite wide and midway up is an entrance to a small chamber. Archeologists believe Yik'in Chan K'awil is buried here. It's an easy ascent up a steel ladder to the summit. From the top, you can see the tips of Temples I and Temple II.

TEMPLE V: Constructed around AD 750 and rising to 187 feet (57 m), Temple V is the second-largest building in the park. During an excavation by Guatemala's Instituto de Antropolgia e Historiá (IDAEH) a royal tomb was discovered here with the remains of an unknown ruler. A 10-year restoration project recently completed by IDAEH rebuilt the temple stairs, allowing visitors to scale the pyramid.

TEMPLE VI: Temple VI is located south of the Mendéz Causeway and is believed to have been built around AD 766 by Ah Yik'in Chan K'awil with the inscriptions finished during the reign of Lord Chi'taam, Tikal's final ruler. At the base of the temple are Stele 21 and Altar 9, which records Yik'in's ascension to the throne. But the temple's real claim to fame is the rear central panel of the 40-foot roof-comb, which contains one of the longest inscriptions found at Tikal with 186 glyphs each two feet high (.6 m) and three feet (.9 m) wide. Some archeologists believed this to be Yik'in's tomb, rather than Temple V.

❖ CAUSEWAYS

❖   Named after famous archeologists who worked at Tikal throughout the years, these causeways or paths connect the various sections of the ruins with each other.

❖   **Mendéz Causeway**: Connects Temple VI (Temple of the Inscriptions) with Group G (Palace of the Grooves). It continues along to Structure 41 to the North Palace of the Central Acropolis, eventually reaching the back of Temple I.

❖   **Mahler Causeway**: Connects Complex P and Group H with Complexes R and Q, continuing on to the East Plaza in the North Acropolis.

❖   **Tozzer Causeway**: Connects Temple III in the Grand Plaza to Temple IV.

❖   **Maudslay Complex**: Connects Complex P, M and Group H with Temple 4.

❖   **Morley Causeway**: Gives access to the Bahren Group.

NORTH ACROPOLIS: The North Acropolis contains a royal necropolis with eight funerary temples one on top of the other dating as far back as 800 BC. The acropolis was built atop an artificial terrace that supported ceremonial buildings. Nearby Stele 31 contains a detailed list of the early rulers and historical events during this period. The tomb of King Curl Nose First Crocodile (AD 379-429) held the skeleton of a crocodile with a carved jade head, three turtle and bird skeletons, stingray spines, shells and several effigy vessels. Nearby Burial 48 contained the remains of Stormy Sky (AD 429-456) alongside two young men, obviously sacrificial victims. Thirty pottery vessels, stingray spines, shells and green obsidian objects were found nearby. Another tomb was found dating back to 100 BC. It contained the remains of a noble woman, along with paintings, jade, shells and other precious objects. The most impressive finds are the two 10-foot masks: the first mask is found under a thatched roof and the second down a short passage. You will need a flashlight in order to see the masks.

CENTRAL ACROPOLIS: This was a huge complex of residential and administrative palaces inhabited by the royal families of Tikal. There are 45 buildings and six courtyards that stretch over 370 acres. Each ruler added his own buildings, so there are layers upon layers of construction here. The best preserved are the home of Jaguar Claw I, Mahler Palace and Five Story Palace. In the past, these buildings were home to the first archeologists who came to Tikal during the 19th century.

SOUTH ACROPOLIS: The South Acropolis has several enormous buildings with seven different platforms that has led archeologists to believe it dates back to the Pre-Classic period. However, it remains to be excavated and studied.

EAST ACROPOLIS: Found behind the Grand Plaza. Archeologists believe this was the location of the ball courts and the main market.

Mundo Perdido (Lost World Complex)

The Lost World has 38 structures arranged in a traditional Maya pattern that indicate this section was an astronomy complex. The broad Great Pyramid is almost 100 feet high and was built between AD 250 and 300. Underneath are four other pyramids, the oldest one dating back to 600 BC, making it one of the oldest pyramids in Tikal. Delicate samples of ceramic pottery were also uncovered here and are on display at the National Museum in Guatemala City (see page 58).

> **AUTHOR WARNING:** *Although robberies have become rare in the park with the introduction of tourist police, you should still exercise caution on some of the more remote paths. Hire a guide, travel in a group and check with the visitor center and with other tourists to see if there are any areas in the park experiencing trouble.*

Practicalities

Children under age 12 may visit at no charge; adults are charged Q70. If you arrive at the park after 3 pm your ticket is good for entry the following day. You should plan for a two-day visit, as it's difficult to see everything in one day. Bring plenty of water and wear sturdy walking shoes, especially if you intend to climb any of the pyramids. Stay out of the sun between 1 and 3 pm, when the heat is the most intense. Try to visit the ruins early in the morning or late in the day, when it's cooler.

◆ Where to Stay

There are three hotels and a campground in the park. All are booked well in advance, often do not honor reservations and will charge higher prices when they are busy. None is a good value, especially considering electricity and hot water are limited. Staying in El Remate may be a better option. However, if you

❖ HOTEL PRICING	
Prices are per person.	
$	Under $25
$$	$26 to $50
$$$	$51 to $85
$$$$	$86 to $125
$$$$$	over $125

are keen to see Tikal at night or in the early morning, then staying overnight is the best way to go. Don't bother trying to convince the guards to let you sleep atop one of the pyramids. It's been forbidden since gangs of backpackers (who all read the same guidebook) started using the Temple IV as a crash pad and ended up defacing the whole area.

Jungle Lodge (Hotel Posada de la Selva), ☎ *502/7-926-0519, fax 502/476-8775, www.junglelodge.guate.com, 46 rooms. $$$.* This attractive hotel was originally built to house the archeological team in Tikal. The deluxe rooms are in duplex bungalows, each with a private bath, two double beds and private patios looking out into the jungle. The smaller and more economical rooms with shared baths are in a separate location. Landscaped jungle paths lead to the main building and a restaurant, bar, lobby and swimming pool shaped like a temple.

Hotel Tikal Inn, ☎ *502/7-926-1917, 24 rooms. Main building: $$$*. Located near the airstrip, this hotel offers rustic rooms with thatched roofs, private baths and Guatemalan décor. The rooms attached to the main building are cheaper and noisier than those in the bungalow. The main building has a charming pool and restaurant surrounded by a lovely garden.

Hotel Jaguar Inn, ☎ *502/7-926-0002, fax 502/3621-4098. Rooms $$; campground $*. The smallest hotel in the park is located next to the museum. The rooms are very rudimentary, equipped with a double bed, clean bath and ceiling fan. There are also dormitory-style beds (four to a room), as well as a small campground with outdoor bathroom facilities. Tents are supplied. 9 rooms.

Tikal Campgrounds, *by entrance and airstrip, no phone – first come, first served, $*. These are by far the cheapest accommodations in the park. During the dry season, camping out can be a pleasant experience; you lie in your tent listening to howler monkeys, birds and other jungle animals. The campground is actually a large open lawn with a few trees and some concrete platforms with palapa roofs and space for hammocks (bring your own). Camping equipment can be rented at the visitor center.

◆ Where to Eat

It's slim pickings and high prices. Most restaurants are located in three small buildings to the right of the park entrance. Known as *comedores*, these small diners serve simple Guatemalan food. The best of the bunch is **Imperio Maya**. Here, the meal of the day is usually roast chicken, rice, salad and fruit, for about US $6. Others include **Comedor La Jungla Tikal, Comedor Tikal, Comedor Sangrado de Jésus** and **Tienda Angelita**. The visitor center also has a restaurant but it is grossly overpriced and the food is terrible.

Uaxactún Ruins

Uaxactún is another one of the older Maya cities, first settled around 900 BC. The oldest stele found in the Maya world, dating back to 328 BC, was found here, leading researchers to believe this is where the Maya perfected their writing system and created their first calendar.

◆ History

The city had the misfortune of being only 12 miles (19.31 km) north of Tikal. As the cities grew, so did their rivalry. For years, the two cities lived as peaceful neighbors under the domain of **El Mirador**, a larger and more powerful northern city-state. However when El Mirador declined in AD 230 an intense competition sprung up between Uaxactún and Tikal. On January 16, AD 378, **Great Jaguar Paw** led his army into Uaxactún carrying a new weapon supplied by its distant ally Teotihuacán in Mexico. It was a spear thrower that allowed warriors to attack from afar. Uaxactún didn't stand a chance. It was defeated and came under the control of Tikal. It would not be free until AD 562, when Lord Water of Caracol brought Tikal to its knees, leaving Uaxactún free to rule itself. Like many Maya cities, Uaxactún was eventually abandoned by AD 900 and was covered by the jungle.

The city was rediscovered in 1916 by the famous team of **John Lloyd Stephens and Frederick Catherwood**, but remained untouched until **Sylvanus Morley** began major excavations during the 1920s and '30s with help from the Carnegie Institute of Washington. Morley came up with the name Uaxactún – Maya for "eight stones" – from an inscription found in a stele. Despite a major plan developed by the Guatemalan government in 1928, which included an airstrip being built, Uaxactún never blossomed into a major tourist attraction. Ironically, it is often added as a supplement tour to Tikal – it continues to live in the shadow of its sister city even today.

◆ Exploring the Ruins

Uaxactún is largely an unrestored site most famous for its small Pre-Classic pyramids decorated with simple stucco masks representing the sun god. It possesses some of the oldest and best-preserved stelae in the area. Ten of the 13 stelae uncovered date back to the Early Classic period (AD 300-500) when the first stone monuments were erected and stucco was used to decorate temples. The Late Classic period (AD 590-889) saw many new structures built with plazas and terraces, decorated with even more elaborate stucco.

The first structure seen by the entrance is a small residential **palace** with a simple layout from the Early Classic period. Nearby is a more complicated **acropolis** with an un-excavated temple that offers a view of the surrounding area. Near the entrance to a broad causeway is **Stele 5**, which records the famous battle that brought Uaxactún under Tikal's power. This leads to Group B and **Structure B-XIII**, which has a beautiful mural dating back to the Classic period (AD 600-900). It depicts a woman on a raised platform surrounded by 25 other figures. Following this is the main **palace**, **acropolis** and Group A , which includes a series of temples and residential compounds layered one upon the other. Some well-preserved stelae are also found here.

Structure E-VII-B in Group E is the most impressive of the buildings, with a four-sided stairway flanked by huge masks and covered with stucco. Three additional **pyramids** align along this eastern edge. It is thought these buildings were used as astronomy labs as the equinox and solstice can be accurately calculated by sighting the sunrise from the eastern stairway.

The modern community of Uaxactún consists of 140 families who survive by hunting and harvesting allspice and xate (a palm used in flower decoration). Through the help of ProPetén, ☎ 502/926-1370, the locals have become active conservationists who recognize their unique role in preserving the forests. By starting up Uaxactún's Forest Society and sponsoring eco-tourism, residents hope to maintain their 80-year record of no timber being cut from the land.

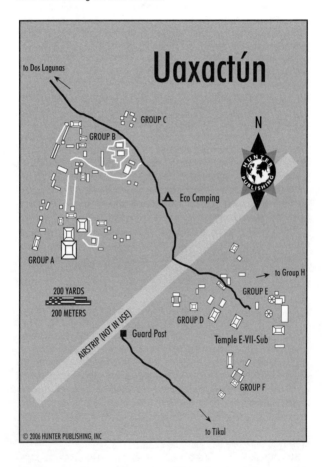

◆ Tours

Uaxactún's hiking and horse trails are open all year and the road from Tikal to Uaxactún has recently been upgraded. Locals offer a variety of tours through the ruins and into the surrounding jungle.

> ### ❖ UAXACTUN TOUR OPERATORS
>
> If you speak some Spanish you can book a tour directly with the tourist collective in the village of Carmelita, **Cooperativa Integral de Comercialización**, Comité de Turismo, Carmelita, San Andrés, Guatemala, Central America, ☎ 502/7-861-0366. There are also several tour companies in Flores and El Remate offering tours to Uaxactún. Prices depend on the number of people and length of stay. Day-trips are the most popular tours. Prices start at about $40.

◆ Where to Stay

Eco-Lodge El Chiclero Camp, in Carmelita Village, no phone, Q30 per person. This is, literally, the only place to stay in town. It has seven double rooms and four singles in small cabañas, which are made with wood from the Bajareque tree and covered with thatched guano palm leaves. There is also a campground with hammocks and mosquito nets.

Their small museum, **Museo Juan Antonio Valdes**, has a good collection of about 350 artifacts (shell, jade, bone and ceramics) dating back to the Pre-Classic period (250-550 BC).

Biotope El Zotz

In Mayan, zotz means "bat," and this biotope was created to protect the thousands of bats that live in the cliff-caves deep in the rainforest. The area is also home to a rare form of anteater, as well as a number of birds, jaguars and howler monkeys. The **Zotz-Tikal trail** is one of the newer trails developed to encourage eco-tourism in the area. It starts at Tikal Park, passes near the bat caves and ends in the small jungle community of El Crucea a Dos Aguados. The actual site of El Zotz has only a few structures and few have been excavated. The most important is the **Pyramid of the Devil** (Pyramid del Diablo). Although covered with mud and moss, you can climb del Diablo where, on a clear day, you can see the pyramids of Tikal. But the real draw in this biotope are the bats that emerge from their caves at dusk, momentarily blackening the sky.

This area requires a special permit to visit so you must book a tour. A typical tour starts in Flores and travels by jeep to Cruce dos Aguadas and continues on pack horses for five hours to the Zotz campgrounds. The bat caves are visited in the evening. The next day you visit the ruins and then take a three-hour jungle trek back to Tikal.

❖   EL ZOTZ BIOTOPE TOUR COMPANIES

Check with **ProPetén**, Calle Central, ☎ 502/7-926-1370, fax 502/7-926-0495 in Flores – they arrange most of the tours along with **EcoMaya**, Calle 30 de Junio, ☎ 502/7-926-4981, www.ecomaya.com. **Monkey Tours-Ni'tun Eco-Lodge**, ☎ 502/7-926-0493, www.nitun.com, in San Andrés, and **La Casa de Don David**, ☎ 502/7-928-8469, www. lacasadedondavid.com, in El Remate also offer excellent tours to this site. Prices start at $145 and vary according to the length of the tour, number of people and time of year.

El Mirador National Park

El Mirador is one of the largest and most important Maya sites. Historians, researchers and archeologists are just beginning work on this massive ancient city and much remains to be explored and deciphered.

◆ History

El Mirador was one of the very first Maya cities, estimated to be over 2,000 years old. The city flourished as a trading, religious and political center from 200 BC to AD 230, dominating all other cities in the area. Because of the large concentration of structures – three square miles covered with massive buildings – archeologists estimate there were over 80,000 people living in this ancient city. Despite its importance, few tourists visit El Mirador and, unfortunately, only the main group of buildings flanked by two massive pyramids has been excavated.

◆ Exploring the Ruins

The city center is marked by two large complexes facing one another. **El Tigre** is the western pyramid. Rising to 141 feet (43 m) and almost 18 stories high, it has a base that is 14 acres wide, the equivalent of three football fields and six times the surface area of the giant Temple IV at Tikal. Directly in front of El Tigre is the **Central Acropolis**, where burial chambers were unearthed. Inside were bodies painted red and surrounded by stingray spines, obsidian lances and other objects of the bloodletting rituals. The Danta complex is found at the site's east end on a natural rise in the land. It has a bottom base that supports three platforms. The widest platform is 68 feet (20.72 m) high and is topped off with three pyramids. Measured from top to bottom the complex is 229 feet (69.79 m) high – one of the tallest in the Maya world.

On April 18th, 2002, the area was recognized as a special archeological zone, and President Alfonso Portillo signed legislation establishing the **Mirador Basin National Monument**. It is hoped the decree will protect El Mirador from the increasing problem of looting and encourage more excavation of the site.

◆ Tours

This site is not easily reached and, unless you speak fluent Spanish, you should book with a tour agency. Most tours take five days and are a combination of horseback riding and hiking. Accommodations are offered in tents or hammocks. Tours depart from Flores by jeep and travel to the small village of Carmelita, 40 miles (64.37 km) north of Flores. Prices range from US \$200 to 300 per person, depending upon the number of people and length of your trip.

> ### ❖ EL MIRADOR TOUR OPERATORS
>
> For tour information contact **ProPetén**, Calle Central, ☎ 502/7-926-1370, fax 502/7-926-0495 in Flores, or **EcoMaya**, Calle 30 de Junio, ☎ 502/7-926-4181, www.ecomaya.com. **Monkey Tours-Ni'tun Eco-Lodge**, ☎ 502/7-928-8469, www.nitun.com, in San Andrés also offers tours to El Mirador. Confident travelers can catch a bus to Carmelita from San Andrés and book their own Spanish-speaking guide for about US \$120. You will have to bring your own food and camping gear. Whichever way you go, you are required to have a local guide accompany you on the trails.

Southeast of the Maya Biosphere

Poptún

Poptún is a municipality made up of 17 small Maya communities. Poptún, the city, is located exactly halfway between Flores and Río Dulce. This area is at the foothills of the Maya Mountains that extend into Belize, and it offers a number of limestone caves in the pine forests and surrounding jungle. Two major rivers – the **Machaquilá** and **Mopán** – provide great swimming and waterside camping. Poptún itself doesn't have much to offer, but a number of lovely eco-lodges offer interesting accommodations and great tours of the area. This is a good place to stop and catch your breath while traveling from Guatemala City to Flores or to Río Dulce.

◆ Ixcún & Ixtontón Maya Ruins

Both of these small ruins are part of the 10-year-old Archaeological Atlas of Guatemala (*Atlas Arqueologico de Guatemala*) project that is gradually mapping the 200 archeological sites in the southeastern Petén. Both sites have received only an initial excavation. Ixcún is half an hour from Poptún near the village of Dolores. It has several nice stelae dating back to AD 790. Stele 1 shows a ruler in ceremonial garb, complete with a head-dress of quetzal feathers. It's set alongside a large ceremonial center with three plazas, an unrestored temple and an acropolis. Several other unrestored structures can be seen in the South Group. The site appears to have been abandoned in AD 800. Ixtontón, a sister city, is four miles from Ixcún along Río Mopán. Initial excavations and research have led archeologists to believe it was major political power and central trading center occupied well into the 11th century. More work is required before the full history can be deciphered.

◆ Adventures on Foot

Caving

There are dozens of caves in this area. However, unless you are an experienced caver, it's best to hire a local guide. Many of the caves are located in the jungle and reached along trails that are difficult to follow. Your hotel can make the necessary arrangements for you. Guided tours usually start at Q50 per person. The only equipment needed is a good sturdy pair of shoes and a flashlight. If you want to go spelunking, you'll need to bring along your own equipment.

NAJ TUNICH CAVES

The Naj Tunich caves are 18 miles (29 km) outside the town of Poptún. They were discovered in 1979. From top to bottom, the cave's sheer rock walls measure 1.8 miles (three km) long and are covered with sacred texts and ancient Maya drawings. People must have painted these markings while suspended from ropes or ladders. The Naj Tunich caves are considered one of the finest examples of ancient Maya cave art and are still considered a sacred entrance to the underworld, Xilbalba, where nine lords reigned. Sadly, vandals defaced some of the paintings in 1989 and some of the caves were closed. They have only recently been opened and all visitors must obtain a special permit from IDAEH to enter. Most local guides have permission to enter and can supply you with your permit. You can't go on your own.

SAN MIGUEL CAVES

Two caves are located near the unexcavated ruin of San Miguel, 15 miles (24 km) from Poptún. The **Cave of the Offerings** (*Cueva de la Ofrecimiento*) was named for the many ceramics and other objects discovered alongside handprints on the walls. The **Cave of the Paintings** (*Cueva de la Pinturas*) has several charcoal drawings of human and animal figures with geometrical designs. The trail to this cave is difficult to navigate. Hire a guide. Contact Finca El Tapir or Villa de los Castellenos (pages 206) for specifics.

LAS CONCHAS CAVES

Las Conchas are a series of caves just off Río Machaquilá. The most impressive is **River Cave**, which has spectacular underground rapids and waterfalls.

Ixobel Cave has some fantastic limestone stalactites and stalagmites. **Echoing Cave** is found along a jungle path and has several hidden chambers and caverns. These caves are close to the Finca Ixobel, ☎ 502/927-7363, which offers tours (see page 206). Prices range from Q15 to Q65 per person.

Machaquilá Forest Reserve

Machaquilá Forest Reserve extends from the village of the same name along Río Machaquilá to some small ruins. The river is an excellent place to swim, with a moderate current and small rapids. Most of the eco-lodges in the area offer guided tours and rent inner tubes for floating along in the river. Trips usually include lunch and transportation and cost about Q85. See *Where to Stay*, below.

The **Machaquilá Ruins** are notable for the finely preserved stelae found here. Not much has been revealed about the nature of this city. The nobility seen on the stelae are richly adorned with jade and other precious metals, suggesting this may have been a prosperous trading center. On Stele 1, dating from AD 630, a young nobleman stands grasping a scepter adorned with jewels and jade. His clothes are heavily embroidered and he is crowned with immense plumes from the quetzal bird. Another carving shows K'inich Chakt'e Ha Ho'Bak, the fourth governor of Machaquilá, wearing a headdress with images of the Maya God Chaac while holding a scepter. There are 106 glyphs on this stele. From what has been deciphered so far, they appear to tell the history of the birth and ascent to the throne of a leader known as Bacab. More research is needed with these glyphs, since Bacab was also a god in the underworld. Also in the glyph is reference to a total eclipse of the sun on June 26, AD 800. The city appears to have been abandoned shortly after that date.

◆ Adventures on Horseback

This area is a combination of pine forest and savanna, making it perfect country for horseback riding. Jungle horseback treks range from short two-hour trips to all-day rides and overnight excursions. They all follow the same trails, and the overnight trips go farther into the jungle to a small camping area by Río Machaquilá. A day-trip usually includes lunch and beverages, while an overnight trip includes hammock, camping gear and all meals. Costs are Q70 for a two-hour trip, Q150 for the all-day trip and Q350 for an overnight trip. Book with **Finca El Tapir**, 3a Calle, 4-74, Zona 3, Poptún, ☎ 502/5-491-9943, 7-927-7327, or **Villa de los Castellanos**, Village of Machaquilá, ☎ 502/7-927-7222, fax 502/7-927-7365.

Finca Ixobel also offers a three- or four-day jungle and camping trek that goes deep into the unspoiled jungle. You travel to the campgrounds by horse and spend the next two days exploring on foot. A local guide offers a botanical tour of the forest where you will learn about the different kinds of plants and animals. You'll also explore a series of caves with Maya pottery and bones. Many have exotic names: **Cave of the Cemetery** (La Cueva del Cementerio), **Cave of the Sacrifice** (La Cueva del Sacrificio), and **Cave of the Mouse** (La Cueva del Ratón). You sleep in hammocks either inside a hut or strung between two trees (check with your guide first). Tasty campfire food is prepared Maya-style, over an open flame. This is an excellent adventure for those who like camping. The three-day trip costs US $75 and the four-day trip costs US $100 (there's a two-person minimum on both trips). Rates include horses, guides, food and all gear.

◆ Where to Stay & Eat

Finca Ixobel, *3 miles south of Poptún,* ☎ 502/5-410-4307, 7-927-8027, *www. fincaixobel.com, 12 rooms, campgrounds, $$.* The very famous Finca Ixobel offers a variety of accommodations but, like many tourist zone hotels, it is often overcrowded and overpriced (it even charges to swim in the river).

❖ HOTEL PRICING	
Prices are per person.	
$	Under $25
$$	$26 to $50
$$$	$51 to $85
$$$$	$86 to $125
$$$$$	over $125

Backpackers gather here in search of the camaraderie that has made Finca Ixobel so well known. The "cool" factor can get overwhelming at times. However, the surrounding pine forest at the foothills of the Maya Mountains is idyllic, and there's an excellent restaurant and bakery serving fresh bread and vegetarian food. Payment is on the honor system, where you cash in your tab upon departure. (Beware, as its adds up fast – average costs is Q100 per day.) The farm offers a number of tours – swimming, caving and horseback riding – at slightly higher prices than normal. If you are on a budget, check at some of the other eco-lodges for better prices. Also, keep in mind that you will be isolated here and must pay for transportation coming and going (which is also overpriced).

Finca El Tapir, *3a Calle 4-74, Zona 3, Poptún,* ☎ *502/5-491-9943, 7-927-7327, 12 rooms, $.* This small campground offers dorms or private rooms in a rustic setting. The accommodations are somewhat secondary to the real focus – eco-tours. The most popular is a jungle trek through a virgin tropical rainforest that includes visits to Maya caves, lessons in the local flora and fauna, swimming and horseback riding. A one-day horseback riding tour costs Q135. Their four-day tour by horse and foot is Q530 (on foot only is Q450). There's also a four-wheel-drive tour for Q530. The staff at the *finca* are really helpful and eager to please. No credit cards.

> **AUTHOR TIP:** *The smaller hotels, especially those in the more remote areas, will only deal in local currency. They do no accept credit cards and if you insist on paying with American dollars your rate of exchange will be lousy. If you plan to travel to the more remote areas, bring small denominations of quetzals. Reservations are not needed for the most part unless you are planning to travel during a very busy season such as to Antigua during Holy Week or to Esquipulas during the January dedications to the Black Christ. Hotels also fill up during the annual patron saint celebrations so you should check ahead before heading out, whether your intended village has anything happening or not.*

Villa de los Castellanos, Village of Machaquilá, ☎ 502/7-927-7222, fax 502/7-927-7365, 12 rooms, $$. This delightful eco-lodge is built on 12 acres of privately owned land right on the banks of Río Machaquilá. The cabañas are made with all natural materials and have thatched roofs, electricity, private baths and two or three double beds. The lodge was built around a lush botanical garden created by Dr Castellanos. It has the most extensive collection of tropical flowers in the area. The owners are devoted conservationists and guests are invited to participate in their reforestation programs. To date, the lodge has planted over 14,000 trees in the area, including Spanish cedar and mahogany. The lodge runs a variety of tours to nearby caves, a river-tubing trip and an excursion to Machaquilá Forest Reserve.

> To read about the local flora and fauna in the area, pick up a copy of **The Ecotraveller's Wildlife Guide, Belize and Northern Guatemala**, by Les Beletsky, Natural World Press.

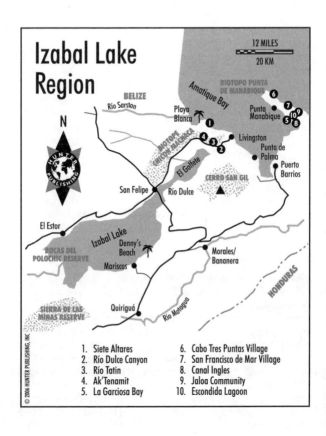

Izabal Lake Region

12 MILES
20 KM

BELIZE

Río Sarston

Amatique Bay

BIOTOPO PUNTA DE MANABIQUE

N

HUNTER PUBLISHING

Playa Blanca

Punta Manabique

⑥
⑦
⑨
⑤ ⑩
⑧

①

BIOTOPO CHOCÓN-MACHACA

④ ③ ②

Livingston

Punta de Palma

El Golfete

CERRO SAN GIL

Puerto Barrios

San Felipe

Río Dulce

El Estor

Izabal Lake

Denny's Beach

BOCAS DEL POLOCHIC RESERVE

Mariscos

Morales/ Bananera

HONDURAS

SIERRA DE LAS MINAS RESERVE

Quiriguá

Río Motagua

© 2006 HUNTER PUBLISHING, INC

1. Siete Altares
2. Río Dulce Canyon
3. Río Tatin
4. Ak'Tenamit
5. La Garciosa Bay

6. Cabo Tres Puntas Village
7. San Francisco de Mar Village
8. Canal Ingles
9. Jaloa Community
10. Escondida Lagoon

Izabal

The department of Izabal has the only stretch of eastern coastline in Guatemala. Due to its proximity to Belize, the area has a distinct Caribbean feel and is perfect for all kinds of watersports, birdwatching, fishing and jungle treks.

CHAPTER HIGHLIGHTS	
➤ Morales-Bananera	210
➤ Río Dulce/El Relleno/Frontera	216
➤ El Golfete	219
➤ San Felipe	226
➤ Lívingston	229
➤ El Estor	235

Lake Izabal is located in the middle of the department. At 227 square miles (590 square km), it is the country's second-largest lake. It's fed by a number of tributaries, including Río Polochíc in the west and Río Dulce in the east. A number of small communities surround the lake. **El Estor** is the largest community on the northwest shore and the town of Río Dulce is the largest on the northeast corner. **El Golfete**, where Río Dulce widens into a bay and eventually meets the Caribbean, is where you will find the Garífuna village of **Lívingston**.

South, on the coast, is the **Bahía Amatiqué**, where the ports of **Puerto Barrios** and **Santo Tomás de Castillo** are found. At **La Ruidosa** the department turns inland toward Morales and Bananera, where the small but beautiful ruins of **Quiriguá** are buried amid banana plantations.

Since this department has both fresh water and the ocean, its main activities are water-oriented. There are miles of waterways to explore and you'll see many yachts moored in the bay. The Río Dulce has been declared a national park and is the gateway to exploring the Petén.

> **AUTHOR NOTE:** Río Dulce is, of course, a river. However, there is a town by the same name and, just for good measure, the entire area is referred to as Río Dulce

Getting Here & Getting Around

Transporte Litegua, Lineo D'Oro and Fuente del Norte offer the best service to Izabal. If you are going to Río Dulce you will have to switch buses at either Morales or at Puerto Barrios. The trip to Río Dulce takes six hours, while the trip to Puerto Barrios is eight, unless you catch an express bus, which is six hours as well. Tickets are between Q25 and 40.

> **Transporte Litegua** leaves Guatemala from 15 Calle 10-45 Zona 1, Guatemala City, ☎ 502/2-251-7092 or 2-253-8169, in Flores 502/ 7-930-5251 . They post their daily schedules on their website, www.litegua.com.

Fuente del Norte leaves from 7 Calle 8-46, Zona1. Buses leave for Izabal four times a day but you will have to check for the times at the station.

Linea D'Oro runs first-class bus service to Izabal. Buses leave three times a day from 17 Calle 9-36, Zona 1.

For shuttle services you can choose from:

Servicios Turísticos Atitlan, 1a Calle Poniente #9, Antigua , ☎ 502/7-832-8581, %/fax 502/7-832-1493, turisticosatitlan@yahoo.com.

Sin Fronteras, 5a Avenida Norte#15A, ☎ 502/7-832-1017, fax 502/7-832-8453, www.sinfront.com.

Turansa, 9a Calle inside Hotel Villa Antigua, ☎ 502/7-832-2928, ☎/fax 502/7-832-4692, www.turansa.com.

Guatemala Reservations/Rainbow Travel Center, 7a Avenida Sur #8, Antigua, % 502/ 5-212-3943, fax 502/7-832-8587, nancy@guatenmalareservations.com.

Río Dulce is reached by **Carreterra Atlántico**, CA-9, the main highway from Guatemala City that passes through Montagua Valley before heading north to the Río Dulce and, eventually, Flores. Most of the secondary roads in this department are in poor shape.

Local transportation is water-based. Dinghies, skiffs and *lanchas* (speedboats) serve as water taxis shuttling between hotels on the river or up to Lívingston. You won't have any difficulty finding a boat – in fact, the boatmen will approach you.

> **AUTHOR TIP:** *A new map produced by the Rio Dulce Tourism Committee has the most up-to-date telephone numbers, services, hotels and restaurants. Look for the map in any of the local travel agencies.*

Morales-Bananera

◆ History

The twin towns of Morales and Bananera are company towns created by the former **United Fruit Company** – Guatemala's original evil empire. When bananas made their way to America in 1890, there was no direct distributor. In 1899, the **Boston Fruit Company** approached railroad baron Minor C. Keith to form the United Fruit Company in order to set up a distribution network. They spoke with several countries in Central America and were granted huge tracts of land in Guatemala. They built a railroad, supplied jobs to the locals and promised to pay taxes. In the meantime, the company built a monopoly that was so powerful it controlled the very destiny of the country. It made Puerto Barrios its major port and all railroad lines led there. Of course, United Fruit controlled the lines and no one else had access to railroads or port without paying exorbitant rates. The company built a small city in the middle of the banana plantation just outside of Bananera. It had schools, shops and grand mansions, but workers lived in the town as virtual prisoners, working long hours in harsh conditions with low pay. The caste system in place meant that whites were always deferred to and a Maya employee could be fired for not raising his hat in respect.

By 1930, the United Fruit had gained so much control over Guatemala's commerce, social system, politicians and economy that it was nicknamed *El Pulpo* (The Octopus). Like most evil empires, it took more than it gave, but its most heinous crime was interfering in Guatemala's democracy movement and setting the stage for the civil war. On October 20, 1944, Guatemala elected the liberal government of Jacobo Arnez, who was sympathetic to land reform, labor unions and free elections. The new government demanded that United Fruit Company start paying taxes (which it had avoided since it began its operations), improve working conditions and return large tracts of unused land to the government. United Fruit Company, frightened it might lose revenue, used political ties in Washington to convince the Eisenhower government that Guatemala was turning communist. In 1954, Congress backed a CIA invasion from Honduras that placed the right-wing dictator Carlos Castillo Armas back in power. Jacobo Arbenz was forced to flee the country, democracy was put on hold and United Fruit Company was back in the saddle. The invasion prompted an investigation by the US Department of Justice and, in 1958, United Fruit Company was forced to return some land and businesses to Guatemala. It merged with United Brands in 1960, but that company collapsed in 1972 and all holdings were sold to **Del Monte**. The subverted liberal movement was to resurface in the country as the leftist guerilla army.

Del Monte is still running the banana plantation, but now at least the workers are free to live where they wish and both wages and working conditions have improved. You can still see the plantation when you visit the ruins of Quiriguá, which also used to be owned by *El Pulpo*. Del Monte maintains its offices, housing, schools, medical facilities, a botanical research laboratory, an airstrip and a golf course.

◆ Quiriguá Ruins

The small city of Quiriguá is the only ruin of its kind in Guatemala. Its giant 3-D stelae covered with exquisite Maya glyphs and zoomorphic carved stones closely resemble the ruins at Copán, Honduras. It is considered one of the most beautiful ruins and is a UNESCO World Heritage Site. Luckily for you, it remains one of the least-visited ruins in Guatemala.

History

The name Quiriguá is from the **Cakchiquel Maya**, meaning "sweet corn" or "sweet food" in reference to the fertile lands that surround the city. Little is known about the early history of this site. It appears to have been settled in the Late Preclassic period between 250 and 300 BC, quite possibly by the **Putun Maya**, who migrated from the north. Hieroglyphics indicate that from AD 300-600 it was a satellite city of Copán. Valued for its trade route on the Río Motagua, Quiriguá developed into a trade center because of its close proximity to jade mines of the Sierra de Las Minas. The city reached its peak during the Late Classic period.

Quiriguá was an ideal location for carving, making use of the large brown sandstone deposits along the banks of the river. Carvers from Copán, Honduras, trained the artists of Quiriguá, which accounts for the similarities in style. There are a number of references to Quiriguá in the stelae of Copán, particularly those associated with the famous **18 Rabbit**. In AD 725, 18 Rabbit placed one of his protegees, **Cauac Sky**, on the throne in Quiriguá. Cauac returned the favor by declaring war on Copán and capturing 18 Rabbit in AD 737, eventually beheading him after keeping him captive for 18 years. Cauac Sky commemorated the beheading of 18 Rabbit and Quiriguá's independence from Copán on the giant stone Zoomorph G. This was one of the first public monuments he commissioned in his 38-year building campaign. He reigned for 60 years and gradually turned Quiriguá into the main power throughout the Motagua Valley. His son, **Sky Xul**, succeeded to the throne in AD 771 and ruled until AD 790 when he was challenged for the throne by Jade Sky. **Jade Sky** ruled from AD 790-840 and Quiriguá flourished during that time. Toward AD 870 the history of the city stopped being recorded and it was abandoned soon afterward.

Quiriguá remained untouched until 1841, when **John L. Stephens** visited. He described the ruins in his book, *Incidents of Travel in Central America, Chiapas and Yucatán* as, "unvisited, unsought, and utterly unknown." Stephens was so impressed with the carvings that he made plans to transport them back to New York. He conjured an elaborate scheme that involved floating the stones up Río Motagua to Puerto Barrios and on to New York by steamship. Fortunately, his plan was never realized as the owners of the site were asking more money than Stephens could afford.

In 1899 the United Fruit Company bought the surrounding land and turned it into a banana plantation. Fortunately, some of its executives were amateur archeologists and they kept the central plaza from being plowed over. In 1910, they designated the area an archeological park and organized the first major excavations under the direction of **Dr. Edgar Lee Hewett** of the Archaeological Institute of America. In 1914, Dr. Hewett organized an expedition to make casts of the stelae at Quiriguá, which he then introduced at a 1915 exposition in San Diego. These replicas are still used to measure the erosion of the originals and are currently on display at the San Diego Museum of Man. Few excavations were done after that. However, because the site was located in the middle of the United Fruit compound it was well protected from looters. In 1978, the University of Pennsylvania completed a major restoration, and in 1981 UNESCO declared it a World Heritage Site.

▶▶ *GETTING HERE: The ruins are 43 miles (70 km) from the Río Hondo conjunction and 58 miles (94 km) from Puerto Barrios. They are located in the middle of the Del Monte banana plantation. There is no public bus service so you must either walk the 2½ miles (four km) or hitch a ride with one of the minibuses that serve the plantation. If you are coming from either Guatemala City or Puerto Barrios, ask to be let off at the Bananera Road to the Del Monte plantation, also known as the Ruins Road. There is plenty of traffic at this crossroads so you shouldn't have to wait too long. A less complicated way to visit the ruins is to book a tour with one of the travel agencies in Río Dulce (see below).*

Exploring the Ruins

Though smaller than Copán, Quiriguá has much larger stelae. **Stele E**, the largest carving found in the Maya world, stands 35 feet (10 meters) tall and weighs 65 tons. The carving, which can be seen throughout the site, is quite impressive and, for the most part, extremely well preserved. The monuments are two basic types – the tall stelae have human figures carved on both sides and hieroglyphic text on the sides, and large, low altars carved into animal shapes with inscriptions on their backs and sides. Each monument is made from a solid block of stone.

GREAT PLAZA: None of the buildings have been cleared, so the main focus is on the impressive carvings scattered around the Great Plaza in an area 328 x 262 feet (100 x 80 meters). Most depict King Cauac in various stages of his life. **Stele D** shows the face of Cauac encircled by gods and animals with glyphs running down the sides. The carvings are so wonderfully executed that this stele was chosen to appear on Guatemala's 10-centavo coin. The monolithic **Stele E** is completely covered with carvings and has a bearded figure wearing a giant feathered headdress. This beard has been the subject of much debate – the Maya don't grow beards. Many of the figures on this stele are full-length and are holding the double-sided scepter, a symbol of royalty. On one end is a carving of Lord Chaac, god of water, while at the other end is the head of a great cosmic serpent. These stelae are so high that scaffolding may have been used to complete the carvings.

Another unusual feature of Quiriguá are the **zoomorphs**. These large blocks of stone have been carved with animal and human figures. **Zoomorph G**, in the center of the plaza, was carved in the shape of a jaguar and shows what is thought to be the beheading of Copán's 18 Rabbit. At the north end, Zoomorph P shows Lord Cauac sitting cross-legged in the mouth of a cosmic monster. Two other altars are carved in the shape of a frog and turtle. Archaeologists believe the zoomorphs were used as altars.

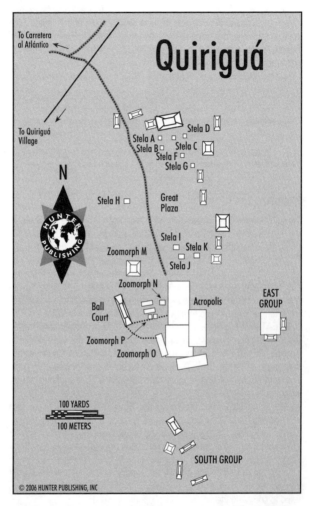

ACROPOLIS: The acropolis is located north of the Great Plaza. Steep stairs lead up to a spacious inner compound with the remains of four walls. This is thought to have been an administrative complex. At the north end are what's left of a palace inhabited by the various kings of Quiriguá. Multiple rooms with built-in benches are connected by passages. Most of the acropolis is devoid of carvings. The one exception is an elaborately decorated ball court wall showing images of K'inich Ahaw, the sun god.

Unrestored structures on the east side are thought to be the location of the old port of Quiriguá, where Río Motagua used to flow. The river has gradually migrated more than one mile from it original location.

The ruins themselves are quite small and can be seen in just under two hours. The main visitor center has a rather dull restaurant alongside an excellent little market selling souvenirs. The ruins are open from 8 am to 5 pm daily. Entrance fee is Q10 per person.

> **AUTHOR NOTE:** *Bring your bug spray and an umbrella. The mosquitoes are relentless here and short bursts of rain are the norm.*

IZABAL

❖ QUIRIGUA RUINS TOUR COMPANIES

An easy way to visit the ruins is to book a tour with one of the travel agencies in Río Dulce. Your ticket includes the entrance fee, lunch and transportation to and from the ruins. Carlos Chocón from **Atitrans Travel**, Turicentro Las Brisas, Río Dulce, ☎ 502/5-218-5950, has the best prices. Tours start at Q120 per person, but vary according to the size of your group.

◆ Where to Stay & Eat

There aren't any hotels close to the ruins or in Bananeras. Most people visit the ruins and return the same day to nearby Río Dulce or Puerto Barrios. If you decide to spend the night, the closest hotels are in the nearby villages of Los Amates and Morales. Unfortunately, most options are dismal and depressing.

❖ HOTEL PRICING

Prices are per person.

$	Under $25
$$	$26 to $50
$$$	$51 to $85
$$$$	$86 to $125
$$$$$	over $125

Hotel y Restaurante Santa Monica, *on the highway just before Los Amates by the gas station, 8 rooms, $.* This decent hotel has basic rooms with two double beds, cable TV and private bath that sometimes offer hot water. The restaurant serves hamburgers, hot dogs and other truck-driver specials. Since it's right on the highway, this hotel can get loud.

Hotel Del Centro, *Avenida Bandegua, Morales,* ☎/fax *502/7-947-8163, 6 rooms, $$.* Rooms are clean without much in the way of décor. All have private baths, overhead fans and two double beds. Rooms are overpriced, so use this hotel only if you are stuck.

Río Dulce

Río Dulce National Park is made up of the El Golfete region that extends to the Caribbean Sea and the area where Río Dulce meets Lake Izabal. The park also includes a half-mile (one km) strip on each side of the river where the twin cities of **Fronteras** and **El Relleno** are located. El Relleno is the smaller village on the south bank, while Fronteras, on the north bank, has more tourist services. The largest bridge in Central America connects the two cities.

The park has over 17,784 acres of wetland ecosystem where egrets, cranes, parrots, hummingbirds, birds, herons, orioles, and pelicans and five varieties of kingfishers come to nest. Smaller rivers, creeks and streams drain into the both the river and Lake Izabal and can be explored for miles in a dinghy or canoe through mangroves, hanging forests and grassy meadows. Sailing, kayaking, fishing and birding are favorite activities.

Unfortunately, the park is also battling an invasion by the aquatic plant *Hydra verticalla*. Although not native to the area, it is slowly overtaking the lake. Local conservationists have started a campaign to clean up the lake and visitors will be asked to participate by following guidelines set up to help eliminate this invasive plant.

Río Dulce, El Relleno, Fronteras

Poor Río Dulce. Not only does it share its name with the river and park, it manages to put its worst foot forward to newcomers. Its main street is actually a highway, CA-9, and it's a chaotic mess of shops, hotels and restaurants. It's often strewn with garbage and snarled with diesel trucks and buses. Aggressive and mildly menacing locals trying to sell boat trips swarm on you the minute you climb off the bus. Most people are so put off by the introduction that they allow themselves to be whisked off to Lívingston or catch the next bus out of town without stopping to explore the area. But once you get past the main drag, Río Dulce is quite lovely. There are some beautiful spots to be enjoyed and it makes excellent base for exploring the region and beyond.

◆ Getting Here & Getting Around

Río Dulce is an aquatic community. The main highway, **Carreterra Atlántico** (CA-9) passes through El Relleno and Fronteras. A smaller road leads to the nearby village of San Felipe and forks off to El Estor, a fishing village on the northwestern shore of Lake Izabal. **Boats** are used for transportation around El Golfete and the lake. Most hotels have a dock

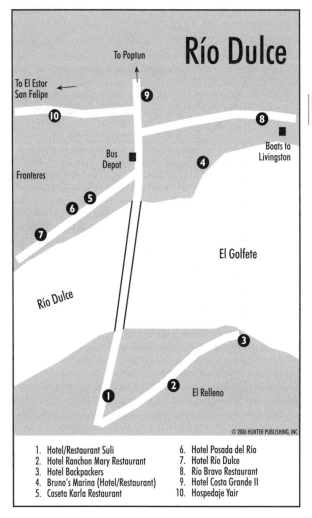

Río Dulce

To Poptun

To El Estor
San Felipe

Fronteres

Bus
Depot

Boats to
Livingston

El Golfete

Río Dulce

El Relleno

© 2006 HUNTER PUBLISHING, INC

1. Hotel/Restaurant Suli
2. Hotel Ranchon Mary Restaurant
3. Hotel Backpackers
4. Bruno's Marina (Hotel/Restaurant)
5. Caseta Karla Restaurant
6. Hotel Posada del Río
7. Hotel Río Dulce
8. Río Bravo Restaurant
9. Hotel Costa Grande II
10. Hospedaje Yair

and *lanchas* (speedboats) serve as the local taxis. They are plentiful and inexpensive; a typical ride will cost Q5-10 per person.

◆ Adventures on Water

Río Cienaga joins the Río Dulce a few miles north of town. It starts as a small lagoon and turns into a picturesque channel that travels north to pastures where cattle and horse graze. The waters of Río Cienaga are crystal clear and you can see six to eight feet (1.8-2.4 meters) to the bottom. The fishing along this river is excellent – snook (robálo), oscars (mojarra), river bass and catfish are plentiful.

> #### ❖ FISHING GUIDES
>
> Fishing trips can be arranged at the main dock or you can contact **Mar Marine**, Km 276 Carreterra al Atlantic, El Rellenos side, ☎ 502/7-930-5569, fax 502/7-930-5091, www.mar-marine.com.

◆ Adventures on Foot

Jardin Botanico el Ciricote/El Hormigo, Ek Cinicote, Río Seja, Km 282, Ruta al Petén, ☎ 502/7-930-2231, fax 502/7-930-5193, www.ciricote. com. Don Emilio Medizábal has spent the better half of his adult life cataloguing the plants in the Río Dulce region. He considers this his life work and has opened his botanical garden to share what he has learned. Trails lead through the verdant jungle he has planted with thousands of plants species. There are several different kinds of ferns, orchids and tropical flowers, as well as a fruit orchard that includes lemons, avocados and pineapples. A visit to the gardens includes an educational walk with Don Emilio who will tell you about the various trees, such as the Santa María (prized for its wood) and the chicozapote tree (*Manilkara achras*), extracts from which are used in the making of chiclets gum.

> **AUTHOR NOTE:** *Socks, shoes and long pants are a good idea for protection against bugs. Bring your bug repellent as well, since mosquitoes are plentiful.*

Probably the most fascinating find on the property is the petrified wood – there are over a dozen samples, several of which have been carbon-dated back 22 million years. The tour is best in the morning when the birds and butterflies are most visible. The two-hour tour costs Q35.

▶▶ *GETTING HERE: The botanical garden is 10 minutes north of Fronteras in the little community of Río Seja. Hop on any colectivo going north and ask to be let off at Km 282, near the garden. The ride will cost Q3 and buses run every five minutes. If you have a large group, Don Emilio may come and pick you up. You can also ask for a guide or directions at the Hacienda Tijax Express office by the main dock in Fronteras. Ask to speak with Carlos.*

Hacienda Tijax Nature Reserve and Rubber Plantation, 400 meters across the bay from Fronteras, ☎ 502/7-930-5505 or 5506, fax 502/7-930-5197, www.tijax.com. This reserve is part of a working farm that includes a hotel with an excellent nature trail. The one-mile (1.6-km) trail makes its way through a pristine first-growth forest filled with orchids, butterflies and many species of birds. It ends at a watchtower at the top of a hill, a spot that offers spectacular views of the entire valley. Horseback riding tours of the farm and surrounding natural sights are now available with a professional bilingual guide. Guided tours of the nature reserve are available for US $10.

The rubber plantation is located nearby. Visitors are invited to see how rubber is farmed and latex collected. It's a lovely outing that starts off at the marsh, travels past meadows and goes down into the valley. Close by is a teak plantation and a spring-fed lagoon. The rubber plantation tour is free.

IZABAL

❖ RUBBER HISTORY

The *Hevea brasiliensis* is a rubber tree native to Central and South America. Most of our rubber comes from petroleum, but 25 % still comes from these trees. The production of rubber in Guatemala began as early as 1736, when sheets of dried sap were sent to France. In 1791, when Samuel Peal discovered how to waterproof material by dipping it into a solution of rubber in turpentine, the industry began. In 1839, Charles Goodyear discovered the process of vulcanization, making the materials waterproof and heat resistant. Although it is not a large producer of rubber, Guatemala has the perfect weather for it, especially in the Río Dulce region which has heavy rainfalls and hot temperatures.

El Golfete

E l Golfete is a widening of the Río Dulce that forms a small bay 10 miles (16 km) wide and between six and 12 feet (9.6-19 meters) deep. The bay is dotted with small islands, most of them inhabited only by birds. Small bays, lagoons and rivers are found along the shore, which is where the majority of hotels are located. Farther east, as El Golfete starts to meet the Caribbean Sea, are several remote Indian villages, including the Garífuna village of Lívingston.

◆ Adventures in Nature

Cayo Grande

Cayo Grande (Large Island), at the east end of El Golfete, is uninhabited and humans are only allowed a short distance on shore. Visitors are not permitted to go inland. A variety of birds, including the colorful toucan, come here to nest. The best times to spot birds are at dawn and dusk; during the day the birds fly to other locations in search of food. You must approach the island by boat, travel through the mangroves to shore and walk a short distance in order to spot the wildlife. Boat tours of the Río Dulce or those going to Lívingston usually make a passing stop here.

Prices for tours start at Q75. You can ask any boatman at the main dock for a tour.

> **AUTHOR NOTE:** *Bring your repellent because the mosquitoes are plentiful and hungry.*

◆ Adventures on Water

El Biotópo de Chocón Machacas (Manatee National Park)

In 1976, Thor Janson conducted a manatee field study in the Río Dulce area and discovered it had the ideal conditions for this sea mammal. He also found that the sea cow was quickly being hunted to extinction. He presented his study to the Guatemalan government who responded by creating this 292-square-mile (7,600-hectare) reserve at the mouth of Río Chocón Machacas. A series of waterways accessible by boat winds through small lagoons and mangroves (the manatee's natural habitat). On land, a nature trail beginning at the visitor's center goes through forests where jaguars and tapirs live. Plants include a lovely combination of mahogany, palm trees and tropical flowers. Camping is permitted, but there are no services so you must bring your own equipment. Boat tours to the reserve can be arranged in Río Dulce and usually cost about US $10, depending on the number of people in your group.

❖ THE SHY MANATEE

Don't be disappointed if you don't spot any manatees. They are notoriously shy, and many locals believe they have left the area entirely. Manatees, also known as sea cows, are mammals that spend their entire life in water. They are a close relative of the elephant and can grow up to 2,000 pounds (907 kilograms). Originally unafraid of man and quite friendly, manatees are now shy and elusive. Can anyone blame them? They were once found in large groups throughout the Caribbean, but are now on the endangered species list after being hunted almost to extinction. Spotting a manatee takes a great deal of time and patience. The slightest noise can frighten them away. You must be willing to sit quietly for several hours in a dinghy or canoe in order to see one.

Hot Sulfur Springs

A few miles up the river, half-way between Río Dulce and Lívingston, is a volcanically heated spring that empties into the bay. You can see steam as the sulfurous hot waters meet the cool waters of the Río Dulce. There is a docking area where you can have a picnic and then relax in the hot and cold waters. Locals believe the water has curative powers. Boat tours of the Río Dulce or to Lívingston usually make a passing stop here. Prices for tours start at Q75 per person. If you want to stop and take a swim, let your boatman know ahead of time.

Río Dulce Canyon

At the point where El Golfete meets the Caribbean, the river narrows into a canyon of sheer limestone cliffs that tower 300-400 feet (90-120 meters) above the river. A living wall of long vines hang down from trees to meet the water and flocks of white heron roosting in the trees show as flecks of white in this canyon of green. The view is quite stunning. Since all boats pass through the canyon coming or going from Lívingston, no special tour is required. The boat to Lívingston, one-way, is Q75.

◆ Cultural Adventures

Asociación Ak'Tenamit

Founded in 1992, Ak'Tenamit is a non-profit organization working with the local Q'eqchí Maya communities providing education, healthcare and community development. They are using an innovative system where locals earn credits for their agricultural goods or manual labor. The credits can then be exchanged for schooling or health services. Using this method, the program has built a tourist facility, schools, clinics and a successful cottage industry that produces handmade paper products now sold throughout the area. Ak'Tenamit and two local Q'eqchí villages also run eco-tours in the area.

Río Tatín Ecotourism Center. This center in El Golfete is 20 minutes by boat from Lívingston and 35 minutes from Río Dulce. It sits beside a beautiful river with crystal-clear waters and is surrounded by lush tropical jungle. There's a small handicrafts shop and working area where women from nearby villages create their paper products and animal masks. Books, postcards, lamps, writing paper and masks are just a few of the beautiful items for sale. A 40-seat restaurant serves typical Maya and Garífuna meals, such as *pachai* fish (flavored with jungle leaves) or brochette of shrimp and vegetables. Prices are reasonable, about Q50 per person.

There are two trails to walk. One runs parallel to Río Tatín until it reaches a small waterfall where you can swim. Along the way, sit at one of the rest stops and try to spot some of the birds and animals around you. Plants and flowers have been labeled with small plaques. This self-guided tour takes about 20 minutes. A second path leads to Ak'Tenamit secondary school, where students from remote villages are offered the chance of education. The trails make for a pleasant afternoon outing.

Asociación Ak'Tenamit has been working with Mayan-Q'eqchí communities since 1992 developing alternative income for the locals. **Plan Grande Quehueche** started in February 2002 and offers several excellent jungle treks from three different locations: Lívingston, Siete Altares or

Ak' Tenamit. Accommodations for the two-day/one-night jungle treks are in a small jungle resort.

Day One: Hike to the Lodge: The shortest jungle trek starts in Siete Altares, just outside of Lívingston, and takes between 40 minutes and 1½ hours, depending on your fitness level. It's an easy, safe trail. You will have to rent a boat to take you to Siete Altares or use one of the *colectivo* boats. The second trail leaves from Lívingston and is another safe jungle trek that takes anywhere from two to three hours to complete. The third and most beautiful trail leaves from the Ak'Tenamit site. It passes virgin rainforest. Your guide will lead you to the Cave of the Tiger (*Cueva del Tigre*), the biggest cave in the area. It has a waterfall in front of its entrance and you must pass underneath or around that to get into the cave. The name refers to a giant jaguar that apparently lived in the cave for a number of years. There have been no recent sightings, but many locals are still reluctant to visit the cave. This trek takes about 1½ hours to complete. Local Q'eqchí guides will point out flora and fauna on the way.

Accommodations are in the village in a four-room guesthouse built in the local tradition. Rooms are shared – two beds to a room – and have crisp linens and screened windows. Bathrooms are also shared and use a special latrine system to avoid pollution. Since the village does not have electricity, everything is solar-powered. The kerosene lamps used at night add a romantic atmosphere. Beside the guesthouse is a small stream that's visited by animals at night – you may even spot a jaguar. Prices include all meals provided by the local women.

Day Two: Cultural Exposure: This is a day of cultural exposure. You can go caving and trekking deeper into the jungle, learn how to weave, make paper or carve. You're also invited to participate in the daily Maya ceremonies of music, dance, song and stories around a campfire. This is one of the most authentic tours offered and is an excellent opportunity to meet Mayan-Q'eqchí. All proceeds go to the community to help preserve their culture and way of life.

The tour is restricted to eight people at a time and no more than 30 per month. Prices are Q300 per person for all activities and Q225 for just the tour and overnight stay. For further information, contact www.aktenamit.org or Paco Enriquez at ecoturismo@aktenamit.org.

▸▸ *GETTING HERE: Ak'Tenamit is 20 minutes by boat from Lívingston and 35 minutes from Río Dulce. You can use one of the private motorboats that charge Q75 per person or jump on a colectivo boat that leaves as soon as it is full for Q30. Just be sure to let them know that you want to get off at Ak'Tenamit. If you are coming from Puerto Barrios, you will also have to pick up the boat in Lívingston. You don't need reservations to visit the center but you do need them for the overnight tours.*

> ❖ **VOLUNTEER PROGRAMS**
>
> Ak'Tenamit also has a highly respected volunteer program. Participants live with the Q'eqchí Maya and help with community development. For more information on volunteering contact: Asociación Ak'Tenamit, 11 Avenida A 9-39, Zona 2, Ciudad Nueva Ciudad de Guatemala, ☎ 502/ 5-902-0608, www.aktenamit.org.

Spanish School

Finca Tatín, banks of Río Tatín, ☎ 502/5-902-0831, www.fincatatin. centroamerica.com. Claudia and Carlos Simónini run this enchanting bed and breakfast Spanish school tucked away in the jungle. The property is surrounded by giant trees filled with exotic tropical birds. The Spanish lessons offered are high in quality and tailored to your needs. Accommodations are either in a dorm or one of five bungalows with private baths. Birding, swimming and lying in a hammock are the favored activities, but there are also some wonderful nature trails close by that follow the river and its tributaries. Cayucos (native canoes) rent for only US $2.50 per day. Tours to the other attractions including excursions to the local Q'eqchí villages, can be arranged. The *finca* is most easily reached from Lívingston. Call from there and they will come and pick you up. Spanish lessons are US $5 per hour, $120 per week.

◆ Where to Stay

All the hotels in Río Dulce are either along the main strip under the bridge or on El Golfete bay. Hotels on the river usually offer boat pick up at the main dock in Fronteras. The more economical hotels are found on the mainland.

> **AUTHOR TIP:** *Prices increase the farther upriver you travel. Competition is fierce, and some people will tell you your hotel has closed in order to get you to their hotel. Call your hotel of choice to check.*

Catamaran Island Hotel, *a half-mile downriver*, ☎ 502/7-930-5495 *or* 7-930-5559, *fax* 502/7-930-5492, *www. catamaranisland.com, 32 bungalows, $$$.* This is one of the oldest hotels on the Río Dulce, originally built to handle tourists from Belize. It has an old-style Caribbean feel to it. Private bungalows

> ❖ **HOTEL PRICING**
>
> Prices are per person.
>
> | | |
> |---|---|
> | $ | Under $25 |
> | $$ | $26 to $50 |
> | $$$ | $51 to $85 |
> | $$$$ | $86 to $125 |
> | $$$$$ | over $125 |

are offered with private baths and balconies that have a lake view. A pathway leads to the tropical gardens where there is a restaurant and a hideaway bar built over the river. You can amuse yourself in the swimming pool or on the tennis court, but the main lobby has the only TV on site.

Tours to local attractions, birding and fishing are offered for an additional charge.

Bruno's Marina, *foot of Río Dulce bridge, Fronteras side,* ☎ *502/7-930-5174 or 5-692-7292, www.mayaparadise.com/brunoe.htm, 11 rooms, $-$$.* Bruno's is popular with the party yacht crowd. It has a swimming pool overlooking the river and a nice restaurant (unfortunately, the food is bland). The building is a bit dilapidated. Still, second-floor rooms come with a great terrace overlooking the bay. They are furnished with single or double beds, a miniature TV, air conditioning and private baths. A smaller building has basic rooms in a bungalow with shared baths and there are also 10 dorm beds available – take these as a last resort.

Hacienda Tijax, *a quarter-mile (400 meters) across the bay from Fronteras,* ☎ *502/7-930-5505 or 5506, fax 502/7-930-5197, www.tijax. com, 5 rooms, 16 cabins, 4 bungalows, $-$$$.* Every town has a place with a bit of magic that grabs you and makes you stay longer than intended. Hacienda Tijax is that place in Río Dulce. This working farm is owned by Eugenio Gobbato, a passionate conservationist who rescued the land from slash-and-burn farming and turned it into a nature reserve with a nature trail and a rubber and teak plantation (see *Adventures on Foot*, page 218, for more details). Take your pick from private bungalows, cabins for three, single rooms and a camping area. The architecture is Thai style and rooms are simple and elegant. Walkways over the water lead to the restaurant and pool. In front is the marina. The restaurant here serves the best food in town. The lodge's Tijax Express will pick you up from the main dock free of charge. Prices include taxes, pick-up and drop-off from town and morning coffee.

Hotel Costa Grande II, *Fronteras Village,* ☎ *502/7-930-5063, 10 rooms, 4 bungalows. $.* This is a decent hotel in the heart of the village. It doesn't have much in the way of ambience, but it is, for the most part, clean. Cheaper rooms have a two single beds, private bath and fan. The private bungalows are equipped with air conditioning, TV, private bath with hot water and small sitting area.

Hotel Río Dulce, *at the foot of the bridge in Fronteras,* ☎ *502/7-930-5179 or 5180, 16 rooms, $.* This is probably the best budget hotel in the area. It's extremely neat and clean and the cozy rooms have large double beds, TV, fan and private bath. You can even get air conditioning for an additional fee. There is not much of a view and, since it's close to the bridge, it can get noisy. Ask for a room at the back. No credit cards.

Hotel Posada del Río, *near post office in Fronteras,* ☎ *502/7-930-5167, www.mayaparadise.com/hotelposada.htm, 9 rooms, $.* This cheery hotel underneath the bridge has a partial view of the river. Rooms are basic, but clean and comfortable, with queen-size beds, private baths and air conditioning. There is excellent security here and the family that runs the hotel is very kind. No credit cards.

Hospedaje Yair, *Fronteras village, road to San Felipe,* ☎ *502/7-930-5131, 11 rooms, $.* A simple hotel with tidy basic rooms but little ambience. Row accommodations open up onto a cement courtyard. All have a double bed, private bath (sometimes with hot water), air conditioning and cable TV. No credit cards.

Hotel Backpackers, *El Relleno, foot of Río Dulce bridge (south side),* ☎ *502/7-930-5480 or 502/7-930-5169, 2 dormitories with 40 beds in each,$.* Well – it's the cheapest place in town, which means it's very popular with backpackers who seem able to endure the impoverished foam beds in a large dormitory room with no privacy and brisk cold showers. The riverfront location is ideal, though, and the property even boasts a lakeside restaurant, a bar and Internet service. The staff isn't happy or helpful. No credit cards.

While staying at Hotel Backpackers, you may hear about Casa Guatemala Orphanage, which the hotel supports. There are rumors about whether the money actually makes it to the children, many of whom appear to be working here. The director has also started a rather controversial program where people pay to volunteer at Casa Guatemala. There have been reports of the volunteers being badly treated.

Denny's Beach, *south side Lac Izabal,* ☎ *502/7-398-0908 or 7-709-4990, VHF channel 63, www.dennysbeach.com, 5 cabañas, $-$$.* The only option on the south side of the lake. Dennis and Lupe Guick run this casual and rustic retreat that features a number of cabañas tucked into the jungle. You can take a bed in the shared dormitory or rent a private cabaña with its own bath. A camping area on the beach has spots where you can pitch your tent or hang a hammock. After Playa Dora, this is the prettiest beach on the lake. The hotel offers horseback riding and tours of the lake, although the favored pastimes are beach volleyball or hammock-lounging. If you are in Río Dulce, you can contact the hotel via their VHF channel – it's the main communication system used here and radios are found everywhere – to arrange a pick-up. Plan to return to town one morning as afternoon winds often make a later return impossible.

◆ Where to Eat

There are plenty of *comedores* in Río Dulce. Some serve simple, hearty meals, while others offer greasy fast food – enjoyable for the first few minutes before heartburn starts.

Río Bravo, *Turicentro Las Brisas,* ☎ *502/7-930-5167, fax 502/7-930-5044.* This dockside restaurant is the best on the mainland, serving terrific pizza and excellent ceviche. Also on the menu are delicious soups, sandwiches, pastas and fresh fish. Drinks are cheap and plentiful, and breakfast is a real bargain. Lots of people end up here because of its convenient location by the dock, where boats to Lívingston and other locations arrive and depart. Q14-45.

Hacienda Tijax, *across the bay from Fronteras,* ☎ *502/7-930-5505, 5506, fax 502/7-930-5197, www.tijax.com.* A great restaurant on the river serving delicious salads, sandwiches, pastas, chicken, steak and seafood. Vegetarians will be especially grateful for the tasty salads and wonderful fruit drinks. Everything is fresh and healthy – a nice change from the usual greasy fare. You also couldn't ask for a better locale either – you can dine overlooking the river and bridge. The staff is as charming as the surroundings. The Tijax Express will ferry you over for free. Q34-70.

Catamaran Island Hotel, *a half-mile downriver*, ☎ *502/7-930-5495 or 502/7-930-5559, www.catmaranisland.com*. If you feel the need to wear that special cocktail dress you brought along, then this is the restaurant to visit. It's got a posh bar where the dress will fit in. The food is decent. Notable dishes include fresh fish, steak and Caesar salad. The biggest selling point at the Catamaran is the romantic river setting. Q70-120.

Caseta Karla, *Fronteras, by the bridge, down from Posada del Río*. This little hole-in-the-wall *comedore* serves excellent grilled fish and grilled chicken. Tacos and coleslaw are the usual side dishes. It fills up fast because it's popular with the locals.

Bruno's Marina, *foot of Río Dulce bridge, Fronteras side*, ☎ *502/7-930-5174 or 520/5-692-7292, www.mayaparadise.com/brunoe.htm*. Come here for standard American fast food. Hamburgers and coffee are the best thing on the menu – avoid the salads. There's a well-stocked bar and a good sound system; folks tend to come here to hang out with other gringo party animals. Q25-65.

Hotel Ranchon Mary, *El Relleno, foot of the bridge*, ☎ *502/7-930-5013*. This open-air restaurant is popular with locals and the yacht crowd. It's nicely furnished all in wood (including the sinks) and serves food that, while not inspired, is consistently good. The hamburgers, club sandwiches and chicken are the best choices. The lakeside location is hard to beat. Perhaps this is reflected in the prices, which are a bit steep. Q40-75.

San Felipe

◆ Sightseeing

San Felipe Village is a small community two miles west of Río Dulce. There are a number of pleasant family hotels here and if you are looking for a quiet base this is the perfect spot. The community doesn't get nearly the same amount of traffic as Río Dulce – most people just come to see the castle.

▶▶ *GETTING HERE: A lovely walkway leads from Río Dulce to San Felipe. It takes about 45 minutes to reach the village. Alternately, catch one of the local colectivos leaving every half-hour from Río Dulce. Tickets are Q5.*

El Castillo (The Castle), a Spanish fort, is about 1½ miles (2.4 km) from the main bridge on a rocky point where the Río Dulce narrows before emptying into Lake Izabal. The towers and cannons against the background of palm trees and a tropical river should not be missed.

❖ HISTORY OF EL CASTILLO

Early in the 16th century when trade was set up between Spain and Guatemala, this area was known as **Golfo Dulce**. Marauding pirates sailed in from the Gulf of Mexico and Gulf of Honduras to plunder the warehouses. In 1595, the governor petitioned King Philip II of Spain for a tower equipped with 12 cannons and 12 soldiers to defend the trade route. Torre de Sande was completed a few years later, but it was destroyed by pirates in 1604. Pedro de Bustamante rebuilt the tower and it was named Torre de Bustamante in his honor. For the next 36 years pirates plundered the fort, damaging a different part each time. But the structure was too important to abandon so, in 1651, Judge Lara y Mogrovejo fixed it up and it became known as San Felipe de Lara Castle. During a 1655 lull in piracy the fort was turned into a prison, but by 1660 it was back in commission. A pirate community on Isla Tortuga became headquarters for Los Hermanos de la Costa (Brothers of the Coast), an international pirate community. For the next six years they pillaged the nearby Río Dulce area, usually stopping off to throw some cannon balls at the fort. By 1672 the fort was so badly damaged that General Francisco de Escobedo was ordered to restore it. He enclosed the entry and expanded the fort, but it did little good. During a 1679 raid on the settlement of Bodegas (now known as Mariscos), the fort was cleaned out.

After this spectacular failure the Spanish government commissioned Sergeant Major Diego Gomez de Ocampo to make the fort work. In 1684, he had just started renovations when the Dutch pirate Jan Zaques attacked the fort, stealing all its ammunition before setting it on fire. From 1684-88 the fort was rebuilt with more ramparts and room for 100 guards. This time, the Spanish finally got it right and for the next 58 years it successfully defended the Río Dulce. Sporadic attacks by English and Irish pirates took place on and off from 1737 to 1779, but there were no significant battles. The last attack on the fort was by a Colombian pirate in 1822. Commerce by then had shifted up the coast and the fort fell into disuse.

The fort remained abandoned until 1955 when the Guatemalan government hired architect Francisco Ferrús Roig to restore it. During an investigation of the General Archives of the Indies in Madrid Spain, he discovered some old fort plans that he was able to use to incorporate the different eras of restorations. The restoration team also uncovered historical artifacts, including the original cannons buried upriver. Visitors can see the original Torre de Bustamante tower alongside the 18th-century improvements.

IZABAL

Today, El Castillo is a tranquil spot. It's a major tourist attraction and offers tours in four different languages. The grounds have been turned into a lovely park with a visitor center, restaurant, pool and picnic area. A nearby dock takes boats arriving from Río Dulce. Open 8 am to 5 pm daily. Q10.

▶▶ *GETTING HERE: If you are staying in San Felipe village, El Castillo is within walking distance. If you are staying in Río Dulce, you can reach El Castillo by colectivo. They leave every half-hour and cost Q4. You can also hire a boat from Río Dulce to El Castillo for Q70 or take a tour of the lake for Q100 per person, which includes a visit to the castle, along with the entrance fee.*

◆ Where to Stay & Eat

All hotels are on the same route, Camino a Castilo de San Felipe de Lara – the only road in town. There aren't any restaurants except those found in the hotels.

Banana Palms, ☎ *502/7-930-5022 or 7-930-3940. $$$$$.* This is an exclusive resort located on the Río Dulce with luxury villas and sculptured grounds. Villas have private decks with river views, Jacuzzi, satellite TV, air conditioning, mini-bars and lavish bathrooms. The grounds have a pool, restaurant, game room and gardens. There is also a private dock with a yacht offering tours. 33 villas.

Hotel Viñas del Lago, ☎ *502/7-930-5053 or 930-5054, fax 502/7-930-5055, www.infovia.com.gt/hotelvinasdellago, 15 rooms, $$-$$$.* Is it the turquoise-colored rooms, the peach-bamboo décor in the dining room or the kidney-shaped swimming pool that makes you feel like you have stepped back to the 1950s? The grounds are quite lush with a small zoo and private dock.

Hotel Changri-La. ☎ *502/7-930-5467, fax 502/7-930-5468, 6 rooms, 2 bungalows, $$.* This is a modern hotel with pool and restaurant. Rooms are rather small but pleasantly decorated with lots of homey touches. All have air conditioning, cable TV and modern bathrooms with great water pressure and hot water.

Hotel Don Humberto, ☎ *502/7-930-5051 or 5052, $.* This is a cheery budget hotel within walking distance of El Castillo. The rooms are basic with a double bed, overhead fan and private bath with no hot water. 8 rooms. No credit cards.

Hospedaje La Cabaña del Viajero. ☎/fax *502/7-930-5062, 8 rooms, $.* A very amiable family runs this small hotel that resembles a bed and breakfast. Rooms in the main building have bamboo windows decorated with lace curtains and furnished with two single beds, fans and private bath. Small bungalows are similar but have small patios and hammocks. There is a minuscule pool with a pleasant palapa café. No credit cards.

Lívingston

Lívingston is a funky village on the Caribbean coast. It is like no other community in Guatemala, with a very Belizean feel, due to its close proximity to that country and the local Garífuna culture.

◆ History

The Garífuna have an unusual history. In 1655, two British slave ships carrying Africans from Nigeria sank off the shores of **St Vincent Island**. The slaves swam to freedom and settled alongside the **Arawak Indians** who were living on the island. The two tribes intermarried and their children became known as the **Garífuna**, or Black Caribes. By 1750, the Garífuna were numerous, prosperous and, for the most part, got along well the **French** colonists who had also settled on the island. In 1763, the **British**, who owned St. Vincent, decided to take back the most prosperous Garífuna farms. This led to the 32-year war. The French left in 1775, but the Garífuna lasted until 1796 when they were deported to the island of Roatan in the Gulf of Honduras. Roatan was owned by the Spanish, who would not allow all the Garífuna to remain. On April 12, 1979, they transported 5,000 men, women and children to the coastal town of Trujillo. From there, the Garífuna spread to Belize and Guatemala, bringing their own language, music, dance and religion.

Garífuna language and culture is a blend of African, Spanish, South American Indian, French and English. As a people, they are most famous for their drums, solid pieces of wood, hollowed out, carved with intricate patterns and covered with the skins of peccary or goats. The drummers use a lead-follow pattern, with one drummer beating a steady pattern while the other plays more intricate rhythms. The accompanying dances and songs are infectious. Their most famous dance is the *Punta*, where couples try to outdo each other in style and movement.

The Garífuna culture is one of the biggest attractions and Lívingston is experiencing some severe problems at the moment. It has become famous not only for its Garífuna culture, but also as a party town where you can get stoned or laid – not necessarily in that order. The influx of tourists has upset the balance in town and many jaded locals have started overcharging for services. Most disturbing are the violent crimes against tourists, which include rape and armed robbery. This is not the place to let your guard down, and you should save the heavy partying for home.

◆ Getting Here

You can reach Lívingston from either Puerto Barrios or Río Dulce. To avoid a rushed visit, plan to stay overnight. The last boats from Lívingston to the mainland leave at 2 pm.

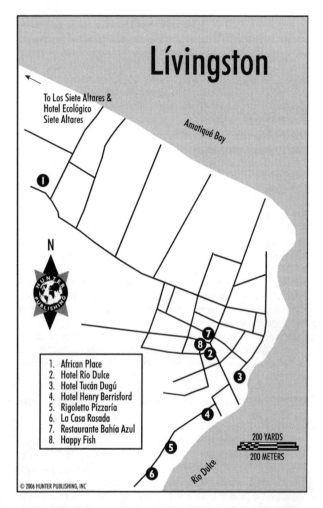

Lívingston

To Los Siete Altares &
Hotel Ecológico
Siete Altares

Amatiqué Bay

N

1. African Place
2. Hotel Río Dulce
3. Hotel Tucán Dugú
4. Hotel Henry Berrisford
5. Rigoletto Pizzaría
6. La Casa Rosada
7. Restaurante Bahía Azul
8. Happy Fish

Río Dulce

200 YARDS
200 METERS

© 2006 HUNTER PUBLISHING, INC

The cheapest way and quickest way to reach Lívingston is via Puerto Barrios. All boats leave from the municipal dock at the end of Calle 12. A public ferry leaves Puerto Barrios at 10 am and 5 pm. The trip takes 1½ hours and costs Q10. *Colectivo lanchas* (public speedboats) leave whenever the boat is full with between 12 and 15 passengers (they usually fill up quickly in the morning, but may take longer in the afternoon). The ride takes 40 minutes (longer if the weather is bad) and costs Q25. Some of the boatmen will try to overcharge. Stand your ground. If you are in a hurry or traveling with four or more people, consider hiring a private *lancha* for Q150.

Getting to Lívingston from Río Dulce is even simpler. Plenty of boats follow this route. In fact, you will get sick of being offered boat rides to Lívingston every time you walk the main street, and the bellicose boatmen are particularly overwhelming when you first get off a bus.

> **INSIDER TIP:** *Don't buy your ticket right away. A favorite trick (aside from overcharging) is to sell you a ticket and tell you the boat is leaving immediately. You trundle off to the dock only to discover you have a two-hour wait. Scheduled departure times for boats to Lívingston are 9 am, 1 pm and 2 pm. All other times are unscheduled, which means the boats leave only when they are have 10 passengers. Some boat operators load up at the main dock and then drive around the river picking up passengers from various hotels. This can easily add several hours to an already long trip.*

If you would like to stop and visit any of the El Golfete sites along the way, ask the boatmen about it *after you have paid for your ticket.* If you ask about a tour before agreeing on a price, they will add a fee without you realizing. You shouldn't pay extra for a stop at Sulfur Springs, Caye Grande or Cañón de Río Dulce, since these are on the way to Lívingston. Without any stops, the ride takes about two hours. With stops it can be anywhere from four to six hours. All tickets are Q75 and there is no room for bargaining. The return boat from Lívingston to Río Dulce is at 2 pm. A favorite route with visitors is to take the trip down Río Dulce and return via Puerto Barrios.

Navigating your way around Lívingston is really simple. There is one main dock at the foot of the hill. The street that starts there is the main street.

◆ Adventures on Foot

Las Siete Altares

Las Siete Altares (The Seven Altars) is a series of seven waterfalls three miles (five km) northwest of Lívingston. During the rainy season, each waterfall forms a small pool at its base – perfect for swimming (there are no falls in dry season). The falls get progressively more spectacular the higher you go, so that by the time you are at the seventh altar there is a giant pool. It's a slippery climb to the top and most people make it only as far as the third or fourth altar.

> **AUTHOR NOTE:** *Be careful if you plan to climb to the top – the rocks hidden by the water are treacherous. The lower cascades are easier to maneuver.*

> ❖ **INSIDER TIP: RED ALERT**
>
> The safer but less picturesque route is to take a boat and ask to be let off at the path leading to the falls. There have been quite a few armed robberies and rapes along the beach path to Siete Altares. Don't take this route alone or in small groups. Check with other tourists to see if there have been any robberies. If there have, avoid the area completely. Leave all money and valuables at your hotel, including your camera. Hire a boat to take you to the falls instead of walking. Restaurante Bahía Azul and Casa Rosada Hotel can refer you to a trustworthy guide. Prices start at Q50.

◆ Adventures on Water

Río Sarstún Reserve

Río Sarstún forms a natural boundary between Belize and Guatemala. It is an area of great bio-diversity, home to the endangered manatee, Colmenero bear, Moreletti's crocodile and sea turtles. It is filled with tropical forests, mangroves, estuaries and lagoons. Thanks to persistent lobbying by CONAP (National Council for Protected Areas) and FUNDAECO (Foundation for Sustainable Tourism and Conservation), 5,556 acres at the mouth of the river has been declared a national reserve. This area is bordered to the north by the Sierra Santa Cruz-Chocón Reserve and to the east by the Bahía de Amatiqué. Eventually, it will link up with Sarstún-Temash National Park in Belize and stretch down to Río Dulce National Park, making it one of the largest protected reserves in the area. FUNDAECO is now working on developing a local office in Lívingston that will offer eco-tours into the reserve and train local fishermen to act as guides. Until then, you can visit in a private boat that can take you as far as the Belizean border. You will see wildlife and pass a number of small communities along the way. Private tours start at Q100 per person, depending on the length of the tour and the number of people. Also, *lanchas* leave Lívingston when full and stop at small communities along the way. It takes 30 minutes to reach the river and tickets are Q20.

Playa Blanca

Just north of Lívingston, between Punta Cocli and Río Sarstún, is a lovely stretch of white sand with crystal-clear waters. Playa Blanca is the perfect place for sunbathing and swimming. It makes up for the disappointing beaches near Lívingston. There is even a small freshwater river nearby. The adjacent Hotel Túcan Dugú, which owns the beach, charges an entrance fee and offers security. The best deal is to take a tour with Restaurante Bahía Azul or La Casa Rosada Hotel, ☎ 502/7-947-0303, for Q90. It includes a visit to Las Siete Altares, Río Cocolí and Playa Dorada and comes with a packed lunch.

Cayos Sapodillas, Belize

The Belize cayes are part of the Great Maya Reef, the second-largest barrier reef in the world (Australia's Great Barrier Reef wins). The Maya Reef starts at the tip of the Yucatán Peninsula in Mexico and extends down into Honduras. Hundreds of small islets known as cayes run parallel to the Belize coast and offer relatively shallow and clear waters. The snorkeling here is incredible and you are often able to see the psychedelic marine life the reef has spawned. A number of tours are offered in town – someone will approach you to sell you a trip. The going rate is Q250 for a day-trip. You have to add on a US $7.50 conservation and a US $20 exit fee paid to the Belizean government. Ouch!

◆ Where to Stay

Hordes of young boys will be waiting to show you the way to a hotel the moment you arrive in Lívingston. They will eagerly carry your bags and recommend the best hotel in town. Of course, they receive a kick-back from the hotels, so don't feel obligated to follow them. If you do go with one, give a tip of Q4 or so. These boys can be pests but, for the most part, they are harmless.

❖ HOTEL PRICING	
Prices are per person.	
$	Under $25
$$	$26 to $50
$$$	$51 to $85
$$$$	$86 to $125
$$$$$	over $125

Hotel Túcan Dugú, *Barrio el Centro (Center neighborhood)*, ☎ *502/7-948-1572, fax 502/7-947-0614, 45 rooms, $$$.* This elegant hotel sits atop a hill up from the main dock. It has tropical gardens, a swimming pool and a bar and could easily be the setting for a novel. Rooms are located in a long, low Caribbean-style ranch house with a thatched roof. They are filled with mahogany furniture, bamboo and natural fabrics. Each has a little balcony overlooking the gardens. Guests have access to the lovely beach farther up the coast.

La Casa Rosada, *Barrio Marcos Sanchez Diaz, a half-mile left of dock,* ☎ *502/7-947-0303, fax 502/7-947-0304, www.hotelcasarosada.com, 10 rooms, $.* This is one of the nicest hotels in Lívingston and it's run by an American couple. It has a lovely riverside garden, a dock and a gazebo. Rooms are in palapa-roofed bungalows with overhead fans and a double bed equipped with a mosquito net. Bathrooms are all shared. The restaurant serves seafood and local dishes. Fishing trips and eco-tours are offered. No credit cards.

Rigolette Pizzeria & Guest House, *on the river a quarter-mile from the dock, 4 rooms, $.* The talented chef María from Mexico runs this little guesthouse and restaurant. Rooms are clean and cozy with shared baths. The nice eating area by the river is a great spot to enjoy the incredible food. No credit cards.

Hotel Henry Berrisford, *by port*, ☎ *502/7-948-1568l, 27 rooms, $.* Henry is not going to win any design awards for this lump of cement in the shape of a giant loaf of bread. The rooms are tiny, but functional, with TV, fan, private shower and double bed. Don't swim in the pool. It's not cleaned regularly.

Hospedaje Doña Alida, *Barrio Capitania, 2 blocks from center of town,* ☎*/fax 502/7-947-1567, 9 rooms, $.* This small hotel is just outside of the main circle and that makes all the difference. It's quiet and private with a gorgeous beach and nice restaurant. The rooms are modest, bright and airy. Some have terraces with ocean views and private baths. Breakfast is available upon request. No credit cards.

Hotel Río Dulce, *top of the hill, no telephone, 5 rooms, $.* Although this hotel has seen better days, it remains a good example of traditional Caribbean style. The two-story wooden structure is one of the oldest buildings in Lívingston. Check your room carefully. Some have mildew and look like they may have critters. Security has been a problem in the past. No credit cards.

◆ Where to Eat

Food has to be brought into Lívingston by boat so everything is more expensive than in other places. The fish and seafood here are incredible. Make sure you try *tapado* – a stew made from fish, crab, shrimp and other seafood that's been simmered with coconut, plantains and coriander.

La Casa Rosada, *Barrio Marcos Sanchez Diaz, a half-mile left of dock,* ☎ *502/7-947-0303, fax 502/7-947-0304, www.hotelcasarosada.com.* This hotel/restaurant has a lovely riverside garden where you can enjoy great vegetarian meals. Fresh fruit drinks and excellent salads are the specialty. Seafood and local dishes are also offered. Q48-64.

The African Place, *Barrio African Place,* ☎ *502/7-948-1585 or 1572.* A favorite place to hang out and watch the people go by. Banana pancakes are the house specialty (try them) and the coffee is really good. For dinner, the African Place offers a variety of local dishes, including *tapado. Q24-48. No credit cards.*

Rigolette Pizzeria & Guest House, *on river near dock, no telephone.* The best food in Lívingston is found here. Chef María can cook just about anything and offers an amazing menu of Italian, Indian, Chinese and Mexican cuisine. They use a woodburning stove for their tasty pizza. Take out is available. Q24-48. No credit cards.

Bahía Azul, *downtown, no telephone.* This is a popular tourist spot that serves good grilled fish and shrimp, as well as fish soup. If you're here at cocktail hour, try their potent piña colada. In the evening, authentic live Garífuna music fills the air. Bahía Azul offers eco-tours in the area. Q32-64. No credit cards.

Happy Fish Resort, *Main Street*, ☎ *502/7-947-0661, www.happyfish resort.com.* It's not just the fish that are happy here. Most tourists are thrilled with the breakfast menu of fruit and yogurt, pancakes, omelets and delicious coffee. Dinner offers a wide range of grilled seafood and fish. The Happy Fish also offers excellent tours in the surrounding area. Q15-60.

El Estor

IZABAL

This sleepy fishing village sits on the northwestern shore of Lake Izabal. For many years, the only way to reach it was by ferry from the other side of the lake, but a new, well-paved road starting at Río Dulce has opened up the area. El Estor is slowly emerging as a center for eco-tourism due to the many pristine rivers nearby and its close proximity to Biotópo Boca del Polochíc.

◆ History

The **Spanish** first settled El Estor as an out-of-reach storage depot. In the 17th century, Río Dulce was plagued by pirates who plundered whatever goods were on hand. To discourage them, local authorities created a storage facility area on the northwestern edge of the lake. Pirates had to first pass by the fortification, El Castillo, at the mouth of Río Dulce, to reach the area. The plan was only partially successful. In 1867, when piracy had declined worldwide, two **British** entrepreneurs, Skinner and Klee, opened a general store in the area. Since it carried the only European goods for miles around, everyone came to shop there. The Brits named their outpost The Store, which the Spanish-speaking locals pronounced as El Estor. The name stuck and the outpost gradually grew into a small, but isolated, community. The original store is now the Hotel Vista al Lago. In the late 1800s the coffee barons of Cobán, Alta Verapaz, built a railroad into the area to transport their coffee down from the mountains to the lake, where it then traveled to Puerto Barrios. The town enjoyed a boom until the main highway south became the new shipping route; El Estor then slipped back to being a sleepy community with fishing as its main source of income. Lake Izabal is the main supplier of freshwater fish in Guatemala.

In early 1960, high-grade nickel deposits were discovered close to El Estor and in 1965 the Canadian nickel giant, **INCO**, announced a mining project to be run by its Guatemalan subsidiary, Exploraciones Y Explotaciones Mineras Izabal, S.A. (EXIMBAL). In order to get a 40-year mining concession, EXIMBAL agreed to invest in El Estor. Over the next 13 years it built the community into a gem of a village with a town square, paved roads, electricity, a school and a medical clinic. However, due to lack of reliable transportation and technical problems, the mine and processing plant was not a success. In 1977 the plant closed, much to the relief of locals who had witnessed the decimation of the surrounding rivers and forests. The deserted mine and processing plant still stand alongside the prefabricated houses built for a workforce that never arrived. Its giant smokestack has become a landmark and residents use it as a reminder of the dangers of letting corporations manage the area. In the mid-1990s there was some discussion about opening the plant in order to mine cobalt from the mountains, but it was quickly abandoned when the community denied access.

Land conflicts and human rights abuses in El Estor have a long and violent history. Indigenous groups have frequently been the victims of illegal and bloody evictions, and those who advocate on their behalf have been subjected to threats and intimidation. In 1978, the nearby village of Panzo grabbed international headlines for a tragic incident when the Guatemalan army gunned down over 100 innocent men, women and children who were attending a community meeting on land reform. The brutality of the incident shocked the world and brought to attention the many human rights violations stemming from the Guatemalan government in the name of democracy and freedom. Amnesty International turned its eye on El Estor in 1999 when a prominent member of the community went missing. Carlos Coc Rax of the Centro para Accion Legal en Derechos Humanos (CALDH) disappeared on April 21, 1999 after working on a land conflict resolution for the local Q'eqchí. His murder has never been solved, but his death rallied the community. When the oil companies wanted to start drilling here, the community formed Amigos de Lago Izabal and successfully fought to keep the oil multinationals off their lake. Locals refused to be seduced by the promise of jobs and riches and proved to be quite savvy in public relations. They invited the president on a tour of the lake, after which he canceled the oil concession. Environmentalists across the county rejoiced. Locals are proud of their success and are now focused on developing eco-tourism to promote conservation and preservation of the area.

◆ Getting Here & Getting Around

El Estor is a 45-minute bus ride from Río Dulce. Buses leave every half-hour and costs Q10. This is the only public transportation to El Estor. The ferry boats from Marisco are no longer running, despite what various guidebooks say. The only way to reach El Estor from the other side of the lake is to hire a private boat. You can also hire boats in Río Dulce to take you to El Estor. Prices start at Q150.

An alternative route for those with strong stomachs and backs is the bus from Cobán, Alta Verapaz. El Estor is only 100 miles (150 km) from Cobán, but the road is so bad that the trip takes between five and seven hours. It travels through the beautiful and very scenic Polochíc Valley. You will probably be the only tourist on board.

> ❖   **MONEY-SAVING TIP**
>
> Bring plenty of quetzals with you to El Estor. American dollars are accepted, but at an extremely low rate. There are no ATMs and neither of the banks offer credit card advances. They accept only American Express traveler's checks. If you do get stuck for cash, your only option is to have someone wire you money via Western Union, which takes a whopping 10% cut. You pick up your money from Western Union at the local bank, just off the main square.

◆ Adventures on Water

Polochíc Delta Refuge

El Refugio de Vida Silvestre Bocas del Polochíc is unique. Three rivers converge on the western shore of Lake Izabal and drain into the lake. **Río Oscuro** (Dark River), named because of its color, drains in from the southwest corner and is a breeding ground for fish. Pristine jungles along the banks of the river are home to howler monkeys. **Río Zarquito** flows along the southern edge of the Polochíc Valley and joins Río Oscuro a few hundred feet up the shore. The water of Río Zarquito is clear, with small lagoons that are breeding grounds for manatees, as well as a bird sanctuary for the rufescent tiger-heron, olivaceous cormorant, snowy egret, ringed kingfisher, American white pelican, greater yellowlegs, least grebe, anhinga and the brown pelican. **Río Polochíc** extends from the Verapaces in central Guatemala down through the Polochíc Valley into Lake Izabal. During the wet season it carries silt and topsoil along its route, creating a delta that forms the second-largest freshwater wetlands in Guatemala.

There is great bio-diversity here – over 250 species of mammals, 350 species, 53 species of fish and 24 species of aquatic plants have been identified so far. Because it forms a biological corridor between the Sierra de las Minas and the Sierra de Santa Cruz, the Polochíc Delta is home to many endangered species. The corridor is part of the larger Mesoamerica Biological Corridor beginning in the Yucatán Peninsula and stretching down to the Panama Canal.

The refuge was declared a protected zone on June 11, 1996. It includes over 962 square miles of humid tropical forest bordered to the north and west by the Sierras de las Minas, on the south by Paxtanto Ruins and on the north by El Estor. The area is managed by the eco-organization **Defensores de la Naturaleza** (Defenders of Nature), which has several ongoing sustainable fisheries and reforestation projects.

Within the reserve is the small Maya Q'eqchi community of **Selempín**. Defensores has worked with the locals to develop a Biological Science Station, offering a number of tours in the reserve.

Their **jungle trek** begins with a 1½-hour boat ride leaving from El Estor and journeying to Río Oscuro. From there it is a short hike up to the Biological Station and two trails. The Cultural Trail journeys through the jungle. It take about 30 minutes to complete. A second trail, La Cotuza, is 2½ miles (four km) long and takes about two hours to complete. Local men from the village act as your guide. You can also rent a bicycle for Q15 per day and visit a nearby African Palm Farm (no admission fee).

The **Aquatic Trail** offers a chance to explore the various channels, mangroves and lagoons in a traditional dugout canoe or inflatable dinghy. Again, local fishermen act as guides. This is an excellent way to spot the shy manatees that inhabit these waters and birdwatch along the way. It's an all-day trip. An inflatable dinghy runs Q40 per day and the fee to do the Aquatic Trail is Q15.

Accommodations at the station are in four rustic cabins that can accommodate up to 40 people. There's a kitchen and common area. All buildings are made from local materials and use solar energy. The women of Selempín provide meals and give demonstrations on how to make corn tortillas. The income from the tour goes directly to the community. The complete tour is two to three days long. Accommodations with meals are Q55 per person; accommodations only are Q30 per person.

Among the options here, all leaving from El Estor, are a private boat, owned by an individual in El Estor, available at Q500 (maximum of six people); the Defensores Boat, for Q700 (maximum of 12 people); and the Public Ferry, at Q40 (Wednesdays and Saturdays only).

❖ **POLOCHÍC DELTA REFUGE TOUR COMPANY**

For more information or to make a reservation, contact **Defensores de la Naturaleza**, 5a Avenida and 2a Calle Esquina, El Estor, ☎ 502/7-949-7237, rbocas@defensores.org.gt.

A few other operations in town offer this tour, but they charge almost double the price and the money does not reach the community. Defensores remains the best place to book ecotours in El Estor.

El Amatillo Lagoon, Bocas de Polochíc

Close to where the Río Oscuro and Río Zarquito meet there is a small lagoon with warm shallow waters that are perfect for swimming. El Amatillo Lagoon is also close to Padre Creek, an area that has excellent fishing and schools of tarpon are so abundant they can be caught by simply putting a net in the waters. A typical tour in a private boat takes three to four hours and includes a visit to El Amatillo as well as a journey through the river channels where howler monkeys, birds and manatees live. Morning is the best time of day to take this tour, since the lake is still relatively calm. Afternoon winds tend to stir up the water, making it choppy and difficult to navigate. The earlier you go, the more animals you will see, particularly the families of howler monkeys who congregate along the banks of the river to watch the sunrise. Cost is Q250 for up to two people.

> **❖ EL AMATILLO LAGOON TOUR COMPANIES**
>
> **Benjamin Castillo Hernandez**, 12 Avenida 1-78, Zona 1, ☎ 502/7-949-7474. Benjamin is a local fisherman and is often out in his boat.
>
> Also try **Doña Isabel de Mane** at Hotel Marisabela, ☎ 502/7-949-7206, to arrange a tour.

Finca el Paraiso

Río Aguas Calientes runs underground through the Sierra de Santa Cruz mountain range before emerging as a waterfall where it meets the freshwater of Lake Izabal. The results are a hot thermal waterfall pouring into a cold freshwater pool that creates a natural Jacuzzi. The waterfalls are located on a private farm, Finca el Paraiso. To reach the river you follow a trail past some fields and into the jungle. The spot is idyllic – perfect for swimming, picnics or lounging on one of the giant rocks along the riverbank. The trail continues up to **Grutas Paraiso**, a series of caves where the river emerges. The caves are fascinating, but difficult and dangerous to explore on your own. You should hire a guide at the visitor's center. The falls get extremely crowded on the weekends when local families come to enjoy the hot springs. Open from dawn until dusk. Admission is Q10 for adults, Q5 for children.

> **AUTHOR NOTE:** *Be careful climbing in and out of the water, as the rocks are slippery. Don't hang around after dark here.*

▸▸ *GETTING HERE: Finca el Paraiso is 45 minutes from Río Dulce. Buses to El Estor leave there every half-hour and tickets are Q10. From El Estor, it's another 15 minutes by bus to the falls. Buses leave whenever they are full (usually every 30 minutes) and tickets are Q5. You can hire a private taxi from Río Dulce for Q150, round-trip.*

Parque Ecológico del Boquerón

Río Sauce empties into the lake on its northern shore just five miles (eight km) from El Estor. At the point where the river meets Lake Izabal, it turns into a canyon with 820-foot (250-meter) cliffs on either side. The flow of water over the large rocks have formed abstract figures in the canyon walls, creating a natural art gallery. The best way to see the canyon is by boat and several *cayuceros* (local boatmen with canoes) will paddle upriver and point out the shapes. The most famous rocks are shaped like a Maya king, an elephant rock and a jaguar. Get off where the river temporarily trickles to a stop and you can hike up to five more set of rapids. En route you'll pass caves that you can explore. The scenery really is breathtaking. Tours of just the rock formation take a little over a half-hour and cost Q10 per person. Hiking to the rapids can take up to three hours and usually costs Q50 per person.

▶▶ *GETTING HERE: Buses from Río Dulce leave every 30 minutes and cost Q10. The ride takes about 45 minutes. Buses from El Estor to Boquerón leave every 20-30 minutes and cost Q5 for the 10-minute ride. You can hire a cab for about Q60, round-trip. You should not visit here at dusk or after dark.*

◆ Cultural Adventures

Asociación Feminina Q'eqchí in Barrio San Francisco is a community project started in 1990 to help the women in El Estor earn a living. The women have been trained to weave and sew using traditional methods that were taught by people from the Highlands. Today, the collective runs a successful business weaving fabric and sewing it into clothing and handbags. Visitors are welcome to visit for a tour of the looms and a demonstration. A small shop sells variety of crafts, including magnificent handbags, at prices that are lower than those in any of the larger markets. The quality just as good. Open daily from 8 am until 6 pm. Donations are welcome. No phone.

◆ Where to Stay

There aren't many luxury hotels in El Estor, but there are a couple of well-run family hotels that are comfortable and affordable. Most of the budget hotels are not pleasant. The best rooms are those by the lake or with a garden. Be sure to get a room with an overhead fan if you don't get the lake breeze.

❖ HOTEL PRICING
Prices are per person.
$ . . . . Under $25
$$ . . . . $26 to $50
$$$ . . . . $51 to $85
$$$$ . . . . $86 to $125
$$$$$ . . . . over $125

Hotel Marisabela, *8a Avenida and 1a Calle, Zona 1,* ☎ *502/7-949-7205 or 7206, 12 rooms, $.* This is the nicest hotel in El Estor, with cushy double beds dressed in lovely linens. The modern bathrooms have hot water and rooms have cable TV. Rooms offer lake views and get a wonderful breeze. One room has five beds, which makes it a great choice for families. A giant terrace with chairs and tables is surrounded by trees and overlooks Lake Izabal. The restaurant serves Italian and Guatemalan lunches and dinners upon request. Their breakfasts are quite good. The owner, Doña Isabel de Mane, speaks English and knows everyone in town. She can arrange boat and fishing tours.

Hotel Los Almendros, *past Texaco gas station off main square,* ☎ *502/7-948-7182, 14 rooms, $.* Nestled in a small garden away from the main square, this hotel is the quietest in town. It has the feel of an old country cottage with its wooden frames and doors. Large rooms, set off a long corridor, have a good double bed, overhead fans, refrigerators and cable TV. It's a 15-minute walk to town.

Hotel Vista al Lago, *6a Avenida 1-13, Zona 1,* ☎ *502/7-949-7205, 21 rooms, $.* This lovely historical building is the original store opened by the two Englishmen (see page 235 for the full story). The rooms on the first floor are extremely tiny and are big enough for only one person. Rooms at the back are dark and get very hot. Request a second-floor room. They are bigger and have a view of the lake.

Hospedaje La Posada Don Juan, *main square,* ☎ *502/7-949-7296, 7 rooms, $.* This is the cheapest hotel in town and it's usually full of backpackers. It's a good place for hooking up with fellow travelers. Small, clean and cool rooms with private baths open up onto a lovely courtyard filled with plants and flowers. This used to be a home before it was converted into a hotel, and it retains a homey atmosphere. The doors close at 10 pm. No credit cards.

Hotel de Central, *main square,* ☎ *502/7-949-7497, 12 rooms, $.* This is a clean hotel with rather generic rooms that have ceiling fans, two hard single beds, TV and showers without hot water. There is a lovely terrace where you can watch all the action in the central square. This is a good family hotel. No credit cards.

Santa Clara Hotel, *2 Calle and 5 Avenida,* ☎ *502/7-949-7244, 34 rooms, $.* The Santa Clara is squeaky clean, but that doesn't stop it from being mildly depressing. Perhaps it is the soft-as-butter mattresses, the windowless and fanless rooms, or the shared bathrooms that offer only cold water. If you need to check in here, get a front room upstairs; they at least have a private bath, windows and a nice terrace with a lake view. The family who runs this hotel is really very helpful. No credit cards.

Hotel Ecológico Cabañas del Lago, *end of Calle 1a along the lake,* ☎ *502/7-949-7546, 4 cabins, $$.* This is the same Hugo of Hugo's restaurant (see below). The cabins are built with natural woods and have small kitchens, a seating area, bathrooms and two double beds. There is no hot water, air conditioning or overhead fans and electricity is produced by a generator. There's a very nice private beach alongside a palapa restaurant where canoes are available for rent. A variety of animals wander the grounds, adding an exotic atmosphere. The property is still being built and so has an unfinished air about it. It's a tad overpriced, but Hugo is open to negotiation. No credit cards.

Turicentro El Paraiso, *50 feet across highway from Finca Paraiso waterfalls,* ☎ *502/7-949-7122 or 502/5-230-3038, 13 rooms, 7 cabins, $.* This charming rustic hotel sits on the riverbank and offers a sandy beach. It has seven basic bungalows that can sleep four people. There are private baths but no hot water. A nice campground has space for tents or a hammock. The restaurant next door serves simple meals like eggs, hamburgers, rice and beans. Food prices are a little bit steep, considering the basic food. No credit cards.

◆ Where to Eat

It's slim pickings in El Estor. No credit cards accepted at any of these restaurants.

Hugo's Restaurant/Sarita's Ice Cream, *main square,* ☎ *502/7-949-7242.* In front of the restaurant is the ice cream parlor selling the delicious

Sarita's ice cream – the best in Guatemala. In back is Hugo's, which has a basic menu of hamburgers, roast chicken, rice and beans and other fried foods. It sometimes offers fresh fish. Q15-40.

Restaurant Vereda, *main square*. This large eatery offers daily specials as well as excellent chicken sandwiches, hamburgers, French fries and salads. They have good fresh *licuados* and fruit juice. Q15-30.

Rancho Tipico Chaabil Restaurant, *Muelle de Piedra, down from main square*, ☎ *502/7-949-7272*. The only fancy restaurant in the area, Rancho Tipico is overpriced. You can't beat the location, though, which is right on the lake. All the furnishings are made from giant rainforest trees and there's even tree-stump tables. While waiting for your meal, count the rings and contemplate how 300-year-old trees ended up holding fried fish dinners. The fish dishes are excellent, but other dishes are not. Avoid the expensive seafood dinners, especially the *tapado* stew, which they claim is a local specialty (it's really from Lívingston, and the folks here haven't perfected the recipe yet). The service is terrible, but friendly. Bring bug spray, because the mosquitoes like this place. Q35-80.

Pacific Coast

Guatemala's Pacific Coast stretches 155 miles (250 km) and is bordered on the north by Mexico and on the southeast by El Salvador. It is best known for its volcanic black sand beaches and mangroves in the departments of **Retalhuleu**, **Escuintla** and **Santa Rosa**. This area is much different from the high-

lands with an extremely hot and humid climate. The rich volcanic soil has made the area very fertile and it has the most farms of any region in Guatemala.

La Boca Costa (Mouth of the Coast) are the foothill of the Pacific Slope that start from the Western Highlands and move down into the **La Costa** (Pacific Coast Lowlands). This is a lush region of deciduous and ever-green rainforest with rivers and streams that meander among four volcanoes. It is famous for its diverse bird populations as many migrating birds make this area their home in the winter months.

The Pacific Coast Lowlands consist of a narrow 25-mile (40-km) strip of land bordered by the ocean and La Boca Costa. The climate is warmer and sunnier than in the highlands and the landscape is diverse. Rivers, lakes, streams, canals and estuaries ply the land, but the largest area is covered by mangrove swamp. Thousands of migrating shorebirds, sea-birds and waterfowl come to nest in La Costa Sur.

PACIFIC COAST

History

This area was one of the very first to be settled in Guatemala, and it was done so by a number of independent tribes from northern Mexico. The very first were the **Olmecs**. They were followed by the **Ocòs** and **Iztapa**, who lived in small villages working in stone and pottery as far back as 1500 BC. Between AD 400 and 900, the **Pipil** invaded the entire coastland, building half a dozen sites and commencing the production of cacao. By the late Postclassic period, the **Quiché**, **Tzutukil** and **Cakchiquel** tribes had also migrated to the area. Unfortunately, many of the original tribal sites have been lost to the jungle or plowed over to make way for sugarcane plantations.

Pedro Alvarado visited this area in 1524 on his way to the highlands, but did not remain long. A handful of Franciscan monks tried to convert the Pipil, but were unsuccessful. The virulent mosquitoes and malaria killed most of the monks and for a while the area was forgotten. In the late 17th century a few settlers came to grow cacao, indigo dye and cattle ranch. But it wasn't until the 1820s that huge plantations of coffee, rubber, banana and sugarcane were planted along the Boca Costa. In order to find workers for their *fincas*, the rich landowners petitioned the government to pass a law that forced all Indians to work four years on a *finca*. This drew a massive influx of people, but few remained after their four-year term was complete. In the early 1880s a railway to Guatemala City and a huge port were built. Puerto San José became *the* Pacific Coast port used by everyone as far north as Mexico and south to El Salvador.

The area remains an agricultural area. Coffee, sugarcane, cardamom, cotton, bananas and cattle are the main crops, and the *fincas*, which stretch for miles, are still in operation, this time with a permanent *Ladino* workforce. The Highland Maya also work here as migrant field workers.

Many of the coastal towns operate as weekend getaways for affluent Guatemalans. Perhaps it is a combination of the heat, humidity and lack of tourists that make parts of the pacific region squalid.

Getting Here & Getting Around

A fast highway in excellent shape runs from Guatemala City all the way to the Mexican border. **Carrterra al Pacificio**, CA-2, can take you from the Pacific Coast to Guatemala City in less than four hours. It is a highway notorious for its dreadful accidents, so drive it with care. Regular bus service departs for Retalhuleu, making it the easiest department to get to. The other departments take several transfers at different villages.

Most of the villages are so tiny that you won't need to take buses to get around. The coastal villages use boats for travel.

Department of Santa Rosa

The department of Santa Rosa's colder and more northern areas are part of the Sierra Madre mountain range, topping out at 5,249 feet (1,600 meters). As you head south, the climate warms up as the land drops to meet the Pacific Ocean. The department is located over what was a volcanic range and is covered with rich volcanic ash. It has four major volcanoes – **Tecuamburro** (6,381 feet/1.945 meters), **Jumaytepeque** (5,954 feet/ 1,815 meters), **Cruz Quemada** (5,545 feet/1,690 meters) and **Cerro Redondo** (4,002 feet/1,220 meters). Between them extensive valleys and plains planted with coffee, citrus fruit and cardamom sit alongside dairy and cattle ranches as the land extends down to the water.

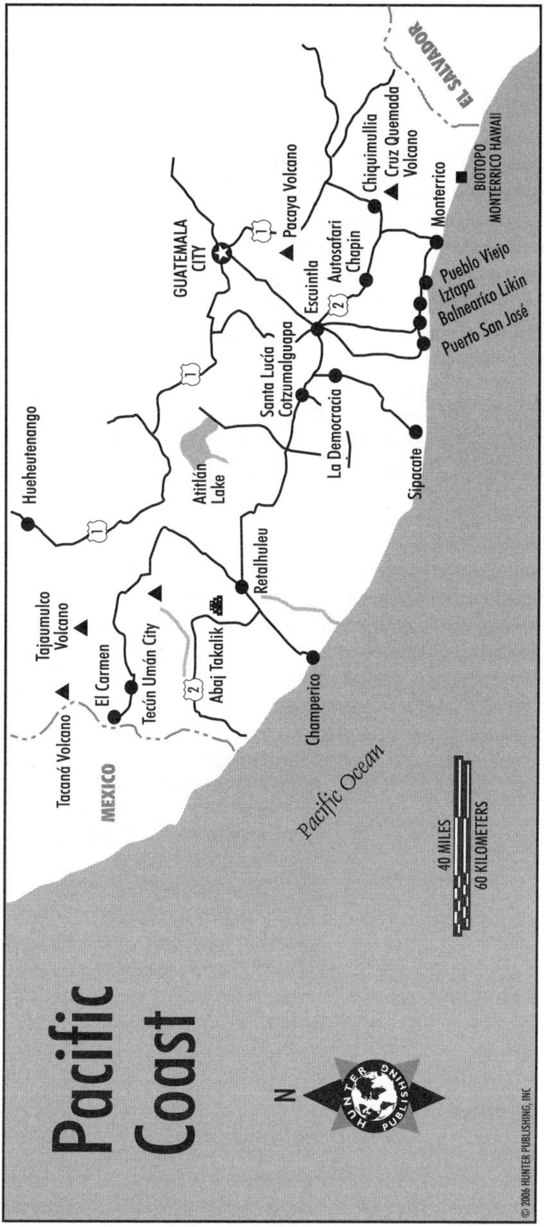

PACIFIC COAST

Santa Rosa doesn't have a lot of tourism and it's two biggest attractions are the volcanoes and the 6,918-acre (2,800-hectare) Monterrico-Hawaii Mangrove Reserve, a sanctuary for marine ocean turtles and migrating birds.

History

Santa Rosa appears to have been settled in AD 100 by the Xinca and Pipil. The **Xinca**, the largest tribe, extended as far east as Jalapa. Shortly after AD 900, the **Pipil** made an appearance in the area and their language (a dialect of Nahua) became the second language. The Xinca kingdom flourished until 1526 when **Alvarado** arrived, meeting with a fierce tribe of warriors who refused to be ruled by the Spanish. Alvarado did leave them in peace, but over the next 33 years later Catholic priests conquered the tribe. In 1570, the area was officially settled with the creation of a tiny village **Nuestra Señora de los Dolores o Candelaria de los Esclavos** (Our Lady of Pain/Candlemas of the Slaves). To open the interior and provide transportation across the huge Río de los Esclavos (River of Slaves), the Puente de los Esclavos (Bridge of Slaves) was started in 1573 and finished in 1592. The department was already a prosperous agricultural and commercial center, and the addition of the bridge elevated it to serve as the main delivery route for tobacco crops from Honduras and El Salvador. Prosperity brought an influx of Spanish and the population gradually changed from Maya to *Ladino*. Today, only two percent of the population is Maya.

The department remained fairly prosperous until the mid-19th century. In 1848, the new Guatemalan government decided to break up the territory into three districts: Jutiapa, Santa Rosa and Jalapa. Santa Rosa was officially recognized in 1852. During this time the country's economy became focused on coffee and bananas and Jalapa grew in importance as an economic center, connected by railroad to Puerto Barrios and the United Fruit Company. Santa Rosa lost its standing. As a result, huge tracks of land were developed into large plantations and Indians were conscripted to work on these plantations as virtual slaves.

There is not much tourism in this department and parts of Santa Rosa are quite poor. The area is famous for its pottery, hats and brooms woven from palm leaves, wood carvings, leather goods and chairs.

PACIFIC COAST

> ## ❖ LEGEND OF PUENTE DE LOS ESCLAVOS
>
> Legend has it that during the construction of the bridge exhausted slaves made a pact with the Devil: their souls in exchange for a completed bridge. The bridge was completed and the Devil went to collect, but during the night one of the slaves had regretted his actions and challenged the Devil using a blessed crucifix as his weapon. The Devil crumbled and could not collect his souls. In a fit of rage, he kicked the bridge so hard that one of the stones fell to the ground. The bridge has been repaired many times since then and that same stone always falls out.

◆ Adventures in Nature

La Boca Costa

La Boca Costa has a warm sunny climate with a dry season between November and May and a humid season from June to October. At 5,000 feet (1,500 meters), it offers a mixed deciduous forest that many birds use as their nesting grounds. The climate and vegetation make this a perfect birding area. Over 380 birds within 58 families have been identified in the region, including the azure-rumped tanager, rufous saberwing, maroon-chested ground-dove and the Pacific parakeet. Warm lowland air and cool highland air meet to create rising thermals for soaring raptors such as the great black hawk, grey hawk, black-and-white hawk-eagle and grey-headed kite.

> ## ❖ BIRDING TOUR COMPANIES
>
> There aren't many organized tours to the area, so you will probably have to make many of the arrangements on your own.
>
> **Guatours**, 20 Calle 5-35, Zona 10, Edificio Plaza Los Arcos, 3rd floor, Guatemala City, ☎ 502/2-337-0019, fax 502/2-333-5769, http://guatours.com, does offer some tours leaving from Guatemala City. See their website for more information.

◆ Volcano Adventures

Cruz Quemada Volcano

This volcano reaches a height of 5,545 feet (1,690 meters) and is no longer active. At its foot is the small village of Santa María Ixhuatán, a community consisting largely of coffee plantations that extend up the volcano. You have to hike midway up the volcano before reaching the giant trees of the rainforest. If the day is clear, you will be able to see over the blanket of coffee plantations as far as the coast. At the summit are radio transmission towers. This volcano is part of the Cerro La Consulta mountain range and the trail is a medium challenge that takes up to three hours to complete. It is best to hire a guide in the village of Santa María Ixhuatán; ask at the taxi stand. Birdwatching is excellent along the trails.

▸▸ *GETTING HERE: There are no direct routes to the village of Santa María Ixhuatán. You will need to take a bus from Guatemala City to Barberena or Aldea los Esclavos and transfer to a local bus for another three miles. From the village, it's a 8½-mile (12-km) hike to the summit.*

Tecuamburro Volcano

Tecuamburro is actually a dormant volcanic complex composed of several peaks, including Cerro La Soledad (Hill of Solitude), 6,053 feet/1,845 meters; Cerro Peña Blanca (Hill White Rock), 6,069 feet/1,850 meters; and Cerro de Miraflores, 6,381 feet/1,945 meters. Cerro Peña Blanca, covered in small openings emitting smoke and sulfur, offers the most interesting climb. This peak is covered with beautiful rainforest made up of giant cypress and pine trees. The forest on all three peaks is so thick that views are scarce until you reach the top. Once above the trees you will be able to see coffee plantations and Cruz Quemada Volcano. Because of the thick vegetation on this volcano trail you should wear pants to protect your legs. The ascent takes between two to three hours. You can ask in Aldea Los Esclavos or in the village of Pueblo Nuevo Viñas for a guide.

Laguna de Ixpaco is a perfectly round lagoon at the base of Tecuamburro Volcano. It is actually a volcanic depression connected to an underground river. The water is a ghostly yellow-green due to the high levels of sulfur and, when levels are high, it can turn to milky-white. Prolonged exposure to the fumes coming off the water can be harmful; people with breathing problems should probably not visit. Nearby are some sulfur hot springs that the locals like to visit.

AUTHOR'S NOTE: *The exact geographical center between North America and South America is found in the capital city of Cuilapa. A monument in the center of town marks the spot.*

▸▸ *GETTING HERE: Tecuamburro is in Pueblo Nuevo Viñas. Catch a bus to Cuilapa, transfer to a bus heading toward Aldea los Esclavos and, at the junction, the bus will head south to Chiquimulilla. Check before you get on; otherwise, get off at the junction and wait for a bus heading south. It's another 10 miles (16 km) to the village of Tecuamburro. Occasionally, the bus does not make it this far, especially after it rains and the dirt road turns to mud. There's a small parking lot at the foot of the volcano.*

◆ Adventures on Water

Río Los Esclavos

Río Los Esclavos runs down the middle of Santa Rosa cutting between Cruz Quemada and Tecuamburro volcanoes and offering numerous hot springs en route. In some places the water reaches 90° F (32° C). Scientists used the exposed volcanic rock along the banks of Río Los Esclavos to categorize the geographical history of the region. This river is becoming popular for **whitewater rafting** because of its five-mile (eight-km) canyon filled with numerous Class III and Class IV rapids, with colorful names such as Crazy Mouse (*Ratón Loco*). Several companies offer day tours along the river.

❖ RÍO LOS ESCLAVOS TOUR COMPANIES

PTP (Promotora Turistica Panamericana), Guatemala Ciudad, 15 Calle, 3-20, Zona 10, Edificio Ejecutivo, Oficina 602, ☎ 502/2-363-4404, fax 502/2-363-4524, www.ptpmayas.com. This company offers a 13-mile (20-km) rafting trip that leaves from Guatemala City or Antigua from July through October. The water fun starts at Santa Rosa de Lima and passes through Class III and Class IV in the canyon. Lunch is a picnic on the banks of the river. The ride ends at Aldea los Esclavos. There's a minimum of six participants. Contact the company for a price list.

Maya Expeditions, 15 Calle 1-91, Zona 10, local 104, Guatemala City, ☎ 502/2-363-4955, fax 502/2-337-4660, www.mayaexpeditions.com. This day-trip departs from Guatemala City or Antigua. The rafting starts at the village of Barbarena before heading down through the canyon to a 200-foot (61-meter) waterfall. There are a number of portages, so you'll need to be in good physical condition. The trip finishes just before the Esclavos Dam project. Offered June through November. See their website for rates and more information.

PACIFIC COAST

◆ Where to Stay & Eat

There isn't much in the way of hotels in this area. The main town is Aldea los Esclavos. You might try the **Turicentro Los Esclavos**, *Aldea los Esclavos, ☎ 502/7-886-5571, fax 502/7-885-5158*. This pleasant hotel has average-size rooms decorated with bright colors and wooden furniture. All have air conditioning (a must in this part of the country), hot water, cable TV and two double beds. There is a decent-sized pool and a restaurant on site.

Monterrico Village

Monterrico is a small undeveloped village along the coast. A number of comfortable hotels set along its main unpaved road are perfect spots for relaxing. The beaches have black volcanic sand. Watch for the riptides.

On the north side of the village is a series of mangrove canals and the Monterrico-Hawaii Mangrove Reserve.

◆ Getting Here & Getting Around

There is no direct route to Monterrico. If you are coming from Lake Atitlán, Antigua or Guatemala City, catch a tourist shuttle from Antigua. They leave every Saturday at 8 am and cost US $12. Reservations are recommended, as many locals use this service for day-trips to the beach. The shuttle back is US$10 per person. See page 70 for a list of shuttle services.

By bus, take the direct line from Guatemala City to the village of La Avellana, where you can hop on a ferry across the Chiquimulilla Canal to Monterrico. From Antigua, Lake Atitlán or Quetzaltenango, take a bus to Escuintla, transfer to another bus in Taxisco and then switch again to a local bus heading to La Avellana village. You can also reach Monterrico through the port of Iztapa in the department of Escuintla. You cross Río María Linda by ferry to Pueblo Viejo and transfer to a bus that travels along a dirt road to Monterrico.

In Monterrico, plenty of small motorboats offer tours of the reserve. You can also rent canoes for exploring.

◆ Adventures on Water

Monterrico-Hawaii Biotópo

Monterrico Natural Reserve and the Hawaii National Park are two combined protected zones along the Pacific Coast. Both reserves have subtropical ecosystems with estuaries of saline water, lagoons and mangrove swamps covering 6,918 acres (28 square km). The mangroves here are nesting grounds to over 110 resident and migratory birds, as well as three species of marine turtles. The region offers a great variety of fish and crustaceans, and birding is excellent.

The beautiful **Chiquimulilla Canal** was built in 1895 in order to navigate through the mangroves, lakes and lagoons that run parallel to Boca Costa. It's possible to travel the entire 55 miles (90 km) that run through the reserve, but the water is partially covered with a reed called "tul," which can make paddling difficult. The plus side is that this reed creates a shelter for a number of waterfowl, so birding is quite incredible. You can rent canoes or hire a boat to explore the many lagoons close by. Flora includes mangrove trees, bulrushes, white water lilies, bromeliads, fruit and timber trees, and several species of iguanas are found here.

Palmilla Lagoon is quite close to the village, though still in the reserve. It serves as a primary breeding grounds for the brown pelican, which favors its mangroves and crustacean- and fish-filled waters. Some of the birds you will spot include the great blue heron, great white heron, common egret, green-backed heron, roseate spoonbill, snowy egret, tricolor heron, white ibis, Chokoloskee chicken, wood stork, white-breasted chachalaca, pygmy kingfisher, brown pelican and the collared plover.

CECON-USAC (Centro Estudios Conservacíonistas de Universidad de San Carlos) runs a rescue program for sea turtle eggs and also has a collection of green iguanas and crocodiles that you can visit. At one time, there were 250 species of sea turtles in the world; only eight remain. Of those, three species are indigenous to the southern coast of Guatemala: the olive Ridley, the East Pacific green, and the green leatherback. All three come to the Costa Sur to lay their eggs in the black sand. When the moon is full, females use the moonlight to guide them. They dig huge pits and deposit up to 25 eggs at one time. Only one or two of the offspring will make it to adulthood. Unfortunately, the eggs are highly sought after for their supposed aphrodisiac properties. The residents of Monterrico support themselves through the sale of turtle eggs and had nearly caused the turtles' extinction until the university developed the turtle rescue project. Now, locals hand back 20% of all eggs collected to the sanctuary and, when the CECON has spare money, it can buy back surplus eggs.

The eggs are placed in guarded nesting spots for hatching. The baby turtles must dig their way out of the pit and dash across the sand to the water. Most are devoured by predators on their way out to sea, but CECON tries to give them a helping hand.

❖ TURTLE RACES

The center has developed a fund-raising turtle race. For Q10, you "buy" a hatchling and watch it race to the sea with its siblings. The owner of the winning turtle gets a T-shirt, a tour from CECON-USAC or a dinner at a local restaurant. The cheering humans also keep the birds, crabs and fish away so the hatchlings can get a head start.

❖ MONTERRICO GUIDED TOURS

CECON runs a number of guided tours through the reserve in either a motorboat or canoe. Take a quiet canoe tour if you want to see wildlife. San Carlos University's Center for Conservation Studies (CECON), Avenida Reforma 0-63 Zona 10 CP 01010, Ciudad Guatemala, Guatemala, ☎ 502/2-331-0904, fax 502/2-334-7664, www.usac.edu.gt/cecom, cecon@usac.edu.gt. There is no way to get in touch with the turtle reserve directly unless you go to Monterrico. Costs for the tours start at Q40 per person.

Sapo Tours is just one of many boat tour operators at the **Tortugario Monterrico Visitor's Center**. Trips last about two hours and cost Q50 per person.

◆ Where to Stay & Eat

Accommodations are quite simple in Monterrico. Seafood and fresh fish are the specialties here. Try the sea bass (*robálo*), shark (*tiburon*) or shrimp ceviche. All hotels are on the beach and the most important things to check for are proper screens and mosquito nets without holes. Mosquitoes are plentiful

❖ HOTEL PRICING
Prices are per person.
$ . . . . Under $25
$$ . . . . $26 to $50
$$$ . . . . $51 to $85
$$$$ . . . . $86 to $125
$$$$$ . . . . over $125

and pesky here. You might also check that your overhead fan works, as this place gets steamy.

Utz Tzaba Hotel, ☎ *502/5-318-9452, www.utz-tzaba.com, 10 rooms and 4 bungalows.* By far the most luxurious hotel in the area. Rooms have palapa roofs with plenty of space and private baths with lots of hot water. The bungalows have fully equipped living and dining rooms, modern kitchens, two bedrooms and private baths. On site is an oceanside pool and three Jacuzzis. The restaurant serves has an international menu specializing in seafood as well as some national dishes. $$-$$$$

Hotel Baule Beach, *first hotel left on Calle Principal*, ☎ *502/7-514-4934,10 rooms, $.* Started by a former Peace Corps volunteer, Baule Beach is now extremely popular with students and backpackers. It's a good place to meet other travelers, but can be noisy. Rooms are comfortable, although they need a good cleaning. All have private baths. No credit cards.

Hotel El Mangle, *next door to Hotel Baule Beach*, ☎ *502/5-514-6517, 6 rooms, $.* A comfortable room in this quiet, tiny hotel might be just what you're looking for. Rooms have fans, mosquito nets and private baths, and the beds are in excellent shape. Outside, plenty of hammocks are lined up for afternoon siestas. No credit cards.

Johnny's Place, *next door to Sea Turtle Center*, ☎ *502/7-812-0409, www.backpackamericas.com/johnnys.htm, 4 bungalows ($$), 20 rooms ($).* This 12-year-old hotel is a favorite with locals and tourists who enjoy the family atmosphere and comfortable bungalows with fully equipped kitchens, private bath and pool. Some rooms also offer private baths. An excellent restaurant serves fresh fish and the pool is open to all visitors. The hotel will gladly arrange tours of the reserve, boat rentals and rent snorkeling equipment.

Hotel Pez de Oro. *On beach close to La Avellena ferry. 9 bungalows. $$.* ☎ *502/2-368-3684.* This is the nicest hotel on the beach with clean and nicely decorated bungalows with fans, mosquito nets, private baths and lovely porches with hammocks to lie in and watch the ocean. There is also a large, clean pool alongside a restaurant serving excellent fish and ceviche dishes. Prices are higher on the weekends. No credit cards.

Hotel "Café del Sol", ☎ *502/5-810-0821, www.cafe-del-sol.com, 12 rooms.* This small Swiss-Guatemalan hotel has very simple rooms on the beach, all with private baths. The terrace has hammocks and the pool overlooks the volcano. The restaurants serves up fresh fish dishes and the bar is well stocked with cold beer and good music. $

Hotel Restaurante Dulce y Salado, ☎ 502/5-817-9046, www. dulceysalado.tk, 3 rooms. Located next door to the reserve, this small hotel offers simple rooms with private bath, mosquito nets, fans and hammocks. Its offers a menu of vegetarian dishes and fresh catch of the day. $

Department of Escuintla

Escuintla is the commercial heart of Guatemala. The slopes of the Sierra Madre Mountains have been turned into cattle and dairy ranches and planted with sugarcane, coffee, cotton, fruits, corn, beans and other vegetables. This is also a manufacturing area that produces articles for fishing, marimbas, furniture, shoes, leather goods and food products. The popular ice cream manufacturer, Sarita's, has its headquarters here. The department's capital of the same name has little to offer the tourist, but it serves as a commercial and transportation hub. If you are exploring the region, you will end up in Escuintla for bus connections. Northwest of Escuintla are the sugarcane fields of Santa Lucía Cotzumalguapa, where a series of ruins have been uncovered. The southern coast caters to sportfishing and has a number of beach resorts for wealthy Guatemalans.

History

Escuintla was one of the first areas to be occupied by the **Olmec** from Mexico. They left a series of statues, small altars and giant carved stone heads scattered throughout the area, many dating to 400 BC that resemble the giant heads found in Mexico. In AD 200, the Olmec built the port city of **Acapán** (since lost to the jungle), which became a major port along the Pacific trade routes. During the Classic period (AD 300-900), the **Pipil** started to take over the established trade routes. By then, the Olmec had disappeared from the region.

Escuintla translates from Pipil language into "Hill of the Dogs" and refers to the paca agouti (*tepezcuintle*), a large rodent raised by natives for its meat. When the **Spanish** conquistadors visited in 1524, they thought the paca were a new breed of dog, which the Pipils found amusing and thus the name. Pedro de Alvarado found the heat and humidity too much and did not linger in the area. Instead, he sent **Franciscan monks** to convert the locals. They built the colonial cities of Gotzumalguapa and Alotec and supervised the first sugar plantations. Colonists and farmers followed, starting up large cattle ranches, indigo manufacturing plants and coffee farms. During this period there were actually two separate departments – Escuintla and Guazacapán. In 1825, shortly after independence, the two departments were combined into one. In 1888 a railway was built connecting the capital to Guatemala City and securing Escuintla's role as a commercial and manufacturing hub. It remains one of the most productive departments in the country.

Escuintla

◆ Adventures in Nature

Lions, Tigers & Rhinos

Autosafari Chapín, Carreterra al Pacifico, Km 87.5, ☎ 502/2-337-1274, fax 502/2-368-0968. This little gem of a place is an unexpected and pleasant surprise just 18.6 miles (30 km) from Escuintla on the road to Taxisco, Santa Rosa. The same family has owned the land for centuries. The original owner, a wealthy farmer, was a big game hunter and covered the walls of his hacienda with the heads and skin of animals he had "bagged" on safari. The latest generation are conservationists and, instead of killing the animals, started bringing them home as pets. The result is Chapín Safari, where lions, giraffes, hippos, rhinos, pumas, deer, antelope, coyotes and leopards wander freely in the habitats created for them. Most are obviously happy since all (except for the rhino) have reproduced. Although you must drive through the safari in either the Autosafari van or your own car, a small walkway leads through a zoo centered on a lake. It houses the local (and much tamer) species, such as white-tailed deer, peccaries, macaws and iguanas. Hardly any foreigners come here and the park is geared toward Guatemalan families who come for day-trips. There is a restaurant and swimming pool on site. Open 8 am to dusk, Tuesday to Sunday. Admission is Q30.

Santa Lucía Cotzumalguapa

Santa Lucía Cotzumalguapa is 35 miles (57 km) east of the capital. This whole area is planted with sugar cane and is of little interest to the tourist except for the great stone heads carved by a mysterious tribe of northerners. Evidence points to the Olmecs, who were the predecessors of the Maya and Aztec civilizations and the originators of many of the scientific and cultural discoveries used by them. No one knows why the giant heads were placed here. The actual city of Santa Lucía is rather ragged and not very pretty but, if you want to explore these ruins, it is the jumping-off point.

◆ Getting Here & Getting Around

Direct buses run from Guatemala City, Escuintla and Retalhuleu to Santa Lucía. A few companies do offer tours out this way, but they sell them at ridiculously inflated prices, almost 200% more than what you pay if you set out your own. The bus ride is not hard and, once in town, you can hire a taxi to take you to various sites for no more than Q70. You can even walk to the ruins, identified by the *finca* where they were found. If you have trouble locating any of the ruins, ask one of the locals for "*las piedras*" (the stones).

◆ Maya Ruins

Finca Bilbao

Finca Bilbao is north of Santa Lucía. The heads here were first discovered in the late 1880s by European archeologists who shipped nine of the best heads to the Dahlem Museum in Berlin. One was lost at sea, but eight made it to the museum in Berlin. Four sets of stones remain at Bilbao and are beautiful examples of the intricate carvings done on the black volcanic stone. Two large stones covered with dots and circles have been identified as the glyphs of the Maya calendar. Farther along in the sugarcane are two more sets of stones, which are much more eroded. One has only its border left, but the second stone has superb carvings of figures, including a ball player surrounded by animals and birds. The final stone is located at the bottom of the field near the second entrance. This stone is a giant face that has been damaged by looters.

▶▶ *GETTING HERE: You can walk to the Finca Bilbao ruins by going uphill from the plaza and following 4 Avenida to a dirt track that runs parallel to the sugarcane fields. Once the path widens, you'll see the heads about 721 feet (220 meters) from there.*

Finca El Baul

Finca El Baul sits atop a small hill surrounded by sugarcane. The site is still used for religious ceremonies and many of the small stone altars are covered with candles and other offerings. The first stone you'll see is a flat relief. Beside it is the most interesting piece, a half-buried figure. This carved head has an odd-looking beaked nose, eyes with no pupils, elaborate headdress and gruesome grin. The top of its head is blackened with soot and candles. They are many beautiful pieces here, but none has been identified or dated.

Close by the ruins is a museum that has an excellent collection of carvings, including a stone skull, massive jaguar and sculpted figures and reliefs. To get to the museum on foot, go back to the unpaved road and walk along the dirt track until you reach a paved road that leads to the *finca* headquarters. Cross over the bridge. You will pass by some houses and

PACIFIC COAST

the sugar refinery before reaching the armed security guards. Ask them if you can visit the museum and they will unlock the doors.

▶▶ *GETTING HERE: El Baul is about 2½ miles (four km) north of the city. You can walk to Finca El Baul, but it will be hot and slow. It's probably best to hire a cab. Follow the road north to the church and go 1.86 miles (three km) to a fork in the road and a sign that reads "Los Tarros" (The Jars). Local buses travel this route as far as the sign. Turn right and go about 1¼ miles (two km) to a dirt road where a hill sticks up in the middle of an otherwise flat field planted with sugarcane. The hill is actually a un-restored temple. On its south side is a road leading up to the heads. A taxi out to the finca and back will be around Q50.*

Finca Las Ilusiones

East of the city is Finca Las Ilusiones, which offers an excellent private collection of artifacts and stone carvings. You will recognize the museum from the stelae located just outside the front door. Inside are thousands of small stone carvings and pottery fragments. Many of the carvings are unusual and resemble nothing else found in the Maya world. Some date to the Olmec period. Unfortunately, nothing has been catalogued. The museum doesn't keep regular hours. Ask around for the person who has the keys that day.

▶▶ *GETTING HERE: This finca is difficult to reach since there are no public buses or proper roads. You can walk here by following Calzada 15 de Septembre along to the Esso Station where the highway begins. Follow the highway northeast for a short distance to an unpaved road. Walk along this road for about .62 mile (one km) to the museum. You can take a taxi from town to the dirt road for about Q35.*

Monte Alto

This is one of the most mysterious sites of the Maya world. It is obviously much older than other sites, and researchers are unsure who first lived here. The giant carved heads and other artifacts point to the Olmecs, who predate the Maya. Researchers did some intense investigation in 1968-1970, but their discoveries only added to the mystery. The large heads with crude carvings, which date to the Olmec period (1500-1200 BC), were found alongside two stelae and two stone altars. But 15 other stelae and other artifacts indicate the area was occupied as far back as 1800 BC. Early to Middle Formative-era (200 BC-AD 200) structures were found mixed with others from the Early Classic period (AD 300-400). The nature of the site has not been determined, but many monuments are built to align with Ursa Major, the Great Bear constellation, during the summer solstice and may have been used for astronomy. Today, most of the interesting artifacts have been removed to the museum in Democracia and there are only the covered mounds left to explore.

▶▶ *GETTING HERE: Monte Alto is in Democracia, 1 km east of the village.*

◆ Nearby Towns

Democracia

Democracia is six miles (9½ km) south of Santa Lucía Cotzumalguapa. There is little to see in this town except the giant Olmec heads that have been taken from nearby Monte Alto site and arranged in the main plaza. The locals refer to them as *chamcos gordos* (fat boys), an accurate description of the large, squat stones carved with simple, childlike faces. These heads are thought to be over 4,000 years old, which would make Monte Alto one of the first settlements in Guatemala.

Museo Rubèn Chevez Van Dorne, facing the plaza. This small but very well organized museum houses some of the area's most interesting archeological finds. The beautiful jade mask you see has just recently been recovered after being stolen in early 2001 and sold on the black market. There are also carved figures, ceremonial yokes worn by ball players, relief carvings, grinding stones, more carved heads and lots of pottery. Open 9 am-noon and 2-5 pm, Tuesday-Sunday. Admission is 35 centavos.

◆ Where to Stay & Eat

You should stay in either Santa Lucía Cotzumalguapa or Escuintla (Democracia has no hotels or restaurants), where most of the hotels are in the budget range.

❖ HOTEL PRICING	
Prices are per person.	
$	Under $25
$$	$26 to $50
$$$	$51 to $85
$$$$	$86 to $125
$$$$$	over $125

Hotel Santiaguito, *Km 90.4 Carr-terra al Pacifico, Santa Lucía Cotzu-malguapa*, ☎ *502/7-882-5435, fax 592/ 7-882-2585, 35 rooms, $$*. This is the most modern hotel in town. It tries hard to be glitzy and sophisticated, but doesn't succeed. Rooms are generic, with two queen-size beds, private baths with hot water, air conditioning and satellite TV. There is a large pool and a restaurant that serves passable Guatemalan fare.

Hotel Costa Sur, *12 Calle 4-13, Zona 1, Escuintla* ☎ *502/7-888-1819, 17 rooms, $*. This hotel is close to the bus terminal and offers simple, clean rooms with private baths with hot water. The restaurant on-site serves reasonable local food.

Hotel La Villa, *3a Calle 3-28, Zona 1, Escuintla*, ☎ *502/7-888-0398, fax 502/7-888-1523, 27 rooms, $*. A quiet hotel with a nice lobby, a swimming pool and a very good restaurant. Very comfortable rooms have private bath (without hot water), air conditioning, small balconies, nice linens and cable TV.

Hotel Texas, *Avenida Centroamérica 156-04, Zona 3, Escuintla*, ☎ *502/7-889-1081, fax 502/7-889-1083, 28 rooms, $$*. This modern hotel has little atmosphere, but its super-clean rooms have double beds, private baths, hot water, air conditioning and cable TV.

Puerto San José

San José is the country's second-largest commercial port (after Puerto Barrios on the Caribbean side). It is connected to Guatemala City via the Pan American Highway (CA-9). Like its sister port, San José is a languid and slightly seedy town catering to sailors and *Ladinos* who like to come and strut their stuff. However, on either side of the city are posh, exclusive resorts catering to wealthy Guatemalans.

◆ History

Iztapa was the first port in this area, built by the Maya but taken over by Alvarado. It did not last long, since most of the shipping done by the kingdom of Guatemala was from Acajutla in El Salvador. In 1814, during the independence movement, the Guatemalan government re-opened Iztapa, but the port was in such disrepair that everything was eventually transferred to San José in 1851. Because San José lacks a natural harbor, a large iron wharf (now an antique) was constructed in 1868 to entice commerce. By 1875, the area had grown to just over 5,000 people. In 1880 the railroad from Guatemala City was extended down to San José. The city has remained a commercial port since then, and now has a population of just under 20,000.

In 1982, Port Quetzal was given a new dock and the iron wharf was abandoned (it is now a place where locals gather to fish, drink beer and hang out).

There isn't much tourism here, but in the last three years San José has been gaining a reputation for sportfishing. An enormous natural eddy attracts the small tuna upon which big game fish like to feed, so the waters are teeming with Pacific sailfish, sought after by fly-fishermen.

The beaches around San José are becoming popular with surfers. During the week an occasional cruise ships stops in, but otherwise the area is deserted, making it the perfect place for lounging. On weekends and holidays the place tends to fill up with Guatemalan families trying to escape the city.

◆ Getting Here

Regular bus service from Guatemala City to Puerto San José takes about three hours. Several shuttle services also come from Antigua to Iztapa, one of the local resorts popular with tourists. Once you have arrived in town, all local transportation is by boat.

◆ Adventures on Water

Beaches

Beaches get very hot because of their black volcanic soil that quickly absorbs the heat. Fortunately, most have small huts that offer shelter, food and drink.

> **AUTHOR'S NOTE:** *Watch the strong currents and take your cue from the locals – if they are not in the water, you shouldn't be either. Don't leave valuables on the beach. Petty thieves are a real problem.*

Balneario Chulmar, 3½ miles (5½ km) west of San José, has the nicest beach in the area as well as several decent *comedores*. You'll need a taxi (about Q40) to reach Chulmar.

Eight miles (five km) east of San José is **Balneario Likín**, a planned residential community centered around canals. The beach here is smooth and wide; it's also deserted during the weekdays. Catch any bus heading out to Iztapa and ask to be let off at Likín.

Big Game Fishing in Iztapa

The ancient Maya port of Iztapa is now the main location for big game fishing. The Maya built this port in the Late Pre-Classic period between 1400 and 1500 BC. When Alvarado landed with his Conquistadors in 1524, they took over and used the port to repair ships. The settlement was abandoned shortly afterwards and was ignored for several hundred years until a brief period between 1815 to 1845, when it acted as a port for the newly dependent Guatemala. When San José took over, Iztapa fell into disuse before being revived as a beach resort.

Most of the country's sportfishing operations are centered in Itzápa because it is only 25 miles (40 km) away from where the big game fish feed. The shortest fishing trip takes two days and one night and the longest lasts one full week. Boats – usually 30-foot (9½-meter) Bertrams – come completely crewed with professional fishermen. For shorter trips, 25-foot (7½-meter) Super Sport Panga Mexican skiffs are used. The two companies that run the fishing tournaments, below, also orgnize the fishing trips. Or you can simply ask for a boat at the main dock.

PACIFIC COAST

❖ FISH-FRIENDLY FISHING

Always check that your company runs a catch-and-release operation. You catch the big fish, get your picture taken with your prize and release it back into the ocean. This conservation program is being practiced all over the world. The largest and most sought-after sailfish are females, but if too many of them are caught and killed, the species may die off. You can't eat sailfish, so it makes sense to let them go.

Trips begin in the early morning and travel 40 miles (64 km) out to sea, where there are plenty of blue and black marlin, sailfish, swordfish, dorado, barracuda, roosterfish, and wahoo.

> ### ❖ FISHING TOURNAMENTS
>
> A number of fishing tournaments held here offer a good opportunity to break into this high-powered sport. For information about what's happening when you plan to visit, contact the **Golden Sailfish and Marina El Capitan,** Lote #3, Aldea Buena Vista, Iztapa, Puerto San José, ☎ 502/7-881-4403, fax 502/2-332-6933, www.sailfishcentralamerica.com. El Capitan also offers reasonably priced fishing trips.
>
> If you would like to improve your sailfish technique, **The Great Sailfishing Company** offers a fly-fishing school. This instructional tour includes four full days of instruction, fly-fishing equipment, accommodations, transportation and all meals. You even get a certificate at the end of the course. The company also offers big game fishing. For more information and rates, contact The Great Sailfishing Company, Sector B, Lote #7, apto. 3, El Panorama, La Antigua, Sacatepéquez, ☎ 502/7-832-1991, 877-441-FISH, www.greatsailfishing.com.

Surfing at Zipacate & El Paradon

This part of the Pacific Ocean has incredible waves that have caught the attention of surfers worldwide. The sport is still in its infancy here, so be prepared for primitive accommodations and basic food. The two favored beaches are Zipacate and El Paredon.

Zipacate's large sandbar along the shoreline creates waves up to 492 feet (150 meters) high and 984 feet (300 meters) long. The area is suitable for all skill levels. To reach Zipacate beach, take a bus from Guatemala City to Escuintla and transfer to a local bus for the village of Zipacate. You'll walk from the town to the beach. You can rent a wooden bungalow at **Rancho Carillo** for as little as US $10 per day. Some have kitchens, but there is also a restaurant on site. Every September this beach hosts the annual surf contest held by the **Guatemala Surf Association**, Alvaro Cruz, President, 17 Avenida 13-67, Zona 1, Guatemala City, ☎/fax 502/2-334-6461.

El Paredon is a popular beach located in the newly formed Sipacate-Naranjo National Park. The shore here has a large beach-break and sandy bottom with waves that match the size of those at Zipacate. Unfortunately, there is no direct bus service, but the new surfing camp here offers shuttle service from Antigua. **El Paredon Surf Camp** is a recent project of the eco-tour company Aventuras Naturales, which hopes to bring income to the locals by developing a haven for surfers. The camp's lodging is still under construction, but a host family offers basic accommodations and meals. The camp offers lessons in both surfing and bodysurfing to people of all ages. For more information, contact **Aventuras Naturales,** Colonia El Naranjo No 53, La Antigua, Sacatepéquez, ☎/fax 502/7-832-3328, http://elparedonsurfcamp.tripod.com.

◆ Where to Stay

It's the two extremes here in San José: ultra-luxury or budget. Check out any of the budget hotels before signing in to make sure they do not cater to the drunken sailor crowd that takes over downtown San José on the weekends. The farther the hotel is from the local bars, the quieter and emptier it will be.

❖ HOTEL PRICING
Prices are per person.
$ . . . . Under $25
$$ . . . . $26 to $50
$$$ . . . . $51 to $85
$$$$ . . . . $86 to $125
$$$$$ . . . . over $125

Radisson Omega Villas del Pacifico, *Final Calle Chulamar, Chulamar Beach,* ☎ *502/7-881-3131, fax 502/7-881-1656, www. radisson.com, 128 rooms, $$$$$.* This all-inclusive resort is an oasis of luxury and elegance. Its location, on the beach with the mangroves out back, affords its guests a view of the spectacular sunsets. Rooms are a combination of cabins and villas and each has two king-size beds, satellite TV, air conditioning and private baths. The décor is tropical, with white rattan furniture. There are two bars and restaurants, along with two pools, a game room, theater and tennis courts. The watersports center offers kayaks, snorkeling equipment and can arrange scuba diving or fishing outings.

Fins 'n Feathers Inn, *Aldea Buena Vista, Iztapa,* ☎ *502/7-881-4035, fax 502/7-881-4955.8 rooms, $$$$$.* This luxury complex has four villas, each with two bedrooms and bathrooms, central air conditioning, a fully equipped kitchenette and sitting room with satellite TV and doors leading to the sundeck overlooking the pool, landscaped gardens and dock. The ocean-view restaurant serves international cuisine. A variety of fishing packages is offered.

Sol y Playa Tropical, *1a Calle 5-48, Zona 1, Iztapa,* ☎ *502/7-881-4365, 28 rooms, $.* This small, family-run hotel is clean and quiet. Rooms are large and nicely decorated with Guatemalan textiles. Each has a double bed, private bath with hot water, overhead fans and cable TV, and all look out onto a lovely pool and garden. No credit cards.

Casa Verde, *Avenida Maquelles and Calle de Esso, San José,* ☎ *502/7-881-1161, fax 502/7-881-1078, 25 rooms, $$$.* This cute establishment offers single or double rooms with air conditioning, two double beds, full bathroom with Jacuzzi tub and a small patio that opens up onto the pool. Behind the docks is a restaurant serving American-style food, including USDA prime steak (they are very proud of this). A fully equipped bungalow that sleeps six is also available. There's a small convention center available for groups and the hotel will arrange fishing trips.

Turicentro Martita, *5a Calle, Avenida del Comercio, Lote #26, San José, PBX 502/7-881-1337, fax 502/7-881-26463, 8 rooms, $$.* This is a very modern hotel offering large, sunny rooms with generic décor, comfortable beds, air conditioning, cable TV and private baths with lots of hot water. Each has a small balcony or patio that looks onto the pool. Although this place lacks character, it is very comfortable and clean. The restaurant serves excellent seafood dinners and the hotel will arrange fishing trips.

Turicentro Agua Azul, *Km 106.5 Carreterra al Puerto, San José,* ☎ *502/7-881-1667, fax 502/7-881-1667, 32 rooms, $$.* Geared toward Guatemalan families, Agua Azul is a well-run hotel. It offers large rooms equipped with two double beds, private baths with hot water, cable TV and air conditioning. There's a very large pool on site, as well as an excellent restaurant serving Guatemalan cuisine. No credit cards.

Hotel Posada del Quetzal, *Avenida 30 de Junio, San José,* ☎ *502/7-881-1601, fax 502/7-881-2494, 18 rooms, $$.* Like Agua Azul, this reasonably priced hotel also caters to Guatemalan families. Rooms are clean and cheery, with one double bed, private bath with hot water and air conditioning. There is a decent-sized pool with a nice restaurant. It's not the most elegant place, but it's comfortable. If no rooms are available, ask about their smaller sister property next door (unfortunately, rooms there don't have hot water). No credit cards.

Casa San José Hotel, *Avenida del Comercio and 9a Calle Esquina, San José,* ☎ *502/7-881-3316, 10 rooms, $.* This is the best budget hotel in town and it manages to stay somewhat quiet on the weekends. It has a very tiny pool and a restaurant. Rooms are basic, with private bath, hot water, overhead fans and cable TV. No credit cards.

◆ Where to Eat

The whole downtown beach is packed with *comedores* offering excellent grilled fish and shrimp, fresh ceviche and, when available, other seafood. The food is simple but good. You can visit any of the hotels listed above, all of which have decent restaurants open to the public. Like the hotel scene, dining here is either cheap with no ambience or expensive with too much ambience.

Department of Retalhuleu

The department of Retalhuleu is where the Pacific and Northern Highlands meet. It shares borders with Quetzaltenango, Suchitepequez and San Marcos. Because it has become a gateway to and from the Pacific, Retalhuleu is the most prosperous of the departments, producing sugar, cotton, coffee, maize, beans, rice, cacao, rubber and fruit. But it is most famous for dairy cattle, considered the finest in the country. There are many wealthy cattle ranchers in this department and they like to relax in the beautiful capital, **Retalhuleu**, usually referred to as Rey. There is also more indigenous culture here with a large population of Quiché Maya. There aren't many tourist attractions, but don't let that stop you. The region does have a famous beach at Champerico, the ruins of Abaj Takalik and the huge Xocomil Aquatic Park.

Getting Here & Getting Around

Direct buses come from Guatemala City to Retalhuleu City. If you are arriving from Panajachel, Lake Atitlán or any of the northern highland villages, catch a bus in Quetzaltenango for a short (36-mile/59 km) ride to the capital.

There is a good public transportation in the city and taxis are cheap and plentiful. Most of the hotels are within walking distance of the downtown central plaza. To visit the ruins or get to the beaches, use local buses.

Retalhuleu

◆ History

The name Retalhuleu is Quiché Maya and it best translates as "Earth Signal." Legend has it that when Pedro de Alvarado arrived he raised his sword in a salute. The metal caught the sunlight and the reflection appeared to divide the territory in two. To the left was the Quiché territory, which they named Retalhuleu (it was also known as the Capital of the New World).

Retalhuleu is the largest city in the Pacific region. It was originally created when the church merged two Quiché villages in the 1540s, but the city did not really start growing until the 1830s, when the area was settled by farmers and ranchers. It developed quickly and by 1849 was a major commercial and agriculture hub. In 1877, the government officially declared Retalhuleu the capital of the newly created department. It has enjoyed a more peaceful history than the rest of the country.

There isn't much to do in Rey except enjoy the easygoing pace of the city. The city's lovely plaza with Greek-inspired sculpture is set in a landscaped park. Off from the plaza is a large, bright white colonial church built by the Franciscan monks. Alongside the church are several ornate municipal buildings.

◆ Sights

Rey is the cultural center for the Pacific, so it often has exhibits and music festivals, along with a number of religious holidays celebrated by the Quiché.

Museo de Arquelogico y Etnologia, 6a Avenida, is a small but well-organized museum with archeological relics from 33 sites in the region. The most impressive are from Abaj Takalik and include small figurines carved from stone and jade. Upstairs is a collection of historical photos dating from 1888 and a mural showing the location of various ruins. Open 8 am-1 pm and 2-5 pm, Tuesday to Sunday. Admission is Q7.

◆ Abaj Takalik Ruins

About 18 miles (30 km) west of Rey is one of the most important Prehispanic sites in Guatemala. The name Abaj Takalik is Quiché for "Standing Stone" and refers to the giant carved heads. The ruins are set in the middle of five coffee plantations owned by the Ralda family. They have donated 22 *manzanas* (neighborhoods) which make up the core of the park.

History

Abaj Takalik may have been occupied as early as 1800 BC. Its first building was erected between 500 and 200 BC. There is evidence of a continual development in architecture and sculpture right up until the Late Pre-Classic period (200 BC-AD100). The giant carved heads found here have been identified as Olmec but the date and origin of other sculptures remain a mystery. Stelae show that Abaj Takalik had ties with the powerful Kaminal Juyú in the Guatemalan highlands and Chocolá on the coastal plains in Mexico. These alliances helped the city develop into a major trade route and become a commercial center. But research indicates the site may have also been used for ceremonial purposes since many buildings are aligned to follow the path of the Ursa Major constellation.

The site was abandoned at the same time as other cities and remained hidden in the jungle for centuries until 1888, when it was re-discovered by a botanist. **Dr. Gustavo L. Bruhl** brought attention to Abaj Takalik, but it took until 1924 before any serious investigation was done. At that time, **Walter Lehman** and **Erick Thompson** began a systematic mapping of the area, employing a method that is still used today. In 1942, **Tatiana Proskouriakoff** laid to rest the argument that the site was not Maya by analyzing some of its hieroglyphics. Since then, it has been recognized as a mixture of Olmec and Maya culture.

In 1976, the University of Berkeley California began a formal excavation that was concluded in 1981. Miguel Orrego Corozo from IDAEH took over the project in 1986 and has been working on it since.

Exploring the Ruins

The ruins are fascinating. Alongside giant heads carved by the Olmecs are stelae carved by the Maya. Many of the buildings have not been cleared, but the largest concentration so far is found in a 5½-mile (nine-km) belt extending north to south, flanked on the east and west by Río

Ixchiyá and Río Xab. This area has nine reinforced natural terraces with more than 70 major mounds and 239 monuments distributed in three principal groups. To date, more than 170 sculptures have been found at this site. Two of the platforms that have been cleared revealed two temple monuments with carved altars and stelae beneath. **Monument 68** has carvings of frogs and toads mixed with hieroglyphics, while **Monument 66** is covered with alligators. **Stela 5**, also found in this area, dates to AD 126 and shows two standing figures separated by a large hieroglyphic panel. **Stela 2** (200 BC) also has carvings and hieroglyphics.

In July 2002, a **royal tomb** was uncovered. While no skeleton was found, there were a number of precious objects, including a jadeite necklace, bracelets, earflares, jade rectangular plaques, three mirrors laminated with a pyrite mosaic and a sculpted greenstone fish. Archeologists Christa Schieber de Lavarreda and Miguel Orrego believe these objects date to AD 100-200 and that the tomb is that of the last ruler of Ajab Takalik.

This site remains a working archeological zone and a visit here offers a fascinating glimpse at how digs are conducted. The local Quiché still use the site for religious ceremonies. If you come across a ritual being conducted, please don't take pictures. Open 7 am to 5 pm, daily. Admission is Q25 for tourists. There are no services, so bring along food and drink.

▶▶ *GETTING HERE: From Rey, take a local bus going to the village of El Asintal, where pickups and taxis provide rides to the ruins for about Q10. Some companies offer shuttle service to the ruins from Xela. Contact **Guatemaya Intercultural**, Quetzaltenango, ☎ /fax 502/7-765-0040; or **Offroad Tourism and Shuttle Service**, Quetzaltenango, ☎ 502/7-761-9924, fax 502/7-761-9576.*

◆ Adventures on Water

Water Park

Parque Acuatico Xocomil, Km 180.5 de CITO-180, ☎ 502/7-772-5763, fax 502/7-772-5780, www.irtra.org.gt. Xocomil translates from Quiché to "Strong wind that blows on the water," a lovely name that has nothing to do with this colossal entertainment park. This is one of the largest water parks in Central America and can accommodate 6,000 people. It's worth coming just to see all the Maya kitsch.

There are 10 water slides that offer a total of 3,937 feet (1,200 meters) of fun. The most thrilling is the Nest of Serpents (*Nido de Serpientes*), which takes you down through tunnels that twist and turn all the way. On the lazy river you float down a 1,771-foot (540-meter) Maya canyon with giant plastic heads of ancient kings that spout water from their noble lips. A massive wave pool is complemented by an artificial beach. The kids' area has its own slides and rides, including the very cool pool shaped like a volcano that bubbles water out of the top. The colossal El Gran Chac restaurant, resembling one of the temples in Tikal, sells overpriced fast food. Comical wall murals depict Maya religious ceremonies.

In 2001 the park was given an award of excellence by the International Association of Aquatic Parks. It's tacky and a lot of fun. Open Thursday to Sunday, 9 am to 4 pm. Admission is Q70 for adults, Q25 for kids.

▶▶ *GETTING HERE: Close to Rey, the park can be reached via public bus. Just ask to be let off at Kilómetro 180.5.*

Swimming at Champerico

The southern coast of Retalhuleu is one long series of beaches: Tres Cruces, El Chico, Manchón, Champerico and Tulate. The only beach with services of any kind is Champerico.

Champerico is, supposedly, Guatemala's third-largest commercial port. But if the rusting pier is any indication, this area doesn't see a lot of action. The beach here is huge and goes on for miles, but you won't see many people swimming far from shore because of a vicious undertow. Be very careful when in the water. Aside from working on your tan, you can eat delicious fried shrimp and fish sold at the small beachside restaurants.

AUTHOR'S NOTE: *Don't stay over because the town is not safe or pleasant at night. Drunk and obnoxious youths from Guatemala City and Rey take over at sunset, driving their cars up and down the beach and through the streets. It's impossible to get any rest and often their parties end in violence. It's better to visit this beach on a day-trip and return to Rey for the evening.*

▶▶ *GETTING HERE: Buses leave from Rey every half-hour for the 20-minute trip to the park. The road is in excellent condition. The last bus leaves from Champerico to Rey at 6 pm. Buses also run from Quetzaltenango every two hours. The trip takes two hours.*

◆ Where to Stay

Since few people visit here, hotels are scarce. However, there are a couple of gems where you will be comfortable. You need reservations only during Carnival and Easter Week.

❖ HOTEL PRICING
Prices are per person.
$ . . . . Under $25
$$ . . . . $26 to $50
$$$ . . . . $51 to $85
$$$$ . . . . $86 to $125
$$$$$ . . . . over $125

Hotel Astor, *5a Calle 4-60, Zona 1,* ☎ *502/7-771-0475, fax 502/7-771-2562, 27 rooms, $$.* Ground-floor rooms at this charming hotel open onto a lovely courtyard filled with flowers. Second-floor rooms have a shared terrace. Accommodations are neat and clean. They have ceiling fans, private bath and cable TV.

Hotel Posada de Don José, *5a Calle 3-67, Zona 1,* ☎ *502/7-771-0180, fax 502/7-771-1179, 25 rooms, $$.* Located jut across from the railway station, this is probably the nicest hotel is town. It's modern without being sterile and has rooms furnished with nice wooden furniture, two double beds, air conditioning, cable TV, private bath and telephone. There's a nice pool as well as a good restaurant. Don José's is the first to fill up on the weekends. If it's full, ask about their new annex up the street. It has 11 rooms similar to those offered here.

Hotel Modelo, *5a Calle 4-53, Zona 1,* ☎ *502/7-771-0256, 7 rooms, $.* The Modelo is a decent budget hotel with clean rooms and shared bathrooms (no hot water). It's extremely basic, but it is clean and safe. No credit cards.

Hotel Costa Real, *Km 182.5, Carretera a Coatepeque,* ☎/fax *502/7-771-2141, 34 rooms, $$.* Set on the outskirts of town, this semi-luxurious property is centered around a nice pool and restaurant. Rooms are bright and colorful, with two double beds, air conditioning, cable TV and private baths (sometimes with no hot water). The restaurant has a decent if uninspired menu.

◆ Where to Eat

The best restaurants are the small *comedores* centered around the plaza. **Comedor Mary** serves excellent Guatemalan meals with rice, beans and tortillas for Q20. **Cafeteria La Luna** also offers good lunches of chicken and fish for Q25.

Hotel Posada de Don José, *5a Calle 3-67, Zona 1,* ☎ *502/7-771-0180, fax 502/7-771-1179.* This very pleasant hotel restaurant is a favorite with locals. You'll find excellent roast chicken, fresh fish and grilled steaks on the menu, all served with soup, salad, rice and beans for Q70. Breakfasts are excellent and include such offerings as fresh orange juice, pancakes and egg dishes. The coffee is really good.

Restaurante Oscito, *5a Calle 4-50, Zona 1,* ☎ *502/7-771-1393.* This restaurant offers traditional Guatemalan food at decent prices. Their *pollo pepian* (chicken in a spicy pumpkin sauce) shouldn't be missed, and they also have excellent grilled fish with garlic and wonderful ceviche. Q40. No credit cards.

PACIFIC COAST

Appendix

Information Services

◆ Conservation Organizations

Conservation is an important issue and a number of organizations actively promoting conservation in Guatemala have excellent resources where you can learn more about the country's protected areas.

Friends of the Forest Association and Wildlife Preservation Trust International (Amigos del Bosque), 16 Calle 6-18, Zona 3, Ciudad Guatemala. ☎ 502/220-7979, fax 502/220-7708, amibosque@hotmail.com.

Center for Studies in Conservation at University of San Carlos (Centro de Estudios Conservaciónistas de la Universidad de San Carlos), Avenida de la Reforma 0-63, Zona 10, Ciudad Guatemala, ☎ 502/331-0904, fax 502/334-7662.

Council for Natural Resources (Comision Centroaméricana para el Ambiente y Desarrollo, CCAD) 7a Avenida 13-01, Zona 9, Edificio La Cúpula, Guatemala City, ☎ 502/360-5426, fax 502/334-3876.

National Council of Protected Areas (Consejo Nacional de Areas Protegidas), 5a Avenida 6-06, Zona 1, Edificio IPM 7a Nivel, Ciudad Guatemala, ☎ 502/238-0000, fax 502/251-8588.

Conservation International, 2501 M St NW, Suite 200, Washington DC, 20037, ☎ 800/459-5660, newmember@conservation.org.

Defense of Nature Foundation (Fundación Defensores de la Naturaleza), 2a Avenida 2-71, Zona 3, Río Hondo, Zacapa, ☎ 502/934-0161. The main office is in Guatemala City, 19 Avenida B 083, Zona 15, Vista Hermosa II, PBX 502/369-5151, www.defensores.org.gt.

Interamerican Foundation for Tropical Research (Fundación Interamericana de Investigacion Tropical, FIIT), Avenida Hincapie 31-31 Zona 13, Mision del Fortin, Apdo. 106, Ciudad Guatemala, ☎ fax 502/333-3555.

Mario Dary Rivera Foundation (Fundación Mario Dary Rivera, FUNDARY), Diagonal 6, 17-19, Zona 10, C.P. 01010, Ciudad Guatemala, ☎ 502/333-4957, fax 502/367-0171, Fundary@intelnet.net.gt.

Fundación para el Ecodesarrollo y la Conservacíon (FUNDAECO), 7a Calle A 20-53, Zona 11, Colonia El Mirador No.1, por Tikal Futura, Ciudad Guatemala, ☎ 502/440-4609, fax 502/440-4605.

ParksWatch – Guatemala, Oficina de Trópico Verde, Vía 6, 4-25, Zona 4, Edificio Castaneda, Oficina 41, ☎ 502/339-4225, fax 502/331-0487, www.parkswatch.org.

Project Petén for Sustaining the Forests (Projecto Peténero para un Bosque Sosteniblen), Calle Central, Flores, Petén, ☎ 502/926-1370, fax 502/926-0495.

◆ Eco-Tourism Agencies

Certain areas in Guatemala are accessible only through eco-tour agencies who have permission to visit the area. The following list is organized by department and area.

All of Guatemala

Maya Expeditions, 15 Calle 1-91 Zona 10, local 104, Guatemala City, ☎ 502/363-4955, fax 502/337-4660, www.mayaexpeditions.com.

Ecotourism & Adventure Specialists, Avenida Reforma, 8-60, Zona 9, Guatemala City, ☎ 502/361-3104, www.ecotourism-adventure.com.

Alta Verapace Department

Aventuras Turisticas, 1a Calle 3-25, Zona 1, or 3a Calle, Zona 3, Cobán, ☎ 502/951-1358.

Hostal d'Acuña. Calle 4 3-17, Zona 2, Cobán, ☎ 502/952-1547.

Caquipec Cloud Forest Trek: Proyecto Eco-Quetzal, 2a Calle 14-36, Zone 1, Cobán, ☎/fax 502/952-1047, bidaspeq@guate.net.

Baja Verapace Department

El Salto de Chilascó: Fundación Defensores de la Naturaleza, 19 Avenida B 083, Zona 15, Vista Hermosa II, Guatemala City, PBX 502/369-5151, www.defensores.org.gt.

Quetzal Biosphere: Fundación para la Conservacíon del Medio Ambiente y los Recursos Naturales Mario Dary Rivera (FUNDARY), Diagonal 6, 17-19, Zona 10, C.P. 01010, Ciudad Guatemala, ☎ 502/333-4957, fax 502/367-0171, Fundary@intelnet.net.gt.

El Petén Department

EL MIRADOR RUINS/SCARLET MACAW TRAIL

ProPetén, Calle Central, Flores, ☎ 502/926-1370, fax 502/926-0495, www.propeten.org.

EcoMaya, Call 30 de Junio, Flores, ☎ 502/926-1363, fax 502/926-3322, www.ecomaya.com

POPTÚN & VICINITY

Finca El Tapir, 3a Calle, 4-74 Zona 3, Poptún, ☎ 502/491-9943, 927-7327.

Villa de los Castellanos, Village of Machaquilá, ☎ 502/927-7222, fax 502/927-7365.

SAXAYCHE & VICINITY

Viajes Turísticos La Moñtana, on the main street, near the ferry, ☎ 502/928-6169, fax 928-6168. Owner: Julian Mariona.

Viajes Don Pedro, on the riverbank, ☎ 502/928-6109. Owner: Don Pedro Mendéz Requena.

SIERRA LACANDÓN PARK

CONAP, 19 Avenida B 0-83, Zona 15, Vista Hermosa II, Guatemala City, PBX 502/369-5151, www.defensores.org.gt.

Fundación Defensores de la Naturaleza , 19 Avenida B 083, Zona 15, Vista Hermosa II, Guatemala City, PBX 502/369-5151, www.defensores.org.gt.

UAXACTÚN

Carmelita, Cooperativa Integral de Comercialización, Comité de Turismo, Carmelita, San Andrés, ☎ 502/861-0366.

WESTERN/NORTHERN PETÉN

Ni'tun Eco-Lodge/Monkey Tours, San Andrés, ☎ 501/926-0807, www.nitun.com. Owner: Bernie Mittelstaedt.

YAXHÁ

Campamento Ecológico El Sombrero, Laguna Yaxhá, ☎ 502/926-5229, fax 502/926-5228, www.ecotourism-adventure.com/sombrero.htm.

El Progresso Department

SIERRA DE LAS MINAS BIOSPHERE/LOS ALBORES

Fundación Defensores de la Naturaleza , 2a Avenida 2-71, Zona 3, Río Hondo, Zacapa, ☎ 502/934-0161. The head office is at 19 Avenida B 083, Zona 15, Vista Hermosa II, Guatemala City, PBX 502/369-5151, www.defensores.org.gt.

MATAQUESCUINTLA MOUNTAINS/VOLCÁN IPALA

Servicios Turísticos Brothers (Brothers Tour Services), Guatemala City, ☎/fax 502/255-2573, www.brostours.homestead.com.

MONTECRISTO TRI-NATIONAL PARK

SalvaNatura, 33 Avenida Sur #640, Colonia Flor Blanca, San Salvador, El Salvador, ☎ 503/279-1515, fax 503/279-0220.

Escuintla Department

SIPACATE-NARANJO NATIONAL PARK

Aventuras Naturales, Colonia El Naranjo No 53, La Antigua, Sacatepéquez, ☎/fax 502/832-3328, http://elparedonsurfcamp.tripod.com.

Huehuetenango Department

HUEHUETENANGO AREA

Unicornio Azul (Blue Unicorn), Hacienda Casco Chancol, Chiantla Chancol, ☎ 502/205-9328.

   PROCUCH, Central Plaza, Huehuetenango City, ☎ 502/771-8139.

LAGUNA MAGDALENA

Paquixena Cooperative, Paquix, Huehuetenango. No phone.

Izabal Department

CERRO SAN GIL

Fundación para el Ecodesarrollo y la Conservacíonde (FUNDAECO) 8a and 9a Calles, 2nd floor), Puerto Barrios, Izabal, ☎ 502/948-7110, 502/440-4615, fax 502/440-4605.

EL ESTOR/BOCAS DE POLOCHÍC

Defensores de la Naturaleza, 5a Avenida and 2a Calle Esquina, El Estor, ☎ 502/949-7237, rbocas@defensores.org.gt.

PUNTA DE MANABIQUE

FUNDARY, Estuardo Herrera, Director, Reserva Punta de Manabique, 17 Calle between 5ta and 6ta Avenida, Puerto Barrios, Izabal, ☎ 502/948-0435 or 948-0944.

RÍO DULCE & VICINITY

Asociación Ak'Tenamit, 11 Avenida A 9-39, Zona 2, Ciudad Nueva Ciudad de Guatemala, ☎ 502/254-1560, www.aktenamit.org.

Mexico

YAXCHILÁN, BONAMPAK, MEXICO

Escudo Jaguar Eco-tourism Center, Frontera Corozal, Municipal Ocosingo, Chiapas, ☎ 01/52/15/350-9600, 201-6440.

Quetzaltenango/Xela

Quetzaltrekkers, Casa Argentina, Diagonal 12, 8-37 Zona 1, ☎ 502/761-5865, www.quetzaltrekkers.org.

Quiché

IXCÁN/MONTES AZULES BIOSPHERE RESERVE

Akianto Travel, ☎ 011/52/9/612-2256 or 011/52/9/614-8333, akianto@prodigy.net.mx.

   Viajes Marabasco, ☎ 011/52/9/613-9776, CI, Chiapas, Mexico, www.ixcan.com.mx, mmorales@ci-mexixo.org.mx.

IXIL TRIANGLE

PRODINT, www.nebaj.org, nebaj@quick.guate.com.

Santa Rosa Department

RÍO LOS ESCLAVOS

PTP (Promotora Turistica Panamericana), 15 Calle, 3-20, Zona 10, Edificio Ejecutivo, Oficina 602, Aldea Los Esclavos, ☎ 502/363-4404, fax 502/363-4524, www.ptpmayas.com.

HAWAII-MONTERRICO BIOTÓPO

CECON-USAC (Centro Estudios Conservacíonistas de Universidad de San Carlos), Monterrico Village, Santa Rosa. San Carlos University's Center for Conservation Studies (CECON), is at Avenida Reforma 0-63 Zona 10 CP 01010, Ciudad Guatemala, Guatemala, ☎ 502/331-0904, fax 502/334 7664, www.usac.edu.gt/cecom, cecon@usac.edu.gt.

◆ Embassies

British Embassy, Avenida La Reforma and 16 Calle 0-55, Zona 10, Edificio Torre Internacional, Ciudad Guatemala, ☎ 502/367-5425-9, fax 502/367-5430. Open Monday-Thursday, 2-6:30 pm, 7:30-11 pm; Friday, 2-6 pm. Closed on weekends.

    Canadian Embassy, 13 Calle 8-44, Zone 10, Edificio Edyma Plaza, Ciudad Guatemala, ☎ 502/333-6102/363-4348, fax 502/363-4208, www. dfait-maeci.gc.ca/guatemala. Open Monday-Thursday, 8 am-5 pm.

    US Embassy, Avenida La Reforma 7-01, Zone 10, Ciudad Guatemala, ☎ 502/331-1541 (8 am-5 pm) or ☎ 502/331-8904 for emergencies (5 pm-8 am), fax 502/331-0564, http://usembassy.state.gov/guatemala.

APPENDIX

Embassies & Consular Offices of Guatemala

CANADA

Embassy: 130 Albert St. Suite 1010, Ottawa, Ontario. Canada, K1P 5G4, ☎ 613/233-7237 or 613/233-7188, fax 613/233-0135, embguate@ webruler.com

Consular Offices : PO Box 70508, Toronto, Ontario, Canada, M6P 4E7, ☎ 416/604-0655, fax 905/831-8164; Hornby Street Suite 760, Vancouver, British Columbia, Canada, V6Z 1S4, ☎ 604/688-5209, fax 604/688-5210, consulguatvan@intergate.bc.ca

UNITED STATES

Embassy: 2220 R Street, NW, Washington, DC 20008, ☎ 202/745-4952, fax 202/745-1908, consulate@guatemala-embassy.org; open Mon.-Fri., 9 am-5 pm.

    The Jurisdiction includes the States of: Delaware, Kentucky, Maryland, Ohio, Puerto Rico, Tennessee, Virginia, West Virginia, Washington DC.

GENERAL CONSULATE OFFICES

200 N. Michigan Ave 6th Floor, Chicago, IL 60601, ☎ 312/332-1587, fax 312/332-4256, conguatch@aol.com. This Jurisdiction includes the States of Illinois, Indiana, Iowa, Michigan, Minnesota, Missouri, North Dakota, South Dakota, Wisconsin.

3013 Fountain View Suite 210, Houston, TX 77057, ☎ 713/953-9531, fax 713/953-9383, consulguat@aol.com. This Jurisdiction includes the States of Arkansas, Kansas, Lousiana, Oklahoma, Nebraska, Missisippi, Texas.

1605 W. Olympic Blvd. #422, Los Angeles, CA 90015, ☎ 213/365-9251/2, fax 213/365-9245, lax@guatemala-consulate.org. This Jurisdiction includes the States of Alaska, Arizona, California, Colorado, Hawaii, Montana, Nevada, New Mexico, Oregon, Utah, Washington, Wyoming.

1101 Brickell Ave. #1003S, Miami, FL 33131, ☎ 305/679-9945/48, fax 305/679-9983, conguafin@bellsouth.net. This Jurisdiction includes the States of Alabama, Florida, Georgia, North Carolina.

57 Park Avenue, New York, NY 10016, ☎ 212/686-3837, fax 212/889-5470, conguatny@aol.com. This Jurisdiction includes the States of Connecticut, Maine, Massachusetts, New Hampshire, New Jersey, New York, Pennsylvania, Rhode Island, Vermont.

I870 Market St. #667, San Francisco, CA 94102, ☎ 415/788-5651, fax 415/788-5653, guate-sf@sfconsulguate.org. This Jurisdiction includes the States of Alaska, Arizona, California, Colorado, Hawaii, Montana, Nevada, New Mexico, Oregon, Utah, Washington, Wyoming.

For more information, contact the Guatemala Embassy at www.guatemala-embassy.org.

◆ Emergency Phone Numbers

Ambulance	123
Fire	123
Red Cross	125
Tourist Police	110 or 120

State Department Bureau of Consular Affairs, ☎ 202/647-5225, fax 202/647-3000, http://travel.state.gov/guatemala.html.

◆ Recommended Reading

A Field Guide to the Amphibians and Reptiles of the Maya World: The Lowlands of Mexico, Northern Guatemala, and Belize, Julian C. Lee; Cornell University Press; ISBN 0801485878; July 2000.

A Field Guide to the Birds of Mexico and Adjacent Areas: Belize, Guatemala, and El Salvador, Ernest Preston Edwards, Edward Murrell Butler; University of Texas Press; ISBN 0292720912; July 1998.

A Field Guide to the Mammals of Central America & Southeast Mexico, Fiona A. Reid; Oxford University Press; ISBN 0195064011; February 1998.

A Forest of Kings: The Untold Story of the Ancient Maya, Linda Schele, David Freidel; Quill; ISBN 0688112048; January 1992.

Bitter Fruit: The Story of the American Coup in Guatemala, Stephen C. Schlesinger, Stephen Kinzer, John H. Coatsworth, Richard A. Nuccio; Harvard University Press; ISBN 0674075900; Expanded edition, August 1999.

Bridge of Courage: Life Stories of the Guatemalan Companeros and Companeras, Jennifer Harbury, Noam Chomsky; Common Courage Press; ISBN 156751068X; Updated edition, June 1995.

Conquest and Survival in Colonial Guatemala, William George Lovell; McGill-Queens University Press; ISBN 0773504338; revised edition, March 1992.

Copán: The Rise and Fall of a Classic Maya Kingdom, David Webster, Anncorinne Freter, Nancy Gonlin; Wadsworth Publishing Company; ISBN 0155058088; 1st edition, October 1999.

Guatemala in the Spanish Colonial Period, Oakah L., Jr. Jones; University of Oklahoma Press; ISBN 0806126035; April 1994.

In Focus Guatemala: A Guide to the People, Politics and Culture, Trish O'Kane; Interlink Publishing Group; ISBN 1566562422; February 1999.

I, Rigoberta Menchu: An Indian Woman in Guatemala, Rigoberta Menchu; Verso Books; ISBN 0860917886; August 1987.

Incidents of Travel in Central America, Chiapas and Yucatan, John Stephen; Dover Publications, ISBN 048622404X; reprinted June 1969, first published 1873.

Maya Art and Architecture (World of Art), Mary Ellen Miller; Thames & Hudson; ISBN 050020327X; November 1999.

Maya Cosmos: Three Thousand Years on the Shaman's Path, David Freidel, Linda Schele; Quill; ISBN 0688140696; Reissue edition, February 1995.

Reading the Maya Glyphs, Michael D. Coe, Mark Van Stone; Thames & Hudson; ISBN 0500051100; November 2001.

Rites: A Guatemalan Boyhood, Victor Perera; Mercury House; ISBN: 156279065X; Reprint edition October 1994.

Searching for Everardo: A Story of Love, War and the CIA in Guatemala, Jennifer K. Harbury; Warner Books; ISBN 0446673625; January 2000.

Secret History: The Cia's Classified Account of Its Operations in Guatemala, 1952-1954, Nick Cullather and Piero Gleijeses; Stanford University Press; ISBN 0804733112; June 1999.

Silence on the Mountain: Stories of Terror, Betrayal, and Forgetting in Guatemala, Daniel Wilkinson; Houghton Mifflin; ISBN 0618221395; September 2002.

Tikal: An Illustrated History of the Ancient Maya Capital, John Montgomery; Hippocrene Books; ISBN 0781808537; September 2001.

The Blood of Kings: Dynasty and Ritual in Maya Art, Linda Schele, Mary Ellen Miller; George Braziller Publishing; ISBN 0807612782; reprint edition, May 1992.

The Ecotraveller's Wildlife Guide, Belize and Northern Guatemala, Les Beletsky; Academic Press; ISBN 0120848112; December 1998.

The Fall of the Ancient Maya: Solving the Mystery of the Maya Collapse, David Webster, Thames & Hudson; ISBN: 0500051135; May 2002.

The History of Coffee in Guatemala, Regina Wagner; Villegas Editores; ISBN 9588156017; January 2002.

The Maya of Guatemala: Life and Dress, Carmen L. Pettersen; University of Washington Press; ISBN 0295955376; May 1977.

◆ Travel Agencies

Antigua

Adventure Travel Center Viareal, S.A., 5a Avenida Norte #25B, ☎/fax 502/832-0162.

Aviatur Travel Agency, 5a Avenida Norte #33, Calle de Arco, ☎/fax 502/832-5067, aviatur@yahoo.com.mx.

Eco-Tour Chejo's, Sergio García, 3a Calle Poniente #24.

Maya Ital Tour, inside Hotel Posade Don Rodrigo, 5a Avenida Norte #19, ☎ 502/832-6502, fax 502/832-6162, mayaital@centramerica.com.

Mayan Paradise Tour and Travel Service, 5a Calle Poniente #6, ☎ 502/832-2071, fax 502/832-1838.

Monarca Travel, 6a Avenida Norte #6A, ☎/fax 502/832-4305, monarcas@conexion.com.gt.

Old Town Outfitters, 6a Calle Poniente #7, ☎ 502/832-4243, www.bikeguatemala.com.

Rain Forest, 4ta Avenida Norte #4 A, ☎ 502/832-5670, fax 502/832-6299, www.rainforest.guate.com.

San Francisco Travel, 4a Calle Ponoenet #9, ☎ 502/832-4020.

Sin Fronteras, 5a Avenida Norte#15A, ☎ 502/832-1017, fax 502/832-8453, www.sinfront.com.

Space Travel Agency, 5a. Calle Poniente #3 A, ☎ 502/832-7143, fax 502/832-7143.

Turansa, 9a Calle, inside Hotel Villa Antigua, ☎ 502/832-2928, fax 502/832-4692, www.turansa.com.

Vision Travel, 3 Avenida Norte #3, ☎ 502/832-3293, fax 502/832-1955.

Guatemala

Mayaventura, 15 Calle 3-20, Zona 10, Centro Ejecutivo 408, Guatemala City, ☎ 502/363-4634, fax 502/333-7266, www.mayaventura.com.

La Vía Maya, Boulevard Liberación 6-31 Zona 9, Guatemala City, ☎ 502/339-3601, fax 502/339-3608, www.laviamaya.com.

Aire, Mar y Tierra (Air, Water and Earth), 6a Avenida 20-25, Zona 10, Edificio Plata Maritima, Guatemala City, ☎ 502/363-3486 or 337-0149.

Guatours, 20 Calle 5-35, Zona 10, Edificio Plaza Los Arcos, 3rd floor, Guatemala City, ☎ 502/337-0019, fax 502/333-5769, http://guatours.com.

Panajachel, Sololá

Servicios Turístico Atitlán, 3a Avenida 3-47, Zona 2, ☎ 502/762-2075, fax 502/762-2246.

Lake Atitlán Resort Association (LARA), Calle Tijon, ☎ 502/219-2755, fax 502/762-2322. www.atitlan.com.

Veleros de Lago, Dragon Lady Cruises, Apartado 45, ☎ 502/906-9344, captain@a1boatsales.com.

Adventures in Education Inc., Posada Los Encuentros, Calle Santander, ☎ 502/762-2326.

Quetzaltenango/Xela

Adrenalina Tours, Pasaje Enriquez, 5a Avenida Sur, Zona 1, 502/761-0924, 761-0922, http://adrenalinatours.xelaenlinea.com.

Quetzal Adventures, Diagonal 12 8-37, Zona 1, ☎ 502/761-2470, www.quetzalventures.com.

APPENDIX

◆ Volunteer Opportunities

If you get inspired to help out and do some volunteer work in Guatemala there are literally hundreds of organizations looking for help. Usually you must commit to at least one to three months and speak a bit of Spanish.

Project Mosiaco Guatemala is an organization that matches international volunteers with 60 organizations in Guatemala working on human rights, environmental issues, healthcare, education and community development. It's a great source of information. Located at 3a Avenida Norte #3, Antigua, www.pmg.dk, ☎ 502/8320955.

Peace Brigades International (PBI), http://peacebrigades.org. A British NGO (non-governmental organization) protecting human rights by sending volunteers to accompany clergy, union leaders, human rights activists and returning exiles.

Website Directory

INGUAT, the Guatemalan Tourism Board, operates the official website, www.guatemala.travel.com.gt. You can contact INGUAT at 4 Calle 4-37, Zone 9, Ciudad Guatemala, ☎ 502/331-1333, fax 502/331-8893 or in the US at ☎ 888/464-8281.

◆ Books/Magazines/Newspapers

Biblioteca Virtual Miguel de Cervantes, **http://cervantesvirtual.com/**. This virtual library has over 2,000 Spanish classics online from both sides of the Atlantic.

EntreMundos, **www.entremundos.org**, is an English-language monthly newsletter for the Quetzaltenango region.

The Guatemala Post, **www.guatemalapost.com**, is an English-language daily.

Prensalibre, **www.prensalibre.com**, is the primary Spanish-language daily.

Revue, **www.revuemag.com**, is Guatemala's English-language magazine, 4a Calle Oriente #23 La Antigua, Guatemala, ☎ fax 502/331-7151.

Siglo, Veintiuno, **www.sigloxxi.com**, is another Spanish daily.

◆ General Information

Http://lanic.utexas.edu/la/ca/guatemala. Site listing all general information websites, research programs, and environmental projects.

http://travel.state.gov/guatemala.html. US Consulate website.

www.cia.gov/cia/publications/factbook/geos/gt.html. Facts and figures about the country.

www.enjoyguatemala.com/hotels.htm. Useful site comparing some of the country's best hotels.

www.guatemalatravelmall.com. A travel site geared to help tourists plan their vacation.

www.guatemalaweb.com. Excellent information site on everything about Guatemala.

www.latinworld.com. Tons of info about Latin America.

www.maya-art-books.org. Volunteer and educational opportunities.

www.mayadiscovery.com. Learn more about El Mundo Maya.

www.quetzalnet.com. Business, tourism and economic statistics.

◆ Health Services

www.mdtravelhealth.com/destinations/mamerica_carib/guatemala.html. The MD Travel Health Directory.

www.cdc.gov/travel/camerica.htm. National Center for Infectious Diseases.

◆ Human Rights Issue & News

www.ghrc-usa.org. Guatemala Human Rights Commission/USA.
  http://peacebrigades.org. Peace Brigades International (PBI).

◆ Destination-Specific Websites

ANTIGUA

Www.aroundantigua.com

CHICUIMULA

www.chiquimulaonline.com

COBÁN & LAS VERAPACES

www.dearbrutus.com/donjeronimo

COPÁN RUINS

www.copanruins.com

Http://www.honduras.net/copan/

ESQUIPULA

www.esquipula.com.gt

LAKE ATITLÁN

www.atitlan.com

MOMOSTENANGO

http://www.geocities.com/momostenango/visitorinfo1.htm

RÍO DULCE

www.mayaparadise.com

QUETZALTENANGO/LOS ALTOS

www.xelapages.com

www.quetzalventures.com

◆ Spanish Language

Learn Spanish, **www.lingolex.com/spanish.htm**
Study Spanish, **www.studyspanish.com**

Spanish Glossary

◆ Days

domingo	Sunday
lunes	Monday
martes	Tuesday
miercoles	Wednesday
jueves	Thursday
viernes	Friday
sabado	Saturday

◆ Months

enero	January
febrero	February
marzo	March
abril	April
mayo	May
junio	June
julio	July
agosto	August
septiembre	September
octubre	October
noviembre	November
diciembre	December

◆ Numbers

uno	one
dos	two
tres	three
cuatro	four
cinco	five
seis	six
siete	seven
ocho	eight
nueve	nine
diez	ten
once	eleven
doce	twelve
trece	thirteen
catorce	fourteen
quince	fifteen
dieciséis	sixteen
diecisiete	seventeen
dieciocho	eighteen
diecinueve	nineteen
veinte	twenty

veintiuno . . . . twenty-one
veintidós . . . . twenty-two
treinta . . . . thirty
cuarenta . . . . forty
cincuenta . . . . fifty
sesenta . . . . sixty
setenta . . . . seventy
ochenta . . . . eighty
noventa . . . . ninety
cienone . . . . hundred
ciento uno . . . . one hundred one
doscientos . . . . two hundred
quinientos . . . . five hundred
mil . . . . one thousand
mil uno . . . . one thousand one
mil dos . . . . two thousand
un millón . . . . one million
mil millones . . . . one billion
primero . . . . first
segundo . . . . second
tercero . . . . third
cuarto . . . . fourth
quinto . . . . fifth
sexto . . . . sixth
séptimo . . . . seventh
octavo . . . . eighth
noveno . . . . ninth
décimo . . . . tenth
undécimo . . . . eleventh
duodécimo . . . . twelfth
último . . . . last

APPENDIX

◆ Conversation

¿Como esta usted? . . . . How are you?
¿Bien, gracias, y usted? . . . . Well, thanks, and you?
Buenas dias . . . . Good morning.
Buenas tardes . . . . Good afternoon.
Buenas noches . . . . Good evening/night.
Hasta la vista . . . . See you again.
Hasta luego . . . . So long.
¡Buena suerte! . . . . Good luck!
Adios . . . . Goodbye.
Mucho gusto de conocerle . . . . Glad to meet you.
Felicidades . . . . Congratulations.
Muchas felicidades . . . . Happy birthday.
Feliz Navidad . . . . Merry Christmas.
Feliz Año Nuevo . . . . Happy New Year.
Gracias . . . . Thank you.
Por favor . . . . Please.
De nada/con mucho gusto . . . . You're welcome.
Perdoneme . . . . Pardon me.

¿Como se llama esto?	What do you call this?
Lo siento.	I'm sorry.
Quisiera...	I would like...
Adelante.	Come in.
Permitame presentarle...	May I introduce...
¿Como se llamo usted?	What is your name?
Me llamo....	My name is...
No se.	I don't know.
Tengo sed.	I am thirsty.
Tengo hambre.	I am hungry.
Soy norteamericano/a	I am an American.
¿Donde puedo encontrar...?	Where can I find...?
¿Que es esto?	What is this?
¿Habla usted ingles?	Do you speak English?
Hablo/entiendo un poco Español	I speak/understand a little Spanish.
Hay alguien aqui que hable ingles?	Is there anyone here who speaks English?
Le entiendo.	I understand you.
No entiendo.	I don't understand.
Hable mas despacio por favor.	Please speak more slowly.
Repita por favor.	Please repeat.

◆ Time

¿Que hora es?.	What time is it?
Son las....	It is...
... cinco.	... five o'clock.
... ocho y diez.	... ten past eight.
... seis y cuarto.	... quarter past six.
... cinco y media.	... half past five.
... siete y menos cinco.	... five of seven.
antes de ayer.	the day before yesterday.
anoche.	yesterday evening.
esta mañana.	this morning.
a mediodia.	at noon.
en la noche.	in the evening.
de noche.	at night.
mañana en la mañana.	tomorrow morning.
mañana en la noche.	tomorrow evening.
pasado mañana.	the day after tomorrow.

◆ Directions

¿En que direccion queda...?.	In which direction is...?
Lleveme a... por favor.	Take me to... please.
Llevame alla ... por favor.	Take me there please.
¿Que lugar es este?	What place is this?
¿Donde queda el pueblo?.	Where is the town?
¿Cual es el mejor camino para...?	Which is the best road to...?
Malécon	Road by the sea.
De vuelta a la derecha.	Turn to the right.

De vuelta a la izquierda. . . . . Turn to the left.
Siga derecho. . . . . Go this way.
En esta dirección. . . . . In this direction.
¿A que distancia estamos de...? . . . . . How far is it to...?
¿Es este el camino a...? . . . . Is this the road to...?
Es... . . . . Is it...
¿... cerca? . . . . near?
¿... lejos? . . . . far?
¿... norte? . . . . north?
¿... sur? . . . . south?
¿... este? . . . . east?
¿... oeste? . . . . west?
Indiqueme por favor. . . . . Please point.
Hagame favor de decirme . . . . . . .Please direct me to...
    donde esta...
... el telefono. . . . . the telephone.
... el bano. . . . . the bathroom.
... el correo. . . . . the post office.
... el banco. . . . . the bank.
... la comisaria. . . . . the police station.

◆ Accommodations

Estoy buscando un hotel... . .I am looking for a hotel that's...
... bueno. . . . . good.
... barato. . . . . cheap.
... cercano. . . . . nearby.
... limpio. . . . . clean.
¿Dónde queda un buen hotel? . . . . Where is a good hotel?
¿Hay habitaciones libres? . . . Do you have available rooms?
¿Dónde están los baños/servicios?Where are the bathrooms?
Quisiera un... I would like a...
... cuarto sencillo. . . . . single room.
... cuarto con baño. . . . . room with a bath.
... cuarto doble. . . . . double room.
¿Puedo verlo? . . . . May I see it?
¿Cuanto cuesta?. . . . . What's the cost?
¡Es demasiado caro! . . . . It's too expensive!

Index

NOTES

ESQUIPULAS

NOTES